Media Culture

by JAMES MONACO

Television, Radio,
Records, Books, Magazines,
Newspapers, Movies

A DELTA BOOK

A DELTA BOOK
Published by
Dell Publishing Co., Inc.
1 Dag Hammarskjold Plaza
New York, New York 10017

ISBN: 0–440–59305–0

Delta ® TM 755118, Dell Publishing Co., Inc.
Printed in the United States of America
First printing—May 1978

ACKNOWLEDGMENTS

"The Decline of Sport" by E. B. White: From THE SECOND TREE FROM
THE CORNER by E. B. White. Copyright 1947 by E. B. White. Originally
appeared in *The New Yorker* and reprinted by permission of Harper & Row,
Publishers, Inc.

"Clay Felker: Requiem for A Winner" by Lucian K. Truscott IV: Published with the permission of the author and of NEW TIMES, the news
feature magazine. Mr. Truscott is a journalist and author who lives and
works in New York City and Sag Harbor, N.Y.

"The Silverman Strategy" by Jeff Greenfield: © 1976 by The New York
Times Company. Reprinted by permission.

"Politics Under the Palms" by Bo Burlingham: Reprinted by permission of
Esquire Magazine, © 1977 Esquire Inc.

"Henry Kloss: Not Your Average Mad Inventor" by Geoffrey Stokes: Reprinted by permission of The Village Voice. Copyright © The Village
Voice, Inc. 1976.

"*Esquire*'s Biggies: Capote, Talese, Wolfe, W. R. Simmons. W. R. Simmons?
Right. W. R. Simmons" by L. Rust Hills: Reprinted from MORE—The
Media Magazine by permission of Namequoit, Inc.

"The Global Bonanza of American TV" by Andrew R. Horowitz: Reprinted
from MORE—The Media Magazine by permission of Namequoit, Inc.

"The Middle Age of British Television" by David Thomson: Reprinted by permission of *American Film* and the author. First published in *American Film*. Copyright © 1977 by David Thomson.

"Kanned Laffter" by Ron Rosenbaum: Copyright © 1975 by Ron Rosenbaum. Reprinted by permission of The Sterling Lord Agency, Inc. First published in Esquire Magazine.

"Harry Makes a Movie" by Robert Alan Aurthur: Reprinted by permission of Esquire Magazine, © 1975 by Esquire Inc. First published as "Hanging Out" column.

"The Making of a Television Series: *Upstairs, Downstairs*" by Charles Barr, Jim Hillier, and V. F. Perkins: Reprinted by permission from MOVIE.

"The Rise and Fall of FM Rock" by Steve Chapple: Reprinted by permission of *Mother Jones* and the author. First published in *Mother Jones*, May 1976.

"The Great Toilet Paper War" by Ron Rosenbaum: Reprinted from MORE —The Media Magazine by permission of Namequoit, Inc.

"The Bobby Bison Buy" by George W. S. Trow: Reprinted by permission; © 1976 The New Yorker Magazine, Inc.

"Mastermind of the Instant Lottery" by Tom Stevenson: © 1977 by The New York Times Company. Reprinted by permission.

"The Next Medium: Intersex" by Robert Russel: First published in *Take One* magazine, Box 1778, Station B, Montreal, Canada H3B 3L3. Used by permission.

"Where Will They Go from Here?" by Roy Blount, Jr.: Reprinted by permission of the author. First published in Esquire Magazine. Copyright © 1976 by Roy Blount.

"This Typeface Is Changing Your Life" by Leslie Savan: Reprinted by permission of The Village Voice. Copyright © The Village Voice, Inc. 1976.

"Missing Hazel" by Nora Ephron: Reprinted by permission of International Creative Management. Copyright © 1976 Esquire Magazine. First published in *Esquire*.

"What TV Does to Kids" by Harry F. Waters: Copyright 1977 by Newsweek, Inc. All rights reserved. Reprinted by permission.

"*Roots* Getting a Grip on People" by Charlayne Hunter-Gault and "*Roots* Has Widespread and Inspiring Influence" by Thomas Johnson: © 1977 by The New York Times Company. Reprinted by permission.

"Post Modernism Is Dead" by Donald Barthelme: Reprinted by permission; © 1975 The New Yorker Magazine, Inc. First published as "Notes and Comment."

For Bob and Marge
—and Megan

CONTENTS

THE EFFECT

THE LAST WORD

THE DATA: WHO OWNS THE MEDIA?

PREFACE

In journalism class at Bayside High School twenty years ago we were taught that there are four distinct categories of newspaper writing: "information, description, analysis, and entertainment." This seemed to be an eminently sensible division of the process, and we set about trying to produce examples of each kind of writing. The result: confusion. Jules wrote a nice little piece describing (or so he thought) the life-style of the local gang, the Bayside West Zombies. We read it and told him it was entertainment. Fay produced what she fully believed to be a strictly informative essay on the Ban the Bomb movement. No, the teacher explained, it was opinionated. It wasn't information; it was analysis. The experiment seemed to have failed.

But it hadn't actually. As neat as the categories looked, they were rooted in false logic. News is entertainment, and to describe an event or phenomenon in detail is to understand it. By the time my generation had reached its majority five years later, this truth formed the basis for the "New Journalism." Communication was understood as a complex continuum, rather than being neatly compartmentalized. We now know that "the truth, the whole truth, and nothing but the truth" is an ideal, a goal that is never actually realized.

Too many factors intervene between the thing or idea itself and the image we receive of it, either in print, or on film, or on television. The medium through which the information is conveyed changes the information subtly but effectively. More important, the people who use the medium impose their own values and biases, sometimes not so subtly.

We still tend to think of communication mediums as somehow secondary to reality: there is the thing itself, and then there is the image of the thing. More and more, however, it becomes clear that in a world pervaded by media, "getting there is half the fun": media images may not be more "real" (the word still means something), but very often they are unmistakably more powerful than the events and people in the real world that they capture and transform.

What, then, is "Media Culture"? In a sense, there is no culture without a medium for transmission of information. Language of some sort is necessary. While griots and grandmothers did a good job for thousands of years transmitting cultures to future generations, the written word is far more effective in this regard than the spoken.

We can mark off historical periods in media terms. The invention of writing was, of course, a major watershed. The development of efficient means of mass printing was a quantitative leap of revolutionary dimensions. For the first time, literary culture—the culture of literacy—was no longer the prized talent of an elite. Ironically, just as the Western World was approaching the condition of full literacy, technical means were being developed to short-circuit language. Photography, movies, and recording—and later radio and television—provide means of capturing "information, description, analysis, and entertainment" and transmitting them even to the illiterate.

Since the beginning of this century we have lived in a world dominated by its means of communication: literary culture has become a subcategory of a pervasive media culture, which includes not only print, but also mechanical, chemical, and electronic means of preserving and transmitting information. Afloat on this vast sea of images, sounds, and language, we find it increasingly difficult to differentiate between various levels of meaning: "fact" and "fiction," once simply defined categories, have been replaced by "factoids" and "faction," "docudramas" and "dramatizations," "nonfiction novels" and "novelizations."

The dilemma is further complicated by the ineluctable fact that the media are industries dealing with products and profits, not just nondiscriminating channels of communication. At the entertainment end of the media spectrum, such quaintly discrete items as "the novel," "the film," and "the recording" have been transmuted into indistinguishable "properties" that can be more efficiently exploited, packaged in whichever medium seems profitable, and then recycled in other media to realize the maximum financial gain.

The book you are holding is a cooperative attempt at a general description of the shape of our media culture now, in the late 1970s. *Media Culture* provides a cogent introduction to the people who mold the media, the product they deliver, and the profound effect that product has had on the way we live now. The special section "Who Owns the Media?" is, I believe, of unusual interest. The data it provides paint a startling picture of the shape of these powerful industries today.

There's no better sign of the success of the "New Journalism," than the work of writers such as Bo Burlingham, Nora Ephron, Jeff Greenfield, Ron Rosenbaum, Geoffrey Stokes, David Thomson, Lucian Truscott (and the others included here). I'm grateful to them all for allowing their work to be reprinted.

I want to thank Virginia Platt for preparing "Authentic Sources and the Media" especially for inclusion in this volume, and H. L.

Masters and Martin Schenker for providing some of the information in Appendix 1. I'm grateful to Cliff Garboden and Fred McDarrah for providing the photos on pp. 99 and 32, and to Ursula Deren for smoothing the way with the redoubtable BBC. Thanks, too, to Alan Reuben of *The Village Voice* for his help. David Lindroth designed the cover. All photo layouts are my own; the authors should not be held responsible.

At Delta Books, Martha Kinney provided much-needed encouragement and advice, and Laura Bernay, Jeri Cummins, Rachel Klein, Giorgetta McRee, Kathy Simmons, Carol Stoddard, and Ann Watson of the Delta staff were especially helpful.

As always, I'm grateful to my wife, Susan Schenker, for her good sense and better humor. My brother Robert Monaco and his wife Margaret (to whom this book is dedicated) have been on the front line of the technological revolution in media for ten years now as computer designer and executive.

Three typefaces were used in the design of *Media Culture*. The basic text face is Times Roman linotype, 9 point set on 10 point slugs. Commissioned by *The Times* (London) in 1931, the design was supervised by Stanley Morison, and since its introduction it has become widely used. Its chief characteristics are clarity and readability. The headnotes are set in Permanent linotype. Designed in 1962 by Karlgeorg Hoefer, it fits the pattern of the clean, sans serif typefaces that became popular in the 1960s. The display type used for chapter and part titles is the famous Helvetica (Max Miedinger, 1957), about which Leslie Savan writes in Chapter 21. The text for *Media Culture* was set by Maryland Linotype Co. The book is printed by Vail-Ballou.

James Monaco
New York City
December 1977

THE SITUATION

1. MEDIOGRAPHY: IN THE MIDDLE OF THINGS
by James Monaco

If you grew up in the 1940s, chances are you remember Froggy the Gremlin. Froggy was the star of a popular Saturday morning children's program that flourished on NBC for eight years, from 1944 to 1952. The official name of the show was *Smilin' Ed's Buster Brown Gang* ("That's my dog, Tige. He lives in a shoe! I'm Buster Brown. Look for me in there too!"), but no one I knew ever called it that. We may have made our mothers buy us the shoes with the little pictures inside, but it wasn't the kid with the pageboy hairdo and his nondescript mutt who got us to tune in every week: it was Froggy.

Invisible most of the time, Froggy had the power to manifest himself if he chose by plunking his magic twanger. Smilin' Ed often had to insist he do so, for Froggy was incorrigible. The format of the program included a number of "regular guests." (It parodied the adult night-time programs, forerunners of television's talk and variety formats.) These were invariably pompous, windy sorts (in short, adults), and Froggy entertained us immensely by keeping up a running commentary on their locutions. More important, he had the strange and enviable power to put words in their mouths.

Shortfellow the poet, for example, might be explaining How to Bake a Cake:

> SHORTFELLOW: Now, children, listen carefully. First, you take the flour and you measure it carefully and you pour it in the bowl. Then you take the milk and you measure it and . . .
> FROGGY: (And you pour it in your shoe!)
> SHORTFELLOW: . . . and you pour it in your shoe! No, no, NO, Froggy!
> ED: *Plunk* your magic twanger, Froggy!
> FROGGY: I'll be good, Smilin' Ed, I'll-be-good, I'll-be-good, I'll-be-good!

Like that. We were enthralled.

The more I learn about that amorphous, pervasive phenomenon

known as "media," the more important memories of Froggy become. It seems to me he gave those of us who were weaned on radio in the late forties a significant advantage over the first television generation that followed. Smilin' Ed's gang had it all over Buffalo Bob's, in a number of ways. The show was not only an emblem of the media experience but also a positive lesson in how to cope with it.

Like most popular children's shows, I suppose, it is a measure of the power of media. Mention Froggy, Midnight the Cat, or Smilin' Ed now to someone who was a regular listener as a child and you will undoubtedly draw a warm response. This is known as nostalgia. Yet ask them the names of the children they played with at the age of five or six and you may well draw a blank. If they do remember them, it's safe to predict that the memories will be neither as detailed nor as vivid, in general, as those of radio and television shows. And this is as it should be: art is supposed to be considerably more intense than reality.

The difficulty lies in the confusion of one with the other. Smilin' Ed's "regular guests" were funny because they were parodies of adults, and the format was essentially humorous because it burlesqued the adult programs. Froggy gave us the gift of power over both—the adults, and their media forms. Paradoxically, at the same time that he was helping to sell us shoes he was also showing us one efficient way to deal with this scam: by actively reproducing our own version of the story. When Froggy got bored with Shortfellow's lecture, he simply imagined a new version of it, and his version had the power of reality. If he could do it, we could do it. And indeed, even today, one of the most obvious ways adolescents (and adults) react against the coercion of media fiction is by quietly providing their own running exegesis: while Kojak proceeds along his own inexorable way, fantasies in thousands of living rooms have him giving up lollipops for grass, or letting his hair grow in and opening a Greek restaurant, or retiring and going into the cop/media business with Joe Wambaugh. This is the equivalent of "body English" in the media experience. It has about as much value as isometric exercises, but it can lead to more decisive actions, such as turning off the set.

Why is Froggy's rebellion so important? For two reasons: one obviously significant, the other less so.

In the first place, none of us controls the media experience. These are others' dreams, not ours, others' worldviews and conclusions, not our own. Media products are written, produced, and directed by others. This need not present a problem in itself, if we are always aware of the biases. Books, letters (and, less commonly, privately made tapes and broadcasts), are clearly the work of individuals, and we approach them as such. There is an inherent dialogue in these mediums between author and reader: a basis of equality. But the more pervasive mediums—the so-called "mass media"—can be insidious simply because they are so ubiquitous and constant that they tend to replace the world as it actually exists in our collective consciousness with their version of the world. There is a *New Yorker* cartoon from several years ago that illustrates this nicely. The cartoon shows a parade passing an intersection, apartment houses on each corner. The windows are large and we can see the people in the apartments watching the parade that is taking place in the street below. They're all watching it on television. The media validate reality.

This is a complex phenomenon. On the one hand, the special reality that media coverage confers on an event, a person, or an idea is perfectly understandable. Once the thing has been covered—written about, taped, filmed, recorded—it exists in history. Without media there would be none. Not only the history, but the mythos of the culture is preserved and transmitted (and sometimes altered) by the media. Thus the question of who controls the media is unusually important. It is not a new one: *Quis custodiet ipsos custodes*? Juvenal asked in the first century A.D. Who watches the watchers?

We've certainly had enough media barons during the twentieth century—Hearst, Sarnoff, Mayer, Paley, Beaverbrook, Murdoch, and others. No doubt, they have exerted powerful control over certain segments of the media spectrum for varying amounts of time. Yet the danger isn't so much the "Citizen Kane" syndrome as it is bureaucratic. Not only in the U.S. and Europe, but throughout the world, the media—newspapers, magazines, films, radio, television, and recordings—have been and continue to be effectively governed by a narrowly defined upper-middle class male white executive caste. This is not to suggest a paranoid theory of media. These people don't meet biennially to revise history and fine-tune the mythos. They don't have to. The fact remains, however, that whole classes of people are effectively prevented from using the media to record and disseminate their own versions of myth and history, and even those few dissenting views that do get through are subtly but significantly attenuated.

Most media criticism in this century—especially the seminal work of the Frankfurt school in the thirties—has focused on this fact. Recently, attention has shifted to a second, more subtle cause of Froggy's rebellion. Even if all of us had perfect access to the media, they would reflect a reality significantly different from the one that surrounds us; for to couch an event, character, or idea in a particular medium is to change it. No way to get around it. We have turned from picturing the world *in* language to picturing it *as* language. No matter who uses the "language" or to what purpose, the language itself has certain rules and qualities that determine what can be said in it and how it can be said. So structuralists and semioticians work to define those rules in order to find out how precisely "the medium is the message." Nowhere is this shift of emphasis more evident than in the endless debate over the effect of television on children. For twenty years, the controversy raged about the effect of content: Do children who watch 918 murders per week on the tube find it significantly easier to take a life? Do they maybe even find the idea attractive? Recently, however, a number of theorists have suggested that more important than content is form. Because television is such an utterly passive experience—it goes on forever, it provides a near-total environment, you don't even have to get up and go out to see it—Marie Winn and others have theorized that it inculcates passivity. That it is, more than metaphorically, a "plug-in drug."

I tend to agree. It seems logical to assume that television provides more sensory information than radio (and that radio provides more information than print) and that, as a result, a consumer/observer has to work harder intellectually to comprehend radio—he has to supply his own images. Likewise, the reader works harder than the listener—he has to supply sound as well. One of the reasons Froggy wouldn't have worked on television is that, although he could easily have been invisible, when he plunked his magic twanger, he would have become all too mundanely visible. He would have been too much with us. Whereas, in radio, Froggy simply shifted from one level of glorious invisibility to another: everybody on radio was invisible. Now, if you believe there is real creativity involved in the work of the listener, or in the work of the reader, then radio obviously gives us a better balance between author and observer (or producer and consumer), and print allows a better balance still. Reading is a creative act, so is listening, so may be watching-and-listening.

Two more myths about media need to be disposed of. At its simplest, the function of the media is to record and distribute information, to get it from *A* to *B* either in space or in time. A humble service, it seems, and most media theorists have warned against taking the service more seriously than its "master," reality. (The *New Yorker* cartoon put this position succinctly.) But, as Raymond Williams* points out in his book *Communications*, we have been wrong to think of communication as secondary. I think it's worth quoting him at length:

> Many people seem to assume as a matter of course that there is, first, reality, and then, second, communication about it. We degrade art and learning by supposing that they are always second-hand activities: that there is life, and then afterwards there are these accounts of it. Our commonest political error is the assumption that power—the capacity to govern other men—is the reality of the whole social process, and so the only context of politics. Our commonest economic error is the assumption that production and trade are our only economic activities, and that they require no other human justification or scrutiny. We need to say what many of us know in experience: that the life of man, and the business of society, cannot be confined to these ends; that the struggle to learn, to describe, to understand, to educate, is a central and necessary part of our humanity. This struggle is not begun, at second hand, after reality has occurred. It is, in itself, a major way in

---

* Williams is, to my mind, the most cogent and provocative media theorist currently working. Two of his books—*Communications* and *Television: Technology and Cultural Form*—should be required reading for anyone seriously interested in media.

which reality is continually formed and changed. What we call society is not only a network of political and economic arrangements, but also a process of learning and communication. [*Communications*, p. 11]

In other words, the result of communication is community. No politics but for the media of debate and law. No economics but for the media of money and advertising.

Theoretically, the media simply record and transmit information, but practically we tend to differentiate between straight information (nonfiction) and that sort of information which is molded to other purposes (fiction). This latter category is popularly subject to a second dichotomy: that between "art" and "entertainment"—but as the boundary between the elite and popular forms of art/entertainment becomes less and less useful, so does the dichotomy, if it ever was. If the media are generally (albeit wrongly) assumed to be secondary to reality, then fiction is likewise considered secondary to nonfiction. Trying to analyze, for example, the effect of television coverage on the American attitude toward the Vietnam War, we concentrate on "news." Yet what was going on in the "pure entertainment" segment of prime time couched between the 7 and 11 P.M. newscasts may very well have had a significant effect on national attitudes, albeit more diffuse and difficult to measure. In 1968, CBS broadcast a tough, honest, succinct "documentary," *Black History: Lost, Stolen, or Strayed*. The show elicited some mild critical and popular interest, yet it was not until nine years later, when Alex Haley's personalized, dramatized *Roots* was shown, that ratings records were set and the national mood toward Black History palpably affected. Partly, this difference was due simply to the passage of time: we were a different country in 1968. Mainly, however, I think the remarkable reception *Roots* received (as book, television show, and record) was due to its dramatic mode. Pure information, after all, does not have the mystic, ritual power of drama. Fiction can capture certain known truths that nonfiction can only allude to, as the professional historians of the National Book Awards committee recognized when they gave Haley a special prize.

Fiction, whether acted or told, has always been a central, binding medium, but until the last fifty years, it has never been available on a regular basis to a majority of the population. Raymond Williams again:

[I]n societies like Britain and the United States more drama is watched in a week or weekend, by the majority of viewers, than would have been watched in a year or in some cases a lifetime in any previous historical period. It is not uncommon for the majority of viewers to see, regularly, as much as two or three hours of drama, of various kinds, every day. The implications of this have scarcely begun to be considered. It is clearly one of the unique characteristics of advanced industrial societies that drama

as an experience is now an intrinsic part of everyday life, at a
quantitative level which is so very much greater than any precedent as to seem a fundamental qualitative change. Whatever the
social and cultural reasons may finally be, it is clear that watching
dramatic simulation of a wide range of experiences is now an essential part of our modern cultural pattern. [*Television*, p. 59]

There is, in addition, an important corollary to this "qualitative change"
in our experience of community. Not only does drama now occupy a
significantly greater area of the spectrum of cultural experience, its
formal influence is amplified elsewhere, as well. The adjective "media"
has become as important as the noun; we are confronted daily by
"media events," "media hypes," "media personalities," "media style,"
and "media ideas." They occur in a half-fictional world, not quite real,
but not completely imaginary either, and they often have a more significant effect on the way we live than what used to be known quaintly as
"real life."

Media has a life of its own. We can see it developing in common
usage. Although the prescriptive guardians of public grammar insist
the word is plural, common usage has it singular as often as not, and a
separate word—"mediums"—is actually more commonly used as the
plural. Everyone knows what the word means; yet few people can
define it with any degree of specificity. Like most important concepts it
is amorphous and pervasive. Yet it seems worthwhile to try at least to
outline its limits.

LEVELS OF THE GAME

Medium in Latin simply means "middle." Nothing could be less
precise. In English the word has taken on the sense of a substance or
agency (a "thing" in the middle) through which information is transmitted.

On the most basic level, performance is a medium, in the sense that
it does convey information. It is, however, the most "nonmedial" of
media, since it changes the information conveyed least: is there any
significant, measurable difference, for instance, between an acted embrace and a real embrace? (If there were, chances are, human relations
would be considerably simplified; but media allow us to lie.)

If performance is identified by its closeness to reality, language is
recognized by its distance from it. Aside from a handful of true
onomatopoetic words, vocabulary is sublimely, utterly arbitrary (and
grammar is entirely abstract). Nothing connects a table with the
sounds we use to convey the idea except convention. Other "languages"
—mathematics and music and painting (when they are languages, not
performance)—are even more abstract and arbitrary: that is their
prime value in science and art.

Most systems considered media are considerably more limited, and more concrete. (That is, you can measure out a batch of any of these media; quantify it.) They are concrete because they are secondary: they were developed to serve the primary media of language and performance. Generally, these secondary media are classified as either "print" or "electronic" (with mechanical, electrical, and chemical media—early phonography, telegraphy, telephony, and photography—being included in the latter category for convenience's sake).

It's immediately obvious that print media serve only language, while the more modern electronic media serve performance as well. This is the crux of the controversy between adherents of print culture and champions of the electronic media. Somehow, during the 9000 years that print reigned in splendid isolation, the idea became established that a description in language of a person, event, or performance had a value that a record of the thing did not, which isn't surprising, since it wasn't until the last century that a direct record—without the intervention of language—was conceivable. On the other hand, the electronic media are considerably less efficient at handling ideas and abstractions: what you see is what you get.

Within each of these broad classifications exist the specific systems, each with particular characteristics. Print: letters, books, magazines, newspapers, flyers, and signs. Electronic: records, tape, radio, photography, film, television, telephony, telegraphy, cable, videodisc, and signs. The categories overlap, merge, and inform each other, but each of them has been developed to serve a specific purpose. On the whole, the history of the media—including print—has been defined by the history of their technologies. It is not, however, controlled by it. The technology of the sound film existed for at least ten years before the birth of the talkies; it simply wasn't economically useful for the studios to initiate sound until 1927. Television could have been wired rather than broadcast from the beginning, had we made a collective decision to do so. The governing rules of media—as with most other areas of life—are economic and political rather than technological.

It's possible to identify certain broad periods in media history, the first of which begins with the development of written language circa 7000 B.C. While writing made it possible both to record and transmit information in language, practically it only permitted one-to-one communication. The ability to disseminate information to a broad audience had to wait for the invention of movable type printing in the fifteenth century (in Europe, earlier in Asia). While the printed book was a significant quantum advance over the handwritten manuscript, it was still not in any sense a mass medium. It was not until the nineteenth century that large numbers of people were literate. Before that, the acquired skill of literacy was a major class determinant, and print, therefore, a particularly elite medium.

Ironically, mass literacy dominated the media for at most 150 years; its major influence lasted less than a century, for at the same time vast numbers of people were first acquiring the skill of reading; the development of photography—and shortly after of recordings, telephony, telegraphy, and moving pictures—was preparing the way for the electronic media revolution of the twentieth century. It was not until 1890 that newspapers and magazines began their dramatic rise. But within thirty years film and records had moved into a leading position as the major media of mass culture. In the 1950s (in the U.S. and Britain, later elsewhere), television moved into prime position. We can expect it to remain there for quite a while, although the rise of cable and videodisc in the eighties should significantly alter its shape.

We tend to think of media as being differentiated by the uses to which they are put: film, for example, an "entertainment medium," newspapers obviously devoted to news; yet, as we've noted earlier, the categories merge indistinguishably. Art (elite entertainment) is separate from entertainment (popular art) only for academicians intent on maintaining the old class structure of the media. Both art and entertainment (fiction) are distinguished from news (nonfiction) only formally, by convention. There isn't a dichotomy between the two; there's a continuum.

The history of newspapers offers an interesting case in point. Of all the media, newspapers seem superficially to be most insistently dedicated to news rather than to entertainment, yet the ideal is honored more in the breach than in the observance. Straight news is only one of ten or a dozen categories of material in the typical newspaper; categories that include gossip, sports, reviews, financial information, features, pictures, crime and disaster stories, and consumer "life-style" stories, as well as advertising—always by far the leader in terms of space. Most publications usually included in this category would be more precisely labeled crimepapers rather than newspapers. This has been true throughout the history of the medium, and recent developments only reinforce this identifying characteristic. In the U.S., *The New York Times* has generally been regarded as the most serious-minded newspaper of record, yet Table X, pp. 299–300, shows just how little space in the "New *New York Times*," as they now style themselves, is actually devoted to international, national, or local political, cultural, and economic news.

If news doesn't sell, what does? The new journalist's rule is: "Sex, power, money, style, but the greatest of these is sex." Crime may be "news" in the sense that it is more or less nonfictional, but its inherent value is almost entirely as entertainment. The newly revived interest in confessional journalism and gossip and the recent flowering of life-style stories (food, consumer goods, travel, gardening, self-help, and the like) neatly cover the spectrum of salable interests. Gossip journalism tells us how other people acquire sex-power-money-style; life-style shows us how we can.

If newspapers are only nominally interested in news, it's also no surprise to discover that they aren't even the prime source of it for most Americans any longer. According to yearly Roper polls, television has been the major news medium for a majority of the country since 1974.

THE STRUCTURE OF MEDIA

The technologies and politics of media interact in a complex variety of ways to produce the individual qualities each medium exhibits. As with other economic activities, the twin foci of interest in media are production and distribution. Since media produce and distribute information about reality, a third category suggests itself: distortion.

In media production, the essential political question concerns access: Who can use the media, and to what extent? As A. J. Liebling put it, sharply and succinctly: "Freedom of the press belongs to those who own one." The new technology of printing has greatly expanded access during the last ten or fifteen years. Offset reproduction, phototypesetting, and especially the new methods of reprography make it possible for just about anyone to produce printed materials, at least in limited quantities. Among the electronic media, the common carriers— telephone and telegraph—have by their very nature been completely open, but of course they only permit one-to-one communication, not wide dissemination. CB radio, however, does allow the individual to broadcast, if only on a limited scale. Likewise, anyone can produce audio or video tapes or discs. In general, access to the means of production in media is quite open. The problem lies with distribution.

The structure is more complicated here. The first governing factor is reproducibility: can a permanent record be made? Tapes and discs and all printed materials are permanent records, of course, but they must be produced and distributed individually. Radio and television transmission (and periodical subscription, too) provide open channels to the public. This is where the question of control becomes evident. In the first place, transmission and subscription cost a lot; capital is a significant factor. Moreover, the technology of broadcasting places strict limits on the number of transmission channels available. If cable transmission ever does reach the point where it can challenge broadcasting on a more or less equal basis, access may possibly be broadened. The number of channels cable could provide (especially with the application of fiber optics technology) is potentially so great as to suggest that cable may be qualitatively as well as quantitatively different from broadcast. But this will only be true if cable systems develop as common carriers. So far, public access has been paid little more than lip service.

The question of audience range is not so simple as it at first appears, either. While access to mass audiences is obviously where the power of media lies, the choice between communicating with a single individual and communicating with everyone is specious. Most kinds of communication that would be of use and interest to those people now effectively prevented from using the electronic media are not massive in nature. The print media already allow this flexibility: one can choose specific audiences for books, magazines, newspapers. The technology exists to address limited segments of the mass audience by cable, as well. Whether or not it will be applied is a political decision.

THE POLITICAL AND ECONOMIC RELATIONSHIPS OF MEDIA

	MEDIA ECONOMICS				MEDIA POLITICS		
Medium	Nexus	Sales Orientation	Channels	Access	Interaction	Distribution Flow	Consumer Control
BOOKS	distribution	object	open	good	unidirectional	discrete	yes
NEWSPAPERS & MAGAZINES	prod./dist.	object, ad space, audience	open	good	unidirectional	semidiscrete mosaic	yes
FILM	distribution	entertainment	open	limited	unidirectional	discrete	some
RADIO	prod./dist.	ad time, audience	limited	limited	mainly unidirect.	continuous	no
CB	manufacture	equipment	limited	excellent	interactive	continuous	no
AUDIO DISCS	prod./dist.	object	open	fair	unidirectional	discrete	yes
AUDIO TAPES	production	object	open	good	unidirectional	discrete	yes
TELEVISION	dist. (prod.)	ad time, audience	closed	none	unidirectional	continuous	no
CABLE	distribution	entertainment	limited	some	mainly unidirect.	continuous	no
VIDEODISC	manufacture	equipment	open	limited	unidirectional	discrete	yes
VIDEOTAPE	manufacture	equipment	open	good	unidirectional	discrete	yes

Nexus: Where does the concentration of economic power lie? *Sales Orientation:* What is the primary product being sold? *Channels:* Are there a limited number of distribution channels? *Access:* How easy is it for someone to gain access to the medium? *Interaction:* Is the medium unidirectional or interactive? *Distribution Flow:* Are the items distributed singly or continuously? *Consumer Control:* Must the consumer/spectator/reader/listener adjust his schedule to the medium's, or can he control the time and location of the experience?

From HOW TO READ A FILM: The Art, Technology, History and Theory of Film Media by James Monaco. Copyright © 1977 by James Monaco. Reproduced by permission of Oxford University Press, Inc.

Feedback becomes important in this context, as well. Not only do the mass media not permit us to talk back, most of them don't even allow us a measure of control over the experience. Discrete products—books, tapes, discs—can be controlled; broadcast products cannot. The development of home videotape systems will help here somewhat. But real interaction with the mass media is again a dream of the cable technologists. Pilot systems of "talkback" television are now in operation, but chances are, most of the "talking back" that cable subscribers are going to do will consist of ordering products in real time.

Now, no one would be worried about the lack of feedback if it weren't for the fact that the media exert such powerful control over the national mythos. Likewise, the question of distortion would not be important if the media record were not so much more durable than the reality which it supposedly records. One of the enduring lessons of the new journalism was the rediscovery that there is no such thing as objectivity in reporting. So long as individual authors are identified, observers can make individual judgments regarding a particular story or analysis. The problem arises with the monolithic front the media present. The only way to deal with this potentially dangerous distortion is to multiply the number of "realities" the media present and to make sure that the new channels of dissemination are not controlled by the same organizations that now control the existing means of distribution. While the hope of a diversified and decentralized media universe is dangled before us in the form of the ever-receding promise of the "wired nation," actual control over the existing distribution patterns of both print and electronic media has grown inexorably tighter.

THE BOTTOM LINE

Who owns the media?

The twelve conglomerates selected for inclusion in Appendix 2 (see pp. 305–315) had total net sales in 1976 equal to half the net sales for all media. Revenue from media operations for the twelve represents 30 percent of net sales for all media and 50 percent of sales for all nonprint media.*

• *Newspapers:* The ten largest newspaper chains listed in Table XI (p. 301) account for 51 percent of total newspaper revenues.

• *Recordings:* Warner Communications, Inc., and CBS Inc., received 65 percent of all wholesale record and tape revenues in the U.S. in 1976.

---

* Although all twelve are best known for their media activities, each is involved in a number of non-media businesses and two, Gulf & Western Industries, Inc., and RCA Corp., are essentially manufacturing conglomerates with strong interests in media.

● *Television:* The three commercial networks account for 69 percent of total television revenues. Eighty-five percent of commercial television stations are affiliated with one or another of the three networks. Although FCC regulations limit television station group owners to seven stations each (5 VHF plus 2 UHF), the top ten group owners in the U.S. (see Table VI, p. 294) have cornered the top markets so effectively that each of their stations reaches an average of 1.8 million homes, and the total number of homes reached by the top ten group's fifty-four stations actually exceeds the number of television homes in the country. (There is notable overlap in the best markets, which accounts for this seeming statistical impossibility.) Twenty-two cable operators cover 51 percent of the market.

● *Film:* In any single year, three of the top five distributors receive more than half of film rental revenues in the U.S. In 1976, Warner Bros., United Artists, and Twentieth Century-Fox accounted for 48 percent of total revenues from rentals; in 1975, Universal, Fox, and Columbia garnered 52 percent of total rental revenues.

● In any year, six media companies—ABC, CBS, NBC, Warner Communications, and any two other film companies—control more than half of each of the nonprint media markets in the U.S. Indeed, in most markets the share of the six is considerably in excess of 50 percent.

These are rough statistics, but the conclusion is inescapable: nonprint media are solidly oligopolistic (and print media are rapidly approaching that state).

So what else is new? Anyone familiar with the histories of broadcasting, film, and the recording industries has marveled at the monopoly wars that characterize each of them. There are relatively simple reasons for the high degree of centralization. First, of course, is the natural tendency of the media barons, involved in new industries without precedents, toward megalomania. If you had the foresight and vision (and they were real) of a David Sarnoff—if your dream was to turn a curious electrical phenomenon into an economic, social, and political tool that would compete directly with the centuries-old technology of print—wouldn't you want to have perfect control? In essence, the nature of the nonprint media requires the standardization that only monopoly provides.

Sarnoff's battle against FM radio is a classic case history. Having invested heavily in the AM system, he was naturally loath to see a competing system (one which provided a notably better signal) gain approval. It took Edwin Armstrong, the inventor of FM, almost ten years to get it off the ground. When Sarnoff "convinced" the FCC to shift the FM spectrum (instantly outmoding all receivers) Armstrong was beaten. He later committed suicide.

But media monopoly isn't entirely a matter of blackguard personalities, as colorful as the stories of the early years may be. Part of the problem is the patent psychology. Having invented (or at least having caused to be invented) a system of capturing and preserving and reproducing moving images, Thomas Edison naturally felt the gimmick belonged to him personally. The trouble was that film wasn't a gimmick, it was a medium of infinite applications. The first thirty years of film history comprise a chronicle of patent wars and trust wars, as first one, then another mini-mogul tried to corner the field. No one succeeded as Sarnoff later did in broadcasting. (Success came later, and for other, unforeseen reasons.) Film was simply too diverse and, during those early years, too structurally immature as an industry to permit true monopoly.

Finally, extreme centralization depends not so much on patent inventions and megalomaniacal entrepreneurs as on two simple economic facts: (1) in a medium, even more so than in other industries, distribution is the nexus: if the means of distribution are controllable (and controlled), then the industry is susceptible to control and centralization. (2) If the industry is capital-intensive (and, especially, if the distribution system is capital-intensive) then captal will out, and those few who control significant amounts of capital will control the industry.

None of the media moguls of the early years really understood all this (except possibly Sarnoff). They stumbled into positions of monopoly power.

The major film studios of the thirties and forties, for example, used to exert a vertical monopoly over production, distribution, and exhibition. A government antitrust suit in the late forties forced them to divest themselves of their theater operations. Gradually, during the fifties and sixties, the studios were forced to sell off most of their production facilities as well. The result was that now, limited essentially to distribution, the modern successors to the studios exert even more efficient control over the film medium than they did in the early days of vertical monopoly.

Anyone can make a film today. Production costs are high, it's true, but the money can be raised. There are more than enough dentists looking for tax shelters. Barbara Kopple recently financed the Academy Award-winning *Harlan County, U.S.A.* with a mixture of grants from church groups, the unpaid help of friends, and Master Charge. The problem is getting the film distributed. As the industry has grown, the distribution arteries have hardened. Only the "majors" have the necessary connections with theater chains and—more important—the significant amounts of capital (often equal to the cost of the film itself) that are needed to properly publicize a feature film. Production is relatively free and open; distribution is tightly controlled.

The same is true in recordings: you can make your own tape or record—maybe you already have—but only Warner's, CBS, and a handful of other companies can get it into the stores and pay for the requisite hype.

From a monopoly point of view, television and radio are ideal. Filmmakers and record producers have to pay to get their product distributed, broadcasters don't. We have given them control of the airwaves and in return ask only that they please, once in a while, show up in Washington to help us enact the quieting charade of regulation. As Lord Thomson put it succinctly, a television license is "a license to print money."

Thomson should know, coming as he did from the newspaper world. One of the main reasons print (including books, newspapers, and magazines) is still relatively decentralized is that the means of distribution are still relatively more open. Newspapers are still essentially distributed by their producers whether they are sold on newsstands or by subscription. While magazine publishers must confront a fairly tightly controlled newsstand distribution system, subscription copies (and that's where the money is, mainly) are delivered by a quasi-governmental organization: the U.S. Postal Service. That distribution system is open to anyone with access to a mailbox, and everyone, from *Time* magazine to the lowliest newsletter, pays the same rates. Indeed, rates are slightly lower for smaller editions—and notably lower for nonprofit organizations. The postal system never looks so good as when it is compared with the means of distribution used by the nonprint media.

But distribution patterns for print are changing too, and not for the better. As second-class rates rise, the "print tax" newspapers and magazines must pay further increases the advantage of broadcast, which uses its medium free. The ostensible rationale for raises in rates is to end the "subsidy" to second-class mailers, yet the obvious solution is never mentioned: tax broadcasters for the use of their medium so that the distribution cost differential between print and broadcast media can be equalized.*

Magazines that rely on newsstand distribution for the bulk of their sales face an increasingly centralized distribution arrangement, and although morning newspapers that are hand-delivered continue to thrive, urban traffic has contributed significantly to the death of most afternoon papers. As the postal service continues to deteriorate, large magazines turn to their private delivery systems, which require significant capitalization, and small magazines are effectively cut out.

Book publishing is perhaps the least centralized of any of the media, yet here, too, the noose is closing. Raw materials are still widely available despite the numerous purchases of paper mills and forests by

---

* Broadcast distribution is not entirely free, of course. The consumer needs equipment to receive the signal, but in general this is simply another source of profit for the nonprint media industry. If we as individuals subsidize second-class mail, we also pay a great deal more to receive broadcast material.

the dominant magazine and newspaper companies, yet the paper "scare" of late 1974, when even major publishers were put on rations by their suppliers, may be an ominous portent of things to come. But distribution is the crux. More and more, small publishers are forced into using the elaborate distribution systems of the conglomerate-owned competitors. They are reduced to producers, with no control over the bottleneck of delivery. Inventory is also a problem in book publishing (as it is in no other medium save recordings). As the cost of maintaining inventory escalates, small competitors are forced out and readers are confronted with notably more limited choices. Books, which used to be valuable because they were available over an extended period, are now approaching the condition of movies: if you don't catch them during the two or three months they are in the bookstores, you'll miss them forever.

Bookstores are, of course, an important link in the distribution chain. In the 1960s, the number of bookstores in the U.S. rose dramatically, a good sign, yet the percentage of stores owned by multi-unit chains increased even more rapidly. Chain stores grew in number by no less than 400 percent between 1963 and 1972. In that year—the last for which figures are available—chain stores accounted for 18.8 percent of all book retail establishments. The rapid growth of computerized operations such as Dalton and Waldenbooks since that time should result in even more disturbing figures in the next census report. The McDonaldization of book sales continues apace.

Yet point of sale is not the crucial problem. The chains don't necessarily sell less nourishing fare than privately operated stores, just a more limited range. And book distribution is by no means limited to stores (as film distribution is to theaters). There are approximately 10,000 bookstores in the country (as opposed to 15,000 cinemas), but books are also sold in drugstores, supermarkets, and at newsstands. Many of the success stories in publishing (books, newspapers, and magazines) during the last fifteen years are tied to these alternative sales points. Mass-market paperbacks, national gossip newspapers, and a number of women's magazines couldn't survive without them.

One of the most meaningful signs that book distribution channels are becoming constricted is the recent notable rise in the category of "Direct to Consumer" sales (see Table V, p. 292). Book clubs have always been a key to best sellerdom; the major part of this increase has been in direct-mail sales to consumers. Producers in ever increasing numbers have turned to the neutral distribution medium of the mails to reach consumers. Assuming that medium maintains a degree of health, this may be a good sign for the book industry. The distribution problems can be circumvented, but this still leaves inventory and the capital expense of advertising as major barriers to small publishers.

In fact, publishing—the oldest of the media—may be setting patterns now for upstarts film and broadcasting. If the videodisc systems now in development work as well as their conglomerate fathers say they do, and if videodisc production licenses are as cheap as they have been promised to be, then film and television will have a significant new distribution medium at their disposal.

So A. J. Liebling didn't quite have it right: freedom of the press doesn't really belong to those who own one—the means of production offer relatively free access—it does belong, however, to the people who own the trucks (or stores, or airwaves) that get the material from the "press" to us. How, exactly, do they exercise that power?

Most media criticism from a left perspective ever since the seminal work of the Frankfurt school of German social criticism has concentrated on ideological control of the media. There's no doubt much truth to the criticism—maybe even as it was phrased in the late sixties by Spiro Agnew from the right, or convicted felon, point of view. Yet the analysis is too crude. Capitalism isn't perpetuated in the media at the expense of socialism because those who control the media are capitalists but because it is the accepted myth on which the country is founded. There is a sense in which the media reflect reality at the same time as they create it. Did television coverage of Vietnam reveal the war for the horrific crime that it was and thus lead to its end? Or did it inure us to megadeaths, search and destroy, defoliation, and strategic hamlets and thus prolong the inevitable conclusion? U.S. involvement in the war hummed along for more than a decade. Would it have lasted twenty? thirty? years without the work of Morley Safer, David Halberstam, and their colleagues? The ideological interrelationship between media and the politics of reality is complex and tricky.

The problem, however, seems to be not so much ideology as non-ideology. With few exceptions, the people in power in the media have only a vaguely liberal stance. The business of America isn't political theory, it's business.

Thorstein Veblen analyzed this phenomenon thirty years before Calvin Coolidge labeled it, and he did so with uncommon insight. Veblen made the important differentiation between "industry," whose function was to produce goods, and "business," whose function was to produce profit. Industry, *si!* Business, *no!* If the early days of the media explosion in this century seem palmier, it is probably because the people who governed the media then were in the game as much for the industry as for the business. The studio system in film, for example, was truly an industry. Because moguls had to produce a certain number of films each year to fill the voracious screens they either owned or contracted for, the aim was to produce the greatest number of goods at the lowest possible cost. The numbers alone were valuable. Now that they no longer maintain ongoing production facilities (whose cost has to be amortized) nor directly control exhibition, they are free to finance and to distribute as few films as they deem financially profitable. There's no studio overhead to justify, no agreements with exhibitors to fulfill. The result: fewer films, fewer opportunities for filmmakers, fewer exhibitors able to remain in business—a continuing downward spiral, despite the fact that financially what little film business remains, is in better health now than it has been since the end of World War II.

Granted, the most equitable structure for any of the media would guarantee not only access to the greatest number but also the widest range of distribution. But given the realities of the contemporary media systems, the key to understanding who controls the media and just how they do it lies in profit-and-loss statements. The danger of conglomeratization is not so much ideological as it is financial. It's not that Charlie Bluhdorn, William Paley, and David Rockefeller meet weekly to decide what the country shall think, it's that the only principles the people in their organizations really care about have to do with accounting.

And the numbers are very beautiful. The annual reports of the twelve major media conglomerates summarized in Appendix 2 are ecstatic celebrations of them. In 1976, for example, Warner Bros. had a profit sufficient to finance an additional twenty-one films (twice that number if they used the cash for leverage or made them more cheaply). Warner Records could have financed 136 major record productions out of profits, and given each of them a first-class advertising campaign. The media businesses, in short, are capable of producing more than double what they do. And the more books, newspapers, magazines, records, tapes, films, and shows produced, the better chance that minority viewpoints will be heard. But so long as those views appear to be unprofitable, they are effectively and thoroughly censored.

Traditionally, book publishing has been not only more industry than business, but altruistic to a certain extent as well. Publishers may have ruled their personal fiefdoms with impunity, but they also felt a certain responsibility to publish poetry, "serious" novels, and scholarly books that would be marginally profitable, if at all. But the conglomerate balance sheet cancels that moral commitment. In the other media businesses, the question isn't "profit or loss," it's "large profit, larger profit, or largest profit." Short of burning the cash in the dead of night, there is no way humanly known to operate a television network at a loss. Costs are known (and artificially deflated: few television producers receive enough to cover expenses; they hope to make their profit in syndication and foreign sales). Income is known: there are only so many minutes of advertising time in the 8760-hour year, and there are far more advertisers than there is time available. Distribution is free. Knowing costs, knowing income, only a fool could lose money.

Distribution, capital, and business profit (rather than industrial product): these are the three keys to understanding how the media are controlled. A more sophisticated analysis of the media economic structure, however, must also include a sense of where the nexus lies. Most media fell into their present patterns almost by accident. Radio programming was instituted originally simply as the carrot to dangle in front of the customer for the radio set. Until the late 1920s there was even what might be called resistance among broadcasters to the con-

cept of advertising. Even Thomas Edison envisioned cinema as a device to be sold for use in the home; as a sideshow entertainment it
seemed to have a bleak economic future.

All modern media have progressed from the stage where the main
profit lies in selling hardware, to the stage in which the tail wags the
dog and software takes control. Even within software there are a
number of crucial stages. The units themselves can be sold (as they are
with books and records), or the material can serve as a medium for
advertising. The advertising, in turn, can be considered as a service (an
opportunity to reach a million readers, ten million viewers or listeners), or it can be further broken down demographically, as it is now,
so that the advertiser is buying not time or space, as previously, but a
certain audience.

Each of these factors quickly shapes a medium, and much of the
problem of constriction and distortion is due not to the ideology of the
owners of the media—not even to the quest for perfect profits—but to
the structural effects of these various elements.

Some examples: When the governing concept of advertising switched
from selling space and time to selling specific audiences, the mass-
circulation magazines—*Life, Look, The Saturday Evening Post, Col-
liers*—which had occupied center stage for a generation, found
themselves at a distinct disadvantage. Within a few years they were out
of business. Magazines like *Time* survived by splitting themselves into
demographically designed separate editions. College students are not
reading the same magazine that executives with more than $30,000 in
income who live in certain upper-middle-class zip codes are.

Likewise the shift to demographics had a significant effect on television programming. James Aubrey had delivered high ratings to CBS in
the early sixties with a schedule that attracted older, more rural viewers. These people do not have as much money to spend on soap and
cereal as younger, urban viewers. By the late sixties, *The Beverly
Hillbillies* had yielded to *The Mod Squad*. Nice for the kids, maybe;
not so nice for oldsters in Kansas. In a real sense, the class that
governs the media is the class with the most disposable income. There
is a significant market for a magazine that is delivered only to heads of
state (it exists). Arms manufacturers will pay plenty to reach those
people. The spate of ethnic magazines in the late seventies has been
made possible only because these books have been able to convince
advertisers that Italian-Americans, Latins, and Single Jewish Women
have money to spend on travel, food, drink, and sundries. They serve
their audiences, if they do, only secondarily.

The differentiation between selling the product and selling advertising is important, too, of course. Both approaches coexist in audio,
audiovisual, and print media: magazines compete with books, radio with
records, broadcast television with film (and soon with videodiscs and
cable). In each case, the nonadvertising medium is less remunerative
than the ad medium, but not by much. Moreover, advertising exerts
pressure even on nonadvertising media simply because those media

must use their ad-selling competitors to announce the availability of their product.

So the national gross advertising budget (see Table III, p. 289) is the fount from which most media financial blessings flow. Yet it is not the only one. The very size of the American nonprint media establishment confers on it certain dangerous and damaging privileges. "Cash flow" permits worldwide dominance. American *Kojaks* and *Columbos* are recut to hundred-minute lengths and recycled as theatrical features around the world. Nearly half of U.S. film revenues come from abroad. If the domestic market is so large it can sustain production of its own accord, then foreign sales are gravy and distributors can effectively undercut native producers.

Television show exporters now get up to $10,000 per hour for their product, yet despite this high figure it's still markedly cheaper for foreign networks to buy dubbed American shows than to produce their own. The BBC, no slouch at cost cutting and the pioneer in television, still has to pay more than this figure for fully 68 percent of its native programming. So trillions of personhours have been spent the world over during the last fifteen years in watching the exploits of the Cartwright family.

Almost in spite of itself, the media establishment is enormously powerful. Everyone knows that, so occasionally there are echoing cries for "reform." Do we not, now, have a Public Broadcasting Service to compete with the commercial networks? The budgets of ABC, CBS, and NBC in 1976 averaged $1.74 billion each. PBS's total revenues for the year from all sources were less than $350 million—20 percent of a network budget.

Reforms are at best meliorative. Media—both print and nonprint— won't begin to realize their full democratic potential until structural changes are carried out.

• All print media must have equal access to an efficient, "subsidized" postal system.

• All broadcast media must be forced to pay rent for their use of public airwaves—not much, a little would go a long way.

• Industrial democracy must be carried to the point where consumers and workers have more control over the business of media than investors.

• Advertising must be organized so that those of us who aren't upscale have something to read, listen to, and look at.

• In short, product has to replace profit as the media motive, and access has to be guaranteed on a basis of equality.

But these are dreams of the future. What about the present?

2. PREPOSTEROUS PARABLES: THE DECLINE OF SPORT
by E. B. White

Nobody has described the media world better than E. B. White did in this perfect *New Yorker* piece from the autumn of 1947. At the time, people probably thought it was a joke.

In the third decade of the supersonic age, sport gripped the nation in an ever-tightening grip. The horse tracks, the ballparks, the fight rings, the gridirons, all drew crowds in steadily increasing numbers. Every time a game was played, an attendance record was broken. Usually some other sort of record was broken, too—such as the record for the number of consecutive doubles hit by left-handed batters in a Series game, or some such thing as that. Records fell like ripe apples on a windy day. Customs and manners changed, and the five-day business week was reduced to four days, then to three, to give everyone a better chance to memorize the scores.

Not only did sport proliferate but the demands it made on the spectator became greater. Nobody was content to take in one event at a time, and thanks to the magic of radio and television nobody had to. A Yale alumnus, class of 1962, returning to the Bowl with 197,000 others to see the Yale-Cornell football game would take along his pocket radio and pick up the Yankee Stadium, so that while his eye might be following a fumble on the Cornell twenty-two-yard line, his ear would be following a man going down to second in the top of the fifth, seventy miles away. High in the blue sky above the Bowl, sky-writers would be at work writing the scores of other major and minor sporting contests, weaving an interminable record of victory and de-feat, and using the new high-visibility pink news-smoke perfected by Pepsi-Cola engineers. And in the frames of the giant video sets, just behind the goalposts, this same alumnus could watch Dejected win the Futurity before a record-breaking crowd of 349,872 at Belmont, each of whom was tuned to the Yale Bowl and following the World Series game in the video and searching the sky for further news of events either under way or just completed. The effect of this vast cyclorama of sport was to divide the spectator's attention, oversubtilize his appreciation, and deaden his passion. As the fourth supersonic decade was ushered in, the picture changed and sport began to wane.

A good many factors contributed to the decline of sport. Substitutions in football had increased to such an extent that there were very few fans in the United States capable of holding the players in mind during play. Each play that was called saw two entirely new elevens lined up, and the players whose names and faces you had familiarized yourself with in the first period were seldom seen or heard of again. The spectacle became as diffuse as the main concourse in Grand Central at the commuting hour.

Express motor highways leading to the parks and stadia had become so wide, so unobstructed, so devoid of all life except automobiles and trees that sport fans had got into the habit of traveling enormous distances to attend events. The normal driving speed had been stepped up to ninety-five miles an hour, and the distance between cars had been decreased to fifteen feet. This put an extraordinary strain on the sport lover's nervous system, and he arrived home from a Saturday game, after a road trip of three hundred and fifty miles, glassy-eyed, dazed, and spent. He hadn't really had any relaxation and he had failed to see Czlika (who had gone in for Trusky) take the pass from Bkeeo (who had gone in for Bjallo) in the third period, because at that moment a youngster named Lavagetto had been put in to pinch-hit for Art Gurlack in the bottom of the ninth with the tying run on second, and the skywriter who was attempting to write "Princeton 0–Lafayette 43" had banked the wrong way, muffed the "3," and distracted everyone's attention from the fact that Lavagetto had been whiffed.

Cheering, of course, lost its stimulating effect on players, because cheers were no longer associated necessarily with the immediate scene but might as easily apply to something that was happening somewhere else. This was enough to infuriate even the steadiest performer. A football star, hearing the stands break into a roar before the ball was snapped, would realize that their minds were not on him, and would become dispirited and grumpy. Two or three of the big coaches worried so about this that they considered equipping all players with tiny ear sets, so that they, too, could keep abreast of other sporting events while playing, but the idea was abandoned as impractical, and the coaches put it aside in tickler files, to bring up again later.

I think the event that marked the turning point in sport and started it downhill was the Midwest's classic Dust Bowl game of 1975, when Eastern Reserve's great right end, Ed Pistachio, was shot by a spectator. This man, the one who did the shooting, was seated well down in the stands near the forty-yard line on a bleak October afternoon and was so saturated with sport and with the disappointments of sport that he had clearly become deranged. With a minute and fifteen seconds to play and the score tied, the Eastern Reserve quarterback had whipped a long pass over Army's heads into Pistachio's waiting arms. There was no other player anywhere near him, and all Pistachio had to do was catch the ball and run it across the line. He dropped it. At exactly this moment, the spectator—a man named Homer T. Parkinson, of 35 Edgemere Drive, Toledo, Ohio—suffered at least three other major disappointments in the realm of sport. His horse, Hiccough, on which he had a five-hundred-dollar bet, fell while getting away from the starting gate at Pimlico and broke its leg (clearly visible in the video); his favorite shortstop, Lucky Frimstitch, struck out and let three men die on base in the final game of the Series (to which Parkinson was tuned); and the Governor Dummer soccer team, on which Parkinson's youngest son played goalie, lost to Kent, 4–3, as recorded in the sky overhead. Before anyone could stop him, he drew a gun and drilled Pistachio, before 954,000 persons, the largest crowd that had ever attended a football game and the *second*-largest crowd that had ever assembled for any sporting event in any month except July.

This tragedy, by itself, wouldn't have caused sport to decline, I suppose, but it set in motion a chain of other tragedies, the cumulative effect of which was terrific. Almost as soon as the shot was fired, the news flash was picked up by one of the skywriters directly above the field. He glanced down to see whether he could spot the trouble below, and in doing so failed to see another skywriter approaching. The two planes collided and fell, wings locked, leaving a confusing trail of smoke, which some observers tried to interpret as a late sports score. The planes struck in the middle of the nearby eastbound coast-to-coast Sunlight Parkway, and a motorist driving a convertible coupé stopped so short, to avoid hitting them, that he was bumped from behind. The pileup of cars that ensued involved 1482 vehicles, a record for eastbound parkways. A total of more than three thousand persons lost their lives in the highway accident, including the two pilots, and when panic broke out in the stadium, it cost another 872 in dead and injured. News of the disaster spread quickly to other sports arenas, and started other panics among the crowds trying to get to the exits, where they could buy a paper and study a list of the dead. All in all, the afternoon of sport cost 20,003 lives, a record. And nobody had much to show for it except one small Midwestern boy who hung around the smoking wrecks of the planes, captured some aero news-smoke in a milk bottle, and took it home as a souvenir.

From that day on, sport waned. Through long, noncompetitive Saturday afternoons, the stadia slumbered. Even the parkways fell into disuse as motorists rediscovered the charms of old, twisty roads that led through main streets and past barnyards, with their mild congestions and pleasant smells.

THE PEOPLE

3. CLAY FELKER: REQUIEM FOR A WINNER
by Lucian K. Truscott IV

There's no doubt now that Clay Felker is the Citizen Kane of the seventies. He's a paragon of the contemporary media mogul—and possibly a parody as well. He, more than anyone else in publishing, established the mode of the decade: sex, power, money, style. But as a businessman, he has had far more style than substance.

Rupert Murdoch's takeover of the Felker mini-empire in early 1977 was possibly the most widely covered media story of the decade. Yet no one, in my experience, got it right except Lucian Truscott in this sane piece of analysis for *New Times*. In most coverage, Murdoch came on as the heavy, yet as Truscott makes clear, he was only playing by the same rules Felker had played by. The difference was that Murdoch knew something about money.

It should be noted, by the way, that George Hirsch, publisher of *New Times*, was a former associate of Felker's. No love was lost between them. Truscott had written for *The Village Voice* before Felker bought it. Both may have had axes to grind. Yet "Requiem for a Winner" seems a far more insightful piece of analysis than the anti-Murdoch cover story *MORE* published at about the same time—"Killer Bee Reaches New York"—by Jon Bradshaw and Richard Neville. Bradshaw was a contributing editor of *New York* at the time, and Michael Kramer, publisher of *MORE*, had just recently been seriously considered for the editorship of the *Voice* under Murdoch's new management! When judging personal political maneuverings in the media world, you sometimes have to make allowances for double reverses.

Of course, in Truscott's piece there's more than a suspicion of the gossipy style Felker made famous. Form follows function, shall we say.

Last summer, Clay Felker was the Concorde of journalism—everybody wanted a seat. With New York, The Village Voice *and* New West in L.A., he was the toast of both coasts. When he walked into Chasen's, tables literally turned. At Elaine's, while he wolfed his fettuccine, writers tapped at him like woodpeckers. For almost ten years, from the outside, Felker looked like a genius: a brilliant editor, a powerful publisher, a successful businessman in the tough world of big-time magazine publishing. His name kept appearing in salty little column items—lunch with Governor Jerry Brown of California; evenings on the town with investment banker and Big Mac chairman Felix Rohatyn; openings with Washington Post owner Kay Graham clinging to his sleeve; nuzzling "frequent companion" and best-selling author Gail Sheehy in the pages of People. . . .

Felker floated his image the way a city in debt floats a bond issue: with hustle, hype, and other people's money. He created a dream, the Clay Felker dream, of instant success, stardom, the pleasures of the temporary life. The Clay Felker dream was a terminal extension of the American dream. The pages of New York, New West, and The Village Voice carried a subtle message to readers: if you want people to believe you're successful, wealthy, sophisticated, act that way. You, too, can be Robert Evans.

In 1968, when Felker started it, New York was synonymous with the New Journalism: Gloria Steinem on The Night Martin Luther King Died; Tom Wolfe on Radical Chic; Gail Sheehy on Speed Junkies; Jimmy Breslin on The Assassination of Robert Kennedy; Adam Smith on Wall Street. As an editor, Felker had a Madison Avenue knack for "now," a nose for the essence of the present tense. But, perhaps, out of a growing sense that "readers" no longer had time to read, he gradually evolved New York into a collapsible magazine filled with disposable articles. Stick-to-your-ribs journalism gave way to fast-food information. Every issue gave you just enough unabashed consumer narcissism to get through next week's cocktail parties—"What! your life isn't working? Get behind the best cheesecake in New York. . . ." Everything about the magazine said the world was on sale, and the sale ended Thursday.

Much to everyone's surprise, even New York Magazine Co., Inc., was for sale, and there is no finer testament to Felker's special brand of journalism than to see Rupert Murdoch, the Australian press baron who bought him out, trying to do Clay's thing without Clay. Slick journalism without Felker is Bloomingdale's without windows, Elaine's without Elaine.

The February 14, 1977 issue of New York is a perfect example: the compulsory man and woman on the cover, very Upper East Side, she with a drink in hand, he with a guide of some sort, no doubt New York itself, in search of the perfect $50-a-head restaurant. Ditto the cover lines: "The City for Lovers: Marlo Thomas Tours the New Trysting Places," "The Most Sinfully Delicious Chocolates in Town," "Do Body Rhythms Really Make You Tick?" Perfect Felker topics. A perfect Felker cover. Open it up, though, and slick turns to slack: the City for Lovers piece consists of one paragraph, a bunch of photos *with long captions and a hype for Marlo Thomas's latest vehicle. The February 14* New York *is ersatz Felker.*

"It's the end of an era," Robert Towbin, NYM Inc.* board member, declared recently. "I saw Gael Greene [New York restaurant columnist] at a party the other night, and she pointed at me and said, 'That's the guy who sold us out! Towbin.' Hell, we didn't sell anyone out," Towbin says almost wistfully. "We were bought out, and so was Felker. The really sad thing is this: it didn't have to happen. Clay could have had twelve good friends on his board, and together we could have withstood any kind of hostile takeover Rupert mounted. Instead, Clay alienated us one by one. . . ."

Another board member put the matter more directly. "Clay Felker," he said, "was the only executive in Manhattan with a self-destruct button on his desk."

Indeed, as the smoke cleared from one of journalism's strangest, swiftest coups, it became more and more apparent that the collapse of Felker's publishing empire last month was hardly what it seemed to readers, staff, and the rest of the media: a sudden and unexpected maneuver by an unscrupulous entrepreneur. The sellout to Rupert Murdoch was just the final step in a process of internal dissent and decay, the last schmalzy scene in a continuing boardroom soap opera that rivaled anything shown on CBS's Executive Suite *or written by* Harold Robbins. Felker's publications marketed the ways of power, preached the gospel of success. How could it have occurred to the million readers of Felker's journalism on both coasts (and in sophisticated pockets in between) that the founder of eat-your-heart-out journalism was himself eating his heart out for more success, more money? How could they have known that Felker's little empire was not the most successful publishing venture since Hefner discovered the airbrush?

Felker was obsessed by power, and because his obsession was reflected week after week in the pages of his magazines, he appeared powerful himself. Appearances were all that really mattered. "Felker got caught in a famous trap in the publishing business," said Edwin Fancher, for twenty years the publisher of The Village Voice *and just one of the many men Felker walked over on his way to power. "His ego was completely involved in growth in a Madison Avenue image sense. To Felker, growth was expanding, blowing up the Madison Avenue balloon. He was much more interested in appearing successful than in real success itself, the numbers at the bottom line."

But Felker explains the waning days of NYM Inc. this way: "I wanted to build rapidly and plow profits into growth. This was the thing which was driving me crazy. We were in a phase of rapid, significant expansion, and it was important for us as a company, to spend three to five years devoting resources to it." But the equation in Felker's mind between spending and growth omitted the bottom line.

---

* New York Magazine Co., Inc., will be hereafter referred to as NYM Inc.—not to be confused with NYM Corporation, a subsidiary of New York Magazine Co., Inc.

The awful truth about NYM Inc. is shown best in dollars and cents.
The Voice *was half as profitable under Felker as it was under its old management.* New York *profits for 1976 are virtually the same as for 1975. "The jury is still out" on* New West, *as Felker's publicists put it, but for the time being, the new California venture has cost NYM Inc. money for four quarters in a row. Stock prices for NYM Inc. in 1976 hovered around the two-dollar mark and didn't move.*

In 1975, the last year NYM Inc. turned a profit, Felker earned three cents for every dollar he spent. This was his idea of growth, finally, and in the end, he admits, it was his empire building that brought him down.

"I guess," Felker reflected recently, "the beginning of the end for me was when we bought The Village Voice."

December 1973: Felker and Alan J. Patricof, chairman of the board of NYM Inc., meet with Peter Tufo, lawyer for Carter Burden, majority stockholder of *The Village Voice.* It is understood that Burden wants to sell. Asking price: $8 million. Patricof thinks this is ridiculous, recommends against buying *The Voice* as "too fragile," a potentially dangerous acquisition. Felker tells Patricof: "The magazine business is going to hell, paper costs are up, it's getting tougher and tougher to make a profit. Newspapers are the future, and we can take *The Voice* national." Patricof disagrees. "You're not supporting me," says Clay. "I'm bringing in Felix [Rohatyn]."

"You've got to understand Clay's attitude," recalls Patricof. "He doesn't know what the word negotiate means. His position is: This is what I want. If you don't give it to me, you're the enemy. So Clay launches a six-month campaign to woo Carter Burden, to bring his price down. Carter wasn't acting all that anxious to sell. Clay was too eager to buy. This is not the way you go about acquiring companies."

Neither Patricof nor Felker knew that Burden had engaged the services of White, Weld & Co., an investment banking firm. Burden *was* eager to sell, so eager, in fact, that White, Weld had put him in touch with Rupert Murdoch. Over lunch at the Carlyle Hotel one day, Burden and Murdoch discussed a possible deal. Nothing came of it. Burden recalls that Murdoch "didn't seem right at the time." But Murdoch apparently decided to play a waiting game. Let Felker acquire *The Voice.* Watch it for a couple of years, see what Felker is able to do with it. Burden won't sell quickly. If he was still interested after he'd had a good look, there would be plenty of time to make his move. Murdoch did exactly that.

January 1974: Felker is moving on Burden. He is trying to convince Burden that *The Voice* could possibly go under within a year, and that he, Felker, could "turn it around." He could jump circulation from its present static 150,000 to 200,000 by Christmas, and to 250,000 by June 1975. All we have to do, Felker assures Burden, is axe the antiquated ways of the old *Voice* and install some "standard, but expensive publishing techniques: promotion campaigns, comprehensive

THE PLAYERS

Felker Enemies

Alan J. Patricof, chairman of the board, NYM Inc., president of Alan Patricof Associates, Inc., a private investment concern. Patricof had been with *New York* since the beginning. He was a "numbers man," and his fights with Felker were frequent and bitter. Patricof owned 25,120 shares of NYM Inc.

A. Robert Towbin, board member, NYM Inc., partner in C. E. Unterberg, Towbin Co., an investment banking firm. Towbin, along with Patricof, was the target of a March 1975 *putsch*. He owned 12,000 shares, and his firm handled a significant block of public shares.

Carter Burden, vice-chairman of the board of directors, city councilman, single largest shareholder with 425,452 shares. Sold *The Village Voice* in June 1974 to NYM Inc. in return for big bucks and 24 percent of the company. Felker *personally* held rights of first refusal on Burden's stock.

Bartle Bull, board member, publisher of *Firehouse* magazine, Burden's college friend. Bull owned 10 percent of NYM Inc., which he got in Burden's *Voice* deal. (Bull was Burden's man at *The Voice*, before Felker.) Felker moved to oust him as publisher and president of *The Voice* almost

as soon as he had Fancher, the previous publisher, out the door.

Peter F. Tufo, board member, partner in Tufo, Johnston & Allegaert, a law firm. Carter Burden's lawyer. Owned 250 shares. Described by Felker as "Burden's hit man."

Felker Friends

Himself, president and board member of NYM Inc. Owned 178,150 shares.

Milton Glaser, vice-president and board member; design director of all three NYM Inc. publications. A founder of the company, Glaser was Felker's right-hand man. Owned 52,180 shares.

Mary Joan Glynn, board member; director of the Borghese Division of Revlon, Inc. Installed as a Felker vote during 1975 *putsch*. Described by three "enemies" of Felker as "Clay's girlfriend." Owned no shares.

Theodore W. Kheel, board member, partner in Battle, Fowler, Lidstone, Jaffin, Pierce & Kheel, NYM Inc.'s law firm. Famous labor negotiator. Describes himself as "close friend and adviser" of Clay. Owned 5000 shares.

James Q. Wilson, board member, professor of government, Harvard University. Owned 500 shares.

Felker (center) with Pete Hamill and Jimmy Breslin in the offices of the erstwhile New York World Journal Tribune *May 5, 1967, the day it folded. Within six months, Felker had resurrected the newspaper's Sunday supplement magazine as* New York. *(Photo © Fred W. Mc-Darrah.)*

marketing techniques, Los Angeles or Chicago sales offices." Today, Burden admits that he was "seduced." Others, principally Bartle Bull, Burden's partner at *The Voice*, aren't so sure. "Carter just wanted the money," Bull says. He was up against the wall on signature loans he had taken out in order to purchase control of *The Voice* in 1970 from Daniel Wolf, Edwin Fancher, and Norman Mailer, who founded the paper.

Finally Burden, without his partner's knowledge, much less the knowledge of Wolf or Fancher, who were still nominally in charge of the paper and who owned large blocks of stock, negotiates the sale of *The Voice* through his lawyer, Tufo. "Can you believe it?" asks Bull in retrospect. "There I was, president of the corporation, paying this guy Tufo his legal fees, signing the fucking checks, and he's selling the floor out from under me."

Mid-May 1974: Before the *Voice* purchase could be concluded, recalls Patricof, "a new contract for Felker became a big part of the deal. Here we were, about to spend a fortune in cash and stock [about $5 million], and Felker wants a raise. I was appointed to negotiate the Felker/Glaser contract. Clay hired a consultant—at company expense. He wanted $125,000 a year, 75,000 shares of stock at two dollars per share with a loan to buy them [$150,000], and a bonus deal based on a 7 percent increase each year; on top of this, the 7 percent represented meeting only 80 percent of *his own budget projections.* He also wanted an unlimited expense account with no provisions for approval by the board. The only thing he didn't get was the $125,000. He got $120,000 instead."

June 4, 1974: Felker and Burden shake hands. Lawyers devise a contract that will eventually give Burden and Bull $800,000 in cash, and control over a third of NYM Inc. stock. (Burden, 24 percent; Bull, 10 percent). The rights of first refusal clause becomes an issue. Patricof wanted the corporation to have the first right to buy Burden's stock should Burden want to sell out. Felker wanted to *personally* have the right to buy Burden out. Felker gets his way.

Question: Just who bought out whom? What was popularly perceived to be NYM Inc. buying out *The Voice* could in another way be perceived as Bull and Burden buying NYM Inc., or at least a significant portion thereof. Felker assumes the first, begins acting.

July 9, 1974: Wolf and Fancher are summarily fired by Felker.

Mid-August–Fall 1974: Felker moves Bartle Bull, the *Voice* publisher, out of his office on the fifth floor to "exile" on the third floor. Felker hires executives at *The Voice* without consulting Bull. Meanwhile, Felker moves to completely change the character of *The Voice.* The paper gets a new "look" à la Milton Glaser (Felker's design director at *New York* and long-time partner). Front pages that once shot at the news from foxholes just beneath the surface of the establishment now blaze with movie star interviews and gratuitous attacks on figures such as Margaux Hemingway and Linda McCartney. Bull looks to support from Carter, does not find it.

Patricof: "I did my share to save Bartle. But Clay was yelling that Bartle was worthless, getting in the way. He was incredible when he screamed about Bartle. You wouldn't believe it."

Bob Towbin: "I was originally in favor of buying *The Voice because* of Bartle. I took a look at the *Voice* figures and said wow! They were unbelievable compared to *New York* magazine. I figured Bartle was helping run things down there, and one good thing we'd get out of the *Voice* deal was somebody who really knew publishing. But Felker hated Bartle. He started undercutting him right from the day we made the deal. Clay said *The Voice* could contribute $1 million a year to our earnings, but only if he was running things. I told him he'd never do it. He would never be able to keep his costs down. Bartle could have helped."

Felker receives a confidential report that projects *Voice* earnings over a three-year period (if the old management had stayed on). Before-tax earnings are projected at $1 million for 1975, $1.2 million for 1976 and $1.5 million in 1977. This is no doubt the source for Felker's statement to Towbin that *The Voice* could account for $1 million or more in pre-tax earnings for NYM Inc.

Winter 1974–75: Felker institutes a new *Village Voice* reader survey to replace the version that had been kicking around the office for a year. Felker's conclusion from the 1974–75 reader survey: "We found that a lot of people in New York simply did not like *The Voice*. I was doing everything I knew how to do, and nothing seemed to work. We were doing huge promotional campaigns, radio advertising, trade-off ads with other publications, every kind of promotion I could think of. We were putting out the best editorial we could conceive of, with the best production, the best graphics. Milton and I worked long and hard on this. Our reputations were on the line. But it seemed as if there was an ingrained hatred for *The Voice* among certain New Yorkers." The survey was suppressed, according to Bartle Bull, who was still hanging onto the publisher's title by his fingernails. Felker was not interested in information that did not support him. He forged on, initiating plans for a national *Voice* that would be even better than the one New Yorkers hated. Four-color covers. More movie stars. More zip. More flash.

Mid-March 1975: Burden tells Bull that Felker will try to vote Patricof and Towbin off the NYM Inc. board of directors at the next day's board meeting. "He called it Felker's *putsch*," recalls Bull. "Carter thought he could make peace with Felker by going along with him. I said, 'This guy is crazy. He's invading Europe. Patricof and Towbin are Poland and Czechoslovakia, and I'm France. I'm next. You're Norway. You're going too.' Carter says, 'No, no. This is going to make me stronger on the board. I'm putting on Gordon Davis. He'll vote with us.' I said 'Yes, and Felker gets his pal Joan Glynn. What good is this?' Clay says Carter will sell out anyone. Now he was going to sell out Patricof and Towbin to get one uncertain vote on the board. I knew I was next."

Patricof's recollection of the *putsch* is similar: "A board meeting was coming, the first one I'd ever missed since 1968. I had to go to Chicago for a board meeting of the Pullman Corporation. I arrived at 9 A.M., and there are messages from Towbin and Kheel. Kheel had met Towbin for breakfast that morning and told him we were going to be replaced by a black and a woman. Towbin went crazy. Clay had been after Carter, badgering him for months about us. We didn't support him; we had to go. I'm in the Pullman boardroom, and the phone is ringing every ten minutes. I left after an hour, caught the 1 P.M. plane back to New York. Towbin was beside himself. He called Tommy Kempner [a director and partner in Loeb, Rhoades & Co., an investment banking firm], and Kempner called John Loeb. Clay always had this image of John Loeb as the President or something. So anyway, Kempner calls Felker and Loeb calls Felker, and all of this is going on while I'm in the air, flying to New York. I got in at 4 P.M., took a cab, and arrived at the meeting at 4:30, half an hour late. I walked in, there I was, the chairman of the board, and I'm shaking like a leaf I'm so pissed. Towbin and Kempner pass me a note that says: 'Relax. Everything is taken care of. Clay is milk and honey. Joan Glynn and Gordon Davis have been added to the board, that's all.' Loeb and Kempner scared Felker off, and the *putsch* was over.

"After the meeting, Milton, Clay and I went into an adjoining room, and Clay goes into his number: 'You fucked me, Patricof. You fucked me back in the beginning. You fucked me out of $5,000 on my contract. You fucked me when I tried to get rid of Bartle. You undermine my management of the company by asking too many questions about the budget.' This would happen every time we had a fight, Felker is screaming and claiming that I was undercutting everything he was trying to do, almost like I was the only one on the board with questions. By this time, almost a year has gone by since we got *The Voice*, and we've all seen the numbers. Circulation is down, profits are down, he's spending money like it's coming up out of the ground. So I told him I was finished listening to him abuse and insult me and I walked out. Things were never the same between us."

May, 1975: Bartle Bull resigns from *The Voice*. "Who's going to fight Felker with me?" asks Burden. "You got in bed with him," answers Bull, "you sleep with him."

Summer–Fall 1975: Planning begins for *New West*. Patricof: "I was in favor of *New West*. Everyone was. But I was concerned that Felker would do the same thing that he was doing at *New York* and *The Voice*. You've got to remember that the first issue of *New York* came out with a hundred pages, and it was put out by thirty people. Eight years later the magazine is still a hundred pages and has a staff of 135. Publishing is a leverage business. Start-up costs are high, but once you turn the corner, every issue should earn some bucks. In 1974, we were operating at an after-tax profit of about 4 percent, and that included *The Voice*, which at the time was more profitable than *New York*. We had revenues of about $14 million, and operating expenses of about $13 million. In other words, for every dollar we spent, we were getting about three cents. Is this any way to run a business?"

In the fall, NYM Inc. board of directors approves start-up money for office space in L.A., a skeleton staff for *New West* and market research. However, Felker hires a large staff and goes far over budget on promotion.

Towbin: "*New West* was an incredible idea, but at the same time, I'm asking myself, why is Clay hiring all these people? It has to do with his obsession with power. The thing which obsessed him, he never really understood. Strange to say, but he never really understood the power of the printed word. He didn't understand that a piece had power because it could change people's sensibilities, or give them a new way of looking at things, like [Jack] Newfield's 'Ten Worst Judges' piece. But Clay never *felt* it. When he walked into his office and saw all those people laboring away in their little cubicles, now that was power to Clay."

December, 1975: Felker wants a new contract. Patricof: "It was exactly like the weeks preceding the *Voice* merger. Here we are, less than a year and a half after he signs his last contract, we're getting ready to lay out a fortune on *New West*—it was budgeted initially at $2.1 million—and Clay is holding us up for more money for him and Milton. He's the genius of the Western World. He's starting a new magazine and it's going to make us a fortune, and if we don't give him a new contract, he's going to quit.

"We meet, and he says, 'I'm starving, I'm in debt, I'm paying off my co-op. I'm underpaid and I can make more money anyplace else.' Then he says, 'I'm holding you *personally responsible* to get me a new contract. You *will* spearhead an effort to get me a significant increase in salary and benefits. You cheated me in 1974'—it's the same old litany—'You tricked me. That bonus arrangement. You *knew* I couldn't meet those budgets.' And I'm saying, 'But, Clay, we took *your* figures, and then we said you had to come within only 80 percent of your own figures and you'd get a bonus.' He didn't get the bonus because he didn't come near the budget. 'But it was a trick,' he says. 'The dividends are a trick.' I said, 'Clay, how can ten cents a share be a trick?' 'It's all applied against my loan the company gave me for more stock!' he screams. 'I never see a penny!' 'But Clay,' I'm saying, 'You got the stock.' And he's complaining that he doesn't own a big enough piece of the stock. Listen. At any point over the years since we started *New York* magazine Clay could have taken equity in the company in lieu of cash. And by this time, equity meant cash. We paid a ten-cent dividend in 1974, and would pay another ten-cent dividend in 1975. If the company was more profitable, we would have been paying more. But Clay was never focused on performance. He was focused on short-term gains: guarantees and fixed amounts. He never understood the basic truth that performance equals profits equals cash. He always said he wanted a piece of his own future, but I'm not sure that he ever really believed it."

Felker: "I was going broke. I was going deeper into debt every year. How was this happening on $120,000 a year? Well, I'm single, and I've always been in the 50 percent tax bracket, so that means I'm really living on $60,000 a year. And I never got a bonus. *Never.* I've been living in the same apartment for fourteen years, since the days of the *Herald Trib.* The combination of maintaining my co-op and the interest on various loans I received over the years to buy stock in the company, well, $60,000 doesn't go very far when you've got a lot of interest to pay. I never had enough money to get into the tax shelters the rest of the board had. I had to use my salary to meet my own expenses. But my main problem with the board back then [winter 1975–76] and right through to the end, the thing which was driving me crazy, was the basic philosophy of the way we ran the company. I wanted to build rapidly and plow profits back into growth, and the board wanted to maximize short-term profits and pay dividends."

Burden: "He was living a total expense account life. At one point, we found out that his maid was on the company payroll. I don't know where his money was going. To tell the truth, I never understood Clay and his thing about his salary."

Meanwhile, according to members of the board, Felker formed an organization within the organization to plead his case: Ted Kheel, on retainer to NYM Inc. at $25,000 a year for "personal professional services," and Jules Kroll, a professional consultant, also paid $25,000 a year.

Felker's final demand was that he would quit if he didn't get what he wanted.

Winter, 1975–76: NYM Inc. board approves a start-up budget of $2.1 million for *New West*. Felker will eventually exceed this budget by more than $2 million. Meanwhile, planning for the magazine continues. Felker is flying from coast to coast, overseeing plans, hiring staff. At the same time, he is meeting privately with individual board members about his contract.

At a party that winter, Felker stayed uncharacteristically late and got uncharacteristically tipsy (he normally drinks very little, if at all). It got to be 12:30 A.M., then 1 A.M., and still Felker was hanging on, talking about *New West*, talking about his problems with the board. Everybody is always so down on him, he is saying. It doesn't have to be that way. Finally Felker corners one of the members of the board, with whom he had often disagreed, and with tears in his eyes, obviously jet-lagged, overwrought from working too hard and sleeping too little, Felker lets go: "Don't you see?" he pleads. "Don't you understand? I know I've been difficult, but I want you to believe in me. I want you to believe that I can be as good as you. Don't you see? I'm a businessman, just like you." Felker is actually weeping. The few people remaining in the room fall silent. No one knows what to do. No one moves. Eventually, Felker goes home.

The next day, Felker calls the board member. He is chipper on the phone, full of ideas for *New West*, as always. It was, the board member recalls, as if the night before had never happened.

Felker's new demands: $150,000 salary; purchase by NYM Inc. of Felker's co-op; $180,000 in a trust fund, payable to Felker at the end of the contract period; $180,000 as a sign-up bonus; turning back his 1974 loan and stock (75,000 shares at $2 per), in return for 200,000 shares of NYM Inc., *free*; a guaranteed annual bonus of $30,000.

"You know the definition of *chutzpah*, don't you?" asked one director. "A guy kills his mother and father and pleads for mercy from the court because he's an orphan. This was Clay with his contract demands."

April 30, 1976: Patricof, Towbin, Burden, Kempner, Davis, Tufo, and Bull meet at the New York Stock Exchange Luncheon Club. According to several of those present, Towbin makes a pitch for the board to accept Felker's demands. "If we don't like what happens with *New West*, we can always fire him," Towbin reportedly says. The others remain unconvinced. Several consider that Towbin has been Felkerized. He's made several expense-account trips to the West Coast with Felker, including one to attend the Academy Awards.

That afternoon, the board meets and Towbin announces that he couldn't get a majority to go along with Felker's contract demands. "You tricked me!" Felker reportedly shouts. "You said you had it all set!"

May 1976: Kheel, Kempner, and Burden form a committee and hire two consultants to come up with a new contract proposal. It is described by one board member as "a deal I would have left my career to accept."

Basically, the proposal gave Felker the following: $125,000 salary; a cash bonus of $30,000 for 1975; a $30,000 bonus for each subsequent year that *The Voice* and *New York* meet the 1975 earnings of the two publications; $3,000 a year for financial counseling; incentive bonuses based on increases of earnings of *The Voice* and *New York* on a sliding scale above 7 percent; 12 percent of annual net pretax earnings of *New West* if actual earnings are within 80 percent of projected earnings. This would apply *for life* (10 percent to Felker, 2 percent to Glaser) if the venture did not exceed $4.1 million in start-up costs.

June 15, 1976: Felker turns the contract down, labeling it another "trick," because his friend Kheel had reservations about two clauses. Two weeks later, Felker says he hadn't turned it down, he'd only wanted changes. But by now, the board is fed up. The contract proposal was potentially the fattest ever offered Felker, and as one board member said, "We just gave up. After that, we knew he couldn't be dealt with. It was insane."

July 22, 1976: Patricof meets with Burden and Bull before a board meeting, at which Felker will make a final pitch for a better contract. Burden reportedly puffs his pipe and says, "Maybe we should sell him out to MCA and watch Lew Wasserman chew him up."

An hour later, Felker stands before a quorum of his board of directors with tears in his eyes. His graying, thinning hair is disheveled. "You don't understand!" he yells. "You're all rich kids! You grew up rich! You've all got houses in East Hampton! You don't know what it's like to come from Webster Groves, Missouri, and make it in New York!"

August 1976: "It was," Alan Patricof said, "the official final beginning of the end for me." For Patricof, spending his first summer in the Hamptons in ten years, it all happened quickly, over one weekend. His closest friend approached him one Saturday and said that Felker was spreading the word all over the island that he was going to "get rid of Patricof." A woman who will be known here as "Deep Hampton" backed up the story. Patricof met her the next day, a rainy Sunday, and she outlined what Felker had said about him at a cocktail party— denigrations of character, threats, general ugliness. "But what she really did for me," Patricof recalls, "was to confirm how public it was. Felker had taken the fight out of the boardroom and into the parties. I decided right then and there that this thing had to stop." Thus began what Patricof privately referred to as the "breakfast campaign."

Patricof continued the breakfasts through August: He wooed

Kempner, Towbin, Wilson, Glynn, Davis. None of the individual board members knew they were the objects of a campaign that ended in late August at breakfast at Carter Burden's, but all were there. Patricof focused on the issues. Costs at *New West* were spiraling upward, showing signs of passing the $4 million mark. A projection for the fall showed cash-flow deficits for September, October and November. Grim data.

Patricof emphasized spending. Editorial costs, legal costs, consultant costs, even messenger costs. (For example, entertainment and travel expenses for NYM Inc. for the first eleven months of 1976 totaled more than $186,000.) An additional and important element was the recent flop of the national *Voice*, a $200,000 loss which Felker had trumpeted as a raging success. This raised questions in the minds of more than one board member about *New West*. Carter Burden: "I was beginning to think that Felker's contract demands were a screen behind which he was hiding his own fear that *New West* would fail."

Still, the board was not ready to fire Felker. So there was discussion on how to exert authority over its own chief executive officer. It was suggested that an "executive committee" be formed to descend into the bowels of NYM Inc. to examine just where the money was coming from, and where it was going.

September 15: A revised contract proposal is presented to the board. The proposal costs-out to about the same as previous proposals (around $2 million) and this time includes a provision for the corporation to buy Felker's New York co-op and allow him to stay in it for free. It is a fat deal. Still, Felker has reservations. A good deal of the cash he could potentially realize depends on his meeting budgets.

September 29: Board meeting. The executive committee forms and is approved by the board, over Felker's heated objections. According to one present, Felker "attacked Patricof viciously." So viciously, in fact, that Patricof later consulted a libel lawyer.

October 1: Felker and Burden, a member of the new executive committee, lunch privately at the Players' Club near Gramercy Park. Unbeknownst to the other directors, Felker has a list of private demands for Burden.

Burden: "It was unbelievable. He'd been talking about this new proposal for three or four months, and he kept telling me, 'It's going to be big. You're not going to like it.' That doesn't begin to describe my reaction. In addition to his previous demands, Felker wanted to restructure the board with Patricof and Towbin off and to 'take the company private'; this would mean raising money to buy all publicly held shares at a time when the company is $4 million into *New West*, and showing cash-flow-deficit projections through the fall. Clay wanted 'absolute working control,' or he would quit.

"Then he said I was to sell him part of my stock. This would be good for me, he said, because he would arrange for the company to pay for my apartment and for a limousine and chauffeur. Then he promised to pay me $50,000 to $75,000 a year, just for sitting on the board, I guess. He told me if I didn't meet his demands by February 1977, he would quit.

"Of course, he'd been threatening to quit for eighteen months. At the September 29 meeting, he stood up and yelled, 'I quit,' but never left the room, so it was never discussed any further. I guess it was at this lunch that I first really began to consider selling my shares.

"I had been satisfied with an investment that would be worth something five or ten years from now. But suddenly, listening to Felker, I began to see my stock hanging at two-dollars per share indefinitely. The thing I had to face was this: How much was my stock worth with Felker, and how much was it worth without him? We set up the executive committee because we felt Felker had deliberately exceeded his authority with the extra $2 million which had been spent on *New West*. That was a very fast $2 million. In the end, I guess both Felker and we on the board were at fault. Felker was less than forthright about the costs of *New West*, but we had let the thing get out of hand.

"Anyway," Burden recalls, "we went down to the NYM offices twice a week and went through the books. Felker was so uptight he would fly back from California the night before we were supposed to visit. One night I was leaving the NYM office and I saw this pathetic figure coming towards me on the street. His raincoat was open, and his head was bowed, staring at the sidewalk in front of him as he hurried along. He looked up and I saw it was Clay. He looked terrible, jet-lagged, worn out. He saw me and pulled me into a coffee shop and began a sob story that we were undercutting his authority, we were screwing him out of money, we were out to get him. It went on and on until finally I got away. The next day I spoke to him on the phone, and he was totally rational, talking about cutting costs, willing to compromise. Bartle used to use Churchill's old quote about the Germans to describe Felker: he's either at your throat or at your feet."

Fall 1976: The word is out on the street that blocks of NYM Inc. stock are up for sale. Approaches are made to Carter Burden by the *L.A. Times* and by McGraw-Hill. An approach is made to Alan Patricof by Wolf and Fancher through an investment banker. Felker is talking to representatives of the Chicago-based Pritzker fortune, which owns McCall's; Peter Sharp, a Manhattan real estate magnate who owns the Carlyle Hotel; the Agnellis, who own Bantam Books; the Times-Mirror Co. Felker admits only to talking with the Pritzkers and Peter Sharp. He wants someone to either buy Burden out and give him the kind of contract his own board "denies" him, or to loan him the money to buy Burden out.

New West has by now made a big splash on the coast, but as one board member puts it: "Listen, I could advance you, advance *anybody* $4 million and you could go out there and make a big splash. Hell, for that kind of money, we could break the world land speed record, we could fly the Spruce Goose."

November 18: Patricof hears from a "quiet yet powerful business friend" that Felker has been wheeling and dealing with the Pritzkers. The friend says the Pritzkers took a good look at NYM Inc. and "weren't turned on by the property." "They met with Clay," the friend asserts, "and said, 'there's no way anybody can deal with this guy. He doesn't know what he wants.' They don't want to inherit your problems."

November 19: The surprise sale of the New York *Post* to Rupert Murdoch is announced by Dorothy Schiff, publisher. It's a handshake deal. Papers have yet to be signed.

November 20: Clay Felker, basking in press reports that he played a key role in setting up the deal between Murdoch and Schiff, invites Murdoch to "celebrate" at Elaine's, the Upper East Side watering hole. Present are: Murdoch; Clay and Gail Sheehy, his "frequent companion"; Pete Hamill and "frequent companion" Shirley MacLaine; Felix Rohatyn and an unidentified female. Murdoch describes the dinner this way: Shirley is badgering Rupert about Australia's relationship with Red China, of which he knows little. Pete is badgering Rupert about Murray Kempton, who should be hired as a columnist, which he eventually is. Gail is scanning the crowded room anxiously, looking for signs of anyone in the throes of a mid-life crisis.

In a cab on the way back to Rupert's Fifth Avenue apartment, Felker tells Murdoch that he "must" see him. Murdoch has heard about Clay's problems with his board, but this time there is an urgency to Felker's voice that catches his ear. Could this be the long-awaited time to move on NYM Inc.? Ever since White, Weld, Murdoch had been playing a waiting game. A lunch date is made.

November 21: According to Murdoch, the day after the "celebration" at Elaine's, Felker called Schiff and told her that real estate man Peter Sharp would pay her more for the *Post* than Murdoch, and would make Felker editor and publisher. Schiff, according to Murdoch, made a note of the conversation and swears to its authenticity. Apparently, Felker believed that by setting up the Murdoch/Schiff deal, he'd have a foot in the publisher's office at the *Post*, in case he lost out at NYM Inc. "It must have dawned on him at dinner at Elaine's that despite his key role in the sale of the *Post*, I wasn't going to make him publisher. So, covering himself, Felker called Schiff with his counteroffer."

Felker admits to his conversation with Schiff, but says his reference to Sharp was made "jokingly," and that he was "never interested in the New York *Post*."

November 29: Murdoch lunches with Felker in the staff dining room at *New York* magazine. Murdoch, recalling the lunch, raises his eyebrows.

"Clay begins by running back over his troubles with the board. So I say, 'Listen Clay, you've got banking friends, Felix Rohatyn in particular, why don't you work it out with him?' Felker listens, but I never got the impression that he was focusing on his problem. He saw it in such narrow terms. Get rid of this guy, get rid of that guy—he figured all he had to do was get some of his friends on the board and everything would be OK. Well, things went on, and Clay let on that he might be looking for a buyer. I told him I had an investment banker who had worked for me in the New York *Post* negotiations. It was Stanley Shuman, and I said perhaps we can work something out. This seemed to perk Clay up. I had the feeling this was the first time anyone had talked seriously to him about buying into the corporation. We left the lunch with a commitment to get together the following week."

Felker's version: "I told him at lunch, 'You're a wiz at making these deals, Rupert. You know a lot about corporate structures and how to *operate*. This is not my great area of expertise.' I had been giving him a lot of advice in relation to the *Post*, names of editors and writers he should hire, all kinds of advice. He'd just call me up and I would give it out. In return, I was asking personal advice on how to get out from under these guys [the board]."

Felker and Murdoch differ significantly on the November 29 lunch. According to Murdoch, Felker was actively seeking a deal. According to Felker, he was simply seeking the advice of a friend.

November 30: Shuman calls Patricof. They talk informally about who the major stockholders are. It is evident that with or without Felker, Murdoch has begun to move on NYM Inc.

December 2: Felker issues memos to his staffs denying an item in *Media Industry Newsletter* that NYM Inc. stock is up for sale. "I wish to state authoritatively and unequivocally that New York Magazine Company is not for sale. We are not negotiating with anyone nor will we. The only way this company can maintain its editorial independence and integrity is to remain independent."

December 3: Patricof meets Kheel at a party, and suggests that Felker should be busy finding a buyer for loose shares of NYM Inc., should make moves to "control his own destiny." Kheel asks: "Can I tell Clay?" Patricof almost chokes on his pastry-wrapped Vienna sausage.

December 9: Murdoch, Shuman, and Felker meet at Murdoch's offices at 730 Third Avenue. As Murdoch recalls it, Clay was panicky. He knew the company was in sad shape, and that some board members were trying to sell it out from under him. "There was open hostility. They didn't trust him, he didn't trust them. The same old story. At lunch the week before, he had been talking about moving to L.A., going back and forth with Gail, keeping the apartment in New York at company expense, but essentially moving his base of operations to the West Coast. So I said to him, 'Listen, Clay, if you can't work with your own board, how can you expect to work with me? Shuman and I have talked this thing over, and we think we have a solution. You want to move to L.A.? Maybe we can make a deal. We'll buy the company. You'll walk away with something like $1 million after taxes. Then we'll spin off *New West*, make it a separate company, and you can buy in with your cash from the NYM Inc. sale. We'll even be willing to lend you some capital to buy yourself and Milton a larger piece of *New*

West. And no matter how large a piece you buy, we'll be willing to give you voting rights over 51 percent of the board.'

"Clay's immediate response was: 'Will I *own* 51 percent?' That would depend, I explained, on how much capital he and Milton were able to raise to buy in. Then he wanted to know if we would be willing to lend the *New West* company $1.5 million in operating capital. I replied that might be arranged, but we would want some control until the loan was paid off. For a while there, I thought we were going to make a deal. But as soon as I mentioned control in return for the operating capital loan, he looked unhappy. The meeting ended, and we decided we'd talk later.

"Meanwhile, Shuman and I have learned that Felker is hawking the company all over town, looking for a deal."

Felker's version: Murdoch proposed a deal similar to the one described above. "But when I asked them about lending us some money for *New West*, he turned to Shuman, and Shuman nodded his head negatively. This is my best recollection. They were talking five dollars per share to buy out NYM Inc., and then spin off *New West* as a separate company for me and Milton."

Shuman, referring to a diary he kept throughout these transactions: "Clay was looking for unfettered control over money and editorial in any kind of deal we made. We told him we'd be willing to buy NYM Inc. and set him up with *New West*. But nothing seemed to make him happy. He seemed to be living in a dream world. The one thing he was definite about was that he would never be able to deliver the board. But by that time, we had figured out the situation. We didn't need Clay to deliver the board. The board was ready to deliver the company without him."

A few days later, Felker called Murdoch and said he didn't "want to take this thing any further." But it was already too late. By now, Murdoch and Shuman are meeting with lawyers and mapping strategy. Their target is Carter Burden and his 24 percent of NYM Inc.

Murdoch: "Clay had really set himself up for the fall. There he was, personally holding the rights of first refusal over Carter's stock, and *he already knew we were moving on Carter.* You know what Gail Sheehy told Byron Dobell [Felker's managing editor at *New York*]? She said it was Clay's midcareer crisis. He was bored with *New York*, bored with the whole thing, but he was blocked. He had no easy way out. When he talked with us, she said, it was Clay's way of breaking through. If that's true, Clay Felker whetted our appetite. The more we looked at the property, the more we wanted it."

December 17: Murdoch and Shuman meet Tufo and his "frequent companion" Princess Lee Radziwill at Parioli Romanissimo on First Avenue.

Murdoch: "Incredible scene. Here we are, sitting around this table, and I've got the Princess on my left, talking to me endlessly, and with the other ear I'm trying to overhear Shuman romancing Tufo, trying to bring the price down. Tufo was talking seven dollars a share, and our idea was around six dollars. So Shuman is laboring away with Tufo—he's much better at these things than I, actually—and I'm having to make two and a half hours of small talk with the Princess, which I'm even worse at. Incredible. Finally, Tufo's two-way radio goes off, and he has to rush to the prison or something, and we're saved. We left with no deal, but we figured that at seven dollars a share, we'd preempt anyone else interested in acquiring NYM."

That night, Tufo calls Burden in Sun Valley and tells him that seven dollars a share was the price, and that Murdoch was definitely interested. Burden instructs him to inform Felker.

December 21: Tufo calls Burden again and says that Murdoch is pressuring him to deal.

Burden: "For the first time, I really had to focus. Until then, I didn't know if my stock was worth anything without Felker. Now they wanted an answer in twenty-four hours. I told Tufo to tell them I wanted ten days, and I told him to inform Felker. I asked Tufo if Murdoch knew about the stockholders agreement and the rights of first refusal clause, and he said, yes, they knew, but all legal opinions indicated that it wasn't in effect, because the company had lost money for four straight quarters. In any case, I wanted to give Clay a chance to make an offer, even though he had failed to inform us of all his dealings with the Pritzkers, and with Peter Sharp and others."

Felker: "I've made my position clear on Carter Burden, and I'll stick by it. He's a goddam incompetent little dilettante."

December 22: Tufo lunches at Felker's apartment, formally announces that Murdoch has offered seven dollars a share, that Burden is actively considering the offer, but that he wants to give Clay a chance. Felker's first response, according to a sworn affidavit from Tufo: *"He can have it."* Felker maintains that he made no such statement. Then, according to Tufo, Felker said he wanted time to work out a deal that would give him 51 percent of the company. "Fine," said Tufo. "Go ahead." Burden has not made up his mind about Murdoch's offer, and has asked for ten days to think things over.

That afternoon, Felker starts to move.

Murdoch: "Felker rang me up—it must have been right after he saw Tufo—and he was incredibly abusive. He was in the bullpen, at his desk in the office. I could hear people around him over the phone. He wanted an audience, and he was really giving it to me. 'I'll sue you, I'll finish you in this town'—he was making all kinds of threats. Then suddenly, after two or three minutes of abuse, he quieted down and was completely rational. He began telling me about his problems with *The Voice*. He said he had 'completely lost it,' lost a sense of what the paper was. The most recent issues had been the worst in the paper's history, he said. Then suddenly he's screaming at me again, threatening lawsuits, and I said, 'Look, Clay, we're serious, but we haven't made up our minds. I'll get back to you.' "

Felker admits to the phone call, but denies having been abusive with Murdoch.

Late that afternoon, Murdoch, Tufo, Shuman, and Burden have a conference call. As Shuman recalls the conversation, "We wanted to begin talking to other large stockholders, but Burden asked us to hold off. He wanted to give Clay his shot."

December 23: Tufo calls Burden and says Murdoch has agreed to hold off and give Burden time to make up his mind.

December 24: Burden, in Sun Valley, phones Felker at the NYM offices, fails to reach him. Burden tries the Beverly Wilshire Hotel, the Beverly Hills Hotel, finally calls the Lyford Cay Club in Nassau—no Felker. Felker had, in fact, gone to Nassau, where he stayed at David Frost's house. Asked why he left town in the middle of a fire storm, Felker replied simply: "I felt protected by my rights of first refusal clause. I don't know how to explain it to you. I just felt protected, that's all."

December 27: Burden finally reaches Felker in Nassau. The connection from Sun Valley is not good. The vacationers have trouble understanding each other.

Burden: "As Tufo told you, Clay, Murdoch is interested. It's a serious offer. But I'll give you a chance to come up with a counteroffer. I'll consider anything you propose, but remember, because Murdoch has promised to buy out all other stockholders at the price he offered me, you'll have to come up with the same sort of deal."

Felker: "You're going to be charged with selling out two New York publications! You're going to be the target of a huge publicity and legal battle! If I were you, I wouldn't want to take on Dick Reeves, let alone Clay Felker!"

According to Burden, Felker was enraged, but "We left it with him promising to come up with something by the end of the week."

Felker's recollection of the conversation completely omits the threats: "That's not the way it happened. It was a friendly conversation. I told Carter I'd buy out him and Bartle at seven dollars a share. I told him I knew Reeves had a particular dislike for him—he was convinced Burden was a phony liberal. I told Carter if he went through with the Murdoch deal, an awful lot of people were going to be mad at him."

December 29: Kay Graham, owner of the *Washington Post*, is about to offer to buy Burden out. Felker calls Burden. From Burden's sworn affidavit:

Felker: "I just want you to know how grateful I am for this opportunity. Maybe now we can finally be friends. I'll have a proposal by Friday [December 31]."

Burden: "The conversation was incredible. Two days before, he had been abusive and violent on the phone. Now he's sounding like he's my best friend. *But he never mentioned any specific deal or offer.* He didn't tell me he was involved with Kay Graham and the *Washington Post* in any way. He never said the *Post* was about to make an offer to buy my shares. I hung up and called Tufo. I was perplexed. I asked him what was going on with Felker. He didn't know any more than I did."

Felker's recollection: "It was a friendly phone call. There was no question in my mind that he had accepted my offer."

Burden's response: "What offer? I didn't even know the *Washington Post* was in on the deal until the following day when I got a phone call from Tufo. He told me he would be seeing Felix Rohatyn, who represented the interests of the *Post*, on Friday, the 31st."

December 30: A series of phone calls. Burden: "Tufo spoke to Felix that night and Felix said the *Washington Post*'s offer would involve dissolving NYM Inc. and making it a division of *Newsweek*. There would be no continuing role for me on the board. NYM Inc. would cease to be an independent company. I called Murdoch. He said, 'Felker is no friend of yours. Did you know he was up all of last night negotiating a new contract for himself with the *Washington Post?*' There it was. Clay and his contract. So I called Clay and said, 'Look, you've said for eighteen months you wanted control, and now you're selling out the whole company to go to work for the *Washington Post*. This wasn't what I had in mind at all.'

"He started screaming. [Burden reads from the affidavit.] 'You have to accept the *Washington Post* offer tomorrow!' he said. 'If you don't accept the *Washington Post* offer, there will be no magazines left to sell! I'm going to go to court to stop you! I'm going to turn the entire New York journalistic community against you!' I told him if he continued to threaten me, I'd sell to anybody but him. I hung up. The irony here is that at that point I hadn't really made up my mind. I called Tufo and told him to call off the meeting the next day with Felix."

December 31: Rohatyn strides into Tufo's office and bids $7.50 for Burden's stock on behalf of the *Washington Post*. Within minutes, Tufo calls Murdoch and Murdoch betters the offer. As far as Burden is concerned, the *Washington Post* is finished.

Informed that Murdoch has bettered the *Post*'s offer, Felker goes searching for somebody to come into the deal with megabucks and stay in. He places a transatlantic call to Sir James Goldsmith (aka Jimmy Goldsmith), a brash, ultraconservative London financier who is looking into publishing. Felker knew Goldsmith through David Frost and Felix Rohatyn.

But in Jimmy Goldsmith, Felker had a problem. Goldsmith was too far right. The Britisher had filed more than a hundred writs of libel in twelve months—said to be an English record—against *Private Eye*, the satirical London biweekly. He'd also filed a criminal libel suit against the *Eye* editor. The analogy is not perfect, but to the extent that *Private Eye* is a muckraking, scandal-mongering tabloid, it is to London what *The Voice* is to New York. Asked why he had turned to Goldsmith, a man he knew would trouble his liberal writers, Felker said quickly, "He would have gone to $8.50 a share; he might have gone to $9. I was scrambling, that's all."

January 1, 1977: Felker obtains a temporary restraining order (TRO) in Federal District Court, barring the sale of Burden's stock to Murdoch pending the outcome of whatever legal battle he can mount. The issues are complicated, but they boil down to this: Felker had a stockholders agreement with Burden giving him the rights of first refusal over Burden's stock, should Burden want to sell it. At midnight on December 31, the fourth quarter of 1976 ended. NYM Inc. had lost money for four quarters in a row. According to the stockholders agreement, this nullified the rights of first refusal held by Felker over Burden's stock. According to Felker, the agreement was null and void due to the enormous start-up costs attributed to *New West*. However, there is nothing in the stockholders agreement excluding start-up costs of new ventures from determining losses over a four-quarter period. Felker's case is described by many as "weak," but it is strong enough to convince the court to issue a TRO.

The same day, Tufo, Shuman, and Murdoch fly to Sun Valley. Upon landing, they are informed that the TRO has been issued. However, none of the principals has actually been served with the order by the court. They decide to go ahead and make a deal with Burden that would become effective pending the outcome of the court case.

At 9 P.M., over a table in a Sun Valley restaurant, Murdoch and Burden sign papers transferring the Burden shares, pending the outcome of the court situation. Murdoch signs a check for $3.5 million and passes it to Burden.

"Let me see it," says Susan Thompson, Burden's "frequent companion." "I've never seen $3.5 million before."

January 2: By the evening of this Sunday, Rupert Murdoch either owns outright or has signed documents giving him control of 51 percent of NYM Inc. stock. "We didn't have to go after them [the other stockholders]; they came to us. Every single one of them wanted to sell. Not one of them was going to stand by Clay," Stanley Shuman recalls.

That night Murdoch phones Kay Graham, informing her that he now controls NYM Inc.

"We'd kept up a warm but occasional friendship over the years," Murdoch recalls. "Once she gave a dinner for me and invited Henry Kissinger. Another time I visited her at her country home, and Felker was there. It was Clay-said-this and Clay-said-that. Every time Clay would suggest something, she'd pick up the phone and call [Ben] Bradlee, or one of her executives at the *Washington Post*, and relay the suggestion. You could almost *feel* the hostility coming back over the line.

"Anyway, when I told her, she was very, very emotional: 'I wanted to buy it [NYM Inc.] for my Clay,' she kept saying. 'You've taken it away from my Clay. You're going to ruin his life's work. All the writers will leave.' She was sobbing. I'd rung to make peace, to tell her I hoped our friendship could survive. She wasn't abusive, but I could hardly believe how emotional she was."

The same evening, Towbin also called Graham to tell her he was selling his stock to Murdoch. (Towbin's 1.5 percent put Murdoch over the top.) "She was crying, and all she could talk about was how we were ruining 'her Clay.' The only thing I could conclude was that the woman was in love with Felker. There's really no other way to explain it."

Shuman: "She [Kay Graham] had been willing to go to $7.50, maybe higher, in the bidding, but all her advisers were against it. Felker was making the same contractual demands on the *Washington Post* that had alienated his own board of directors."

January 3: After a tumultuous board meeting, during which Murdoch and Shuman are installed, Felker retreats to the offices of *New York*. There, he finds the support so lacking on his own board.

January 4: The staff of *New York* issues a press release denouncing Murdoch on "moral" grounds, supporting Felker and threatening to walk out if Murdoch takes over. Principal spokesmen are Richard Reeves and Ken Auletta, Felker's chief political writers. But neither Reeves nor Auletta bothers to check that Felker had, only a month before, been actively negotiating with Murdoch in the fruitless attempt to sell *New York* and *The Voice* in return for a major share of *New West*. Nor do the *New York* staffers bother to inform themselves of the Jimmy Goldsmith connection.

Shuman: "The irony of him hiding behind his writers during the fight that first week in January, when he'd already cut their balls off—it's just too much."

January 6: The staff of *New York* magazine stages a work stoppage, a walk-out in support of Felker. That afternoon, Felker and Glaser go to the offices of the magazine, look around, and announce that it is impossible to put the magazine out.

At the same time, lawyers for Murdoch are in court. They report to the judge that Felker has refused to meet with Murdoch, as he had been urged to do earlier in the week, when the TRO was issued. The judge, who on Saturday issued the order barring sale of Burden's stock to Murdoch, now apparently realizes that Felker is simply using the federal court as a delaying tactic to maneuver. He orders Felker to meet with Murdoch to see if they can reach an agreement.

January 7: At 4:30 A.M., Friday, about the time Bartle Bull was pasting up the last house-ad to fill the last hole in a very peculiar issue of *New York*, the deal went down. That afternoon, the court lifted the TRO, thus completing the sale of Burden's stock to Murdoch. Felker sold his 10 percent of the company to Murdoch at $7.50 per share, netting $1.2 million. *New York* magazine and Clay S. Felker were no longer synonymous. Loyalists who left the magazine with him, and who stayed behind to answer the phone while he vacationed for ten days in the French West Indies, answered his home phone with the words: "Clay Felker's office." It truly was the end of an era.

Shuman: "Clay's position right to the end was: 'I can't make a deal with you because the writers will consider that I sold them out. You either go away, or I'll litigate.' The truth was, he sold them out a long time ago. The amazing part of it is that he really believed what he was saying. It was a kind of tragic madness."

Murdoch: "What Clay never realized was the simple fact that there are ways to deal with a board of directors. He could have had them to lunch twice a year at the offices of *New York* with the governor or Teddy Kennedy or somebody. He could have flown them all to the West Coast for the founding of *New West*, given them a dinner at the Beverly Wilshire, introduced them as 'my colleagues and friends.' With a few simple moves, he could have kept them happy. Instead, he made enemies of them, one by one. They were all threats to his authority. He was afraid of them."

Felker, over scrambled eggs and vegetable soup at Stark's on Madison Avenue: "These guys have been lying about me for years. I'm going to defend myself the only way I can—legally. They're lying to cover up a dishonorable act. I'll sue for libel. I'll sue anybody who tells a lie about me. It's the only recourse I have left. I'll sue. . . ."

A few months after Truscott's analysis appeared, Felker bounced back. With the substantial financial help of Vere Harmsworth—a British newspaper magnate and Murdoch competitor—Felker and friend Milton Glaser formed a company that bought Esquire magazine, where Clay had begun his career as an editor years before.

4. THE SILVERMAN STRATEGY
by Jeff Greenfield

If there is one class of people responsible for the style of American television, it's programming executives. In the fifties, Sylvester "Pat" Weaver at NBC developed "specials" to compete with series. In the early sixties, James Aubrey at CBS pursued the lowest common denominator of sitcoms single-mindedly. The late sixties were best characterized by CBS's Mike Dann, who projected the "nice guy" image at the same time he put together an impressive string of ratings wins. Fred Silverman is the programmer of the seventies, no doubt about it. Jeff Greenfield profiled him for *The New York Times Magazine* in the spring of 1976, shortly after he had moved over to the third-ranked network from perennial leader CBS. ABC was not in third place for long. At least some of the credit must go to Silverman. For the last two years ABC ranked well ahead of its two competitors. In early 1978, Silverman announced a switch to NBC, then the third-ranked network. If he wins there, he'll have performed a unique network "hat trick."

The corner office on the thirty-eighth floor of the American Broadcasting Company's corporate home on the Avenue of the Americas looks directly out across Fifty-third Street at the far more imposing glass-and-granite building of the Columbia Broadcasting System. Only a few hundred feet separate the two buildings, but, by other measures, the distance between the two companies is enormous.

For twenty years, the CBS television network has been the godfather of American commercial broadcasting, drawing more viewers and making more money than NBC-TV or ABC-TV. For more years than that, ABC has been the industry's stepchild, a perennial last-place entrant in the ratings race. Until three years ago, the network had gone more than a decade without making a profit: in 1974, the spread between CBS's pretax profits and those of ABC was more than $60 million. And in the fall of 1974, ABC's prime-time schedule had been the laughingstock of the industry. As an expression among insiders had it, "in broadcasting, CBS is Bloomingdale's, NBC is Gimbels, and ABC is Korvettes."

Now, however, ABC is making its most ambitious bid for network parity. Since the start of the mid-January "second season," it has won the race for the highest ratings every week. Its new shows are almost all hits, three of them appearing among the top ten shows, one of them—*Laverne and Shirley*—twice winning the highest ratings of any series. And, barring a sharp change in viewing habits, ABC will beat out NBC for second place in the viewing averages for the whole season.

A keystone in this effort is the man who occupies this corner office, a programming executive whose commercial instinct and competitive drive are something of a legend. After thirteen years spent helping to keep CBS the most-watched of the three networks, thirty-eight-year-old Fred Silverman was lured across the street—with a salary of $250,000 a year, stock options, a paid-up $750,000 life-insurance policy, and corporate "perks" on both coasts—to become president of ABC Entertainment and help build ABC into a fully competitive network.

At stake are millions of dollars in advertising revenues, hundreds of millions of dollars in rising—or falling—stock prices, the reputations and careers of powerful corporate executives. And something else is at stake too. The three networks are all run by privately owned corporations which derive their revenue from supplying programs to publicly licensed television stations, stations occupying airwaves that are, in theory, publicly owned and operated in the public interest. By examining the tactics and assumptions of so highly regarded a programming talent as Fred Silverman, by watching how ABC is so rapidly moving into network parity, we may learn something about what the incomparably powerful public resource of broadcasting has become—and why.

Fred Silverman is the living repudiation of the stereotyped television executive. Instead of the soft-spoken, sleekly groomed, evasively polite man in the gray flannel suit, Silverman is a blunt, combative, overweight pulling guard. His hair is indifferent to style: his shirt, suit, and tie are rumpled and out of fashion. When he is crossed—by the sloth of a subordinate or a challenge to his judgment—his temper can be explosive. He is also candid about his failures (*"Me and the Chimp,"* he said, "represented a new depth in television programming"), and a man whose willingness to make quick decisions has won him the respect of television's creative community.

Mike Dann, who first hired Silverman for CBS and whose job as the network's programming chief Silverman inherited, calls him "the least political executive in the history of broadcasting, and the best all-around program bureaucrat I have ever seen. There were *three* CBS network presidents who wanted to fire Freddie. But he is absolutely brilliant in putting together a winning schedule."

Unlike other programming executives, who came to television from theatrical talent agencies, or from the networks' sales or research departments, Silverman is a "pure programmer": He has done nothing else in his adult professional life. His master's thesis at Ohio State was a study of ABC-TV's programming through the 1950s; his first job was at an independent Chicago station, WGN-TV, in 1960. Two years later, with his sole network experience a summer in ABC's mailroom, the twenty-five-year-old Silverman was hired as director of daytime programming at CBS by Mike Dann, who had been impressed by the insights into network television expressed by Silverman in his master's thesis.

"Fred was always very commercial," recalls Mike Filerman, a Playboy-TV executive who worked with Silverman in Chicago and later in New York. "He was a perfectionist at picking promotions; what pictures we'd run in *TV Guide*, what the logo of the advertising should look like. He would box out every hour of every day: how our shows would flow, what the competition was doing."

Ethel Winant, who was a CBS talent executive throughout Silverman's tenure with the network, remembers that, even when he was running CBS's Saturday morning children's programming, "he had plans, charts, cards. He'd broken everything down. He was totally compulsive. He'd go over a script or story line again and again and again. Someone would say, 'We just did that, Fred,' and he'd say, 'Let's do it again.' It was like psychoanalysis. Repeat and repeat until you see something you didn't see before."

After seven and a half years supervising the daytime gold mine of soap operas, game shows, and Saturday morning cartoon shows filled with rock music, monsters, and animated violence, Silverman inherited the top programming job in 1970, after Dann quit. In that time, CBS scrapped its rural shows (*Hee Haw, Beverly Hillbillies*) for the more sophisticated urban comedies of the Norman Lear and Mary Tyler Moore studios. Although some industry sources downgrade Silverman's success because, "with the Lear and MTM spin-offs any network would be first," virtually every television producer I talked with regards Silverman as a uniquely skilled commercial programmer.

Part of his reputation rests on sheer hard work. "He reads everything," says Universal-TV vice president Tom Tannenbaum. "Every script, every story line. He is on top of every phase of the show, from casting to the story to the promotion and advertising." And several producers tell of receiving telephone calls in Los Angeles from Silverman, who is based in New York, at 1 A.M. or later East Coast time, offering script or casting suggestions.

Producer Gary Marshall (*Happy Days, Laverne and Shirley*) observes that Silverman "doesn't spend time with small talk at meetings. The other guys will ask where you got your jacket or whether you played golf. With Freddie, it's 'What have you got?' "

He is also willing to commit his network to decisions, without the dissembling appeals to research and committees. When Bud Austin, head of Paramount-TV, tried to pitch ex-*Mannix* star Mike Connors, the networks wouldn't accept his terms. Silverman called Austin into his office at ABC and said, "Bud, before you leave this room, we'll have a deal with Mike." They did. "When Fred wants something," Austin says, "he'll get it."

He also lets producers know exactly where they stand with prospective pilots, either assuring them "this is gonna make it to the air," or telling Norman Lear that he wasn't taking *Mary Hartman, Mary Hartman* because "I hate it."

It is not, however, Silverman's decisiveness that makes him so highly valued (and highly priced) a programmer. It is, rather, his commercial, competitive instinct about what performers and schedules will work. He himself says, "It's a screwy world—there is no science to what we do." To build a successful TV show, "you either start with a unique idea, or a personality, and you take it from there." It is Silverman's gift that he can size up what kind of personality will appeal to the mass audience better than any other programmer—and he can put that show in the right time period to win the biggest possible audience. "He doesn't believe in premises as much as *people*," Gary Marshall says. "He'll suggest *this* actor, *that* actress."

Thus, Silverman suggested to producer Quinn Martin that the portly William Conrad, seldom thought of as a leading man, could work as a hero-detective in *Cannon*; that Buddy Ebsen would make a countrified Columbo in *Barnaby Jones*. He called Norman Lear after one Bea Arthur appearance on *All in the Family* to suggest that Maude would make a good character on her own. Sonny and Cher and Tony Orlando and Dawn were signed by CBS after Silverman had seen their acts once. In his first days as CBS programming head, in the summer of 1970, he saw a rough cut of the first Mary Tyler Moore show and moved it—at an unusually late date—to Saturday night, where it has anchored the successful CBS comedy bloc for six years.

Further, a typical Silverman success will feature very strong personal and family bonds, at home or at work. Ethel Winant suggests that "Freddie is very much a believer in home, family values, the middle-American silent majority in a society that puts it down. He has a conservative, old-fashioned morality." He is prouder of *The Waltons* than of any other show he helped develop and, coincidentally or not, many shows developed during Silverman's tenure at CBS feature the extended family that is rapidly vanishing in real life. Mike and Gloria (*All in the Family*) finally leave the Bunker home—and move next door. Bob Newhart's sister comes to Chicago—and falls in love with Newhart's next-door neighbor. Rhoda Morgenstern moves back to New York—into the same apartment building her sister lives in. Doc rents out the apartment in his brownstone—to his daughter and son-in-law.

Silverman's insights into what will work on television do not exist abstractly. Even as a graduate student at Ohio State, his judgments and values were linked to the maximization of profit. He wrote scornfully of those who demanded higher quality shows:

"Television critics and pasteboard programmers have all the answers (on paper) though they fail to realize that network television is basically a business with profit and loss columns, stockholders' meetings and annual reports." ABC's biggest successes in the 1950s, Silverman noted, came with shows that had "a leading man with whom the audience can easily identify. They are all distinct personalities—flesh-and-blood characters who possess an intangible quality which makes them real and believable. . . ."

It is his capacity to turn this general insight into specific judgments —about personalities and programs—that has made Silverman a winner in the commercial television universe. A producer who has worked closely with him says, "Freddie's not out to put 'better' television on the air. Freddie's out to *win*." "It's like a *war* with him," Gary Marshall says. "And he says, '*This* is how we'll win the war.' "

If any institution needed an executive with a reputation for winning, it was the American Broadcasting Company. It has been the industry's kid brother, last among unequals, throughout its twenty-five-year history. It was born when the Federal Communications Commission ordered the National Broadcasting Company to divest itself of one of its two radio networks in 1941. After years of court challenges, NBC finally sold off its weaker "Blue" network to Edward Noble, the "Life Saver king," keeping the far stronger "Red" network for itself.

SILVERMAN'S FAMILIES: *Mary Tyler Moore and friends at the wedding of Ted Baxter and Georgette.*

SILVERMAN'S FAMILIES: *Sally Struthers and Rob Reiner as the younger generation of* All in the Family *with Archie's grandchild.*

SILVERMAN'S FAMILIES: *Isabel Sanford and Sherman Hemsley as the Jeffersons with son and friends.*

SILVERMAN'S FAMILIES: *The* Good Times *clan—Florida (Esther Rolle) with James Evans (John Amos) and young Michael (Ralph Carter): a second-generation spin-off.*

SILVERMAN'S FAMILIES: *The cast of the ill-fated* Beacon Hill. *By far the largest of Fred Silverman's CBS families, this one was a blatant imitation of* Upstairs, Downstairs, *but English class sensibilities couldn't be translated into American terms.*

The inherent imbalance worsened when commercial television began after World War II. A combination of money, reputation, and prior ownership of desirable big-city channels made NBC and CBS far more powerful than ABC, both in talent and in network size. To this day, ABC has thirty-five to forty fewer stations in its lineup than either of the other networks. And even though ABC got an infusion of capital in 1953 when United Paramount Theatres bought the network, the gap has never been narrowed. For more than twenty years, Leonard Goldenson, who engineered the merger and who has served as chief executive of ABC ever since, has witnessed an endless struggle to achieve equality that has never fully succeeded.

There have been successes: ABC was the first to lure the Hollywood studios into television production, first with *Disneyland* in 1954, then with Warner Brothers' products such as *Cheyenne, Sugarfoot, Maverick, Colt .45* and *77 Sunset Strip.* In 1960, in 1965, and again in the early 1970s, the prime-time program lineup, with a heavy dose of violence-tinged, action-oriented shows, gave NBC and CBS ratings problems.

But there was, in one current executive's words, "no consistency of performance." Constant management shake-ups gave the network a permanent air of instability. Leonard Goldberg, a former programming executive who now co-produces three ABC shows, remembers that "when I took over as head of programming in 1966, I told another executive that we needed a three-year timetable. The guy told me, 'You don't understand—if we don't get better ratings by next Tuesday, we ain't gonna *be* here.' "

Still by the fall of 1974, ABC was in respectable shape. Under its president, Elton Rule—brought in after the collapse of a widely criticized merger attempt with I.T.T. in the late 1960s—the company was making a $50-million profit on revenues of just under $1 billion. The television network, the dominant source of company revenues, had strengthened its news division with the signing of Harry Reasoner; its sports programming, including the Olympics and *Monday Night Football*, was more than competitive with that of the other networks, and its *Close-Up* documentaries had won its public affairs division critical acclaim. But the heart of a commercial network is its prime-time schedule. And in the fall of 1974, ABC-TV experienced what Elton Rule calls "The Debacle."

In a sharp departure from ABC's traditional emphasis on urban, fast-paced action-dramas aimed at the eighteen-to-forty-nine-year-old audience, the network scheduled a string of shows with settings in the old Northwest, Alaska, Kansas, with names that suggested a berserk typewriter: *Kodiak, Kung Fu, Nakia, Kolchak*. One Hollywood executive explained that "Marty Starger [then programming chief] had reached the point in his career where he wanted to do prestige things, good things that had no chance for the ratings." And Michael Eisner, the network's thirty-three-year-old vice president for program development, acknowledged mistakes in piecing the schedule together. "There was no way," he said, "that any sane person could have watched our Friday night schedule."

The disastrous performance in the fall of 1974—when ABC was averaging two million fewer viewers than second-place NBC—began the network's most serious effort to cure its inferiority complex once and for all. In November 1974, forty-two-year-old Fred Pierce was named president of ABC Television. A twenty-year veteran of the company, Pierce had always been placed in a subordinate role. As one executive said, "It took an enormous failure for ABC to wake up and see who its strong horses were. They were forced to go with Pierce—the one man who knew the most about broadcasting—and put him in a position of responsibility."

Under Pierce, January 1975 saw a return to the urban, action-oriented ABC style with *S.W.A.T.* about a special Los Angeles police team whose uniforms, automatic weapons, and style reminded some viewers of storm troopers, and with *Baretta*, starring first-rate actor Robert Blake in the role of a streetwise cop. With *Barney Miller*, a funny smart comedy about a New York police precinct, the network also had its most appealing comedy.

In addition, Pierce developed a shrewd—and sound—theory for the fall of 1975. Reasoning that the new family hour would make the 8 to 9 P.M. time period one of mass confusion, Pierce decided to make his strongest schedule at 9 P.M., with familiar returning shows to attract the disoriented adult audience. This gave the network an aura of stability and made its fall schedule work to the limits of the available shows. In addition, Pierce, Mike Eisner, and Marty Starger developed new shows with unexpected appeal—*Welcome Back, Kotter; On the Rocks* —and turned one marginal show, *Six Million Dollar Man*, into a smash hit by moving it to 8 P.M. Sunday.

Finally, Pierce reached out to Fred Silverman, whom he had first met when Fred was a graduate student studying ABC. The network wanted to give the industry—and Wall Street—the strongest possible signal that it was moving toward an all-out challenge to its rivals. And Silverman, tempted by the chance to help build a network into supremacy instead of keeping it there, and feeling, according to colleagues, that his work at CBS has been somewhat taken for granted, crossed Fifty-third Street and joined the kid brother.

While Silverman had nothing to do with devising fall 1975's ABC schedule, he did supervise the execution of the new shows. In so doing, he brought one of his principal theories to bear on the new efforts. Because his emphasis is on people, rather than promises, Silverman emphasizes their likability. Norman Lear remembers that, at CBS, "Freddie worried that we had George Jefferson a little too abrasive in *The Jeffersons.* When we made *One Day at a Time,* he said, 'Don't make the young woman so abrasive.' He'd like everybody to be lovable."

One of ABC's new shows, *On the Rocks,* was set in a prison, a hard place to find lovable people. John Rich, a one-time Lear colleague who adapted the series for American TV from a British original, declares that "the show was originally harder. ABC changed it to a minimum security prison from medium. Silverman said, 'Stay away from the hard stuff. Don't scare people away.' It hurt us to water it down a bit, but in the long run it helped. Freddie understood that you had to like the characters first—then you could get rougher."

For the midseason schedule in January 1976—the one which has pushed ABC into first place in the ratings—Silverman gave ABC a solid string of early-evening youth-oriented shows by using another of his favorite techniques: making characters attractive to a national audience by showcasing them on already popular shows.

Thus, Silverman noticed the characters of Laverne DeFazio and Shirley Feeney, two working-class girls in the 1950s, on a *Happy Days* episode, and immediately spotted the twosome as a possible series. He also scheduled *Laverne and Shirley* directly after *Happy Days* and kept the highly popular Fonzi from *Happy Days* around for the new show's first two episodes. *The Bionic Woman* is simply a character introduced and killed off in one episode of *Six Million Dollar Man*, then "brought back to life" on her own show, surrounded by characters from the parent show. In the world of Fred Silverman, familiarity breeds acceptability.

Silverman does not accept the argument that this kind of schedule is repetitively old hat. He sees the new ABC schedule as "diverse. There isn't one new show that's like any of the other new shows." He concedes that *The Bionic Woman* is "derivative" but counters this admission by calling attention to the Donny and Marie Osmond show. "It takes a certain degree of boldness to put them on the air," he asserts, "a couple of kids, eighteen and sixteen, who've never done a show of their own." And of *Almost Anything Goes*, which features dozens of contestants climbing greased poles and falling into vats of viscous liquids, he insists, "A show like that has as much validity as *60 Minutes*."

It is not that Fred Silverman doesn't like different kinds of shows altogether; his last CBS schedule did include the high-risk *Beacon Hill*. Further, ABC in 1975–1976 had both critical attention and commercial success with *Eleanor and Franklin*, the impressive Winter Olympics coverage, and *Rich Man, Poor Man*, which, while more soap opera than profound drama, is at least attempting to tell a story wider in scope than a car chase. Starting in early 1976, the network presented the first of six episodes in a new dramatic series, *Family*, with an unusually prestigious roster of talent—Sada Thompson as star, Jay Presson Allen as writer, Mike Nichols as producer, Mark Rydell as director, and Laszlo Kovacs as cinematographer.

The point is that Silverman is acting both out of conviction and personal preference when he helps turn the vast majority of prime-time programming over to weary and conventional forms. "In the TV universe in which I work," he says, "the chances of coming up with new forms are remote . . . If there are two ways to go, and they're equally valid, it's insane not to do something that would involve less risk."

Thus, when he was asked why the appealing male-buddies chemistry of *Starsky and Hutch* wouldn't be successful outside the form of guns-and-screeching-tires police melodrama, he laughed. "What should they be?" he asked. "Architects? Then what happens to them? If you try to develop twenty-two story lines a season, you find yourself reaching, after the first four or five."

Beyond this reasoning, however, is the apparent fact that Silverman, in contrast to many other network programmers, simply likes what he sees. Mike Dann, his predecessor at CBS, says, "Freddie has a total passion for everything that's on the air." Ethel Winant recalls, "Once when he was on vacation in Europe, I talked him into coming to Ireland. The best time he had was in Dublin after dinner; he would sit in the hotel and watch two and a half hours of American reruns. If they put *life* on television, Freddie would enjoy it more."

However, Silverman says that, after spending thirteen hours a day in the business, "there are better things to do than look at television"—by which he specifically means spending time with his wife (and former secretary), Kathy, and their three-year-old daughter, Melissa. For all his professional dynamism, Silverman is something of an introvert. "There are very few people with whom I have a personal relationship," he says. "There are some very private people, and I'm one of them." Silverman lives with his family in a luxury apartment on Central Park West; with the mid-season schedule in place, he intends to step back from his demanding pace, slow down, and lose weight. "I have a very strong imperative," he says. "My doctor says if I don't, I'm gonna die."

Meanwhile, Silverman benefits from an ironic circumstance. The schedule he left behind at CBS proved to be extremely weak, with a Friday night lineup that has already been completely scrapped, and a conspicuous lack of success among the new shows (which might possibly be traced not to Silverman's selections but to his absence during their development). At ABC, the team of Pierce, Eisner, and the now-departed Starger built a strong fall schedule which gave Silverman breathing space to develop the new January shows and spin-offs that will give the network its best seasonal ratings in at least a decade. With Jackie Gleason, Nancy Walker, Carl Reiner, Mike Connors and other talent waiting in the wings for next fall, ABC will have its best chance in history to finish first over the course of a season. [It did.] (NBC, which entered this season with high hopes of finishing first, had a full-scale programming disaster and is now all but resigned to finishing last.)

Oddly, the potential success of ABC may only ensure that the overwhelming majority of network television will grow increasingly cautious. Lee Rich notes that one reason *The Waltons* was put on CBS's schedule was that the network was so clearly in the ratings lead that it had nothing to lose by trying this relatively innovative show. "Today, with the competition tightening, nobody can afford to take a new form."

While Mike Dann, now a consultant with Children's Television Workshop, asks wistfully, "Shouldn't there be *some* programming for the minority audience on a regular basis some of the time?" the three commercial networks continue to battle for the greatest number of viewers all of the time, for numbers mean revenues, dividends, and profits. "That's the nature of the business," Silverman says. "If you don't like the system, you can get out of the business."

5. POLITICS UNDER THE PALMS
by Bo Burlingham

There's a bit of an air of fiction here, but then consider the characters Burlingham has to deal with. In the New Hollywood, Jane
Fonda hosts the Academy Awards, not Bob Hope, and people rise
for a standing ovation at the drop of a yellowing blacklist. Co-opta-
tion? Perhaps. More important is the sense in this typically ram-
bling *Esquire* story of the smudged line between reality (played in
this episode by Huey Newton) and star-studded fantasy.

Burlingham's previous piece for *Esquire*—a jaundiced portrait of
Richard Goodwin—had resulted in lawsuits.

It certainly seemed like a raw deal for Harry Reems. After viewing his
performance in *Deep Throat*, a Memphis jury had awarded him a two-
year sentence for conspiracy to transport obscene material across state
lines. But never let it be said that Hollywood sat idly by while the Feds
sent poor Harry to the pokey. On June 1, 1976, Warren Beatty threw
a benefit for him at a small bar on Wilshire Boulevard, and *everybody*
came to stand up and be counted. Marjoe Gortner was there, and
Bobby Morse, and Lorne Greene, and Gail Fisher from *Mannix*. Dave
Garroway sipped a martini in the vestibule. Sally Quinn interviewed
Jack Nicholson about the sex life of Governor Jerry Brown. Hugh
Hefner walked around in a denim jacket, sucking nervously on his pipe.
Buck Henry waved and smiled, and Louise Fletcher blew kisses at
random. Rod McKuen stood before a microphone. He was wearing a
rumpled blue work shirt and rumpled trousers. He ran a rumpled hand
through his rumpled hair. "This time they get Harry Reems," he said.
"Next they'll do away with *All the President's Men*. I myself wrote
a poem with the word 'fuck' in it. I don't want to go to jail for that."

In the darkest corner of the dimly lighted bar, a tall, thin man sat
hunched over a table and observed the festivities. He wore Lee slacks
and a navy-blue shirt, open from the neck to a point well down his
torso. A handsome fellow, he looked Mediterranean, like a Greek

prince, with curly golden brown hair, delicate hands, a pronounced Adam's apple and a striking face—long, narrow, tan, with high cheekbones, sleepy blue eyes and thick lips. His name was Bert Schneider and his mood was sour. "What's going on here?" he muttered. "What is this, anyway? A fund raiser or a media event or what?"

Schneider is one of the more successful producers of the new Hollywood. His second motion picture, *Easy Rider,* is said to have revolutionized the industry, and he followed it with two more hits (*Five Easy Pieces* and *The Last Picture Show*), as well as several duds. In 1975, he won an Academy Award for *Hearts and Minds,* the documentary about U.S. involvement in Vietnam, and achieved some notoriety by using the occasion to read a message to the American people from the Provisional Revolutionary Government of South Vietnam. Coming on the eve of the Communist victory in Indochina, the action caused a commotion among the stars, though it did not surprise many of them. By then, Bert Schneider was known as one of the most committed—if elusive—activists in Hollywood.

Like Jane Fonda, Schneider became involved in radical politics in late 1969 and early 1970, at a time when the protest wave of the sixties was nearing its high-water mark. As the tide receded during the next four years, his activity—like hers—increased. But while she played to the gallery, ignoring the catcalls and jeers, he stayed backstage, generally preferring to manipulate the action rather than star in it. He shrouded his role in mystery. People talked and wondered but knew little more than that his name sooner or later appeared in association with most of the leftish causes that sought succor in Hollywood.

Most, but not all. In the spring of 1976, Schneider was keeping his distance from the cause of the moment, Tom Hayden's campaign for the Democratic nomination to the U.S. Senate. Jane Fonda had mobilized dozens of Left-Liberal stars for her husband. They gave money, held fund raisers, appeared in commercials, went out on the hustings. But Schneider held back. Much as he disliked the incumbent, Senator John Tunney, he did not contribute a nickel to Hayden's candidacy. Some said that he had tried to promote Shirley MacLaine as an alternative.

On the other hand, he did support Harry Reems. He had offered to testify at the trial. He even deserved some of the credit for this benefit's success. More than any other individual, he had helped foster that strange blend of guilt and nostalgia through which Hollywood tries to atone for its sins of silence during the McCarthy era. Nonetheless, from his corner of the bar, Bert Schneider found the spectacle quite distasteful. At length he rose from his seat. "I guess I should do my duty," he said. "Where is Harry Reems? What does he look like, anyway?" He ventured a few steps into the main room, packed with revelers and drunks trying—as best they could—to stand up for Harry Reems. The noise and the glitter soon proved too much for him. He retreated. "If you see Harry, tell him I was here," he said and left.

I waved good-bye, watched him go, and went back to gazing at the stars. In the end, I spent three weeks observing them at cocktail parties and rallies along the campaign trail. But then and later my attention kept returning to Schneider. Friends and critics alike found him fascinating. They would tell me the rumors of his strange alliances and daring deeds, mingled with gossip about his unorthodox life-style—his dope, his girl friends, his parties. And then, as often as not, their voices would drop; their eyes would lower; they would glance stealthily from side to side; and I would hear once again the bizarre tale about a producer, the disappearance of a black revolutionary and the death of a young man named Artie Ross.

THE PRODUCER

Bert Schneider lives in Beverly Hills, off Benedict Canyon Drive, in a spacious house with a sauna, a swimming pool and a breathtaking view of Los Angeles. At night, he can sit beside the water and watch the city lights flicker below, listen to the locusts, and breathe fresh country air. By day, it takes him half an hour or so to drive to his office on La Brea in Hollywood.

Inside the office building, the signs read B.B.S. (after Bert Schneider, Bob Rafelson and Steve Blauner), the partnership that made Jack Nicholson a star and heralded the rise of the independent filmmaker. B.B.S. does not function anymore, but Schneider and Rafelson continue to share the premises. Schneider works out of a suite on the third floor, in which I am now sitting. "This is no ten-by-twelve office," he points out. It is, in fact, more like forty by fifty, complete with a white Tiffany chandelier, a billiards table and an antique nickelodeon. A plush sofa stands next to the door and faces Schneider's desk. Two photographs are on the wall behind him. In one of them, Bert beams as he stands with his arm around an equally radiant Huey P. Newton; in the other, Bert smiles alongside Fidel Castro. I can see on an adjacent wall an even larger photograph of Newton alone and next to it a pair of poems he wrote, typed up, and gave to Schneider. A map detailing "The Input/Output Structure of the United States Economy" fills another wall, and then there are the posters, some Cuban, some European, most about films (*L'Amour l'après-midi*; *The Gentleman Tramp*), and one that shows the crouched figure of a *guerrillero*, a rifle to shoulder, and around him the words: "GUATEMALA—9 AÑOS DE LA LUCHA ARMADA."

Hollywood has not seen much armed struggle in recent years—a circumstance that has not fazed Schneider. He has kept active enough to earn himself a fat FBI file, portions of which have recently come into his possession. He pushes a button on his desk and asks his secretary to bring in a copy.

He tells me of his introduction to radical politics. "I had read Richard Fariña's book *Been Down So Long*, and identified with the story. So I arranged to meet his widow, Mimi. She showed up with Alan

Myerson, the director, who was working with a San Francisco theater group—The Committee. We wound up connecting. I remember a discussion we had over dinner. We were sharing antiwar sentiments. Alan asked me some probing questions. How deep was my commitment? What would I do to stop the war? I recall one very clearly. Would I lay my body down in front of a draft board?

"Well, he made me question myself, you know, just how full of shit was I? It's something I've asked myself many times since. I'll give you my current answer: still a lot. It seems like I'm always measuring my performance against my convictions and coming up short."

His secretary brings in the FBI file. He sits down on the couch and thumbs through it. "Here, look at this," he says, showing me a description of one "Berton J. Schneider," with "black hair, sometimes dyed blond . . . weight 200 pounds." (In fact, Schneider's brown hair does have a blond tint—from the sun, I suspect, rather than peroxide. He is, moreover, quite skinny, weighing no more than 170 pounds.) Schneider, the report continues, is often seen in the company of a certain "starlet"—no doubt Candice Bergen, with whom he lived for some time. "Bergen went crazy over that," he says with a smile, and flips the pages. "This is my favorite: 'Sources described Schneider as being about thirty-eight years of age, tall, manly, wears long hair, mod clothing, and has outspoken nature.' "

I inquire if I might look through the file. He declines, then shows me another page. "Recognize that date?" he asks. August 21, 1971. "Look," he says, "they had someone reporting every four hours on my movements. I was in Nevada at the time, and they watched every step I made." He paused. "The day George Jackson was killed." In the course of an escape attempt. What was Bert Schneider up to, anyway? "I'd rather not go into it."

He puts down the FBI file. I ask more questions about his life. He grows slightly impatient. "Why don't we talk politics?" he says. "You want to know what I think of the Presidential candidates?" He stands up, walks around the office and rattles off his assessment of the Democratic field. But "electoral politics is all a lot of crap, really. Now everyone is talking about this Humphrey-Hawkins bill to solve unemployment. What a shuck! It doesn't come close to solving the problem. Look, there's only one solution in the long run."

"What's that?" I ask.

Standing in front of his antique nickelodeon, facing his pool table and chandelier, he smacks a fist into his palm and says, "The fucking working class has got to get off its fucking ass."

THE PRODUCER GROWS UP

Schneider was born forty-three years ago in New York—"with a silver spoon in my mouth," as he puts it. His father, Abraham, the son of poor immigrants, had worked his way up from messenger boy to executive at Columbia Pictures. (He eventually became president.) The family lived in Westchester County. Bert remembers himself as a rebellious youth, the black sheep, hanging out with the caddies on the golf course and the help in the kitchen. His father had been a Roosevelt Democrat through the war but turned conservative with the rest of the country in the late forties. He disliked Communists and felt the Hollywood Ten should go to prison. Schneider recalls heated arguments over the dinner table, in which he challenged his father's McCarthyite views.

Such tensions notwithstanding, Bert and his brothers, Harold and Stanley, carried away an awful respect for the old man. Abbie Hoffman tells a story about attending a heavyweight championship fight many years later with Bert, Harold, Bob Rafelson and Jack Nicholson, among others. They arrived early to take their ringside seats at Madison Square Garden. They remained seated as the fighters entered the ring. They remained seated as the national anthem was played, and then as the boxers slugged it out. But when Abe Schneider came by to say hello, his sons leaped to their feet.

Bert went from prep school to Cornell University, where he majored in government. He did not last, however. "I was thrown out for bad marks, gambling, and girls." The Army beckoned. In filling out his selective service form, he confessed to marginal association with groups of dubious loyalty. An investigation followed. Ultimately, he avoided the draft and went to work for Screen Gems, a Columbia television subsidiary, in New York City. There he rose steadily from production assistant to vice-president and treasurer—"with a healthy assist from my family background"—earned a good salary, married, settled down. "I was into the American dream," he says. "I pushed my political instincts into the background. I wanted a family, career, money, the whole bit."

In 1965, Schneider quit Screen Gems and moved to California. where he went into business with his boyhood friend, Bob Rafelson. Raybert Productions soon struck gold. Capitalizing on the Beatles trend, they found four personable, all-American mop-tops, put guitars in their hands, dubbed in an accompaniment, and called them The Monkees. They milked the phenomenon for three years. Then, following The Beatles' success with *A Hard Day's Night*, they decided to make a film "to commemorate the rip-off and bury The Monkees." The result was *Head*, which appeared in 1968, produced and written by Bob Rafelson and Jack Nicholson, directed by Rafelson, with Bert Schneider as executive producer.

Meanwhile, Dennis Hopper and Peter Fonda were working on a film called *Easy Rider* about two free-spirited hippie bikers and their adventures among the red-necks. When problems developed with their sponsor, American International Pictures, Jack Nicholson suggested they take the project to Raybert. They did, and Bert Schneider became executive producer. Jack Nicholson, as an alcoholic Southern lawyer, turned in a brilliant performance and began his rise to stardom. As for

Easy Rider, it cost only $375,000 to produce and wound up grossing more than $35 million. The major studios became convinced that there were hefty profits to be found in sponsoring low-budget, independent movies that were aimed specifically at the large youth market.

Schneider seized the time and concluded a deal with Columbia, where his brother Stanley was now president and his father, Abe, chairman of the board. Under the arrangement, B.B.S. Productions (which superseded Raybert) would make—and Columbia would pay for and distribute—six films; so long as the budget did not exceed $1 million per film, B.B.S. could produce whatever it pleased, without having to seek Columbia's approval.

At thirty-six, Bert Schneider had hit the jackpot. He had wealth, power, independence, a happy marriage and two children he loved. And when the press wrote about the "New Hollywood" in 1969, it was referring to Schneider and his friends. (*Esquire*, for one, did a cover on the subject—depicting a cathedral with an *Easy Rider* marquee—which Schneider framed and put in his office.) They believed their good notices—you always do—and fancied themselves avant-garde. Whether they were or not, they certainly comprised a fast crowd—handsome men and beautiful women, sharp clothes, flashy cars; swimming pools and saunas, travel, excitement, glamour. And dope—the best, in fact, that money could buy. Schneider acknowledges its impact on his life. "You can't really measure the impact of any one factor, but drugs—marijuana and the psychedelics, I mean—did awaken in me other, new ways to look at the world."

HOLLYWOOD, 1969

To the extent that a film like *Easy Rider* had a political message at all, it was thoroughly insipid, mainly wrong, and new only to Hollywood, which had passed unscathed through a riotous decade. Movie people had shied away from the movements of the sixties. Antiwar rallies in Los Angeles drew small crowds compared to those in New York and San Francisco. As late as the summer of 1969, the politically active Hollywood left was minuscule and did not include any New Hollywood stars.

Probably the most committed radical in the film community was a Canadian citizen, Donald Sutherland's wife, Shirley, an actress herself and a prime mover behind the Friends of the Black Panthers. It was a tame group, which held Sunday brunches to raise money for the Panthers' Breakfast-for-Children program. At 4 A.M. on an October morning in 1969, a commando unit of the Los Angeles Police Department broke into her sumptuous home, waved guns in the faces of her children, and hauled her off to jail. TV reports showed her wearing a fur coat as she entered police headquarters to be booked for illegally purchasing a case of hand grenades. She denied the charge. The police destroyed the evidence, then produced a single grenade, which they said had been saved from the original batch. The case dragged on for several years before Federal District Judge Warren J. Ferguson threw it out, saying that Shirley Sutherland was the victim of White House Plumbers-style dirty tricks. In the spring of 1976, the Senate Intelligence Committee revealed that a week before her arrest the FBI had named Shirley Sutherland a prime target of its Counterintelligence Program (Cointelpro) against the Black Panther party and had circulated leaflets with a deprecating caricature of her. But by the time the report appeared, the Panthers had changed and so had their Hollywood contacts. Shirley Sutherland was out; Bert Schneider was in.

THE PRODUCER GOES LEFT

In the sixties, Schneider attended some local anti-war demonstrations and worked on a Beverly Hills peace referendum. But he did not really commit himself to the peace movement until the November 1969, moratorium. At the time, B.B.S. was producing *Drive, He Said,* based on the novel by Jeremy Larner and directed by Jack Nicholson. Larner—a former speech writer for Eugene McCarthy—suggested that they organize a movie moratorium on November 15, urging filmgoers to give their money to the peace movement instead. In lining up sponsors for the strike, he and Schneider focused their efforts on the stars of the three "buddy" movies of 1969—*Easy Rider* (Fonda and Hopper), *Butch Cassidy and the Sundance Kid* (Paul Newman and Robert Redford), and *Midnight Cowboy* (Jon Voight and Dustin Hoffman). Only Redford and Hoffman declined to join, because—says Larner—they considered it an ineffective gesture.

They were, of course, correct. Nonetheless, the event launched Schneider on his voyage left. He went to Washington for a press conference. When he arrived at the moratorium headquarters, he introduced himself and offered his help. Someone mentioned that the telephone company was planning to suspend service because of an unpaid bill. Schneider wrote out a check for the full amount—$40,000 or $50,000, to the best of his recollection. The press conference received scant attention, but—as he himself later observed—the money opened doors. He began to meet the stars of the antiwar movement: Sam Brown of the moratorium, Allard Lowenstein, Abbie Hoffman and, through Hoffman, other members of the Chicago Seven. They fascinated Schneider, and not only because of their idealism. Alan Myerson says, "Bert's art is manipulation—people, events, ideas. He is extremely skillful at it. . . . These people were involved in manipulation on a scale he had never thought of, in areas he had never explored."

Schneider regards these experiences—the moratorium and his introduction to the Chicago Seven—as turning points in his political life. There was a third factor as well: Jane Fonda. She had been living in France with her husband, Roger Vadim, and their daughter, Vanessa.

Except for some slight contact with American deserters and draft resisters, she had stayed clear of politics. But in the fall of 1969, she returned to America and before long threw herself into the movement.

Schneider met Jane Fonda through her brother, and they were close for a time. She introduced him to Shirley Sutherland and the Panthers. Since then, rivers of bad blood have come between them, but he still describes Fonda as an "inspirational figure for me" in 1970. "She was not prepared to take things lying down. She put her commitment to the test and accepted the consequences."

His politics were even more eclectic than hers in those days. Abbie Hoffman's book *Revolution for the Hell of It* pushed him toward the Yippie left. He began to criticize the moratorium as too tame. "He saw personal gestures as political action," recalls one former associate. "He used to smoke dope in front of the Columbia executives. To him, this was a radical act. He boasted about it. Then he would argue that promiscuity was revolutionary, that monogamy was bourgeois. At about this same time he was flipping for Baba Ram Dass." His marriage, meanwhile, was on the rocks, and he began to be seen with Candice Bergen.

SHIRLEY SUTHERLAND'S POLITICAL PARTIES

It was a peculiar season for the New Left—the long, hot winter of 1969–70. It began with the conspiracy trial of the Chicago Seven and it ended with Kent State. The Weathermen emerged in October, then quickly disappeared underground. The peace marchers gave way to the street fighters. Buildings were bombed, burned, and trashed. Brand-new movements appeared overnight. But most important were the weekly fire fights between Black Panthers and police, during one of which Panther leader Fred Hampton was shot to death while sleeping in his bed.

Most of the Panther leaders who survived wound up in jail or in exile. The others devoted themselves to raising money for bail and legal defense. These efforts often took them far from the ghetto turf—to Leonard Bernstein's town house on the Upper East Side, to Herschel Bernardi's cottage on Fire Island, and to the gorgeous mansions of Hollywood. It was, in short, the season of Radical Chic.

Shirley Sutherland organized a benefit at her home. Bert and Candy came, as did Warren Beatty, Peter Fonda, Jon Voight, James Earl Jones, Paul Mazursky, Bobby Darin, Waldo Salt, and Dalton Trumbo, among others. A lawyer named Luke McKissick presented the Panthers' case. Beatty cross-examined him at length, then announced that he would not help the cause until he had heard the other side from the Los Angeles Police. (He never did contribute. "You would have thought we were buying guns," says Shirley Sutherland, "but the checks were made out to McKissick, for God's sake. It was all for *legal* defense.") Peter Fonda offered to donate a copying machine, and did.

Later, however, he threatened to sue if Shirley Sutherland did not put up half the cost. Most people gave money. "We were asking for one-hundred-dollar donations," Shirley Sutherland says. "Jack Nicholson, he must be a good soul. He came down the hill with his hundred dollars and left. A lot of people brought it in cash. This puzzled me for a long time. Then I would hear that so-and-so had a non-American wife or something."

Shirley Sutherland planned a second party following Academy Awards night. Jane Fonda called to say that Elizabeth Taylor and Richard Burton were throwing a losers' party that same evening. That year, Fonda was a loser with *They Shoot Horses, Don't They?* but she assured Shirley she would attend the Panther benefit instead. "I said, 'No, you won't,'" Shirley Sutherland recalls. "'You go there and invite all the losers to our party.' Well, she did and they came to the fund raiser, announcing that Elizabeth Taylor had promised to donate six thousand dollars to the Panther defense. I said, 'What do you mean, promise? You call her and say we need the money now.' She telephoned, using some excuse. We needed to show the check around or whatever. Don went down to get it. He ran into Burton first, who wrote out a check for three thousand. Then Taylor came stumbling around and wrote out another. I think they'd had a lot to drink. The next morning, we were at the bank by nine fifty-five. Later they told David Frost we had hijacked the money."

TONY CURTIS GOES TO A PARTY FOR TOM HAYDEN: A DIGRESSION

A couple dozen people stood in clusters around the Bel Air living room—most of them middle-aged, wearing expensive, casual clothes and HAYDEN FOR SENATOR buttons. They sipped cocktails and chatted. In one corner, a combo played mellow tunes, all but drowned out by the blare of a rock band in the backyard. Around the room were scattered statues of women in various poses; abstract paintings hung on the walls; a collection of Oriental objets d'art filled a large Indian cabinet. And right there in the middle of the living room was a reflecting pool, its surface so smooth as to resemble glass, or perhaps clear plastic. A young woman in black velour pants waved to someone, began walking across the room and stepped into the water. She blushed and withdrew her dripping foot. The hostess appeared with paper towels to mop the floor. A few moments later, another woman wandered into the room. She drifted toward the combo and splash! The hostess reappeared with more paper towels. A white-haired man in a seersucker suit and white shoes was talking earnestly to another fellow. He edged toward the pool. Without thinking, he lifted his leg to rest it on the water. More blushing, more paper towels.

Out back, the rock band wailed. A black theater group performed some outrageously racist skits. A barbecue dinner was served. Finally,

Hayden arrived. As he spoke, I spotted Tony Curtis. "I've always admired Tom," he said. "Back in the sixties, you know, I identified with the things he was saying and I couldn't say. Then, of course, he married Jane, who is my friend. And Henry, such a wonderful man. It became, you know, a family thing, more touching than other campaigns." Later I learned that Jane Fonda had known him only slightly before the campaign.

THE BLACK REVOLUTIONARY

Huey P. Newton—minister of defense of the Black Panther party— was serving two to fifteen years in San Luis Obispo, having been convicted of voluntary manslaughter in the shooting death of a policeman in 1967. On May 29, 1970, the California Appellate Court set aside his conviction and ordered a new trial. On August 5, he was released on bail.

Jane Fonda was filming *Klute* in New York with Donald Sutherland. At the suggestion of Mark Lane, her mentor of the moment, she offered Newton her apartment on the Upper East Side for a press conference. It turned out to be a foolish idea. Newton spoke to the media as he sat in a white, green and gold antique chair, his image reflected in ornate, gold-framed mirrors. He wanted to drum up support for the Panthers on trial in New Haven, but news reports focused on Fonda's gilded furnishings. Afterward, she began to receive death threats and had to hire a bodyguard.

Bert Schneider met Huey Newton in September and came to regard him as "the most charismatic and special figure I have ever met. . . . He has probably had the most profound effect on my life of anyone I have ever known. He was the first person I'd met who didn't have any hate. He understood that revolution had to do with love." Their friendship went beyond politics, Schneider says. "We couldn't have been friends if our politics were too removed. Actually, we approach politics in similar ways. But it became a deep, personal relationship. We made a strong connection."

Fonda, on the other hand, did not connect with Newton. She moved away from the Panthers and gave herself to the anti-war movement instead. Likewise, Shirley Sutherland found other projects that needed her more, notably the nascent prisoners' union.

GROUCHO MARX STUMPS FOR TOM HAYDEN: A DIGRESSION

On a bright Wednesday morning in late May, Groucho Marx took the stump for Tom Hayden. He appeared at a rally in the Fairfax district, the Los Angeles version of Flatbush. He wore a gray leisure suit, a turtleneck shirt and a navy blue golf cap. An attendant held him erect, and his words were barely intelligible, but earlier he had sent the following telegram:

DEAR TOM, YOU CAN BET YOUR LIFE THAT YOU HAVE ALL MY SUPPORT INCLUDING MY ARCH SUPPORT FOR YOUR WALK THRU CALIFORNIA. I WOULD LOVE TO HOT-FOOT IT WITH YOU BUT I AM PLANNING TO CAPTURE YOUR WIFE JANE AND SMOTHER HER WITH KISSES THE WHOLE TIME YOU ARE AWAY. ABSENCE MAKES THE HEART GROW FONDA. I AM 90 PERCENT WITH YOU THE OTHER 10 PERCENT GOES TO THE WILLIAM MORRIS OFFICE. YOU ARE A BRILLIANT SPEAKER AND AN HONEST MAN. YOU HAVE MY ADMIRATION, MY RESPECT AND MY VOTE. DON'T STOP. YOU ARE THE BEST MAN FOR THE JOB. THE SECRET WORD IS HAYDEN AND TELL 'EM GROUCHO SENT YOU.

HOLLYWOOD, 1970

In the fall of 1970, *Variety* ran a full-page advertisement announcing a public meeting to organize a protest against the Vietnam War. Jane Fonda, Donald Sutherland, M.I.T. professor Noam Chomsky, and welfare-rights leader George Wiley were featured speakers. The sponsors had reserved a large room at a Los Angeles hotel, but no one anticipated the crowd that showed up. Hundreds and hundreds of stars filed into the auditorium and found seats. Most of them filled out cards for the mailing list, which read like a who's who of Hollywood: Alan Arkin, Gregory Peck, Ray Bradbury, John Cassavetes, Warren Beatty, Carl Reiner, Hal Holbrook, Barbra Streisand, Herb Alpert, Robert Wise, Burt Lancaster, Norman Lear, Diahann Carroll, Elliott Gould, Mr. and Mrs. Sonny Bono, Walter Matthau, Jack Lemmon, Dory Previn, Bert Schneider, Goldie Hawn, Neil Diamond, Candice Bergen, Gower Champion, James Coburn, Martin Landau, Abby Mann, Leonard Nimoy—and many, many more. After twenty years of silence, Hollywood was ready for action. Instead, it got speeches and arcane political discussions, and before long the crowd began to thin.

Even so, the meeting produced a new organization, the Entertainment Industry for Peace and Justice (EIPJ), and a plan: to hold a spectacular peace rally in the Hollywood Bowl, a nine-hour marathon with speeches, poetry, music, dance, and theater—choreographed by Gower Champion, with a score by Quincy Jones and musical direction by Henry Mancini. It would coincide with demonstrations in Washington on May Day 1971. Bert Schneider donated office space; Robert Wise donated his studio; Burt Lancaster donated his time to make commercials for it.

Fonda, Donald Sutherland, and the other organizers began with a burst of energy, most of which went into meetings. There were big meetings at the Hollywood Roosevelt and little ones in the office. Often they came to order at 6 P.M. and ran until 3 A.M. The participants criticized and self-criticized; they raised consciousness; they figured out their politics; they discussed, for instance, whether or not Gower Champion might create sexist choreography; then they explored the meaning of sexism. In the course of it all, they neglected to organize the peace extravaganza, and they shunned most of the stars who had presented themselves for duty. Finally, when the city council threatened to deny them the Hollywood Bowl, they gave up the whole idea.

"I had been away for the weekend," recalls Shirley Sutherland. "When I came back, I found Don and Jane in the kitchen. 'Haven't you heard?' they said. 'We're not doing the Hollywood Bowl.' Well, I was so angry, I threw them out of the house. The arrogance! They could have had the ten hottest bands, the ten biggest choreographers. But no one was radical enough for them. Those were crazy times. Don and Jane did great things for the antiwar movement, but we all made mistakes, and that was certainly a mistake."

Fonda had entered her super-radical phase. Donald Sutherland tagged along. Together they would listen reverently to Mark Lane and rap for hours on end. They devoured the literature of the left. Having attended scarcely a single union meeting in his life, Sutherland laid plans to run for president of the Screen Actors Guild. He lobbied for votes, proposed bold action, demanded a shop steward on every set, predicted a smashing victory—and lost in a landslide to John Gavin. The race did nothing to enhance the role of radicals in the guild, but no matter. Sutherland and Fonda had other things to do.

HUEY NEWTON COMES TO HOLLYWOOD

According to Bert Schneider, Huey P. Newton was not attracted to Hollywood. "He used Bobby Seale as the front man." Nonetheless, he began to spend more and more time there, lounging beside the pool or in the house with Schneider and his friends. He did not match their fantasy image of the black revolutionary. He dressed stylishly—in bright, flowered shirts, mod pants and shoes—and he had a shy, gentle manner. His voice did not betray his street wisdom; it was smooth, intelligent, almost refined. By and large, they liked him. Jack Nicholson, for one, still considers Newton a friend. Rafelson thought him charming, though he sometimes wondered why a revolutionary would hang out in Hollywood. Alan Myerson believed that "Huey was one of the few radical media stars who was able to take what he wanted from Hollywood and not get sucked into the game." Warren Beatty found him "bright and energetic. He had a remarkable sweetness, a vulnerability that surprised me."

To his enemies, however, he was not so vulnerable. He traveled with an enormous and dedicated bodyguard named Robert Bay, who could easily squash any attacker he did not shoot first. Newton did in fact need protection, especially after his split with Eldridge Cleaver in

February 1971. Egged on by the FBI's Cointelpro operatives, the factions went to war; several Panthers on both sides suffered grisly deaths; Newton himself was a marked man.

INTRODUCING ARTIE ROSS

Schneider also introduced Huey Newton to Artie Ross, his twenty-five-year-old friend and protégé from Big Sur. Ross thought the Panther leader a sincere, pleasant, stimulating fellow, in contrast to Abbie Hoffman, who struck him as dishonest. This was no reflection on their respective political beliefs, in which he could not have been less interested. Though he had spent most of the sixties in Berkeley—as a student at the University of California—Artie had avoided the radical storms that swept through the bay area. Instead, he had been drawn to the hip counterculture and now fancied himself a whole-earth man, living off the land, in direct contact with the cosmos, above politics.

Like Bert, he had been born to a wealthy New York Jewish family. His father was a successful Wall Street businessman. His mother served as a trustee of Brandeis University. Her best friend was Bert's mother-in-law. In 1963, Artie went to Berkeley, where he majored in drama and joined a fraternity, Sigma Alpha Mu. He made a name for himself as a campus hotshot and drove around in a late-model Mustang—"the definitive Jewish frat rat," as one friend recalls. After the Schneiders moved to Los Angeles in 1965, Artie looked them up and became a frequent visitor.

In the meantime, the bay area was turning psychedelic. Artie Ross reflected the change; he turned in his resignation from SAM and let his hair grow, sometimes decorating it with roses. He smoked pot and dropped acid and went to rock concerts. He attracted women—he was handsome, lean, muscular, with a high forehead that grew higher every year as his hairline receded. But there was something else as well. "He was incredibly perceptive and articulate," says one of his former girl friends. "He had a knack for pinpointing other people's states of mind. You felt he was constantly searching you. And he projected a very romantic image of himself as a kind of a rake or a scoundrel. When he wanted to impress a woman, he exposed his vulnerability. He expressed his emotions. It always worked because, you know, it's a great technique, right?"

Others, however, found him brash, competitive, and egocentric. "A lot of people resented him," the girl friend went on. "They thought he insinuated himself into scenes. He had an ability to define a social situation. He would look for the center of the action, gravitate toward it, assimilate it, and leave. But he never meant to hurt or to take advantage. It was just his growing process."

Artie hungered for adventure. He also enjoyed the outdoor life. While still at Berkeley, he met Rob Keystone, who was building a trimaran (a boat with three hulls) in Marin County. After his graduation, Artie moved across the bay into a house on Melvin Belli's estate and spent most of the next two years working on the boat. In his spare time, he earned pocket money through a variety of small enterprises. Once, for example, he made a tidy profit on a cheese-and-bread booth at Marin's famous Renaissance Fair.

Ross and Keystone finished the boat in 1970 and sailed it south. They stopped briefly in Los Angeles to see Schneider, then headed toward Florida via the Panama Canal. Artie, who had literary ambitions, kept a journal. (Later he wrote a novel based on their voyage; it was never published.) By the time they reached Miami, the hurricane season was approaching. They left the boat with friends.

Artie next turned up in Big Sur, south of San Francisco. In the early seventies, the area was a counterculture capital on the decline, though the Esalen Institute still drew people from all over the country to its warm sulfur baths and its consciousness-raising sessions. Schneider often visited Big Sur with Candice Bergen. Artie served as host and guide. He arranged accommodations for the couple and took them to points of interest, notably the communal baths. There they would sit for hours, naked and steamy, absorbing the good vibrations.

BERT SCHNEIDER PAYS HIS DUES

On August 21, 1971, officers at San Quentin shot and killed George Jackson as he fled the maximum-security unit, where he had been awaiting trial for allegedly murdering a white guard at the Soledad Correctional Facility. Incarcerated for twelve of his twenty-nine years, he had come to personify the black liberation movement, largely on the strength of his book *Soledad Brother*. On August 28, the Black Panther party buried him in a solemn ceremony. Schneider and Bob Rafelson paid for the funeral.

The Panthers, however, were already turning away from the revolutionary militancy that Jackson symbolized. Upon his release from prison, Huey Newton had found the party in deep trouble—isolated from the black community, facing extinction in its war with the police. He soon began to overhaul and revamp the organization. He purged some members and brought the rest to Oakland. There he set about building a reform-oriented, ghetto-based political machine, with its own newspaper and school. The turnabout happened quickly enough to startle the left. Less than a year after Jackson's funeral, Bobby Seale was running for mayor of Oakland under the slogan "If you want a job, vote for Bob."

With the change in political direction came a change in style. The Panthers started referring to Huey as the supreme commander or the supreme servant of the people. His telephone-answering device informed callers, "The servant is not in." He moved into an expensive apartment beside Lake Merritt—for security reasons, it was said. Meanwhile, the party spent $10,000 on architects, who designed a

The George Jackson saga was subject matter for a Hollywood film, but Bert Schneider didn't do it. Edward and Mildred Lewis produced Brothers *(1977), directed by Arthur Barron. A semifictionalization using invented names, the film came in for the usual amount of criticism on the left—as any Hollywood film must— but the performances of Bernie Casey (as the Jackson character) and Vonetta McGee (as the Angela Davis character) could not be gainsaid. Despite ideological problems, the film was a vivid, if romantic, portrait of two revolutionaries.*

fortress for him. (It was never constructed.) He had a valet to attend to his needs, and some Panthers urged him to buy a Rolls-Royce. He ruled it out as too ostentatious, opting instead for a late-model Buick with a telephone.

There was a practical explanation for all this. The party needed an infusion of capital to establish itself as a power in Oakland politics. Some members argued that wealthy benefactors would be more comfortable—and more generous—visiting Newton in his luxury suite. Moreover, the Panthers felt they had to shed their image as fire-breathing revolutionaries. Perhaps the new Black Panther party merely reflected the times. The so-called exploitation films were playing to packed theaters in black communities. Super Fly, the stud cocaine dealer, was displacing Malcolm X and George Jackson as a symbol of black resistance. The message was clear: you commanded respect by flaunting your wealth, power and class. And so, when Seale ran for mayor, a chauffeur drove him from place to place in a black limousine. At public events, he wore a suit, a tie and a broad-brimmed fur hat. Likewise, the elite Panther soldiers stashed their leathers and dressed to kill—usually in three-piece pin-striped suits with red carnations in the lapels.

The Super Fly craze so captured their imagination that Seale and Newton wanted to make their own black exploitation movie, based on a supposedly real incident in Illinois. Newton planned to write the screenplay, and Seale would have a starring role. Huey also talked to director Paul Williams about doing an allegorical film about his conflicts with Eldridge Cleaver. To be titled *I Never Thought of It That Way Before*, it would have told the story of two ghetto blacks who survived the riots and became a television news team—reporter and sound man—connected by a wire. Nothing came of that idea, either.

Schneider was not involved with Newton's film plans, but he played an important role in the new Black Panther party. When Huey decided to take the suite on the twenty-first floor, Schneider helped put together a consortium of Hollywood philanthropists to pay the rent. He then telephoned a bay area hi-fi store and ordered a $5,000 stereo system. Schneider regarded the gift as a palliative. "Huey felt like a prisoner up there," he says. "He was happiest on the street."

Schneider also supported the party's political projects, such as the school and the newspaper, and in the spring of 1972 he made his greatest contribution to date. As they mapped out strategy for the approaching campaign, the Panthers hit on an idea to broaden their base of support. They would hold monster rallies called survival conferences, with speeches and entertainment. Tower of Power—a rock group from Berkeley—would appear; so would blues singer John Lee Hooker and comedian Richard Pryor and the Sisters Love. Congressman Ronald V. Dellums agreed to talk, and the Reverend Cecil Williams of the Glide Memorial Church and, of course, mayoral hopeful Bob Seale, and city council candidate Elaine Brown, the Panther minister of information. But the main attraction was a mammoth giveaway of food and shoes, free for the asking, first come, first served. Bert Schneider offered to pick up the tab—to the tune of $300,000.

It was an ideal arrangement. It made everyone happy—the poor people of Oakland because they got the merchandise; the Black Panthers because they got the credit; and Schneider because he got the right to regard himself as a real member, a radical activist. In fact, the only unhappy ones were the opposing candidates, who won anyway.

Though he did not boast of his generosity, Schneider let others know that he was more than a dabbler in Left Wing politics. At Hollywood parties, he referred to the Panthers in the first person plural and made snide remarks about liberals and Uncle Toms. From time to time, he commiserated with his rich radical friends about movement "rip-off artists," but he did not include the Panthers among them.

JANE FONDA GOES TO VIETNAM

In the meantime, Jane Fonda and Donald Sutherland were taking the U.S. Army by storm. From the ashes of EIPJ had risen the FTA Show, a radical counterpart to the USO tour. (FTA signified Free Theater Associates, or Free the Army, or Fuck the Army, or whatever else disgruntled G.I.'s cared to make of it.) The troupe included

Fonda, Sutherland, Dick Gregory, Peter Boyle and director Alan Myerson, formerly of The Committee. The military authorities guaranteed the show's success by trying to ban it. When it finally opened in March 1971, FTA played to houses packed with enthusiastic G.I.'s. The material sometimes read like the minutes of the Eighth Congress of Soldiers, Workers, and Peasants, but they performed it with gusto, and the show was a smash.

That spring, Sutherland and Fonda were also working out a deal with Warner Bros. to do a movie called *Steelyard Blues*, in which they would star with Boyle and which Myerson would direct. The studio reluctantly agreed to set aside $100,000 in the budget as a donation to the peace movement, in exchange for which members of the cast and crew accepted less money than they would otherwise have earned. At about the same time, *Klute* was released and Jane Fonda became a ranking star.

By then, Schneider and Fonda were already moving apart. They had committed themselves to different causes, and they approached politics with different attitudes. Schneider made no effort to alter his life-style to fit his ideological beliefs. "I get high on the contradictions," he said. Then again, he never became a Left Wing sectarian. He often went out of his way to help film-industry radicals with whom he had bitter political disagreements.

Jane Fonda, on the other hand, rejected the usual accouterments of stardom. She did not live in Hollywood or flaunt her wealth, such as it was. But despite her best efforts, the contradictions remained. The crew of *Steelyard Blues* found it amusing that she would frequently announce in a loud voice, "There are no stars here." They knew that the film was being made only because she was starring in it. Moreover, she *behaved* like a star, whether consciously or not. She surrounded herself with loyal retainers—six or seven radical women from the bay area—who followed her around, advised her on lofty issues, did her bidding and basked in her glory. Yet she barely acknowledged the workers on the set. Meanwhile, she referred to her daughter's hippie nurse as "a member of the collective."

Within the movement, she began denouncing other radicals as Trotskyite—a category that grew to include members of Trotskyite sects, other people whose views did not coincide with her own, and those who associated with either of the above. After the filming of *Steelyard Blues*, her coterie purged Alan Myerson from the FTA collective because of his "bad politics." The show then continued its tour of military bases, while he kept busy in the cutting room.

In the spring of 1972, Myerson set up a final session to polish the film. Fonda came, though she was leaving the next day for Paris and then North Vietnam. "She was snotty to everyone," Myerson recalls, "utterly disdainful of their functions. She didn't want to be there, but neither did anyone else. Most of us decided to make it as pleasant as possible, but she just made it worse. Finally, I called a break and asked Jane to join me. We walked out to the parking lot. For the next hour or so, we really went at it. I attacked her for her attitude toward the people with whom she worked. She only understood ideology; she lacked humanity. Frankly, I resented her as a public spokesperson, since she didn't back up her words with action in her personal life.

"I next saw her at a slide show Hayden was giving on Vietnam, a few weeks after her return from Hanoi. She threw her arms around me. She said she had thought about our argument all through North Vietnam, and she wanted to thank me for my criticisms. Actually, I did see a tremendous change in her. She had stopped her ideological posturing. She was in love with Tom Hayden. For the first time, I found her to be natural."

Fonda and Hayden began living together and eventually founded the Indochina Peace Campaign, through which they continued to work against the war long after most others had quit. The next January they were married. When their son was born, they named him after Nguyen Van Troi, a hero of the Vietnamese resistance.

HEARTS AND MINDS

By 1971, B.B.S. seemed to be losing its touch. *The Last Picture Show* was a success, but its next two films—*A Safe Place* (1971) and *The King of Marvin Gardens* (1972)—drew mixed reviews and small audiences, despite Nicholson's presence in both. Perhaps the times were out of joint. The B.B.S. films tended to depict alienated protagonists seeking alternatives to drab, hypocritical, plastic, violent, bigoted, unjust workaday America. It was a popular theme in the late sixties, but by 1972, it seemed to be losing its box-office appeal. As Mitch Tuchman, a chronicler of the Hollywood Left, observed, the films "had all the earmarks of youth-market pictures—except, increasingly, youth."

Moreover, the partnership was weakening. Schneider wanted time off from the movie industry, a chance to think about his life and decide on his future. Rafelson wanted to make his own films. Steve Blauner wanted to leave Los Angeles. In the meantime, Daniel Ellsberg was preparing to go on trial in Los Angeles for his theft of the Pentagon Papers. Schneider volunteered his help on the Pentagon Papers Peace Project. The propaganda wing of the defense fund. "I was meeting with members of the project," Schneider recalls, "and I was thinking about the trial and the war, more so than before. I realized that I could never be useful as a propagandist or researcher, but I could help by making a movie about the Pentagon Papers." So he put off his vacation from the film business.

Schneider had an idea; he set about finding a filmmaker. Rafelson suggested Peter Davis, a young director who had done several documentaries for CBS, notably *The Selling of the Pentagon*. Davis liked the project but felt the film should look beyond the Pentagon Papers to the broader questions of American involvement in Indochina.

Schneider agreed. In July 1972, Davis began filming. Denied access to North Vietnam, he and his camera crew spent two months in South Vietnam. After returning to the United States, they filmed some interviews and events, assembled stock footage, and—in the summer of 1973—began to put the documentary together.

Schneider, meanwhile, had other worries. His father and brother were in trouble at Columbia. Under their leadership, the studio had poured millions into clinkers (*1776, Lost Horizon, Nicholas and Alexandra, Oklahoma Crude*) and, by 1973, was deeply in debt. (According to one estimate, Columbia lost as much during the six years of Abe Schneider's administration as it had made in profits during its other forty-four years combined.) In June 1973, Stanley announced that he was departing with a large settlement on his contract and a multi-picture distribution deal; Abe ascended to the purple, as honorary chairman at $300,000 per year. Other Schneider stalwarts soon tendered their resignations.

Bert had been visiting China with Candice Bergen. On his return, he was confronted by a new regime at Columbia, which had announced a policy of lowered expectations. It would sponsor fewer films and review all production contracts on the books. In November he met with his family's successors to discuss the state of *Hearts and Minds*, which he had promised to deliver by December 31. At about the same time, he began pressuring Davis to finish a rough cut and soon found himself at odds with the entire staff.

Daniel Ellsberg, one of the central figures in Hearts and Minds.

They had harbored mixed feelings about their producer from the very beginning. As anti-war partisans, they felt a political commitment to the film that they knew he shared. But he was different from them, and not just because he had more money. He believed in hierarchy. He would review their work, then retire to discuss it with Davis—leaving behind the two editors, both of whom happened to be women, to twiddle their thumbs in the screening room. Then he would suggest changes without consulting them. (Schneider had always had a reputation as a producer who generally did not interfere with his filmmakers. According to one story, he did not know Peter Bogdanovich was shooting *The Last Picture Show* in black and white until the film was well into production. "Wouldn't it be better in color?" Schneider asked. "No," Bogdanovich replied.)

Schneider had given the staff a mid-December deadline to complete some work. They labored around the clock to meet it, fighting off exhaustion, spurring each other on, and were ready on the appointed day. They waited all morning and into the afternoon. Schneider did not appear. Finally, he telephoned from a Rocky Mountain resort. He was skiing, he said, and could not make it back. They would get together on his return.

The staff was in revolt. They believed Schneider had exploited them, working them to the brink of collapse without offering a nickel extra, then mocking their efforts. They grew angrier still when, two weeks later, Bergen showed up at a New Year's Eve bash with Henry Kissinger.

Then came an incident that seemed to crystallize their resentment. At a meeting in Schneider's office, several staff members argued with him over the role his friend Ellsberg should assume in the film. They believed that Ellsberg lacked credibility. Schneider accused them of deserting Ellsberg because of negative publicity. "That's liberal," he said. He pulled open a desk drawer, picked out a booklet and handed it to Lynzee Klingman, one of the film editors. "Here, read this," he said. "I got it in Peking." It was a copy of Mao Tse-tung's essay *Combat Liberalism*.

The discussion grew heated. Schneider turned to the other editor, Susan Martin. "What are your political credentials?" he asked.

Martin's jaw dropped. An image of Schneider's Beverly Hills mansion appeared in her mind. She began to laugh.

"What's your revolutionary training, anyway?" he asked.

She exploded. "My fucking life is my training. What's yours?" She walked out.

When the staff got around to reading Schneider's booklet, they were not appeased. The man had no shame. He ran his employees ragged while he lived like a king and then quoted Chairman Mao in their faces. The chutzpah! They Xeroxed the booklet and posted it.

Somewhat later, Alan Myerson came by to view the rough cut. Afterward, he and Schneider talked in private. He returned alone to the studio and, in a quiet but firm manner, proceeded to chastise Davis for allowing "collectivism" to run rampant and impede progress on the film. Davis's subordinates watched horrified as Myerson publicly humiliated their boss. Overcome by guilt, they promised to follow orders henceforth. They crossed out *Combat Liberalism* on the posted pamphlet and wrote COMBAT COLLECTIVISM above it in big red letters.

BRENDA VACCARO LEAFLETS FOR TOM HAYDEN: A DIGRESSION

As the 1976 primary campaign entered its final week, Tom Hayden rolled some of his big guns into Santa Monica for a noontime rally on the beach: Jane and Henry Fonda, Lee Grant, Brenda Vaccaro and Nichelle Nichols, the black actress who stars in *Star Trek*. At eleven-thirty or so, workers set up a stage on the sand near the pier. A crowd began to gather—mostly young people in their twenties and thirties, wearing swimsuits and T-shirts. They basked in the sun and listened to rock bands and folk singers until one o'clock, when the rally began without Brenda Vaccaro. She arrived as it ended and made her apologies. "I overslept," she said, grabbing a stack of campaign literature. Then she walked along, shaking hands, distributing flyers, and urging everyone to vote for Hayden. A car was stopped at an intersection. She went over to leaflet the driver and returned in a huff. "Can you imagine?" she said. "That man called Tom Hayden a Communist! That's the most ridiculous thing in the world!"

I asked why she supported Hayden. "Well, I've known Jane for ten years now," she said. "She invited me to see that G.I. show she was doing. I loved it. I thought it was hilarious! Wonderful! I gave some money. Then she called me to support Tom. She wanted me to go on a walking tour of San Francisco. Well, of course, I overslept and missed the most important thing, a rally for—what is it?—the Chicago Seven? No, you know, in Marin County. The San Quentin Six! That's it! Well, I missed it, a historic occasion, but I did get to walk with Tom. We went to these marvelous Irish pubs. It was quite fabulous. And you know you just have to work for change, but your attitude has to be balanced."

ARTIE ROSS MOVES TO HOLLYWOOD

At Big Sur, Artie Ross had learned about a new spiritual discipline called Arica, which was rapidly winning converts among many tuned-in people in America. Under the guidance of Oscar Ichazo, a Bolivian guru, Arica followers went through an intensive program of physical and mental exercise that seemed to open up fresh paths to inner peace. Artie took the course, became a devotee, and moved into an ashram in San Francisco, where he lived and taught until mid-1973. He then headed south to Los Angeles to carry on his work. Bert invited him to stay at the Benedict Canyon house. He accepted and moved into an empty bedroom. But while Arica took up his time, the motion-picture business soon captured his fancy. He spoke to Schneider about learning the trade.

As it happened, Schneider had just launched another project. He had acquired the distribution rights to Charlie Chaplin's old movies in 1971 and wanted to do a film biography of the great comedian. Chaplin had held out for two years before giving his consent. In late 1973, Schneider began work on *The Gentleman Tramp*. He named Artie Ross associate producer and sent him off to England, where Artie served as Schneider's surrogate, sometimes solving problems, often referring them to higher authority. Schneider was happy to let his protégé shoulder as much responsibility as possible, for he had problems of his own in Hollywood.

THE PRODUCER PRODUCES

Beginning in December 1973, the new leaders of Columbia Pictures moved to eradicate the vestiges of the Schneider regime. They withheld some royalties B.B.S. was earning on its previous films. They tried to cancel the six-picture deal. They took the 16 mm. rights on B.B.S. productions away from R.B.C. Films—a Schneider outfit—and reassigned them to another distributor.

Nonetheless, the studio still owned *Hearts and Minds*. In April 1974, Bert approached David Begelman, his brother's successor as president, about taking the film to the Cannes Film Festival. Begelman approved, and Columbia began designing posters. But then Begelman had second thoughts. He asked for a copy of the rough cut to show the board of directors. Schneider rejected the request as "weird." In May, when Begelman saw *Hearts and Minds* for the first time, he withdrew his support of the Cannes showing. Schneider proceeded with it anyway. Columbia insisted that its logo be removed from the film.*

Meanwhile, Schneider had trouble on another front. Former Kennedy-Johnson adviser Walt Rostow was incensed about his role in the picture. He had agreed to an interview with great misgivings and only after receiving a promise that he could review his segment. From their four-hour conversation, Davis selected three short clips in which Rostow arrogantly recited the official justification for the war. The editing, Rostow believed, made him look like a buffoon.

By then, Peter Davis and his crew had virtually finished their work on the documentary. As a reward, B.B.S. flew Davis, Klingman, and Martin to France, where they had their first opportunity to observe Schneider in action, trying to make their film a success. Whatever ill

---

* In mid-1977 David Begelman left Columbia abruptly. There were strong rumors of embezzlement.

will they still held began to dissipate and eventually gave way to admiration, as Schneider proved himself a promotional genius.

Schneider later told one reporter that there had been talk at B.B.S. of cutting down the Rostow interview because the film ran too long. Recognizing the media value of a lawsuit, however, they had decided to let it stand, though the court battle would delay the picture's release and exacerbate the problems with Columbia. Schneider had a strategy. He would try to orchestrate the publicity around *Hearts and Minds* so as to create the impression that it was being suppressed for political reasons. This was not exactly true, of course: Rostow objected to the fact that he came off as a pompous fool; Columbia had serious doubts about the film's commercial prospects and a history of bad blood with the Schneider clan.

Nonetheless, the strategy worked. At Cannes, *Hearts and Minds* played to rave reviews, one of which—by Rex Reed—was killed by the New York *News* but appeared elsewhere. Someone sent a copy to Representative George Brown Jr., an anti-war Democrat to whose reelection campaign Schneider had contributed in 1972; he reprinted it in *The Congressional Record*. *The New York Times* and *The Los Angeles Times* ran articles suggesting that the film was a victim of political censorship. B.B.S. sued Columbia for its royalties and 16 mm. rights and for release of *Hearts and Minds*. It won back the former, and the studio agreed to sell the latter for $1,000,000. Finally, an outfit called Rainbow Pictures—founded by Schneider's old friend Henry Jaglom—bought the film and arranged to have Warner Bros. distribute it. A special Los Angeles showing in December, 1974, qualified it for an Academy Award nomination.

THE REVOLUTIONARY DISAPPEARS

These were hard times for Schneider, his family and his close friends. He split up with Candice Bergen, whom he still loved. Facing certain conviction and a long sentence for selling three pounds of cocaine, his friend Abbie Hoffman fled underground in April. In July, two taxicabs collided in Greenwich Village; one of them skidded onto the sidewalk and killed Peter Davis's wife, Johanna, as their young son looked on.

Meanwhile, strange things were happening in Oakland. A black disc jockey had brought an assault case against Huey Newton, who—he claimed—had beaten him up. Then, on July 31, two black vice-squad officers visited a Panther-run bar to investigate a report that prostitutes were soliciting customers there. Newton offered to buy them a drink; they refused it. According to the police account, Newton and his bodyguard, Big Bob Heard, a 400-pound, 6-foot-8-inch Bostonian, proceeded to jump the officers. When the dust settled, eight people were under arrest. Booked on four separate charges, Newton posted $5,000 bail and walked away.

But, on August 17, he went back to jail. This time, it was charged that he had pummeled his tailor, a fifty-two-year-old black man named Preston Callins. Apparently Newton had called Callins to his lakefront suite to fit him and Heard for new suits. The tailor arrived and began to measure. Something he said displeased the Panther leader, who allegedly proceeded to pistol-whip him into unconsciousness. Callins sustained two skull fractures but survived. After arresting Newton, the police searched his apartment. There they said they found evidence that linked him to the August 6 shooting of Kathleen Smith, a seventeen-year-old black prostitute. Newton was charged with two more counts of assault and released on $47,000 bail. On August 23, he failed to make a court appearance. The judge revoked his bail and issued a bench warrant. The FBI soon added his name to its wanted list.

Later, some reports put him in Cambodia. Others put him in the back seat of a car from which a shotgun was fired into an East Bay restaurant, killing four. According to one rumor, Huey was fleeing not only the law but a group of bay area pimps who had put out a $10,000 contract on him. In any event, he had apparently relinquished day-to-day control of the party. Elaine Brown took command in his absence, while Bobby Seale faded from view. He was said to be in hiding, afraid for his life. As for Kathleen Smith, the prostitute, she lingered in a coma for about three months, during most of which time the authorities did not even know her name. Toward the end of October, she died.

Bert Schneider followed these developments closely and did not hide his concern for Newton's safety. Then again, his own troubles were not over. Late on the night of January 17, 1975, the police raided a party at his home—in response, they said, to neighbors' complaints of noise and traffic congestion. They confiscated marijuana, hashish, and three amphetamine pills, and arrested seven adults (including Schneider) and twenty-six juveniles (some of whose parents were well-known Hollywood figures, according to newspaper accounts).

Less than a week later, on January 22, Stanley Schneider died suddenly of a heart attack. He had been working on *Three Days of the Condor*, his first effort as an independent producer. He was five days shy of his forty-sixth birthday.

There came a point that winter when the pressure got to Bert Schneider. Elaine Brown was in town for a benefit at the American Film Institute. One who saw her said she "looked like the cover of *Vogue*"—ravishing, in a long dress, furs, and a towering African hairdo. She had the thankless task of explaining why the supreme commander had vanished and why Chairman Bobby had "resigned." A Los Altos restaurateur served a sumptuous meal; a film about the Panthers was shown. Most of the guests enjoyed themselves—but not Bert Schneider. He sat off to one side and wept, talking incoherently about the death of his brother and the disappearance of his best friend.

*   *   *

ARTIE ROSS WRITES A SCREENPLAY

In the meantime, Artie Ross had begun another project. As *The Gentleman Tramp* had neared completion in the fall of 1974, he had talked with his friend, director Paul Williams, about coauthoring a screenplay—a contemporary American *Casablanca*, perhaps. If only they could find some sufficiently evil force around which to construct the story. . . . They gave up; searched for another idea.

One day, while they were experiencing the pleasures of LSD, Artie began discussing the people he had met through Bert: Candy, Abbie Hoffman, Huey, Bob Rafelson. . . . Really, you know, it might make an interesting movie—the producer, the starlet, the radical and the whole-earth kind of guy. They would have to figure out a plot, of course, some action to bring the characters together. They tried to improvise a story, without much success. Then, as luck would have it, Artie found himself in the midst of a thrilling adventure, and the pieces just fell together.

In March 1975, there were reports from Havana that Huey P. Newton had shown up in Cuba—washed ashore, to be more precise. Local militia units had spotted a man in a dinghy approaching the island. The boat had landed. The man had been arrested and jailed. He had identified himself as the founder and leader of the Black Panther party, now a fugitive. The authorities had transferred him to Havana. He was given to understand that he could stay in the country so long as he lived modestly, maintained a low profile, and worked. He gladly accepted the terms.

That spring, Artie Ross completed a draft of his screenplay, entitled *West Coast*. It contained an intriguing story. There were four main characters: a handsome forty-year-old Hollywood producer; his starlet girl friend; his whole-earth protégé from Big Sur; and his comrade-in-arms, an aging sixties radical, obviously modeled on Abbie Hoffman—white, Jewish, and facing heavy drug charges. The plot centered around the producer's efforts to get the radical to Cuba. One way or another, his friends become involved in the escape. After much wrangling and several close calls, they sneak the fugitive into Mexico, and from there he travels to Havana.

Artie passed the script along to Paul Williams for polishing. Copies began to make the rounds of their friends. Schneider liked it, though he did not identify with the producer and found the portrait of the radical too critical. Candice Bergen wanted to play the starlet. So did Julie Christie, who was considered a better actress. Christie was slated for the part. Richard Dreyfuss agreed to do the radical, on condition that he could rewrite the character. He worked up some new dialogue. Abbie Hoffman obtained a copy. He sent word that he was pleased overall and thrilled about Dreyfuss in the role, though he, too, suggested changes. Huey Newton read the screenplay in Cuba. He praised it, saying Ross and Williams had "taken a complicated idea and made it simple."

The Hollywood moguls, however, did not agree. With Schneider's help, Williams saw top men in every major studio and presented each with a package deal: Ross's screenplay, Christie and Dreyfuss as stars, himself as director. All but one turned him down cold. John Calley, then president of Warners, expressed interest, but—after consulting with his board—he, too, declined, telling Williams the story was too complex. According to Calley, the studio felt "the audience would not understand it. And anyway, who gives a shit about a bunch of Beverly Hills exotics and their interaction with revolutionaries?"

Despite his failure to find backing for the movie, Williams continued to work on the screenplay, and copies continued to drift around Hollywood. Along with them went a story, which eventually dozens of people heard, most of them believed, and everyone discussed in hushed tones with each other, with curious journalists, and with anyone else who showed interest.

According to the gossip, Artie Ross had written *West Coast* while participating in the real-life escapade on which it was based. But he had altered some of the details. The fugitive was black, not white, fleeing a murder rap, not a drug bust. And the producer had long since separated from his girl friend, who was thus not involved; it was said that he sought help from a radical movie star and her husband, an erstwhile movement leader with senatorial aspirations. They refused assistance. So the task fell to Artie Ross and a couple of his closest friends.

Artie Ross immediately recognized the story's movie potential. He considered filming the getaway, then decided against it because the cameraman felt queasy under pressure. Artie divided his time between working on the escape and writing about it in his script. He eventually produced a tale of thrilling adventure, but rumor had it that the true story more nearly resembled *The Lavender Hill Mob* than *The Great Escape*. He purchased a boat to sail the fugitive to freedom, but the boat sank. A Cuban exile was hired to fly the fugitive to Havana, but the pilot tried to sell the information to the Mafia. Artie obtained a rifle for protection, but the gun exploded in his hands as he examined it. Finally, he drove the fugitive to Mexico, rented a fishing vessel, took him as near to Cuba as they dared venture, and set him overboard in a dinghy. Artie himself then returned to Los Angeles.

Or so it was said.

BOB HOPE LOSES HIS TEMPER

By April 1975, *Hearts and Minds* was a cause célèbre in Hollywood. Schneider felt confident it would win the Academy Award for Best Documentary. Five days before Oscar night, he told antiwar activist Cora Weiss, who was leaving for Paris, that he expected to have a national audience the following Tuesday. If so, he would be delighted to deliver a message from the Vietnamese liberation forces to the American people. On Awards night, the crowd at the Music Center cheered as Davis and Schneider approached the stage to accept their award. Davis delivered a quiet, moving tribute to his wife. Schneider choked as he mentioned his dead brother, then made his statement. The audience applauded. The two men returned to their seats.

Meanwhile, Oscar emcee Bob Hope was fuming. He conferred back-stage with Frank Sinatra and together they talked to Howard Koch, producer of the awards program, who agreed that the academy should dissociate itself from Schneider's action. Sinatra went before the cameras with the disclaimer, which received a mixed response from the crowd. Warren Beatty, who had just presented the Best Picture award, mumbled an oblique criticism of Sinatra: "You old Republican, you." Shirley MacLaine confronted him backstage. "Why did you do that?" she said. "You can't speak for the Academy." Raquel Welch found the whole episode disgraceful and denounced Schneider. Francis Ford Coppola, on the other hand, rose to his defense, noting his recent run of hard luck.

Schneider himself enjoyed the ruckus he had raised. "Sinatra made the event. Without him, there would have been no headlines, scarcely a ripple. As it turned out, I got to read the statement four or five times more for television and the press. I loved it."

Schneider, it seemed, had regained control of his life. Shortly after winning the Oscar, he disposed of his January drug bust by pleading guilty to a charge of trespassing. He put the final touches on *The Gentleman Tramp* and began his long-delayed vacation from movie making. That spring he severed his remaining ties to Jane Fonda and Tom Hayden.

ARTIE ROSS TAKES LAUGHING GAS

After finishing the screenplay of *West Coast*, Artie Ross took a job as a traveling promoter for Paul Williams's film company, Pressman-Williams, which was re-releasing a movie called *Sisters*. He based himself in Los Angeles, where he lived in the bottom half of a house in the Hollywood hills. It was one of those odd pink stucco Spanish-style places. The street-level floor rested on Artie's apartment, which sloped down a steep embankment. The apartment had three levels, connected by a network of staircases. Despite all the climbing, it was a pleasant place to live—light, airy, cozy, with a view of the valley and a wild garden out back.

From his hillside abode, Artie conducted promotional sorties into the American heartland, particularly the South. He managed to save money and planned to set up his own movie production company. He had also developed an interest in radical politics. He began to read voraciously—Mao, Fanon, Huey Newton, Edgar Snow. Many of his friends were surprised. Artie had spent the sixties in the eye of the storm, untouched by the political turbulence around him. What accounted for this sudden hunger?

In June 1975, he returned to Los Angeles from a barnstorming tour. He seemed happy, if somewhat jealous of Schneider, who was leaving for Havana in a few days. But there would be other trips.

Artie had a new toy. He had obtained a tank of nitrous oxide (laughing gas) and a mask of the sort doctors use to administer pure oxygen to their patients. Though known to cause brain damage, nitrous oxide is a relatively safe, nonaddictive drug in small quantities. When inhaled, it displaces the air in the lungs and causes a sensation of euphoria. But it is an inert gas; it cannot substitute for oxygen in the blood. Thus it leads to loss of consciousness. Most nitrous-oxide freaks employ a balloon or beach ball filled with the gas. When they black out, the balloon or ball slips away; air fills the lungs; they regain their senses. Artie, however, thought he could prolong—maybe amplify— the high by using the oxygen mask, which would not drop when his muscles relaxed.

One afternoon, he placed the tank in a closet that opened onto a staircase. He then strapped on the mask, took a seat on the steps, and turned on the gas. Later he told friends he had never had an experience to equal it. He had felt himself getting higher and higher. He had seen the "white light." It was mystical. When he came to, he was lying at the bottom of the stairs. He had fallen, and the weight of his body had ripped off the mask.

His friends were shocked. You can't do this, they said. It's too dangerous. You'll kill yourself. He dismissed their warnings.

Bert Schneider was planning to have dinner on June 20 with his ex-wife and his daughter. They invited Artie; he accepted. At five that afternoon, a friend telephoned Artie, and they spoke for several minutes. At 6:15 P.M., another friend knocked on his door. There was no answer. On entering the apartment, the caller heard a hissing sound, shouted Artie's name, then looked toward the staircase. There he lay, slumped on the steps. The mask was attached to his face; the tank was in the closet; the gas was turned on.

The friend telephoned Schneider saying, "You better get over here. I think Artie is dead."

Schneider postponed his departure a few days while he helped arrange a small funeral. He himself delivered a eulogy. "Artie lived on the edge," he said. "There are many ways to measure the fullness of life besides quantity. Artie packed several lifetimes into his thirty years."

Later, Artie Ross's friends would wonder about the loose ends of his life. Did he commit suicide? Those who knew him best thought not. He left no suicide note; he had not been depressed; but neither was he a fool. He understood the risks of his final trip. Why was he courting death? How did he evaluate his recent adventures in the Hollywood left? Where was he heading? What did he think about in those final moments?

Paul Williams discussed some of those questions with a friend. Then he shrugged. "Well, we know this much," he said. "Artie Ross died laughing."

HAVANA

Bert Schneider left for Havana shortly after the funeral. Over the next nine months, he made three trips to Cuba, accompanied by his closest friends and associates—Paul Williams, Peter Davis, Lynzee Klingman, Susan Martin, Candice Bergen, one of his lawyers, his secretary. He invited Warren Beatty, who declined, and Francis Ford Coppola, who accepted. On their return, the travelers praised the Cuban revolution and told amusing stories of their visits. They said Huey Newton was doing just fine.

6. SONNY GROSSO: COPPING IN

by James Monaco

If Hollywood is now peopled by inherited nobility, that's only half the story. A larger percentage than ever of today's media product has roots in reality of one sort or another. Sonny Grosso has made a career of recycling cop stories. I profiled him in this piece for *MORE* in February 1977. Since Grosso's was not exactly a household name at the time, *MORE*'s editors thought it was necessary to find a hook to hang the story on. They ran it under the headline "Why Is Kojak So Tough?" even though the bald loudmouth is only a sidelight in the story. Six months later, partly due to this story, Grosso was a minor celebrity in his own right, doing the talk show circuit.

Sonny Grosso is an ex-cop with nineteen years on the New York City force, thousands of arrests to his credit, a long string of awards and commendations from the department, and a reputation for being what his official biography calls "the scourge of the drug underworld." Since leaving actual police work, he's become a kind of Renaissance man of the media cop world: an actor in *The French Connection* and many other cop movies and TV cop shows, a writer of cop dramas for TV and film, story editor for cop-show plots, technical adviser and producer for film and TV cop projects, and currently coauthor of a cop novel. Through all these works, Grosso has added his own identifiable stamp to the changing image of the cop—that of the tough, independent maverick.

In his attractive East Side Manhattan office, which serves as a center for his media operations, Grosso at forty-three still displays the quick, spare, tense moves of a guy who's been on the beat most of his adult life. He still talks the studied, hip lingo of the streetwise city cop, even if he sometimes forgets himself and reveals a literate, sophisticated intelligence when he's trying to explain, say, a particularly nice turn of phrase in one of his scripts or the psychological intricacies of a character he's created or played. Grosso's carefully barbered beard betrays some of the distance between the media cop packager he's become and the cop he used to be: mustaches may be *de rigueur* now in the New York City Police Department, but Grosso's carefully trimmed goatee is too elaborate for the station house. After years of playing roles in the line of duty, Grosso now plays the detective role.

He eased into this new career six years ago with the success of *The French Connection*, a landmark film that significantly changed the way cops are portrayed in the media. Grosso has had a lot to do with those changes. *The French Connection* was based on Grosso's most famous case—he was the real-life partner of Eddie Egan—the one that got him promoted to detective first grade faster than anyone else on the New York force before or since. Not only was Grosso the Cop a character in the film (Roy Scheider played Grosso opposite Gene Hackman's Eddie Egan), Grosso also played a cop character himself (Detective Phil Klein), and most importantly, as technical adviser, Grosso did a lot to give the film its final effective shape.

Back then Grosso had no idea how valuable his cop experience, and his ability to articulate it, were to the media. The next-to-nothing deal he made for all his services on *The French Connection* taught him something of a lesson. "Everyone asks me why didn't I make a better deal for myself with all the millions of dollars that *The French Connection* made," says Grosso. The way Grosso tells the story of the deal, the answer has something to do with John Wayne and Grosso's own innocence. Robin Moore, who had just finished writing *The Green Berets* and had begun *The French Connection* book, invited Grosso to meet with him at Toots Shor's. With Moore at Shor's that night was John Wayne, who was soon to appear in the movie version of *The Green Berets*. Grosso was in no mood to fight for a percentage of the gross. "At that time to sit down with Robin Moore and John Wayne, who was . . . right underneath *God* to me. . . . You know, I mean I would have given *him* money to write about me! We made a very bad deal. We made no deal at all on the movie. . . ."

During the last six years Grosso has learned how to deal. Since *The French Connection*, he has worked on a dozen different projects, including *The Godfather* (technical adviser and script consultant), *Kojak* (technical adviser for the first season), *Baretta* (technical adviser for the second season, as well as writer and script consultant), and at least six projects that were directly based on his own experiences. These included a pilot for a television series called *Mr. Inside and Mr. Outside*; the 1973 film *The Seven Ups*, in which Roy Scheider starred in the Grosso role; a 1974 pilot for a show called *Strike Force*; a TV movie, *The Marcus-Nelson Murders*, based on the Wylie-Hoffert case of 1963, on which he'd worked (but *everyone* worked on that case); and the TV film *Foster and Laurie*, the story of two well-liked Lower East Side cops who were ostensibly killed by the Black Liberation Army. (Grosso had a personal involvement in the aftermath of that case—a shoot-out on a Bronx street in which Grosso and partner

Randy Jurgensen shot and killed a machine-gun-armed suspect in the Foster-Laurie case. He recently turned *that* experience into a novel.)

In short, Sonny Grosso has had a hand in most of the major cop films and television series of the 1970s. "It could only happen in this country," he notes with a mixture of wonder and embarrassment at what he knows sounds terribly like a cliché. "That something like this could happen to a guy like me." A guy like Grosso was born and raised in East Harlem and became the head of the family at fifteen when his father died. Grosso raised his sisters, took good care of his mother, and joined the police force after the Korean War when a friend who was about to sign up brought along an extra application.

Personally, Grosso is something of a boy scout as well as a tough cop—he's self-effacing, friendly, thoughtful.

Grosso certainly makes money from his media deals these days, but he makes a convincing case that he's not in it for the wheeling and the dealing and the money alone. He can speak with a kind of evangelical fervor about the importance of accurately translating the cop reality he experienced on the force—the way the job shapes the man—into the cop media experiences he shapes these days.

He first got a sense of the impact he could have during the shooting of *The French Connection*. Originally the whole thing was a lark, but as the job wore on and he spent more time shepherding star Gene Hackman and director Billy Friedkin around, he began to discover a mission. "We showed the way cops *are* in that film," he insists, "better than anybody had done it before. And we had a big effect. My desire was finally culminated when Hackman and Friedkin at different times both said to me, 'I still hate your job, I hate what you do, but at least now I understand why you do what you do.' That's all I ever wanted. Walk a mile in my shoes."

Grosso's projects all share certain attitudes and stylistic quirks that graduate students of media may someday call "Grossovian subtexts." Of course there are other media cops and other subtexts. Grosso's former partner, Eddie Egan, has carved a career for himself as an actor, most recently appearing in a continuing role in *Joe Forrester*. Dave Toma is the model for Baretta. Grosso's most recent partner on the force, Randy Jurgensen, has acted with him in most of the movies he's made and appears with Grosso's cinematic alter ego, Roy Scheider, in Billy Friedkin's *Sorcerer*.

But the most significant rival to the Grosso media cop style has been the work of novelist Joseph Wambaugh, a former sergeant in the Los Angeles Police Department. Wambaugh has been notably successful in bringing a little more realism to the cop genre, showing, as Grosso explains, "that policemen like apple pie and have mothers and that 'pull-over-and-give-me-your-license-and-registration' isn't the only thing they know how to say." While Grosso and Wambaugh share this desire to change the image of cops in the media, to make them more human, in other respects their work contrasts markedly. Wambaugh's novels (*The New Centurions, The Blue Knight*) and television shows

RIGHT: *Grosso as detective. Police mug shot, 1960.*

ABOVE: *Grosso as actor, playing "Phil Klein" with cast on the set of* The French Connection *(1971). Actor Roy Scheider (center) plays the character based on Grosso, "Buddy Russo."*

BELOW RIGHT: *Grosso as character, with former partner Eddie Egan, as Det. Phil Klein and Lt. Simonson in a scene from* The French Connection.

BELOW LEFT: *Grosso as technical advisor on the set of* The Godfather *with James Caan (1972). He is in costume for a small part in the film.*

ABOVE RIGHT: *Grosso as technical advisor on the set of* Report to the Commissioner *(1975).*

ABOVE LEFT: *Grosso as cop in a recent photo.*

BELOW: *Grosso as writer in his office on East 63rd St. (1976).*

LEFT: *Grosso as star. His 8x10 glossy.*

(*Police Story*) focus on foot cops, while Grosso's have dealt exclusively with detectives. The difference is more than just a matter of subject; there is a sharp contrast in attitude, as well.

Philip Rosenberg, a writer who is currently collaborating with Grosso on a "nonfiction novel," sees the difference between the Wambaugh cop show and the Grosso cop show as related to the historical contrast between the NYPD and the LAPD. In Los Angeles (and most other American cities, for that matter), the entire force is organized under the civil service. In New York, the detective bureau is a separate entity; the people who work for it are not subject to civil service rules, but rather serve at the will of the commissioner. This is the result of a nineteenth-century reorganization of the force intended to isolate the free-roving tradition (that prevailed within the entire department at that time) strictly within the bounds of the detective bureau. The net effect was to preserve the tradition of the detective as independent operator. So, whereas the typical Wambaugh cop is pictured as a "working stiff" who has to cope with the boredom and idiosyncracies of the civil service bureaucracy, as well as basic human concerns such as marriage and divorce, the quintessential Grosso cop is far more independent—an outsider and a more intriguing character for it.

The East Coast tradition has always been more action-oriented. Jules Dassin's 1948 movie, *The Naked City*, was the prototype. In the early sixties the television spin-off of the film and David Susskind's *NYPD* further emphasized the downbeat *film noir* tradition of the Eastern cop show. It was only left to *The French Connection* and then *Kojak* and *Baretta* to further accentuate the central character of the tough cop as outsider, almost beyond the law.

Of course, Grosso is not entirely satisfied that the final products reflect his conception of cop character. Censorship and commercial demands distort the new realism of TV cop shows, he says. He has discovered that whatever eventually reaches the screen is inevitably the result of numerous compromises. In television, the biggest problem is language. As Sonny says, "Cops don't talk unless they talk in 'fucks.' " Even such mild expletives as "hell," "damn," "jesus" and "christ" quickly fall to the censor's blue pencil. Moreover, the physical violence of police life—essential to an understanding of the quality of the experience—is still inappropriate for TV; nightsticks may not touch heads, guns are not allowed to be shoved in faces, knives may not enter bodies. One of the subjects that Grosso most wants to treat in a television show is cop suicides—police have the highest rate of any profession. But this subject, like many others, is still taboo.

Sometimes the degree of realism Grosso desires can have ethical, legal, and potentially violent implications. Grosso is now developing a set of stories based on his own cases (to be packaged as novels, films, TV series—whichever happens to fit). The stories could explode in his face if he oversteps the boundaries of fiction. The reason: criminal charges are still pending in one of these cases; another may result in a $250,000 suit for false arrest against Grosso and partner Randy Jurgensen. "It's not like Robin Moore doing a 'property.' People get killed." There is also pressure from the force. Also, not every cop wants to be a character in a Grosso project. Names may be "changed to protect the innocent."

For these as well as more technical reasons, most of Grosso's numerous "recycling" projects fall somewhere in the middle ground of the media continuum: they certainly aren't pure fiction, but neither are they factual documentary narratives; they're "fictionalizations," "dramatizations," "docu-dramas"—Grosso is intrigued by the media jargon names given to his various projects, and the subtle gradations between fact and fiction they are supposed to represent.

In the midst of all of this, Grosso feels there is one major aspect of police work that so far has been ignored almost entirely in media images of the job—the sense of police work in its communal context. He thinks that media cops tend to be overdrawn heroes isolated from their communal, political settings, heroes who seldom need the help of their colleagues, much less the people on the streets around them. He says that any cop who has thought about his job will tell you that he doesn't create his personality or his job in the abstract—the streets around him do.

The first stage of the cop story renaissance has been to communicate a more accurate image of the police personality. The second stage is going to involve a more precise and sophisticated analysis of the function of the job itself. It isn't enough anymore to show that cops are human. It's necessary now to show how they relate to the people around them.

7. HENRY KLOSS: NOT YOUR AVERAGE MAD INVENTOR

by Geoffrey Stokes

With Edwin Land, Henry Kloss is the last of the breed of inventor/ industrialists whose stories are closely woven into the fabric of media history. But, as Geoffrey Stokes's *Village Voice* profile points out, it isn't as easy as it once was to combine business with invention. Kloss wanted to make products, not profits.

Henry Kloss shows me to his living room. A spare gray rectangle, it is perhaps a little less cluttered and fussy than the living rooms of other Cambridge academics who have managed not to take decor seriously, but otherwise unremarkable. Except for the thing in the corner.

The thing is a 24-square-foot viewing screen, curved and jutting out from its stand like an attentive hawk. Perhaps a dozen feet in front of it, squat and ugly, is a toad. Kloss flicks a switch, the toad hums, its eyes light up, and an image appears on the screen. It is a car. It is megacar. The camera swoops in on it, caresses it with the obscene attention of Anger's camera in *Kustom Kar Kommandos*, probes its velvet interior . . .

Kloss turns the sound up, and I realize that this is only another commercial for an all-new-1977-custom-whoopee. But it really doesn't matter. I am drawn in, captured by the camera, possessed by the sheer power of the image. I am watching the Advent 1000, the latest off-spring from the incredibly fertile brain of Henry Kloss, and in these few seconds I already know, like it or not, that it is going to change our lives. It's already changed Kloss's. For the worse.

At forty-seven, a rumpled, energetic Humpty Dumpty of a man, Kloss is practically a caricature of the mad inventor. A compulsive coffee drinker—"I learned to work in the plant one-handed," he says— he offers me a cup. Fumbling about the detritus on his kitchen counter, he also comes up with an ashtray. It's not an ashtray at all, it turns out

"A rumpled, energetic humpty-dumpty of a man. . . ." Henry Kloss poses with his Advent video projector. (Photo by Cliff Garboden.)

(he doesn't smoke), but a large concave lens. "Optical experiment," he apologizes.

Then through the dining room—a Calder lithograph skewed crazily inside its perfectly plumb frame, a half-dozen open magazines strewn among the books that cover the long table—to the back porch, where he begins to discuss the events that led to the Advent 1000.

As he talks, with a fluent coherence not all that common among specialists in the higher reaches of electronics, the mad inventor gradually fades. In his place, an even more impressive figure emerges. Kloss is a genius, of course, but he's also the shrewd entrepreneurial founder of three successful businesses. And despite the painstaking thoroughness with which he answers my questions, he obviously wishes he were spending this brisk October morning patrolling his laboratories and factory. Unfortunately, there is really very little for him to do but watch the leaves blow across his lawn. Henry Kloss is unemployed.

Seven months earlier, he had been effectively removed from control of the company he'd founded; a week ago, finally sure that the Model 750—a somewhat less spectacular, lower-cost version of the set that dominates his living room—was see-worthy, he quit.

"I first got involved in audio systems in a kind of backhand way," he begins. "I was working my way through M.I.T. by operating a small woodworking shop and some people from the acoustics division asked me to build speaker cabinetry for them. . . ." A few years later, in 1953, Henry Kloss was among the founders of Acoustic Research, the

Cambridge-based firm at which he participated in what he now calls "the seminal event" of the burgeoning hi-fi industry.

"If you look around New England now," he says, "you'll see that almost every company in the speaker business, with the exception of Bose, is second- or third-generation AR. It was the springboard, and the bulk of the people now working on the forward edge of the industry were associated with it at one time or another."

The event Kloss refers to was the first commercial air-suspension speaker, the AR 1. Cheaper, lighter, and above all smaller than the rigid-cone models which had dominated speaker manufacture up to that time, it still delivered full low-frequency sound. Yet, despite its undoubted contribution to the revolutionary shift of hi-fi from the hobbyists' to the consumers' market, the AR 1 wasn't actually new. Kloss points this out in his generous credits to a number of pioneers while giving a brief disquisition on the history of speaker design: "So what we did at AR can perhaps best be described as rediscovering an overlooked way to make the *obvious* speaker. The difference is that we got some attention."

Kloss considers the AR 1 as "the crude, but definitive statement. Real commercial success came in with a less perfect, but more affordable, model that delivered unprecedented sound-per-dollar." That speaker, the AR 2, was for years the standard against which all other air-suspension models were measured. "I delivered it," says Kloss, "the day I left AR."

That was in 1956, and a year later Kloss used his share of the firm's profits to join with two other friends in establishing a new audio company. Since that time he has been most conveniently identified as "the K in KLH." During the ten years that Kloss was associated with KLH, the company was perhaps best known for its innovations on the low end of the price scale. Its speakers featured the clean natural New England sound (and included a special-quality cone that resulted from Kloss's two-year study of the paper-manufacturing business), but its fundamental strength lay both in its array of compact, affordable stereo systems and in what is still damn near the only listenable table-model radio. But that's not all KLH did.

Prompted by Kloss's Left/humanitarian politics, KLH not only regularly hired a significant part of its work force right out of Walpole Prison, it created an on-site school—the KLH Child Development Center—in an effort to open the job market to women. "Like the AR 1," says Kloss, "it seemed a natural kind of thing. You want a business to make a profit, of course, but one also wants to be some sort of effective force in the community. A lot of what we did then is now legally mandated, but I just thought of it as right."

But he doesn't think of the on-site school as an unqualified success. "It was a good school," he says, "my daughter went there for two years, and she got a fine education. And to the extent that it minimized absenteeism and turnover among our workers, it was obviously good for the company as well, but we never really managed to show that it was in industry's self-interest. To the extent that it wasn't a totally convincing pilot program, you'd have to call it unsuccessful. An on-site school is still viewed as something you have to make a corporate contribution to—like the United Way, I guess."

Still, KLH was a very successful corporation, doing some $17 million in annual sales by the time the Singer Corporation bought it out in 1967. Soon afterward, Kloss founded the Advent Corporation, a company known to some extent for audio innovations like a Dolbyized cassette recorder, but primarily as the creator of the quintessential bookshelf speakers. Which wasn't what he had in mind.

"Advent wasn't intended *at all* as a speaker manufacturer," Kloss says. "I started the company because I was interested in moving over from audio to television. But the development time on the video projection system was longer than I'd hoped it would be, and when some people from KLH unexpectedly became available . . . You know, you do what you have to in order to make money.

"During the twenty-three years that I've been in this business," he continues, "There's been a steady evolution of *breadth*—of quality sound becoming more accessible because we gradually lowered the cost of performance. Eventually, you get to a point—which was sort of reached a few years ago—where a genuinely large number of people can afford to purchase equipment which—if someone doesn't come along and worry them and unconvince them with a lot of needless 'improvements'—they can live with forever. Which wasn't so much a design breakthrough—the Advent is really built on the AR model—but one of minimizing the cost in manufacture and distribution.

"Beyond that particular point—with the possible exception of time-delay circuitry—there's not that much more you can do. Or to put it another way, there's no driving need for new product, and you're just into the 'Detroit syndrome.' I never wanted to do that, though, believe me, if I thought I could deliver real *value* in a $200 speaker, I jolly well would have. But for a lot less money, Advent provided a speaker that I like to describe as necessary and sufficient. So, as things now stand, you could fairly say that I'm—finally—uninterested in loudspeaker design."

A number of younger—and non-AR—engineers may disagree with Kloss's assessment of their work, but it's clear that for him, as it has been ever since he started Advent, video is the frontier. "At the end of KLH, I was absolutely sure that the company was going to continue to grow—all you had to do was look at record sales. I was right about that, but I also thought that the industry as a whole would eventually be dominated by the giants—the Sylvanias and Magnavoxes. On that, I was wrong. They tried—at one point GE had a pretty good receiver, as I recall—but they had been so thoroughly discredited that it was too late for them. And though my prediction was wrong, I must say that struck me as a rather heartening development.

"Anyway, at that time ten years ago, the circumstantial evidence for an analogue to television was already there. Color had really become a large business, and the economics of that size business meant that at least *some* of the sets that the major manufacturers put out had to be of the minimum cost and quality they could get away with. But they were all technically *very* similar—they are still—with the differences between the 'best' and the 'worst' insignificant.

"And because they're all built on a very low level, I saw the same thing happening in TV that happened in sound. The only reason nobody complained about having a bad set was that no one had ever seen a good one."

And so at Advent, Kloss began work on a "good" set: one that, in his words, "would make television as rewarding as an evening at the theater—or, for that matter, an evening reading."

That seems a worthwhile enough goal, but the analogy is at least strained. Kloss himself has talked about the importance of the long-playing record to the hi-fi explosion, and there are, of course, nearly an infinite number of books; no matter how attentive the viewer may be to his splendidly engineered set, television simply doesn't offer the variety and depth of the media to which Kloss compares it. But, he claims, it will. "I get so *annoyed* when I hear that argument," he says. He leaves his chair and leans against the wall, rocking back and forth against it. "Admittedly, if you want to turn your television on at a particular time of night, there's likely to be nothing on worth watching, but the good stuff in any given week is way out of joint with the time available to watch it.

"Now I'm assuming here that watching television is an *activity*, rather than something you do as background to whatever else 'important' you're doing. The reason that we think of it as background is only the short-term requirement of the technology which trivializes it by showing it on that tiny screen.

"Think for a minute again about going to the theater. I always buy the best seats, because if I go to the theater, I want to get as much out of it as I possibly can.

"The same thing is true for watching television. The world is expanding so rapidly that now there's almost an unlimited choice of activities for us on any given evening. But time doesn't expand. So if I'm going to put in an hour watching television, I might as well get *everything* that hour can possibly give me.

"And I *don't* have to waste that hour watching junk," he continues. "Videodisc is right on the edge of being here, and you can already buy a first-class videotape system for no more—allowing for inflation— than a comparable sound recorder would have cost fifteen years ago. Not too far in the future, people will be able to choose what they watch in pretty much the same way they now choose what they listen to or read. It's inevitable; video is *going* to go in the direction of reading."

As Kloss cites other examples of the trend—sales figures for Sony's Betamax system, for increasingly sophisticated video games, and the developing market for preprogrammed videotapes—he grows visibly more excited. But, at the moment, for the first time in twenty-three years, he is not part of the electronics industry's future, but of its past.

Advent's troubles were partly technical—the projection TV simply took longer to perfect than Kloss had anticipated—and partly managerial—when the new television finally went into production, there were errors in pricing and marketing. The details are complex (and are fascinatingly recounted by Paula Span in the October 26, 1976 issue of the Boston *Phoenix*), but the bottom line is all too clear. Though Advent's sales were growing steadily, its profits—first as a percentage of sales, and then absolutely—were shrinking. By 1975, they had disappeared entirely, and the company lost almost $3 million. Early 1976 brought no improvement. Suppliers were getting restive, the firm's bank was on the edge of hysteria, and Advent was all but officially bankrupt.

Enter, on an apparently white horse, Peter Sprague—a millionaire industrialist of liberal pretensions who specializes in "rescuing" financially troubled companies. With a major infusion of his own capital and a reputation that led the same bank which had refused credit to Kloss's Advent to invest in Sprague's, he stabilized the firm's shaky finances. He also brought in his own president, one Pierre Lamond, and kicked Kloss upstairs to a tightly compartmentalized research function.

"Dammit," says Kloss. "I'm not one of those lonely-inventor-in-a-cellar types. I'm a guy who brings a team of talented people together—marketing and sales people as well as technicians. I've been in business for twenty-three years, and in every year but one, I've made money. And that one year, we had tremendous start-up costs manufacturing a product—the projection television system—that is going to make Advent profitable for years to come."

Perhaps. Certainly, as Henry Kloss's dream machines continued to come off the production line, Advent turned around. Despite losses early in 1976, the company realized an overall profit of more than $200,000 for that year. By all estimates, 1977 will be even better. And given that he still holds a large chunk of Advent stock—several million dollars' worth, on paper—one should not feel too sorry for Henry Kloss.

One's sympathy should better go out to us. For Kloss's failure to hold on at Advent (and the State Street Bank's unseemly eagerness to pull the rug out from under him) means that the coming video industry is likely to be very different from the existing hi-fi market. Instead of a handful of inventor/entrepreneurs constantly trying to gain a competitive edge in a highly fragmented market (either by developing new technologies or lowering the cost of existing ones), the video market is all too likely to be left to a handful of giants. The costs of entering it are just too high. Instead of executives whose joy in their work is part of their reward (Kloss paid himself $60,000 annually as Advent's president; Lamond's annual compensation *begins* at $75,000), the industry will be dominated by conglomerates which measure their divisions' success by return on investment. Inevitably, it seems, we will have shoddiness and the Detroit syndrome.

A straw in the wind, perhaps, is Advent's recent decision—a few miles from the original site of the KLH Child Development Center—to have some of its products assembled in Mexico. Where labor is cheap.

THE PRODUCT

8. *ESQUIRE'S* BIGGIES: CAPOTE, TALESE, WOLFE, W. R. SIMMONS. W. R. SIMMONS? RIGHT. W. R. SIMMONS.

by Rust Hills

Esquire was the magazine of the sixties, as *New York* has been the magazine of the early seventies. But something happened after Harold Hayes, editor in the sixties, left. The magazine rolled along all right as a subsidiary of Gulf & Western. The decline in editorial matter didn't hurt too much. But magazines have ratings too. Rust Hills, fiction editor, explained what happened when *Esquire* ran afoul of W. R. Simmons. (Lee Eisenberger has since left the magazine. Byron Dobell, from *New York*, took his place. Dobell then left when his ex-boss Clay Felker bought in.)

"It's the rumors themselves that are killing us," says Geoff Norman, articles editor of *Esquire*. "I called a writer the other day and said, 'Hey, where's the piece?' He said, 'I heard rumors you guys were folding, so I put off doing it.' So I told him, 'C'mon, we're holding a spot for it, get it in.' And he is. But who needs all these goddamn rumors?"

"It's the Simmons report," I tell him. Everyone I've spoken to seems to agree that the fate of the magazine may not exactly stand or fall but will certainly teeter-totter on the outcome of the next Simmons report.

"I don't understand all that about the Simmons report," says Geoff, shaking his head, obviously not interested in the damn thing, and off he goes to a Dubies meeting in Lee Eisenberg's office.

At the Dubious Achievements Awards meeting, it's all new people, but they're still cracking one another up in the same old way. Lee Eisenberg is behind the desk, Harold Hayes's desk from '63 to '73, Don Erickson's desk from '73 to March '76, Lee's since then—the editor's desk. Eisenberg's feet are up on it, which seems to be part of that desk's destiny. A half-dozen editors have dragged in chairs and have their Xeroxes of the "roughs." It's a two-step process: each of the editors brings in rough write-ups of news items and the group decides which are dumb enough; only later, when they're rewritten, do the editors start putting headlines or comments on them. This is a business of trying to top one another for a funny line, and they keep going, giggling and groaning, until they get something Lee thinks will do. Nora Ephron is funny, Gordon Lish is funny, they *all* get funny. The feature is scheduled for January 1977. There was a rumor around a while back that December was going to be *Esquire*'s last issue, but no one knew where it came from, and it's pretty much forgotten now. Still, it's not a very comfortable way to work.

Surely everyone who reads *Esquire* has noticed that the magazine over the last few years has been less, say, "exciting" than those scathing, snotty, outrageous, big-read, fascinating issues of the Harold Hayes decade. When those issues were coming out, though, there was always some proportion of management and ad staff who felt that all that almost deliberate bad taste and controversiality were driving advertisers away. But the irony is that it was *after* Harold Hayes, when they got at least a somewhat more amenable, "service-oriented" editorial product, that their big troubles began. Since—if not because— Hayes left, ad linage has dropped disastrously, to little more than half the 1280 pages they had in 1973.

But no one there, so far as I could tell, feels they need to get Harold Hayes back, the way David Smart, the original publisher, finally felt he had to get Arnold Gingrich, the original editor, back in the early 1950s. Some do blame what happened on a lackluster editorial policy, but more speak of circulation problems. Still more are ready to blame the last wretched Simmons report. There's not much they can do about the Simmons report, except wait and worry about the next one, but meanwhile they're repositioning the magazine in the other two areas.

Over lunch, Lee Eisenberg speaks eloquently of how he's going to make *Esquire* into a magazine that men and women will need, like, even "love"—although I keep telling him not to use that word. Lee is now thirty, has been at *Esquire* forever. "As a baby," he says, "I learned how to write those *Esquire* copy blocks that describe a big beautiful automobile and end, 'It's $42,000. Fuck you. You can't have it.' I could do it in my sleep, right to the exact character count. I want to take that abrasiveness out of the magazine. I want to make it into something people of my generation will need."

But I'll believe it when I see it. People have been trying to get the snottiness out of *Esquire* for years. Snottiness seems to be the magazine's institutional imperative.

Anyway, gentling down *Esquire* now can't really help much with the next wretched Simmons report. If readers liked the magazine more, it might actually hurt them more, as I'll explain in a minute. Meanwhile, *Esquire*'s made some changes in circulation that would help, all things being equal, which they're not.

Esquire's problems with circulation go back to a bad decision made in the mid 1960s. Between '66 and '75 they shot the circulation up from a million to a million and a quarter. This was done as a result of pressures from the advertising sales staff, who felt they couldn't

JULY 1969
PRICE $1

Esquire

THE MAGAZINE FOR MEN

' Esq., Inc.

© Esq., Inc.

Eskie, the Esquire *logo, went through a series of transformations over the years before being dropped from the magazine's nameplate in the middle seventies at about the same time the subtitle "The Magazine for Men" was killed. Corporate profits went into decline soon after. When Clay Felker bought the magazine in the summer of 1977, he cannily promised a return to the image of "man's magazine."*

achieve the pages and revenue goals set by the corporate management unless they got that kind of circulation, which would make them competitive with the big magazines like *Time* and *Newsweek* and so on. But this was done, as Don Erickson points out, without any regard for the discrepancy between what the magazine actually was, on the one hand, and what was being presented to the advertisers and readers, both, on the other. There may be a million people who want a semi-literary magazine like *Esquire*, but that extra quarter million just *don't*.

So they've cut circulation now, *back* to a million, and of course it's better for them, just as it's presumably better for *Playboy* now that they've cut down from 6.5 million to five. The *Esquire* renewal rate has stayed the same, or even gone up a bit, despite the fact they've eliminated all those costly, self-destructive subscription deals. Also, that good newsstand circulation is up 15 percent for the first half of '76. And of course when the quarter million was cut, they did it so as to improve the demographics. Now they've positioned themselves to be competitive with *New York, The New Yorker, Psychology Today, Harper's,* and *Atlantic,* and feel more comfortable about it. But when you start cutting circulation, the rumors start flying that you're in real bad trouble.

"We knew that's what everyone would say, but we felt we just had to do it," says Gil Chapman, president of Esquire, Inc.'s two-magazine publishing group. (The other magazine is *Gentlemen's Quarterly,* which has always seemed to me the dumbest thing going, but is a red-hot book these days due to the American male's New Peacockism—fancy underpants and a lot of things you and I don't understand.) *GQ* has been changed from a part-trade to an all-consumer magazine, and a lot of apparel manufacturers find its $3,000- to $4,000-page rate a lot more attractive than *Esquire*'s $9,000 to $14,000.

The people who made the wrong decisions about circulation have gone, and no one left has to defend them, which makes things more pleasant. David O'Brasky, who left *Esquire* space sales to become publisher of *Gentlemen's Quarterly* and is generally credited with that magazine's success, has now returned to be publisher of *Esquire*. He gets along with Lee Eisenberg, and it's a nice, if rare, thing for the editor and publisher of *Esquire* to get along. Don Erickson, who was the previous editor, is now called editor-in-chief, but Eisenberg is really the editor. Erickson's role is perhaps awkward—either supervising while not seeming to or else *not* supervising *while* seeming to—but he feels at least partially responsible for Eisenberg's promotion and ad-mires and likes him and Chapman, and they *all* apparently admire and like the hell out of one another and everything would be jolly, jolly, jolly for a change there—were it not for the everlasting Simmons report.

I imagine more than half the people there don't know what the Simmons report is, or what it did to them. But they all know it's what they have to worry about, and they're right. It makes a nice, mysteri-ous outside menace. The curious thing is that for those there who *do* know what happened, the matter is equally mysterious and even more menacing.

The theory and origins of the Simmons report go way back to those bleak days in the early fifties when television began to make an impact in advertising and compete with the magazines. The audited ABC circulation of the magazines was a known fact, but it could not com-pete on a cost-per-thousand basis when the networks, through the Nielsen survey and others, began presenting huge numbers—of not just *sets* but *viewers*. The magazines answered with the concept of pass-along readership—not just *copies* of each issue of the magazine, but how many *readers* each copy had. *Life* magazine, in cooperation with Alfred Politz, did a "total audience" survey on *Time, Reader's Digest*, some of the women's magazines, and other big ones.

In the early sixties, some agency people—BBDO and others—began asking for the same information on *all* magazines. In response to the agency requests, thirty-five or forty magazines sponsored a survey done by Willard R. Simmons.

Simmons set up a basic sample of 20,000 households from U.S. Government census sources, and they go to great lengths to get the exact household selected, and not just the people next door. And you should be glad they don't ask you, because it all takes a long time. They ask you everything: age, occupation, children, income, and about all sorts of products, liquor, cigarettes, cars, and so on forever. Magazine readership is surveyed as if it were just another product.

The Simmons interviewer shows you a loose-leaf notebook. On each page of the loose-leaf notebook are five logos of the magazines being surveyed—maybe ten pages of logos, five to the page, got it? They're in alphabetical order on the page, but the order of the pages is rotated. Now, as I flip through this book, I ask you: "Can you tell me if you ever happened to read any issue of any of these magazines in the last six months?"

Okay, I believe you, but we don't leave it at that. The typical number of magazines read or magazines *said* read is six. For the magazines you've said you've read only, I pull out a stripped copy from my interviewer's bag of fifty or so stripped copies of the different magazines.

A stripped copy is the cover, *not* the front-of-the-book; *does* include the central editorial sandwich, up to twelve of the lead spreads, but less when there *are* less; and *not* the back-of-the-book. I take you through it, page by page, and then I ask you: "Have you read this particular issue of *Esquire*?"

If you say yes, then you are considered to be a reader of *Esquire*, no matter how it happened that you saw it. Whether you're a subscriber, bought it on the newsstand, found it in the doctor's office or lying by the side of the road—none of this matters. As it works out, each person who says, "Yes, I saw that issue," increases the total audience of that magazine, as projected by Simmons, by 10,000 readers.

Obviously, the pass-along readership varies with the kind of magazine, *The National Geographic*, for instance, does badly in total audience studies because subscribers save their copies, keep *decades* of them there on the shelves, all gleaming yellow in the sun. They keep *Reader's Digest*, too, God knows why. But with the weeklies, especially the news-magazines, even *Sports Illustrated*, it's exactly the opposite. People feel they have to get rid of them, there'll be another in next week. Thus the relationship between what's called "primary" readership (by the purchaser or someone in his household) and "nonprimary" is about 50-50 for a magazine like *Esquire*, but it's about 25 percent primary to 75 percent pass-along for *SI, Time, Newsweek*, and so on.*

Nevertheless, *Esquire* managed a pretty high ratio of readership to circulation, by monthly magazine standards, being pretty much on a par with *The New Yorker*'s five, nearly six, readers per copy. From 1965 to 1973, the numbers grew, reflecting the increase in circulation, so that by the eleventh Simmons, in 1973, *Esquire* had seven million readers on a circulation of 1.25 million.

In 1974 there were changes of ownership at Simmons. After some delays, they came out two years ago, in November, with the "1974–75 Simmons," and that, as they say at *Esquire*, "was when the shit hit the fan."

---

* Could this be the reason Clay Felker's first editorial decision was to make *Esquire* bimonthly?

The 1974–75 Simmons used the same basic methods, but based on the 1970 census instead of the 1960 census. It had always been a random sample, the 20,000 households, rather than a stratified, match-up representative sample, and it had chosen different households each year, unlike Nielsen; but now it was based on different "sampling points": instead of using Suburb A of Pittsburgh, it used Suburb B. The differences are more complicated than they are significant.

But for some reason, the new Simmons came up with very different figures for some few magazines. *Sport* magazine fell somewhat, so did some others, but there was no rhyme or reason to which were affected. Not all monthlies fell. Not all men's magazines. Just a few, just especially *Esquire*. *Esquire*'s total audience dropped from seven million readers to four million readers "in one fell swoop." That's what they say at *Esquire*, then they shake their heads sadly and say it again—"in one fell swoop."

Esquire people rushed over for some heated discussion with Simmons people about this incredible drop. Frank Stanton, the new director, told them, "It's inexplicable." He said he could not explain the change because all the records of the previous studies had been destroyed and there was no way to check what was different. All he could tell them was that when the logos had been shown, about the same proportion had said they'd read a copy of *Esquire* in the last six months, and that the trouble had come when the particular issue, the stripped copy, had been shown. Discussion grew more heated.

So much so, that when the list of magazines participating in the next Simmons appeared, *Esquire* was not included, and Stanton told them he'd assumed from their attitude that they didn't want to participate. *Esquire* filed suit to get back in, asking for $1 million in damages for being excluded. Stanton said the new study was already started, and he couldn't put *Esquire* in. *Time*, meanwhile, had sued Simmons on technical grounds, claiming the study hadn't been up to the standards it had paid for and had been improperly conducted. Then in the spring of 1975, Stanton said he would not put out the study *Esquire* had been excluded from, so the suit to get into the study that hadn't been done was dropped. Stanton announced a new study.*

Of the drop in *Esquire*'s readership from seven million to four million, just common sense would have to say that either Simmons was wrong before, or they're wrong now. It's just not conceivable that a magazine's readership would drop from seven million to four million in one year on virtually the same circulation—the quarter million circulation take-off having been done much more recently. You'd think everybody could just discount it as a mistake, but they can't, because of the uses the Simmons report is put to.

The report is published in thirty volumes, two or three mimeographed pages to each volume, each page a complex and detailed table of figures. You can look up any sort of tiny specific figure you want on

---

* *Esquire*'s Simmons report for 1976 was up to 4,643,000 readers; in 1977 it dropped to 3,693,000 readers.

these charts, like what percentage and/or actual projected number of adult male (over eighteen) *Esquire* readers drank any Scotch whisky in the previous month. But more importantly, far more importantly, you can use these figures the other way: by feeding them to the computer.

That's what Simmons was developed for: the concept of media selection by computer. Once you put all that Simmons comparable data into the computers you can ask it questions far too subtle and sophisticated for mortal men, or even you and me. If you've got an amount of money to advertise Scotch whisky and it's not just a matter of cost-per-thousand, but also "reach" and "frequency," subtracting "overlap" or maybe not subtracting overlap, plus all the demographic considerations and jargon, jargon, jargon, the computer speaks your language and tells you in five seconds which magazines to buy—one, two, three, say, in terms of "efficiency" above the cutoff point in the client's budget.

But no matter how complicated it all is, sooner or later you have to mix in the cost-per-thousand. It's easy to see how the figures are skewed by a difference of three million total readership on the same buy. You take the page rate, and if you divide it by four million readers instead of seven million readers, the answer is going to come out disastrous for *Esquire*, no matter what the question.

And it *has* been a disaster. In the first six months of this year, they took a real beating. They deny the rumor that they're losing $5 million a year, but they don't deny the report in *Media Industry Newsletter* that the magazine dropped $2 million in the last fiscal year. They feel they've "bottomed out" now: *Esquire* was up in ad pages in August and September, and will be up in December, and the December issue will run over a hundred ad pages, for the first time they've broken a hundred in fourteen months, and the first quarter of '77 looks good, and things are looking better, especially in Detroit, where it counts, they say, and so on. But of course you've got to bottom out with some real bounce-back from a $2 million loss.

Meanwhile, the rumors have been killing them. The only one that seems to be true is that Gulf & Western made a run on the stock. The rumor that Fairchild was trying to buy *Esquire* was apparently pure rumor. There seem to be small grounds, or none, for rumors that either Harold Hayes or Clay Felker was trying to take over the magazine. [But small grounds, apparently, were enough.] Maybe I got conned into thinking all the rumors about *Esquire* folding soon were wrong, but if so, I was glad to be conned that way.

A lot does seem to depend on the imminent Simmons, but not perhaps everything. David O'Brasky somewhat discounts its importance. "A lot of people didn't want to be in *Esquire*," he says, "and I think they may have just used the Simmons figures as an excuse for staying out." To some extent this may just reflect how much he admires and likes the new Eisenberg *Esquire*, and how sure he is he can sell it. Yet when I asked Chapman why *Esquire* had not just paid but sued to get back into a syndicated research program that had mauled them so badly, he replied: "You have to be in the computer." Simmons is the only game in town, and if you're not in it, you're not playing. It isn't that the actual life or death of *Esquire* hangs on the next report— or at least they don't acknowledge thinking that way there now. It's just that if the next Simmons is as bad as the last one was, more "adjustments" will have to be made.

With Marvin Krauss, who is *Esquire*'s expert on research and has dealt most directly with the Simmons problems, I got to musing about what possible directions these "adjustments" to the editorial approach would have to take in order to please the computer. It seemed to me that any good magazine, one that a subscriber would want to read carefully and possibly want to save because it was so interesting or attractive, would be at a great disadvantage. To get a higher readers-per-copy number, you'd have to make the magazine *worse*.

"You know, Rust," Marvin Krauss interrupts me. "The sad thing, the *terrifying* thing to me about all this, is that if you were deliberately to design a magazine to accommodate to this pass-along readership concept, what you'd come up with is a magazine exactly like *People*."

9. THE GLOBAL BONANZA OF AMERICAN TV
by Andrew R. Horowitz

Nothing emphasizes the essential commodity nature of media entertainment products more than the international trade in them. The U.S. has dominated world trade in film, television, and recordings for decades. In this incisive piece of analysis written for *MORE* in 1975 and based on research completed by The Network Project (see Appendix 3), Andrew R. Horowitz helps explain why and how.

There is perhaps nothing so incongruous as a television set in a mud hut or slum shack. But this incongruity does exist in many countries around the world. It may do more to change the world more quickly than any development since the invention of the wheel.

> —*Leonard Goldenson*
> *Chairman of the Board, ABC (1964)*

From 1959 to 1973, Ben Cartwright and his sons—Adam, Hoss, and Little Joe—roamed the plains of the Ponderosa and the screens of American television. In a total of 359 episodes (25 a year for almost fourteen years), *Bonanza* reassured millions with its good, clean fun and weekly doses of frontier justice. Meanwhile, away from the ranch, the American Way of Life was steadfastly protected by determined cops (*Mannix, Highway Patrol*), dedicated doctors (*Ben Casey, Dr. Kildare*), vigilant intelligence agents (*Man from U.N.C.L.E., Mission Impossible*), and a whole parade of just plain folks (*I Love Lucy, Father Knows Best*).

In the United States today, most of these programs have now been replaced by "new" concoctions of the entertainment mill. But though the Cartwrights may be hard to find in the U.S. these days, last week they were seen by more than 400 million viewers in ninety countries. Indeed, for the past decade, *Bonanza* has offered the single most common cultural experience around the world, leaving one hard-pressed to disagree with NBC's boast that Ben Cartwright and his sons are "truly the first television family of the world." And not far behind are the other programs that once filled American screens five, ten, and even twenty years ago. This TV culture, former ABC International president Kevin O'Sullivan assures us, is "the most sought after, the most desired programming in the whole world."

UNESCO recently estimated that the total number of hours of American TV programs exported abroad each year ranges anywhere from a base of 100,000 to as many as 200,000, or well over twice the number of hours exported by all other nations. The longest American series include over 500 episodes with a total broadcast time of close to 400 hours. *Peyton Place*, which leads the pack with 514 episodes, can be viewed abroad for ten years if each one-half hour segment is shown weekly. In the early sixties, the largest foreign consumers by far were Great Britain and Germany. Today, American television culture abounds in Latin America, Africa, Asia, Western Europe, and Canada. Except for the People's Republic of China, Mongolia, Albania, the Democratic People's Republic of Korea, and Cuba, American programs currently are seen in almost every country of the world. By 1970, 115 countries were receiving programs syndicated by NBC. CBS, whose foreign clientele included 105 countries, and ABC, which in 1969 was distributing almost 900 programs in more than 90 countries, were not far behind.

In 1971, however, the Federal Communications Commission ruled that the networks could no longer syndicate programs in the United States and also restricted their exports to those few programs they produce and finance entirely on their own* The official explanation for the ruling was that the networks commanded too much control over which programs were seen on American screens. The decision came, however, at the height of the Nixon Administration's attack on the "liberal bias" of network news coverage. Whatever the motives, the ruling moved the networks to sell off their extensive film libraries and distribution services. NBC dealt off its division to National Telefilms Associates (NTA), a former motion picture syndicator. CBS and ABC also sold to independent companies, albeit ones run by the same executives who had operated the syndication divisions at each network. Indeed, the former ABC executives even kept the name of the network's old service—Worldvision.

But even if the FCC had not ruled in 1971 and the networks had continued their foreign syndication activity, their efforts would still have been dwarfed by Hollywood. For the past decade, over 80 percent of all American programs exported have come from the studios of some 160 motion picture companies. Ninety-nine percent of the global marketplace, however, has been—and remains—the exclusive province of ten California-based multinational entertainment conglomerates:

---

* Since the networks produce so little entertainment fare themselves, the FCC ruling has limited their foreign catalogue to news and public affairs—categories that account for only 9 percent of all American material exported.

Allied Artists, Avco-Embassy, Four Star Entertainment, MCA, M-G-M, Paramount, Screen Gems, Twentieth Century-Fox, United Artists, and Warner Brothers. This "Hollywood 10," with program sales offices throughout the world, has turned the foreign distribution of old U.S. serials into a $100-million-a-year business. Warner Brothers, for example, serves up such enlightenment as *The FBI, Kung Fu,* and *Superman* through no less than 52 foreign subsidiaries that syndicate the series to 117 nations. MCA, with 24 foreign subsidiaries serving 115 countries, offers such TV Americana as *Marcus Welby, M.D.* and *Leave It to Beaver.*

Unlike the networks, whose income is derived almost exclusively at home, the revenues these film companies receive from foreign sales often mean the difference between profit and loss. Television production in the United States is often a deficit operation. The sale of a series to a network usually covers only the cost of production; rarely does it return a profit. According to most film industry sources, U.S. television film producers earn about 20 percent of their revenue through exporting.

While television was slowly coming of age around the world, American firms were there first with the most. Once a new broadcast system had been built in a country, the problem of filling air time remained. Rarely could this need be met with the limited financial resources available in most foreign countries, which, in many cases, lacked even the most primitive production facilities. Such countries were easy targets for Hollywood distributors. These companies had money, talent, technicians, and facilities, not to mention an extensive backlog of ready-made programs. They could supply an essential product in a market where virtually no competition existed.

Nor was Hollywood eager to see any competition develop abroad. To discourage the possibility, all major distributors have resorted to "price cutting"—offering a foreign broadcaster a program for much less than it would cost to produce a homemade product. The practice dates back to 1956 in Australia, where a number of U.S. distributors had begun to experience some competitive pressure from a handful of Australian production companies that were using every money-saving device possible to produce half-hour films on Australian history and contemporary life for $20,000 each. The American response was to offer Australian broadcasters one-hour episodes for as little as $1,000 and half-hour programs for $500. These prices not only allowed local station managers and advertisers to pick up slick U.S. products for a fraction of what it would cost to produce locally, they also guaranteed them a ready supply of programming that had successfully passed the all-important test of viewer popularity. As Erik Barnouw, the Columbia University communications scholar, has noted, Australian broadcasters received these early bargains with comments like this to local producers:

Look, I can get *Restless Gun* for $1400 an episode. It had an audi-
ence rating of 31.1 in the United States. According to *Sponsor*
magazine, it had a CPMHPCM [cost-per-thousand-homes-per-
commercial-minute] rating of $2.34. That's some CPMHPCM rat-
ing, isn't it? Now what can you offer?

The local producer could offer ideas, perhaps talent, but certainly not a
bargain certified by a CPMHPCM rating.

Since the fifties, TV producers around the world have been overwhelmed by a vast, cheap supply of American exports. Most vulnerable have been the poorer countries of Latin America, Africa, and Asia,
where TV production is still in its infancy. For instance, one-hour U.S.
programs could be purchased in many countries in 1974 for as little as
$75 (Haiti and Honduras). In Thailand, the bargain price was $500.
Even in Kuwait and Saudi Arabia, with all those petrodollars, the figure
was as low as $250. The prime-time programming in Nigeria ($35–40
for half-hour episodes; $80–110 for the longer ones) was wall-to-wall
Hollywood: *Mission Impossible* (Sunday), *The Big Valley* (Monday),
Mannix (Wednesday), *Bronco* (Thursday), and *Bonanza* (Friday).
The impact in Nigeria, as elsewhere, has been to wipe out the economic base for local program production.

The film industry long has known the strategic value of efficient
organization and centralized control to serve its global designs. In 1922
it formed the Motion Picture Association of America (MPAA) to
handle both the domestic and foreign syndication of its members'
films. In 1960, the "Hollywood 10" established a similar entity, the
Motion Picture Export Association of America (MPEAA), and vested
it with the authority to represent its membership in negotiations with
foreign governments and entrepreneurs for the sale of U.S. television
programs.

The MPEAA operates as a single bargaining unit with foreign customers. Such activity would be prohibited in the United States on
antitrust grounds. It flourishes abroad, however, under the protection
of the Webb-Pomerene Act of 1918. The act permits businesses overseas to function as monopolies, with a single sales agent empowered to
set prices and arrange contracts. This is the way it works with the
association which, in addition, itself restricts members from entering
into separate negotiations with foreign buyers. The MPEAA's functions, scope, and methods are not unlike those of the Department of
State. One of its regular quasi-governmental duties includes lobbying
against foreign legislation that would hinder the impact of its members'
programs. When an Argentine bill was proposed a few years ago that
would have required U.S. programs shown in Argentina to be dubbed
in that country, the MPEAA sent down a delegation to oppose the bill.
Although this legislation hardly could have been considered grounds
for any major concern, the MPEAA worried that if the bill were
passed, then similar bills would be proposed in other Latin American

countries, thus making the export of programs to that hemisphere more difficult. The bill was defeated.

Though the American TV bombardment abroad is heavier than ever today, a few nations are beginning to rise up against the aggressive sales tactics of U.S. producers. Until recently, for example, prime-time programming in Canada was almost a replica of that seen in the United States. A 1965 government-appointed commission, after surveying the state of Canadian television, was left with this question: "Does not a population of twenty million people have something of its own to say?" In 1969, the Canadian Parliament passed a law permitting only 40 percent of the country's programming to be produced abroad, and only 30 percent from any one country. Other nations, including Great Britain, France, Italy, Denmark, Sweden, Australia, and Japan have also imposed quotas—albeit less stringent ones. Because those industrialized nations have well-developed television resources today, they are less vulnerable than the developing (and more populous) nations of Latin America, Asia, and Africa. In the end, however, it is merely a matter of degree. For the impact of the American TV series, wherever it appears, extends well beyond the propagation of American symbols, characters, and patterns of behavior.

Like the missionary campaigns of the eighteenth and nineteenth centuries, America's exported TV culture has served as a herald of empire. Its message has helped grease the international proliferation of U.S. business interests since the early fifties. While the American TV package has supplied the world with images of the good life, foreign subsidiaries and affiliates of American consumer goods industries have amassed fortunes in providing it. Procter & Gamble (which currently earns $3 out of every $4 abroad), Bristol-Meyers, Colgate-Palmolive, Coca-Cola, Pepsi-Cola, Ford, and General Motors for years have sponsored American programs abroad—ever since the Esso Corporation (now Exxon) began experimenting with television advertising in Cuba in 1951. When a TV campaign launched by the oil company a few years later increased sales by over 20 percent in a period of only twelve days, a huge economic surge abroad followed, with other firms enjoying similar successes elsewhere. As one Max Factor executive put it in 1959, the year his company sponsored thirty-nine U.S. programs in Brazil, "to ignore the power of television is to ignore the most powerful advertising force the world has ever known."

Not until the sixties, however, did the global interests of U.S. broadcasters and consumer goods industries truly begin to merge on a large scale. The union was spearheaded by ABC, which spent the entire decade integrating scores of stations around the world into a single international network, Worldvision. Although ABC no longer operates this network because of the aforementioned 1971 FCC ruling, its efforts played a crucial role in spreading commercialism worldwide. What Worldvision offered the international advertiser was a centralized sales apparatus enabling him to market his merchandise on an unprecedented scale. From 1965 to 1969, ABC extended its reach to

HOOKING UP THE SYSTEM

Before any American TV program could reach its intended foreign audience, national television systems had to be built and management and technical personnel trained to operate them. This became the task of the three American commercial networks, which, by the mid-fifties, had begun exporting an economic framework of broadcasting built on the American experience. Their efforts resulted in television's sweeping the globe. By 1973, broadcasters in 130 countries were transmitting signals from more than 33,000 stations to more than 330 million television sets; and in 90 countries, some form of commercial broadcasting had been introduced.

The earliest, and most direct, type of American influence abroad involved investing in foreign broadcast systems, a practice initiated with NBC's purchase of stock in an Australian TV station in 1953. But given the reluctance of foreign governments to relinquish ownership of their valuable broadcast properties to outsiders, only a modest share of the networks' surplus capital ever found its way abroad in this form.

Where the networks *did* make a considerable impact abroad is in pioneering the construction and expansion of foreign television systems. CBS entered this field in 1959, when it provided technical assistance for the creation of a second German television network (Freies Fernsehen). The network was declared unconstitutional and dismantled a year later. Nonetheless, it set the stage for further projects, including, among others, a contract signed with the Italian Broadcasting Corporation (RAI) in 1961 to supply management expertise in the areas of program production, news, public affairs, and sales promotion. CBS's largest project, however, involved construction of Israel's nationwide television system in 1966.

But it was NBC that emerged as the biggest U.S. supplier of management and technical aid to foreign broadcasters. Invariably, they were broadcasters whose systems were being built with equipment purchased from NBC's parent company, RCA. Activity in this area began in 1958, when the company provided managerial and administrative assistance to television systems inaugurating some form of commercial operation in Portugal, Peru, Sweden, and Yugoslavia. NBC then went on to build TV stations in Egypt, Argentina, and Hong Kong, assist in the formation of Italy's second television network, and design national broadcast systems in Kenya, Sierra Leone, the Sudan, Uganda, and Nigeria. (Nigeria's system, in fact, was managed by the company's international management services coordinator, J. Robert Myers, from 1962 to 1965.)

NBC also put together the largest single television project ever undertaken by an American firm: construction of a thirteen-station network in Saudi Arabia, started in 1964 and finished two years later under joint contract to the U.S. State Department and the U.S. Army Corps of Engineers. In 1966, again with U.S. government support, NBC built South Vietnam's national TV system, to which the company continued to supply equipment and advisory support.

ABC has by far the most widespread connections abroad. With CBS and NBC concentrating primarily on maintaining a firm command of television markets at home, ABC eagerly pursued less competitive situations abroad. The company owns stock in five Central American television stations, three Japanese stations, and one each in Australia and the Philippines; and in program production companies in Mexico, Great Britain, and West Germany. In addition, ABC maintains minor holdings among some fifty-four other television stations around the world, to which, over the years, it has supplied assistance in the areas of administration, sales promotion, and programming. Like both CBS and NBC, it also has been active in the development of foreign broadcast systems. In 1960, ABC built Ecuador's first TV station, and later assisted both in the creation of the Philippine Republic Broadcasting System and in the formation of the Arab Middle East Television Network, comprised of stations in Syria, Lebanon, Kuwait, Iraq, and Jordan.

60 percent of all TV sets outside the United States where some form of commercial broadcasting was permitted.

The genesis of the network dates to 1960, when ABC invested $250,000 in five Central American television stations (Costa Rica, Honduras, Guatemala, El Salvador, and Nicaragua). The company then organized these stations into the Central American Television Network, to which it offered three important services: program buying, sales representation, and networking. The plan called for each station to relinquish its prime-time evening viewing hours to ABC, which, in turn, would supply it with "free" programming sponsored by American companies operating in the Central American market. In this way, ABC sold such programs as *Batman, The Flintstones,* and *My Little Margie* to an advertiser and then placed them alongside designated commercials in any of the countries the sponsor wanted them to appear.

The scheme proved enormously profitable. According to the U.S. Department of Commerce, scores of U.S. corporations flocked to Central America to take advantage of these new market opportunities. By 1963, ABC had signed on thirty-one U.S. multinational corporations as advertisers, which, in the words of a company brochure, then reached an audience "with upwards of $136 billion in disposable income." Throughout the sixties, ABC added stations and advertisers to its Worldvision network. By the end of the decade, the network comprised sixty-eight stations operating in twenty-seven countries.

Today, America's television culture is firmly entrenched as a global salesman for more than 200 multinational U.S. firms that do $200 billion a year in business overseas. ABC's satellite coverage of the 1972 Olympic Games in Munich was watched by an estimated one billion people in a hundred countries—more than one fourth of the world's population. Coca-Cola, International Harvester, Sears Roebuck, Schlitz, Prudential Life Insurance, among other companies, paid ABC nearly $20 million to beam their advertising messages to a waiting world. Back in the sixties, Marshall McLuhan enthusiastically predicted the arrival of this "global village." More accurately, it seems to have become a global Ponderosa.

10. THE MIDDLE AGE OF BRITISH TELEVISION

by David Thomson

Despite American dominance of world television markets, other national TV systems do manage to make their mark occasionally. German television and Italian television (both essentially state owned)
have coproduced a number of films by important cinema directors,
serving as a financial cushion for hard-pressed native cinema industries. British television, split between commercial and noncommer-
cial networks with the latter financed by a unique tax system
(which separates it from undue government influence), is generally
regarded as the best in the world. As David Thomson makes clear
in this piece originally written for *American Film* in 1977, the British
export product which has succored American public television is
only the tip of the iceberg. There's a lot of dry rot on British TV, too.
Nevertheless, the BBC was the first television system to begin
broadcasting, having celebrated its fortieth anniversary in November 1976, and the best British programming has had a profound
effect on the "art" of television worldwide, if not the business.
See Chapters 13 and 22 for more on British TV.

Television sets are the same all over the world: the fronts bulging with
stress, the corners rounded, the interiors filled with gray jelly. Often,
the programs are the same also, but they acquire different meanings in
different countries. In Britain, television shares many programs with
America, yet the experiences are so unlike that one is forced to
concede how far the medium responds to its setting.

In 1976, British television celebrated American independence and
carried the look-away conversations between Ford and Carter. But it
has been most proud of itself. The year marked forty years of television in Britain and twenty-one of "commercial" or "independent" television, which came into being in 1955 under the Independent Broadcasting Authority (IBA) after an initial monopoly by the British
Broadcasting Corporation (BBC). Britain still has only three channels

z cars: *British success in an American genre, the cop show.*

to choose from, but virtually the entire audience of fifty million has access to them. Television reaches the majority of the population simultaneously, further emphasizing the smallness of the country. The medium portrays less and less the distinct localities of Britain. Instead, there is a glut of programs—some comic, some dramatic—that are affirmations of little England, obscure to foreigners, determinedly oblivious to Britain's decline in international terms, and set in some middle class where no offense is given or taken. Domestic drama and comedy seem to concern families whose television set has been taken away for an operation, pitching the members of the household into farce or tragedy, or both.

An example of this form, entertaining but instantly forgettable, is the comedy series *George and Mildred*, often the top-rated show in Britain. It is about a childless couple on the brink of middle age; he is an impotent layabout, she a frustrated bourgeois lady. They live in a tidy never-never land which could be in any part of Britain. Their class basis is blurred: George is probably working-class—except, like so many of Britain's workers, he is unemployed—and Mildred has the nervy gentility of the nouveau poor, trying to keep a "nice" house on less money. They are visited by relations or bicker with neighbors, but there is only one joke: Mildred's waspish regret that the limp George won't or can't have sex with her. From week to week, the characters become more familiar, but never shallow, and Yootha Joyce and Brian Murphy are examples of the television performer who is recognizable but who has no personality.

The nature and effect of advertising on television have always been under scrutiny in Britain because one of the two most popular channels is funded by commercials, while the other is not. The BBC is a state enterprise, although its board of governors and director general have surprising freedom, and no one has ever impeded the right or necessity of the BBC to examine and criticize the running of the country. BBC-TV is financed by the license fee: anyone possessing a television receiver must pay the government £12 a year for a black-and-white set and £18 for a color set. There are now about eighteen million licenses. Stores selling or renting sets pass on the addresses of their customers, and there is an inspection system and fines for those without a license. The BBC advertises on commercial television the domestic horror of a knock on the door after dark, when an illicitly enjoyed *Columbo* is interrupted by a drab Hitchcockian inspector. The accumulated licenses fees (£230 million a year) pay for the entire radio operation as well as two television channels: BBC1 and BBC2.

BBC2 honors the corporation's tradition of providing for small, elite audiences. The third television channel was awarded to the BBC on the understanding that it would carry some "difficult" material and not be fearful of modest audiences or abnormal length. BBC2 transmits for a relatively small portion of the day with foreign films (subtitled) and Hollywood classics, programs made for the Open University courses, and documentaries which are more specialized and less sensational than those on the other two channels. BBC2 carries live coverage of

MONTY PYTHON: *"Nobody expects the Spanish Inquisition!"*

sports and nearly continuous transmission from the three-party political conferences held at the end of the summer. There is also "Open
Door," a slot for minority interest groups to use studio facilities and to
make documentaries about themselves.

BBC1 is diligently set on entertainment and digestible information:
news, documentaries, plays, recent films, talk shows, and situation
comedies and action series imported from America. (*Kojak* is relished
in Britain, and George Savalas is shamelessly featured in advertisements for a British hamburger less sustaining than his brother's lollipops.) The tempo and mood of BBC1 only begin as people return
from work. During the day, it has school programs, nursery games for
infant children, magazines for women at home, and horse racing—a
popular sport on British television. Sometimes BBC1 will even close
down and give way to music and the trade test pattern that enables
shops selling television sets to demonstrate fine tuning.

Herein lies a striking difference between television in Britain and
America. The succession of game shows and soap opera on daytime
television is unthought of in Britain, where the medium remains primarily an evening diversion. Not a night game, however: it is rare for
a channel to continue more than thirty minutes after midnight. Television in Britain takes it for granted that its viewers want to go to bed,
and that they have better things to do during the working day.

Such fastidiousness testifies, I think, to an underlying suspicion of
television in Britain, and of what it might do to popular taste. The
BBC has only grudgingly extended viewing hours and often adopts a
lofty, if not hypocritical, attitude toward its own competition with
commercial television. There is still a lot of "dignity" clinging to the
BBC, most evident in the authority and reassurance of the corporation
between programs: announcers onscreen, the BBC insignia of a globe
slowly revolving, giving measured introductions to every program. In
America, by contrast, the medium runs itself, and programs are glued
together with commercials. BBC-TV separates programs and leaves a
definite pause in which we can choose to go on, pick up a book, or
even turn off the set. I doubt that many viewers exercise such options,
but the channels offer the possibility of it. It also politely withstands
what Britain considers the reckless vulgarity of American television—
canned studio laughter, commercials appearing before a program has
properly begun and more often during it, game shows where prizes
dwarf the intellectual tasks, meaningless amiability of quizmasters and
hosts, and police series of routine violence.

Not long after commercial television had begun in Britain, a government committee set up to assess its performance administered a
prim rap on money-grubbing knuckles and called for higher standards.
Independent television is controlled by the Independent Broadcasting
Authority, which coordinates a dozen or so companies set up on regional franchises. Several commercial companies contribute programs
to the network, their own series or plays, or packages bought from
America. Independent Television News is carried by all the commer-

cial companies, and financed by them, but it is autonomous. The commercial companies are financed by the advertising they carry: a maximum of three commercial breaks an hour, as compared with four or more in America. In 1975, advertising revenue was £176 million. The advertisers buy time in certain programs—as in America—but they cannot sponsor programs. Thus again, the channel impresses a character upon its product, and every program is preceded by a fanfare and a company trademark.

In the 1960s, especially, the commercial companies were immensely profitable: It was in Britain that Roy Thomson, newspaper owner and stockholder in television, said that commercial television was a license to print money. Britain flinched at that candor, years before profit became as elusive as it is today. But with a stagnant economy, advertisers are thin on the ground, and in recent years the BBC has been winning the larger part of the popular audience. Some commercial companies have been under economic pressure, and nowhere is this better dramatized than in the way the BBC lately has overrun Saturday nights with two programs: *The Generation Game*, a family game show in which contestants participate in everything from making pastry to sketching with the host, Bruce Forsyth; and *Starsky and Hutch*, in which the muted homosexual implications come through more clearly in Britain, where sexual jokes and behavior are handled casually on television.

Britain now submits to a daily litany of its own hard times in newscasts—in most of which the pound is measured against the dollar, thus fostering anti-American feelings. But commercials in Britain have seldom been so in awe of their own products as those on American television. Hollywood always aspired to glamour with a directness that embarrassed the British, and many commercials in this country are humorous, even to the point of teasing the larger process of advertising. That could make them all the more successful as inducements to buy; the Englishman may be a sucker for irony, just as the American eats up conviction and sincerity. Still, I find British commercials subtler and more engaging than those in America. There is one small gem of a British commercial now worth describing, if only because commercials may be the true staple of the medium. Two men are watching horse racing on television—the ad is for a particular color model—and they come up to the set as the race ends, admiring the lifelike tones of the reception. The camera is at the back of the set and, as they chat, a flap is lowered and a miniature stableboy leads a miniature winner out of the set while the two astonished giants stare down at the threshold of the real and the absurd.

Disruptive humor has an enduring place on British television. In the early sixties, the BBC mounted a late-night (i.e., after 10 P.M.) live program, *That Was the Week That Was*, which sprang David Frost upon the world and prompted the description "satire." *TW3* and its successors lasted several years before growing institutional anxiety persuaded the BBC that people were weary of satire. The program was always hit-or-miss, shocking only in a very conservative Britain. But it demonstrated that real issues and politicians could be discussed with wit, partiality, and virulence. It was controversial, and, sadly, it is no more. British television is more respectful than it was ten years ago; the BBC is more cautious of the awkward ground between its charter and government sensitivity, and the other channel is more apprehensive of alarming the consumers that advertisers require. The need for "balance" has diluted what little radical journalism television encouraged. "Objectivity" excuses increasingly restrained investigation.

Most Americans, however, still find British television opinionated, demanding, and outspoken. Talk-show hosts give their guests a rougher ride than ingratiating U.S. hosts, and political interviewing on British television has sometimes jolted its leaders out of their anodynic routines. Twenty years ago John Freeman's *Face to Face* established a precedent for a subject being turned into victim, his frailties exposed and his reputation scrutinized. Politicians and show business personalities can cope with that treatment, of course, but I recall two startling revelations of Muhammad Ali in Britain—once where he walked off

THE FORSYTE SAGA: *Nicholas Pennell and Susan Hampshire as Michael Mont and Fleur Forsyte. The twenty-six-episode series was one of the most influential television programs of recent years, establishing the limited series as an important form.*

TALKING TO A STRANGER: *The television play has had far greater success in England than in the U.S.*

the set because an interviewer kept asking an awkward question, and again when his potent racial comments got out of control and hushed a studio audience disposed at first to like him.

British comedy shows can be raw for Americans. Sex is harped on lewdly, and nudity is not uncommon. Popular comedian Frankie Howerd works largely through innuendo. *Till Death Us Do Part* and *Porridge*, I think, were funnier and closer to reality than their American cousins *All in the Family* and *On the Rocks*. Alf Garnett in the first was a working-class Fascist, drunk on Churchill, and ranting against "nig-nogs." The humor in the show grew out of shrewd character studies, and, when we laughed at the blatant prejudices, nobody was sure whether we were exorcising or substantiating Alf's attitudes. Real risk was involved, and the BBC dithered between liberal reservations and high ratings.

The comedy show that disturbed most people was *Monty Python's Flying Circus*, one of British television's most eccentric achievements. Many people were viscerally uncomfortable; others laughed at its anarchistic abuse of television genres and at the randy violence that fulfilled surrealism's belief in the shattering of convention. The Python gang were not out to please. There was a brazen, refreshing insolence about them which was capable of impaling staid audiences. Television often treats the audience as if it were a short-tempered emperor. "Monty Python" knew it was a stupid, dozing beast. That it flourished speaks better of audiences than of programmers and indicates a public wish to be surprised more often.

Police series are popular in Britain, and viewers follow Kojak, "Pepper" Anderson, Columbo, Cannon, and several more of the sentimental personality cops from America. The native crime series are less rigid in plot formula, more alert to character, and far less confident that the police are on top of their job. *The Sweeney* is as violent as an American series, and funnier than *Kojak*, but its London Flying Squad heroes are scruffy, morose men, shorn of a private life and aghast at the impossible task of keeping up with crime. Television crooks in Britain sometimes get away, and the cops creak with strain. On *Softly, Softly*, there was an intelligent episode about a decent but harassed detective who rigged evidence to nail a man he knew was guilty. *Softly, Softly* is the latest spin-off from *Z Cars*, a landmark series begun in the early sixties, originally in the Liverpool area, that exposed police fiction to the rigors of neorealism.

In Britain there is a stronger tradition of documentary on television, and by now many miles of film of atrocities and street fighting in Northern Ireland have been unreeled. News programs are parochial, and newscasters more reserved personalities than in America—not soothsayers or celebrities, but pained go-betweens for the bad news and an overwhelmed public. Newscasts make more use of interviewed spokesmen than America does, and seem to expect the public will make up its own mind. But, of course, political parties and doctrines are active in Britain and only intermittent in America, and there is a greater faith in public debate. Moreover, two men running for the highest office in Britain would have been more pungent, more amusing, and more eloquent than Carter or Ford were prepared to be. In Britain they appeared as nervous as people offering only themselves, alien to a system that still considers ideas and issues as important as the men who debate them.

Another advantage in Britain is the amount of drama available. That means not only the classics and serializations of novels—John Galsworthy's *The Forsyte Saga*, in twenty-six episodes—but television plays commissioned from good writers. Many leading British dramatists have done original work for television: Harold Pinter, David Mercer, Dennis Potter, Peter Terson, Peter Nichols, and John Hopkins, who began on *Z Cars*. The quality of British television drama does something to make up for, and may be stimulated by, the dearth of a contemporary British cinema. Many of these plays end up on the tube as films. *Talking to a Stranger*, written by John Hopkins for the BBC in the mid-sixties, was four ninety-minute plays describing the disintegration of a British family. It was a pungent antidote to television's tendency to inflate and bowdlerize the family beyond all reality. *Talking to a Stranger* was so moving and engrossing that it seemed a withering mirror for the English living room.

It was more shattering than any British film of its time and proof of television's use of the best talent around among writers, actors, and directors. One of the most promising of young English directors is Stephen Frears—he made *Gumshoe*—and he is usually to be found on television with unexpected, personal films. Frederic Raphael, an established movie writer, has never surpassed *Glittering Prizes*, a series of plays written for television. He was also involved in a recent project that showed how easily the BBC could become a major producer of movies. He adapted, and Clive Donner directed, a version of *Rogue Male* (the source of Fritz Lang's *Man Hunt*) with Peter O'Toole in the lead. It was fondly imitative of Hitchcock's British movies, but effortless, atmospheric, and gripping. Its aims were clear and sensible, it had given scope to talented people, and it was sure of an audience—the conditions so fleeting in the British cinema.

Yet if British television is not often compelling as television—rather than as a substitute cinema—it is a boon to the film fan. Not as many films are shown as on American television, but on the BBC they are intact and uninterrupted, a condition the BBC has kept to faithfully. Even films on the commercial channel are only nibbled at to fit time slots. Moreover, BBC2 is adventurous in its choice of movies. Recent weekends have provided *The Devil Is a Woman* (without an apology for being in black-and-white), the rarity of Michael Curtiz's *The Mad Genius*, Visconti's *Death in Venice*, Jean Harlow in *Red Headed Woman*, Eric Rohmer's *The Marquise of O* (before it opened in a London cinema), the complete version of François Truffaut's *Mississippi Mermaid* (benefiting from a color system better than that in America), Erice's *Spirit of the Beehive*, Abdelsalam's *The Night of Counting the Years*, Pasolini's *Teorema*, and Marcel Ophuls's four-and-a-half-hour *The Memory of Justice* (with only one intermission).

I have been praising British television, despite an overall discontent, slowly amounting to contempt with myself for watching. The implication is that only in addressing American readers can I find so much good. British television is subtler than American; it expects more involvement from the audience. Yet, within this island, I am dismayed by the way television seems happy merely to mollify an uneasy people.

Confronted by the total pattern of American television, the British might see more clearly the range of subjects their television attempts and the relative freedom from gridiron scheduling. As I have said, the American is taken aback by British television, just as I was disappointed in America by the gap between unequivocally time-killing television programs, so interrupted as to be incoherent, and films that are daring, accurate, and beautiful. Perhaps American movies would not be as good if American television were better, while in Britain television compensates for our despair with the national cinema.

Television is not so much entertainment or information as a habit, perhaps even an alternative to living life to the full. In both Britain and America, I believe, it is to be endured, like poverty or bad weather. We watch its insipid, neurotic flicker and the shriveling of our own sensibility with equal bitterness. After forty years of television, the most pregnant speculation about it remains: "Suppose it did not exist. . . ." Britain will soon have a fourth channel, and the BBC and the IBA are dutifully competing for it. But the consumer may think enough is enough. We hardly need one more channel like the others. It would be better to turn it over to the recording of Parliament—if those bashful democrats consented—or for some quite fresh purpose.

Perhaps television does sustain our goods-buying democracies; perhaps it only props them up with delusions. Amid the BBC's celebration of itself in 1976, it revived *Cathy Come Home*, a dramatized documentary about homeless families that shocked public and politicians alike when it was first shown a dozen years ago. It is still poignant, still a challenging use of actors and real squalor; it still angers. Yet after it was shown again, a bleak credit admitted that there were now more homeless people than ever. And if America congratulates itself that newsreels from Vietnam curtailed that senseless war, in Britain the years of Northern Ireland on television have only persuaded the British that the problem is insoluble, and excuse enough for the escapes offered by *The Generation Game* or *Starsky and Hutch*.

11. KANNED LAFFTER
by Ron Rosenbaum

One of the more intriguing aspects of video history is its curious relationship to the older medium of film. To a large extent, film still sets the pattern TV follows. It's not only that feature films provide much of the product for the voracious tube, nor that the film studios produce more than three quarters of the dramatic and comedy series seen on TV. More subtly, the film experience provides a model for the video experience: hence laugh tracks. Comedy, the theory goes, does not work without an audience. It's a communal experience. The best sitcoms are filmed or taped before a live audience. The rest depend on *communitas ex machina*—a programmable robot community. Actors are still required in the flesh, apparently, but the other half of the dramatic equation—the audience—can be replicated electronically. Another great advance for modern science: audiences, live ones, were always so . . . unpredictable. Where are you, Froggy, now that we need you?

First at *Esquire*, then at *MORE*, Ron Rosenbaum has been responsible for much of the best media criticism of the 1970s. He did this piece for *Esquire* in 1975.

It's been an uphill struggle for Ralph Waldo Emerson III and his canned laughter machine. Since 1970, Ralph's been trying to convince TV producers that the super-sophisticated laugh machine he designed can lay down laugh tracks light-years ahead of the leading laugh maker in the business.

For as long as anyone can remember, the laugh-canning industry has been dominated by that one man, the legendary and secretive Charlie Douglass, "King of Canned Laughter," and Charlie's patented laugh machine.

"Charlie's got into a position in this business where he can do no wrong," Ralph grumbles. "It's become an automatic thing: you want laughs you go to Charlie, he's got the golden ears, they all say."

Ralph thinks the "golden ears" mystique has deafened TV people to
the declining quality of most of the canned laughter you hear these
days. "What they don't realize is what you get when you get Charlie to
do your laughs are Charlie laughs . . . you get that universal Charlie
Douglass sound. And it's sad, because some of his material is very old.
Very tired."

But Ralph Waldo Emerson III—a direct descendant, he says, of
Emerson the New England poet and philosopher—has more than mere
technological gripes about Charlie's laughs. He has *philosophical* objections.

That universal Charlie Douglass sound creates a profound "detach-
ment" between the TV viewer and the ghostly host of canned laugh-
ers, Ralph says. "You get the feeling that here's the performer and
here's this black box making laughs. There's no feeling of *oneness* with
the audience," Ralph complains.

Ralph and I are chatting in an ABC-TV sound-studio control room
and Ralph is preparing to demonstrate for me his machine—the one he
believes can bring oneness back to canned laughter.

"You are looking at the most sophisticated, most versatile machine
of the bunch," Ralph tells me as he unbolts the waist-high blue-and-
chromium-cased laugh box. He selects some cassette cartridges of
laugh loops from his carefully coded laugh library, loads them into
slots in the laugh machine, and plugs the machine into his Rapid Cue
master control console.

"I've got eighteen grades of laughter here," he says, turning to the
console, which is covered with red, white, and yellow rows of square
buttons.

"Listen—this is a number one." He touches a red button and someone starts chuckling. A few more people break into pleasantly indul-
gent after-dinner laughs which mingle with sporadic throaty chortles
and incipient giggles. A muted, curiously comforting and intimate
sound fills the nearly empty studio.

"That's your basic chuckle track," Ralph says. "Now I'm gonna
bring in some more people, give it some more body. Here's a number
nine." He touches another red button, then reaches over to the right-
hand side of the console and slides a few arrow-shaped fader knobs up
and down in their slots.

"Here now you've got the body of the audience going, and what you
can do with the faders is bring up some chuckles or accents or whistles
and cheers, and down here you've got your giggle track and you can
trail off into that, and this one here, this number nine on the white
row, is the most powerful—I call it my 'pants-dropper.' "

After the screaming gasps of the pants-dropper die out, Ralph fades
down to a mixture of giggles and exhausted whimpers on one of his
taper-off loops, then builds back up to a rhythmic full-bodied roar,
comes down to chuckles again and lets me take over the controls.

To put his laughs on the sound track of an actual show, Ralph just
hooks the speaker of his laugh machine into the tape of the show, sits

at his console watching the show on a monitor, and plays his laughs and applause directly onto one of the eight tracks of the show's master tape. "Without being arrogant," Ralph confides, "I think I know what's funny and what isn't, but more important I know what's *supposed* to be funny."

There's no show on the monitor this morning, just an empty studio and the two of us pushing buttons and making wave after wave of phantom studio audiences crack up. And the strange thing is that it's pretty funny all by itself, this straight dose of unadulterated canned laughter. No silly jokes to get in the way. Very infectious stuff. I couldn't help myself, I broke up and began laughing along with the machine.

Ralph smiles proudly. "I can take anyone and sit 'em down here and in a minute I can have them laughing. I could prove to the biggest doubter that he's not standing on solid ground because if you're sitting here laughing at this stupid machine . . ."

It was five years ago that ABC executives urged Ralph to take on the Titan of Titters. A daring project. Charlie Douglass may not have invented canned laughter itself, but he patented the machine that has made laugh tracks a household sound in America. Charlie and his laugh machines still produce most of the "sweetened" laughter and applause you will hear on prime time tonight. That's right, "sweetened." The people who produce shows like *The Mary Tyler Moore Show, Cher, M*A*S*H,* etc., don't like to say they use "canned laughter." They prefer to say that they augment their studio-audience sound with "electronic sweetening," which usually means laughs from Charlie Douglass's laugh machine. Even those shows which boast of being "recorded live" before a "live studio audience" still use a bit of prerecorded sweetening here and there to help out "lines that get a laugh in the dress rehearsal, say, but for some reason don't in the final taping," as one sitcom producer explained to me. "It's not a cheat using it that way. Well, it's only *half* a cheat." And sweeteners are slipping into some of the most traditional live shows on TV. The network people, both of whom refused to be identified for fear of losing their jobs, told me that the Rose Bowl Parade often uses sweetening to create that "smattering of applause" effect as each floral float goes by, and that ever since a well-known comedian bombed with his monologue on an Oscar broadcast, the Academy Awards show has standby sweetening on tap for laughter and applause.

It all started around the time of *My Little Margie,* in 1954. Or maybe it was 1955, with *Our Miss Brooks.* You hear different stories. But sometime in the mid-fifties, Charlie Douglass, a CBS radio and TV sound man, left the network and took a laugh-track machine to Desilu studios. Desilu was just beginning to turn out the first of the filmed non-audience comedies that would soon take over the airwaves. With his machine, Charlie was able to transform himself into a one-

First of the laughtracks: My Little Margie, *with Gale Storm, Charles Farrell (and friends).*

man studio audience for hire, the kind of audience that would laugh at just about anything.

From the outset, Charlie surrounded his laugh-making business with an aura of mystery and an apparent obsession with secrecy. He put padlocks on the laugh machine, refused all requests for interviews, discouraged publicity. It was rumored that his early contracts pledged him to a vow of silence to protect the identities of certain comedian and celebrity clients who swore publicly they never used a laugh machine. Rival laugh men suggest that all the secrecy is just a clever merchandising gimmick to make Charlie's laugh-making technology seem more complex and mysterious than it is. They're convinced that the padlocks conceal nothing more than repeating loops of prerecorded laughs activated by the keyboard on the outside of the laugh box.

Those first Desilu laugh tracks, the ones that established that unmistakable "canned" sound—who *are* those people and why are they laughing in that peculiar way?

I've heard it suggested that some of the laughs on Charlie's classic early laugh tracks were taken from tapes of old Burns and Allen radio shows—the cruel corollary being that, by now, half the people you hear yukking it up on any given rerun of *The Gale Storm Show* are dead.

But several rival laugh men had a more interesting explanation.

"The way I heard it," one of them told me, "they'd get an audience in a preview theater, put cans on their head, put an *I Love Lucy* show on the screen and let Charlie mike the house."

"Put what on their heads?"

"Cans—earphone headsets. They run the audio into the headsets so that when you mike the house for laughs you don't get the audio from the show mixed in with your laughs. You get very clean laughs that way; that's what Charlie was known for from the beginning—he always had really clean stuff."

Picture yourself in one of those early preview theater audiences. There's a blown-up kinescope of *I Love Lucy* on the screen, and you are surrounded by strangers with headsets on and wires coming out of their ears. Enough to make you laugh all by itself. But will it be your normal laugh or will it be a little nervous, a bit hollow? And when you *do* laugh you might as well be laughing alone in a cave, because your padded earphones isolate you from the sound of the laughter of the can-heads around you. None of that mutual jollying, none of the infectious crosscurrents you find in any ordinary audience. That special "canned" resonance, perhaps even the phrase "canned laughter," may be traced to these very cans.

But any chronicle of canned laughter, however brief, cannot fail to cite the daring conceptual breakthrough made manifest by such shows as *The Real McCoys* back in the mid-fifties, the breakthrough that made possible the canned laughter takeover of the airwaves.

Grandpa McCoy goes out into the pasture to milk a cow. Real pasture, real cow. Something funny happens like maybe the cow steps on Grandpa's hat. Suddenly there's a big roar of laughter from out of nowhere, well, from out of Charlie's laugh machine. Now, nobody watching *The Real McCoys* on his home screen is expected to believe that the laughter he hears is the real McCoy—that there's a real audience out there squatting in the cow pasture and yukking it up. All pretense to realism in canned laughter was abandoned. People who could accept the idea of an ethereal laugh materializing in a cow pasture could get used to the idea of a laugh materializing anywhere, even after the lines of a show like *My Mother, the Car*. Canned laughter became pure sound, Mirth Muzak. Before long, any new sitcom pilot that wanted a chance with the network biggies had to come to the screening room equipped with a lush Charlie Douglass laugh arrangement if it expected to be taken seriously.

Ralph Waldo Emerson III was by no means the first to challenge the King of Canned Laughs. There was the NBC hippo-roar machine, for instance.

Back in 1957, NBC put together a team of their best sound-effects men and told them to come up with a laugh machine for the network's own use. The intensive search ultimately led ace NBC sound man Austin Beck to Disneyland to check out a machine called the MacKenzie Repeater. Disneyland technicians had installed the Repeater inside certain simulated wild animals—the half-submerged hippo in the jungle river of Adventureland, for instance—in order to get them to roar on cue.

While NBC electronics technicians worked feverishly to adapt the hippo roar to the roars of canned laughter, veteran NBC sound man Monty Fraser (he's known in broadcasting as the man who produced the sound of Fibber McGee's closet) compiled a basic laugh library of audience laughs from the old George Gobel show. The NBC laugh-machine team even came up with an added device especially to please Milton Berle: a flickering neon bulb placed on top of the camera, wired to the newly adapted MacKenzie laugh machine; the bulb flickered as long as the machine laughed and Berle could know exactly how long his canned laugh lasted, so that he wouldn't step on it with the opening line of his next joke. But despite all its efforts and many improvements, NBC never has been able to lure a substantial number of clients away from Charlie Douglass with its hippo-roar machine, a fact that continues to pique some NBC laugh men.

"It's kind of a clique thing," one of the NBC laugh men tells me. Billy was part of the original NBC laugh team and he still does laughs for the network. "A clique in the sense that all the old comedians, like Burns and Hope, they stick together and they stick with Charlie. He's kind of like the Cadillac of the business. He's got the name; it doesn't matter if his material sounds older."

Ralph Waldo Emerson III is about to play a very special reel of tape for me. Ralph has just removed the reel from a padlocked file drawer in his laugh laboratory, and he's threading it into the lab's big Ampex 440 playback machine.

What's on this special reel? Not Ralph's own laughs. In the past few hours he's played enough of them to convince me of their quality. In the past few hours he's also revealed the three main sources of canned laughs for the entire ABC network (two obscure and canceled situation comedies—*A Touch of Grace* and *Thicker Than Water*, and *The Jonathan Winters Show*). He's confided to me the philosophical principle which guides the sweetening style ("What I do is give you the live-sounding laugh that *would have been there* had the show been done before a live audience. Nothing phony about that"), a kind of *ex post facto* existentialism.

He's told me how he's confronted and resolved the moral qualms he feels about making his living from canned laughter. "Somebody's got to do it," he told me grimly. "Like I said to my wife before I went into it. This is the one chance I'll have in my life to take something I really hate and take it away from caricature and turn it into an art form."

And he's told me about the hard times when they laughed when he sat down at his laugh machine. "When I first started I had to audition. I'd play my laughs and people would say, 'What's that?'—they were so used to Charlie they'd lost contact with what real laughs are. I had to really come on strong, I had to be ten times better than anything else available."

And he's tried—not entirely successfully—to convince me that he's not really preoccupied with Charlie and couldn't care less about the mystique surrounding Charlie's laughs.

"That there's a mystique at all is the amazing thing to me. What's the mystery? It's shit. What am I worrying about it for? The stuff I've got is much better. But there is no animosity between Charlie and myself. It's more like I'm Avis and he's Hertz."

But despite all this talk the tape Ralph is about to play is going to be the real clincher. Ralph was able to make this one-of-a-kind tape as a result of an unprecedented head-to-head sweetening contest with Charlie Douglass himself. The occasion was the production of an ABC Julie Andrews special. Union rules forbid independent laugh contractors like Charlie from working on network property. But several Charlie loyalists among the guest stars insisted on taking the show off the network lot to have their own segments sweetened by Charlie himself. "There was a big flap over who was gonna sweeten the show, me or Charlie. Incredible battles," Ralph recalls.

When a truce between the rival laugh men was finally negotiated, Charlie was awarded the sweetening of two thirds of the show, Ralph one third. Toward the end of the somewhat bitter sweetening contest that ensued, Ralph decided to isolate and thoroughly study his opponent's legendary laughs. He took a master tape of Charlie's two thirds of the show, isolated the sweetening track, and made a high-quality recording of Charlie's laughs in action.

"That's what's on this reel," Ralph says as he switches it on. "Pure Charlie tracks. I wanted to study them, see if I could figure out what the secret is, what it is about Charlie's stuff. Listen, you can hear for yourself."

A familiar-sounding wave of applause washes over the laugh lab. More applause. Ralph works the fast forward. Some laughs now.

Ralph proceeds to take me on a guided tour of these Charlie tracks, clinically analyzing all the weaknesses he believes he's discovered. He even has an unkind word to say for the silences between the laughs: "If you listen carefully you can hear those awful mechanical things going on inside the machine."

Then Ralph takes off the Charlie reel and threads in a reel with his third of that memorable Julie Andrews showdown.

"Listen to this and tell me you don't hear the difference," Ralph tells me.

I listen and I hear the difference and all at once I understand why Ralph has been having trouble breaking Charlie's monopoly. Ralph's laughs do seem to have a greater clarity, more natural-sounding beginnings, more naturally tapered "tails," as he calls them. And some of the Charlie laughs he played for me do tend to roar on and roar off in a homogeneous blur, and they do tend to taper off into some very familiar and repetitive-sounding hollow chuckles, and Charlie's applause can sound more like the roar of the ocean in a conch shell than an audience. But there's something warm and familiar and comforting about these Charlie tracks. They don't sound like real laughter, but they do sound like real *canned* laughter, the kind we're conditioned to accept, not as audience response but as soothing background noise. After Charlie's comforting confections, Ralph's naturalistic attempts to imitate a "live," "real" audience sound jarring and unnatural.

Ralph complains that "Charlie's sound has been around so long people don't know what real laughter sounds like anymore; they don't like it when they hear it." For the TV world it's a case of he-who-laughs-first-laughs-best, and Charlie laughed first.

But Ralph did come away from that canned laughter contest with one consoling, if ironic, triumph.

Ralph switches off the tape and smiles. "You want to know what happened at the end of that Julie Andrews sweetening? One of the producers who wasn't really in touch with who was sweetening what ran in here one day and he's listening to a segment of the show—a comedy sketch by Alice Ghostley—that I had done the laughs for. Well this guy listens to it and announces to everyone, 'Those are great laughs; that's what makes Charlie Douglass great.' You shoulda seen him when I told him who did those laughs." Ralph chuckles at the memory. It has the unsweetened sound of a last laugh.

And what of the legendary Charlie Douglass? He was somewhere in Germany the first time I tried to contact him. Someone had unloaded a batch of early Dean Martin-Jerry Lewis comedy-hour shows on a German TV station. The German station had Charlie flown to Munich to dub some of his laughs onto the sound track so that they would follow the new dubbed-in-German Jerry Lewis punch lines.

Charlie's secretary assured me that even if he were around the corner from me in Hollywood he might as well be in Munich because he never, never talked to reporters about his business. I begged her to get Charlie to call me after he returned from the Munich sweetening, just so I could hear the sound of his voice.

A week later I received a phone call. The voice on the line identified himself as Charlie Douglass and told me politely that he had never varied from his no-talk rule and wouldn't make an exception for me.

I tried to counter by telling him that other laugh men were talking openly about their work. Why did he persist in being so secretive?

"I think they're foolish to open up anything like this," Charlie told me. "You might have the best intentions, but there are many others who would jump on us. They'd crucify us. Then the government would get ahold of it and you'd never know what was happening."

"What would the government want with sweeteners?"

"You never know. I just think for everybody's welfare it would be better if nobody talked, and I'm not going to."

As a last resort I asked the voice on the phone if I could just meet with him in the flesh, to verify that the elusive Charlie Douglass himself was real and not canned.

"I'm sure there are lots of people who will verify I'm real," Charlie said. But he wouldn't say who.

12. HARRY MAKES A MOVIE
by Robert Alan Aurthur

People don't write books or screenplays or musical comedies anymore. They write properties. The key to success in today's media
market is to produce a piece that easily translates from one medium
to another. Then the producers take over. But they no longer produce movies, plays, or series. They produce packages. The package
consists of property, star, and director—or any two of these: a
combination that looks like it will generate enough media energy to
make a profit. Here Robert Alan Aurthur describes Harry Engle's
quest for the proper package. He is, as they say, the last of a dying
breed.

You want to produce a movie; it's a thing you just have to do. But
without major studio backing, without owning a best-selling novel or
hit play, and without a partnership with one of the few bankable
superstars, how do you get a picture made? Perhaps if we follow the
single case of New York-based Harry Engle you may find some answers. The project described is purely fanciful while altogether proto-
typical, and though Harry Engle is not his real name, Harry is, be
assured, a real person, a man dedicated to making movies, an independent producer since 1959.

At fifty-eight Harry Engle has spent all his working life in the movie
business. When he was nineteen, through his Uncle Charlie who managed a small chain of movie houses in Westchester, Harry got a job in
the foreign-sales department of a major studio's New York office.
Twenty-seven dollars a week; but after six months he was sent to the
Paris office, raised to thirty-five dollars a week, and for three years,
until the outbreak of the war in Europe, Harry learned about the
movie business. In 1941, drafted into the U.S. Army, Harry spent the
subsequent war years at the Army film studios in Astoria, Queens.
There he helped make more than two hundred training films, learned

how to budget a picture, found himself rewriting scripts and working nights at Moviolas.

The war over, Harry went back to the major studio's New York office, still in international sales, a hundred and a quarter a week, a reasonable raise every year. Then came the important break, when the federal government brought an antitrust action against the majors, forcing the film companies to divest themselves of their theater chains. No longer could major producers prevent an independent from booking his picture into any movie house in the country. And so in 1950 Harry accepted an offer from a company created by three men who owned an extremely successful toy business and wanted to produce movies. With access to heavy sums of money the partners were wise enough to make participation deals with successful film directors and stars who yearned to operate out from under major studio strictures. Paid five hundred dollars a week, Harry was also given 10 percent of the company. In 1958, having made eleven pictures, having bought and arranged distribution of a number of foreign films, having pioneered in the sale of a lot of schlock movies, bought for nearly nothing, to late-night television, the partners sold out for a capital gain to a major film company, which was now part of a burgeoning conglomerate. After taxes, Harry's end was a million one. At forty-two, a millionaire with a wife, a son in private school, and a Park Avenue apartment, Harry Engle was determined to stay in New York and produce pictures that represent the best of East Coast filmmaking: real, tough, unslick, and *meaningful*. He knew how.

Well, these days Harry Engle is mostly morose. In fifteen years Harry has managed to produce five pictures, all of quality, none to bring shame. Two lost money, one broke even, one was a moderate success, and one a hit. But because Harry's pictures must be financed and distributed by a major company, and because the bookkeeping is controlled by that company with charges inflated for overhead, distribution costs, prints, and advertising, even the hit, which cost a million eight to produce and was reported in *Variety* to have grossed nearly nine million dollars, brought Harry little profit.

A combination of his losers, years when he had no income at all, and the plunging stock market has reduced Harry's 1958 million one to a 1974 three hundred thousand, give or take a few dollars. But is Harry Engle discouraged? Not at all. He and wife Rene have taken a smaller Park Avenue apartment; his son Charlie (named for his late greatuncle) is out of the house and into a law firm which specializes in show business; the Engles have their beach house in Quogue and the Mercedes 450, and Harry just *knows* that his next picture will be a blockbuster, so big that even the most artful bookkeeping can't hide the kind of profits that will make him a rich man.

A few days from now Harry Engle will take a stack of worn books out of the New York Society Library. Unable to spend a half million dollars for a current best-seller or a hit play, Harry must find his sources in older books. He reads selectively, choosing categories that he believes might catch the upcurve of a popular trend. He once made a spy picture, but spies are out now; his big hit was in the youth area, but youth pictures have also become unfashionable. Comedies? Too hard to find. And so he carries home a half-dozen private-eye novels when . . . zap! He hits one. A faded dust jacket tells him that one of the books, *The Spiraling Pigeon*, was written in 1937 under a pseudonym by Raymond Chandler. Fantastic: a great story of a retired Los Angeles cop drawn into a political campaign when one of the candidates is accused of murder. Fifteen minutes after closing the book Harry has decided that updated (because he doesn't want the costs of making a period film) and moved to a New York locale (because he won't produce out of a Hollywood studio) the story will work like a charm.

At nine thirty the next morning, afraid he will learn that *Pigeon* is owned by one of the studios, long buried on a dusty shelf in California, Harry calls son Charlie, who has access to all information on film literary rights. While waiting for Charlie's return call Harry rereads *Pigeon* twice. What the book lacks in sex, the author regains in profundity; preserving the latter, Harry will see to it that the obligatory seventies sex is added. Tastefully.

At one thirty Charlie calls with the relieving news that no film company owns the book. Charlie also tells his father the name of the California agency representing the author's estate and the woman agent to be contacted. Two weeks later, after some dozen expensive phone calls, charges all carefully noted, Harry owns a one-year option on *Pigeon*: five thousand dollars against a final purchase price of fifty thousand. With heavy fingers Harry writes his personal check for the five, but his intention is to lay this money off immediately with a distributor; and certainly the forty-five thousand will be paid out of production funds long before the year is up. Instantly, then, Harry calls an executive friend at the New York office of Continental Artists, which, like United Artists, owns no studios, produces no films of its own, but finances and distributes independently made pictures worldwide. On the phone Harry sets a lunch date with his Continental Artists friend, Harvey—tomorrow, one o'clock, La Grenouille—then cabs to Charlie's office where his son's secretary runs off Xerox copies of the book. Free.

At lunch the next day Harry gives Harvey one of the copies, explains that the film can be made for a million five, that to buy the book, have a script written and involve a director will initially cost Continental Artists a mere seventy-five thousand dollars. The million five estimate does not of course include a major star like Redford, Newman, Hoffman, McQueen, Warren Beatty or Stanley Stunning, any one of whom would be perfect for the leading part. Harry does not tell Harvey that he plans to put himself in for a hundred-thousand-dollar producer's fee plus expenses of about fifteen thousand, but he does emphasize that he will charge nothing, maybe a few office expenses, for developing the project to the point of production. Right now Harry owns 100 percent of the deal, but naturally he's prepared to surrender the normal 40 percent to the distributor plus whatever other percentages are necessary to get a name actor and director. Harvey listens politely, allows Harry to sign the sixty-two-dollar lunch check, leaves with the book.

Four days later Harvey phones Harry to tell him that while he found the book interesting, he also found it very much like *Chinatown*. That's good, Harry says. No, that's bad, says Harvey. Well, says Harry, it can be changed so as not to be like *Chinatown*. Fine, says Harvey; when Harry has a script he'll be happy to read it, and if the script attracts an actor like Newman, Redford, McQueen or Hoffman. . . .

For the next three weeks Harry canvasses every motion picture company with offices in New York, but not one offers Harry any more hope or aid than Continental Artists. *If* they see a script, *if* a star will commit . . .

Because Harry knows Paul Newman and Dustin Hoffman personally, he is able to call each on the phone and get a promise from each to read the book instantly. Both warn the producer that they are booked a couple of pictures in advance, but Harry says he'll be happy to wait. He has to get to McQueen and Redford through agents, but because he is Harry Engle, a man with a good reputation and a lot of friends, he's assured the stars will be urged to read the book right away.

Within five weeks Harry has gotten polite turndowns from all four stars. Yes, the book is interesting, *maybe* a little too much like *Chinatown*, but *if* they see a script, and *if* their schedules allow . . .

Every Thursday night Harry plays in a poker game where one of the regulars is Paddy Chayefsky, and the next Thursday, while sandwiches from the Carnegie Delicatessen are being distributed, Harry tells Paddy about the book. Chayefsky says he no longer works on material that isn't his own, but if he did he would charge four hundred thousand dollars. Harry laughs, then pulls in a hundred-sixty-dollar pot, forty-five dollars of which were Chayefsky's. Paddy tells Harry that he should try to get Walter Burns, another New York screenwriter, who, Paddy says, is available.

At twelve thirty the next day Harry meets Walter Burns for lunch at the Russian Tea Room. Harry knows that until 1969, a year when the movie business sort of went into the outhouse, Burns's price for a script was a hundred fifty thousand dollars, but now, like most screenwriters, Burns works for short front money and a lot of promises. Old acquaintances, Harry and Walter have a jolly lunch, and the writer leaves with a copy of the book. At ten that night Burns calls Harry at home; he likes the book, sees a way to make it much different from and even more meaningful than *Chinatown*.

Now Harry has a problem. He knows what the deal with Burns will be: forty thousand dollars for the script—ten thousand on signing; fifteen on delivery of first draft; ten on delivery of second draft; and five thousand dollars after a final polish. *If* the picture is made, Burns will get another sixty thousand on commencement of principal photography, an additional twenty-five thousand out of (possible) first profits, and 3 percent of (highly improbable) subsequent profits. The problem is the first ten thousand dollars, to be paid immediately, not to mention the remaining thirty thousand.

On Tuesday nights Harry plays gin at the Friars Club, where one of the regulars is a socks manufacturer named Lenny Gross, a man in his sixties enamored with show business. Lenny has always had great respect, even awe, for Harry. He has seen all of Harry's pictures, and on ladies' nights at the Friars when Harry has taken Rene to dinner, Lenny is always there with his young blonde wife, always insists on picking up Harry's check. For years Harry has thought of Lenny as somehow, someday, being a saver.

In a meeting that lasts exactly twenty-five minutes, Lenny agrees to become Harry's partner in the development of *Pigeon*. Agrees? He *begs*! In return for underwriting the five-thousand-dollar option money and the forty-thousand script fee, plus a call on thirty more for unforeseen expenses, like perhaps front money for a director, Lenny will get one third of all of Harry's action, including his production fee. When the film is made, Lenny will recoup all his advance out of the production money. Harry leaves Lenny's Thirty-sixth Street office with a signed letter of intent and two dozen pairs of French-lisle socks.

And so the script gets written, but not as quickly as Harry hoped or as Walter Burns had promised; secretly Burns had taken a fast rewrite job for another producer, as well as sneaking in a movie-of-the-week for television. And so, a script promised in eight weeks is delivered in fifteen, during which time Harry gets a lot of phone calls, all friendly, from his not-so-silent partner Lenny Gross. Winter becomes summer before Harry has his first look at the initial draft of *Pigeon*. Promising, but needs a lot of work; not a script to show a distributor, a star, or a socks manufacturer. Bringing Burns to the house in Quogue, Harry and the writer work for nearly a week, agreeing on substantial changes, after which, vowing exclusivity, Burns leaves to work on a second draft. Six weeks later the draft is delivered, and Harry is pleased; but with more work to be done Harry decides to spend the polish before submitting the script to anyone. In three weeks Burns is finished. Harry is happy; Walter Burns has done a fine job. For a fee of fifteen hundred dollars, paid by Gross, a production manager budgets the script to a total of a million six. Not bad, and Harry knows where he can cut some fat if necessary.

Over the next three months, for varying and to Harry mystifying, reasons, the script is rejected by every top star, every hot director, and every distributor who reads it. The stars are too busy, or the part isn't right; all the directors are booked two or three years hence; and no distributor will take a chance without a top star and/or director. Harry is worried, and the phone calls from Gross have turned ugly. Harry no longer plays gin at the Friars. In some desperation Harry goes back to Harvey at Continental Artists; Harvey is on record as liking the script a lot, and maybe a deal can be salvaged. Yes, Harvey says, he does think the script can be made into a fine picture, and *if* Harry can get a director of talent, and *if* he can sign a second-rank star, and *if* he can budget the picture for under a million dollars . . .

Two weeks later Harry gets a commitment from director Perry Franklin; rising out of live television in the fifties, Franklin had made some respectable and profitable films in the sixties; his last three pictures, however, lost money. Harry proposes that like himself Franklin work up front for no money, but the director insists on a payment of ten thousand dollars against a fee of a hundred fifty thousand plus 15 percent of the profits. Afraid to call Gross personally, Harry prevails on son Charlie to contact the manufacturer's lawyer; and after some transmitted complaints and a demanded meeting with Franklin, where the director expresses no doubts that the picture will be made, Gross turns over the ten thousand.

Harry pares the budget. Working over the script with Franklin the two professionals trim scenes; an entire sequence is cut, expensive location moves changed or eliminated, the cast total reduced. Harry chops his producer's fee by half, and the budget is now under a million dollars. But the final block, the leading actor, proves insurmountable. Harry submits a dozen names; none is acceptable to Continental Artists. The mention of George Peppard brings a frosty smile, James Garner a cynical laugh. In three weeks Harry's option on the book will lapse; the agent for the author's estate is not interested in extending a free option, and there is no possibility that Lenny Gross will pick up the full cost of the book. In fact, Lenny's last phone call carried a veiled threat of vicious men coming to lean on Harry.

So, a miracle is needed, and of course a miracle occurs. No film is ever made without at least one miracle. Ten days before Harry is completely dead with *Pigeon* he gets a call from the California agent of, well, not Warren Beatty but a star of equal magnitude, Stanley Stunning. Stanley has read the script and is *extremely* interested in being the star of *Pigeon*. Harry is thrilled and stunned. Knowing that Stanley was booked until 1977, is even now supposed to be starting production with a film made by his own company, Harry hadn't even bothered to send Stanley a script. What happened? Well, the agent says, a series of unforeseen disasters, among them an unshootable script, have caused the star to cancel the current picture. He's available and willing to work. Stanley gets a million dollars, plus two thousand a week expenses, against 10 percent of the gross; is Harry prepared to talk a deal? Putting the agent on hold, Harry calls Harvey at Continental Artists. Harvey puts Harry on hold and calls the president of his company, a man who maintains his office by virtue of his ability to make a decision. The word is go!

To prove his vital interest, Stanley Stunning skies in on the red-eye from L.A. to meet with Harry at noon the following day in a suite at the Sherry-Netherland. All morning Harry meets with the people at Continental Artists. Forget the under-million budget, restore the original script. With Stanley the picture can go to four million and no one will complain.

At the Sherry, Harry has coffee while a sleepy but extremely charming and enthusiastic Stanley Stunning eats a breakfast steak. Showing all his splendid teeth, thrilled to meet Harry at last, eager to work with a producer he respects, Stanley has a swell idea for the girl to play opposite him—Greta Gorgeous. Who? You know, says Stanley, that new Canadian chick who was so great in Paul's last picture. Stanley has never met her, but he'd be glad to call Greta personally to ask her to make the picture with him. Fine, says Harry, and meaning it; Greta Gorgeous is perfect for the part.

Still smiling, Stanley says there are a couple of little problems, and Harry, smiling back, says like what? Like the director, Stanley says. Perry Franklin is fine, but Stanley prefers to work with Jerry Shaw, who was to direct his canceled picture. The fact is, Stanley admits, Shaw's commitment is still on; he's on the hook to Jerry for three hundred grand, and he has no intention of paying it himself. Let Continental Artists settle with Franklin and pick up the tab for Shaw, a *great* director.

What else? Harry asks. Well, says Stanley, he doesn't want to work in New York. Not that he wants the Los Angeles look, he says quickly, which would be bad for the picture, but San Francisco would make a fine location. But that would require a rewrite, Harry says, and Stanley answers that those changes can easily be made along with other necessary changes. Changes? says Harry. Yes, says Stanley; the thing is, he won't play a cop, even a private eye. Too much like Jack in *Chinatown* or Steve in *Bullitt* or Paul in *Harper*. The guy should be a newspaperman. But that's a big change, Harry says, and Walter Burns is already on four new jobs, totally unavailable. Forget Burns, Stanley says, he's got a writer who'll make all the changes in two weeks, and it'll cost the picture only fifty thousand dollars.

Silent for a moment, Harry pours a third cup of coffee. There are certain things he knows. He knows he's fifty-eight years old with shrinking capital, and most films today are produced by long-haired youths who sit around Beverly Hills offices wearing jeans, sandals, and blowing grass all day. He also knows that Continental Artists will happily pay for a rewrite as well as settling with Perry Franklin. Harry will lose a friend but gain a picture. It won't be easy, though. In two weeks, when he needs Stanley's signature on contracts, the star will be shacked up with Greta Gorgeous in the Canary Islands. Because Stanley is a monumental pain in the ass, a picture which should take twelve weeks to shoot will probably stretch to sixteen. There is little doubt that at some point, bugged by Harry's daily demands to maintain schedule and budget, Stanley will have him barred from the location. But if Stanley will work, really work, if he won't just walk through the picture to collect his million dollars at the other end, *Pigeon* can be a *good* film. Yet even then Harry will have a hassle. He'll have to fight Continental Artists for an important and tasteful ad campaign, and he'll especially have to fight for a prestige release: an East Side house in New York, not a multiple release in drive-ins. And he'll have to fight for an honest count, which is a joke, but there's always the chance the few points he has left will be worth something. At worst, by getting the picture made, Lenny Gross will recoup his money and Harry can pay the bills for another few months without dipping into capital, maybe even replace the Mercedes through a deal on the picture. And so Harry Engle, a good poker player who knows when to fold his hand and wait for another, who knows when simply to call, smiles at Stanley Stunning and asks if there are any other problems. Stanley tosses his long locks, laughs, and says none that he can think of for the moment. Well then, Harry says, putting out his hand, let's make the picture.

13. THE MAKING OF A TELEVISION SERIES: *UPSTAIRS, DOWNSTAIRS*
an interview
by Charles Barr, Jim Hillier, and V. F. Perkins

If British export television doesn't have the enormous profitability of American export TV, it nevertheless has class—in both senses of the word. BBC costume dramas have established themselves as models of middlebrow entertainment the world over—and have been better than that at their best. In the U.S., the Public Broadcasting System owes much of its growth to British imports and has in fact been so successful at attracting an upper-middle-class audience with the likes of *The Forsyte Saga*, serialized Victorian novels, and, most important, *Upstairs, Downstairs*, that major corporations who want to reach this opinion-making audience now find it worthwhile to contribute several million each year to "funding" (rather than "sponsoring") such shows, receiving only a subdued credit and logo frame at the beginning and end of the programs.

There have actually been two influential British forms in the last few years. While the serial format established by the 1967 series *The Forsyte Saga* (seen in scores of countries around the world) has proved most popular, the Music Hall tradition of anarchic comedy has perhaps been even more fruitful, from *The Goon Show* radio program of the fifties through *Monty Python's Flying Circus* of the seventies. Other variations—*Till Death Us Do Part* in particular—have served as models for American popular sitcoms of the seventies.

Upstairs, Downstairs was a production of London Weekend Television, which with Thames Television (producers of 1977's superb *Rock Follies* series) shares the commercial channel in the London area. Basically an attempt to capitalize on the milieu and charm of the extraordinarily popular *Forsyte Saga*, the show was conceived by two actresses, Jean Marsh (who plays Rose) and Eileen Atkins. *U,D* was commissioned for thirteen episodes in 1971, but proved so popular it was renewed for four more seasons, finally coming to conclusion in 1975. Thus *U,D* combines elements of the British closed-end series and the American open-ended form. The second season, as befits a show that was supposed to deal with Edwardian

England, ended with the death of the King in 1910. The third series extended the story line to the outbreak of World War I, the fourth to the end of the war, in 1918. The fifth came to an exhausted conclusion in 1930. In all, the series consisted of sixty-eight episodes (the last season being expanded from thirteen to sixteen).

The direction, production, and scripting of *Upstairs, Downstairs* are of interest not only for themselves but for what they show us about the much more elaborately dramatized serial, or closed-end series. American series run as long as they can, production is standardized, eighteen to twenty-six weekly episodes are churned out on a seven- or eight-day turnover. Plot development and character development are to be avoided at all costs. Characters are established early on and maintained throughout the useful life of the series. Generally, major events—weddings, divorces, but never deaths—are permitted only when it is thought the series needs a hype, or when a minor character is spun off to a series of his or her own.

The British system, which tells a story no matter how long and detailed, with a beginning, a middle, and a conclusion, yields a much more complex and rich dramatic experience. Viewers get to know and understand characters in more depth and detail in a twenty-, thirty-, or fifty-episode series than in any other medium except the multinovel saga (which first served as a model for this sort of programming).

Barr, Hillier, and Perkins interviewed the producer, John Hawksworth, script editor Alfred Shaughnessy, two of the team of directors and writers who produced *Upstairs, Downstairs* (Bill Bain and Rosemary Anne Sisson), and others, with an eye to investigaing how the collaborative process works in such a complex and lengthy undertaking.

The interviews took place during the filming of "Joke Over," the episode in the fifth season, in which Cousin Georgina, running with a "fast" group, accidentally kills a man during an early-morning drive in the country.

SETTING UP SERIES V

SHAUGHNESSY: Towards the end of Series IV, it was quite clear that London Weekend wanted to continue. We'd got to the Armistice at the end of the First World War, so the natural thing was to start turning our minds towards the 1920s. A great range of literature was read by John Hawkesworth and myself, and as with any other series we sat down and started to think of all the things that would happen to the Bellamys. One starts with the characters.

What we were faced with was a situation where Richard had a new wife, the house was still there with the servants in it, James was a

REGULAR CHARACTERS

Upstairs

RICHARD BELLAMY (David Langton): Liberal M.P., living in Eaton Place; raised to the peerage in Series IV.

LADY MARJORIE (Rachel Gurney): Richard's first wife, died in the *Titanic* at the start of Series III.

VIRGINIA (Hannah Gordon): Richard's second wife; introduced as a widow with two children during Series IV, married at the end of Series IV.

ELIZABETH (Nicola Pagett): Richard's daughter; prominent in Series I and II, then sent to America.

JAMES (Simon Williams): Richard's son; a professional soldier before the war; owner of the house after his mother's death; wounded in the war and awarded the Military Cross.

HAZEL (Meg Wynn Owen): James's wife; introduced at the start of Series III as Richard's secretary; married James during Series III, died at the end of Series IV.

GEORGINA WORSLEY (Lesley-Anne Down): unmarried ward of Richard, living in the house since late in Series III; a nurse in the war.

Downstairs

HUDSON (Gordon Jackson): butler.

MRS. BRIDGES (Angela Baddeley): cook.

ROSE (Jean Marsh): head housemaid.

EDWARD (Christopher Beeny): footman, now chauffeur; married since early in Series IV to

DAISY (Jacqueline Tong): housemaid.

RUBY (Jenny Tomasin): kitchenmaid.

widower and slightly damaged by the war, very moody and rather lost, and Georgina had come out of the war, having nursed in a military hospital in France, very much grown-up and matured. That was the starting point.

What I had to do as script editor was to write the first episode to line up all the pieces in the right order. It's rather like getting horses in line, at the tape, for the off. It was a question of maneuvering the events so that you could end up with a household all set to go through the twenties: Lord and Lady Bellamy, and James and Georgina, living there, and the staff operating as before. John Hawkesworth and I put down a number of ideas of what might be the nucleus of a story. We discuss everything together. We had all sorts of ideas about the twenties and what might happen. For instance, there might be something to do with flying, James could take it up. There would be wild parties, perhaps, in which they would be involved, as bright young things. There would be the possibility—an early thought I had which turned into a very interesting episode—of James standing in a by-election,

PRODUCTION TEAM

JOHN HAWKESWORTH Film producer and writer from 1947 (producer and writer of, for example, *Tiger Bay*, 1950), then television producer. A director of Sagitta Productions, which developed the original *Upstairs, Downstairs* property. As well as producing, he now also writes several scripts in each series.

ALFRED SHAUGHNESSY Started in films at Ealing after the war, subsequently a writer for Group 3, then director of several films (including *Cat Girl*, 1957, discussed by David Pirie in "A Heritage of Horror"). Playwright and television writer; script editor and writer for *Upstairs, Downstairs* from the start.

ROSEMARY ANNE SISSON Playwright and television writer, now working on films for the Disney Organization. Has written for *The Six Wives of Henry VIII* and *Within These Walls*, and for *Upstairs, Downstairs* since Series I.

BILL BAIN Australian-born television director, working on both one-off plays and series. One feature film, *What Became of Jack and Jill* (for Amicus, 1972). Has directed for *Upstairs, Downstairs* since Series II, including the play in Series III which won the Emmy award.

trying to exploit his leadership of men and his MC, and feeling that he ought to be doing something useful. We discuss all these loose ideas in terms of what will probably happen to them in the end, who will marry whom, and so on. What you are really doing is working out a line of destiny for every character and what the resolution will be, and then you devise stories which will advance that in a sort of progression—at the same time looking for all the most interesting and typical kinds of situation and event which are special to that period of the twenties, which are not like any other period.

So you start with a grid of characters, against which you put a grid of events?

SHAUGHNESSY: To a certain extent, yes. What we very much try to do is have a good story for each main character somewhere in the series, so that none of the main characters goes through a series without what you might call a leading role. Thus, we have a very strong and interesting episode about Hudson. Hudson is always *there*, he's absolutely the rock and anchor of the whole thing, but his part is often quite small: he is a link between upstairs and downstairs, but he doesn't often become the center of the whole story. Here we have one in which he does, we have two in which James is centrally involved, and so on. And we have, inevitably, a story of how the General Strike in 1926 affects the Bellamy household.

When we've planned the stories, I sit and write the whole lot, all the outlines, right through in considerable detail before we ever start, and submit them to the Controller for his approval. This is before we commission any writers; the stories are approved first.

When you started Series V, was it already plain that this was the last one?

SHAUGHNESSY: Yes, we thought it was, and we said it was; in fact, we said the same at the time about almost every series. But the last story is now clearly a wrap-up of the whole thing.

WRITERS

SHAUGHNESSY: We've got down to our regular four writers by a process of elimination. We started the series off years ago with a very wide range of writers, then we found one or two of them didn't quite come up to it, or weren't quite right for it, so they were dropped off and perhaps a new one came in. The process went on, and we've now whittled the number down. John Hawkesworth and I found that between ourselves, and with Rosemary Anne Sisson and Jeremy Paul, who both absolutely understand the series, are used to it and are reliable and good craftsmen, we can be sure of getting the quality we want.

I have my own very definite views about the theater and the sort of drama I like—some people think it quite old-fashioned. I believe in what I call the middlebrow, good-quality theater, the theater of Priestley, Noel Coward, Rattigan, John van Druten, N. C. Hunter, that sort of thing. I'm a great believer in "good theater," good strong dramatic situations, with heart and emotion, and construction: I think you've got to build to a good end of act with a situation where you want to know what happens next. I think naturally one tends to cast the kind of playwright that one admires and who writes in the kind of style one likes, who can draw character in a certain way and is not too eccentric, too offbeat. Any playwright working on a drama series like this, under such rigid guidelines, with so many things *given*, has to be first and foremost a good dramatic craftsman, able to be given an outline and turn it into a play by sheer technique, with a sense of how long a scene should be, what you go to next, and so on: the carpentry of making plays.

A lot of talented writers don't want to work on this type of series because it's too restricting. It's a craft where you are told to put the flesh on some bones which are given to you, to think of how to do it well and economically, with the minimum number of sets and characters, and keep the audience hooked and interested, an audience of millions.

How much freedom do writers have in picking their own stories?

SHAUGHNESSY: I'm not too dictatorial about who writes what. We have an early meeting between the four of us about the way the series is going to go. This is after the outlines have been approved at executive level, and before any scripts are commissioned. They've had a look at the outlines, and we all meet, and someone will say, "Could I please do the one about the General Strike?" and so on. One allocates them by agreement. There are sixteen stories in this series and we've ended up doing four each.

Obviously we each have our own particular line. Jeremy Paul is much the youngest of the four, and the least in touch with the *Upstairs, Downstairs* kind of world; but he's learnt by research, and watching, and has picked it up as he's gone along, and does a very good job. Since he's young and a bit more radical than us, one finds his work is slightly more modern in its approach: for instance, he did the General Strike story, and did a very good job of putting the two points of view. He didn't by any means do a totally right-wing account of the Strike, from the Bellamys' point of view, but saw it from below stairs too, with perhaps even a little bias on that side. Which is a good thing.

Rosemary of course, being a woman, has a streak of romanticism in her; not *all* women writers do, but she certainly has, and she tends to be particularly good with rather emotional, romantic relationships. John Hawkesworth's strongest line is probably his comedy: he's good at all of it, but he has a particularly strong line in below-stairs comedy scenes, for Mrs. Bridges and Ruby, and so on. Also the crisper sort of upper-class situation like divorces and hunting-field scandals, which are his world . . . I suppose we all have certain stronger areas, based on our experience of life and what we know about and care about.

With just the four of us writing it, we've been able to sort out a lot together as we go along. We've written three or four scripts, and then had a pause and met together for the whole day, the four of us, discussing the *next* group of stories, ironing out who's going to take care of which element, allocating the threads. The four of us can then go away knowing exactly what the others are going to be doing.

DIRECTORS

How much does allocating a particular director to a particular story depend on meshing in with the director's other commitments, and how much on a decision that Bill Bain, say, would be right for it?

SHAUGHNESSY: You may be surprised to hear that they are not cast in relation to the writing or planning of the stories. The very first thing that happens when we're going to do a new series is that directors are booked for dates, and we get a whole series of director dates. So you know from the start that, say, episode four will be directed by Chris Hodson, because you know the studio dates; and then the stories are written for those dates. All you can do then is see how it falls on the table: there are the directors, there are the stories. We look and see, and if there's something *patently* wrong, then we might try to adjust the stories if we can. What we can't adjust are the directors, because they are terribly busy and have to be booked so far ahead. I can't say at this stage, "Episode five is a story that wouldn't be suitable for this director, so can we have another director?"

But you can switch stories around?

SHAUGHNESSY: We had an occasion very early on, in Series I, when a very hard, rather masculine political story fell into the lap, as it were, of Joan Kemp-Welch, and a very romantic story, of Lady Marjorie having an affair with one of her son's friends in the army, fell into the lap of a director whose forte was the absolute antithesis of that kind of romantic stuff. It might have been a good idea to cast them against their styles, but it was obvious that Lady Marjorie's affair was really tailor-made for Joan Kemp-Welch, so on that occasion we switched the stories over. They went out, of course, in the original order, but the recording order was changed. I hate it when that happens, it terrifies me when we get all over the place: it's very difficult when you're trying to keep all the threads clear. So we try to avoid these switches.

MAKING "JOKE OVER"

"Joke Over," written by Rosemary Anne Sisson, was planned as the eleventh of thirteen stories. After the extension made to the series, it became number thirteen of the sixteen stories. This is the story we followed in the studio, and to which the more specific areas of the interviews refer.

All the main characters of the series appear in "Joke Over" except for Rose, the head housemaid. The play also features one semi-regular character, the Bellamys' solicitor, Sir Geoffrey Dillon (Raymond Huntley). One important new character is introduced, along with several others who will not reappear after this story. A subplot deals with the chauffeur, Edward, and his attempt to resign his job. The main line of the plot is apparent in the accounts which follow of how it developed from idea into script.

SHAUGHNESSY: I originally wrote an outline for an episode in which what was put down on paper was: at some stage of the series Georgina, as a bright young thing getting caught up in the mad social world, would have a nasty accident and be brought up short. There would be some unpleasantness in the newspapers, her name would be slightly tarnished, it would embarrass Richard in his political situation, and so forth. I first thought, rather obviously, of a motor accident, and then someone pointed out that in *The Great Gatsby*, which was running at the time we did the outline, there was a thing about a car killing a man: Could we avoid that? So I went away and thought of a drowning accident on the river: a bit of fooling around in punts at Maidenhead, in which someone got drowned, partly through Georgina's fault. And then practical considerations loomed up, visions of a complicated night location with arc lamps on the river and crowds of people—it became rather a major operation. So we went back to the concept of a motor accident. We still did it on location but it wasn't so complicated.

At what stage did this come together, with Georgina meeting the new young man?

SHAUGHNESSY: Much later on. We had also said that towards the end of the series Georgina would meet this young man. In the end it fell into episode eleven for their first meeting to take place. Rosemary thus inherited this boy as well, so he was threaded by her into the party which resulted in the accident: he was kind of half involved, and was able to appear at the inquest and give evidence and get her off the hook.

So Rosemary Anne Sisson was simply given these two elements to knit together, or had she come in at an earlier stage?

SHAUGHNESSY: She was given them. What happens then is, she finds her way of knitting them together, which we discuss in committee. And then she goes away and writes it.

THE WRITER

When you came to write "Joke Over," how much had already been defined?

SISSON: They'd written an outline. At that stage, really, we all grab. They have such a gift for outlines, marvelous stories, that the four of us tend to sit around the table saying, "I'd like that one," like greedy children; and then you suddenly think, "Well, I can't write all thirteen." So, gradually, they shake down, and John Hawkesworth tends to say, "Well, I thought Rosemary would probably write this one, and Jeremy probably write that one," and in the end we're pretty happy.

Was Edward's crisis always a part of this play?

SISSON: No, it wasn't. It started with the general theme of the play, which in this case was mainly Georgina and Robert Stockbridge; and then I always tend to want a lot more plot. We all have our different tendencies, and I like a tremendous lot of plot in my plays. I like a main plot and two subplots; so that once I got Edward's subplot into this I was happy, then it began to take shape.

The "Joke Over" episode of Upstairs, Downstairs: *Georgina and friends have the damned unfortunate luck to run over someone early in the morning.*

When you came to your Edward subplot, how far did you need to clear that with the general structure of the series?

SISSON: The nice thing is that the four of us have a continuing series of meetings. We've had three all-day meetings on this series, and at the second one I told them, "I haven't got a subplot in this one, I'm not going to be happy." So I suggested the Edward theme, we discussed it, and it was integrated into the total scheme.

   You start off with what the story broadly contains; and it's a mysterious thing, the moment when the imagination takes over and it begins to move strongly in one direction or another. That's when John and Freddie give us freedom. It's a very subtle process actually, this good, hard skeleton they offer you, and the freedom they give you to put your own particular face and flesh on it; and that's why it's a joy to work with them, because you keep your creative freedom.

When would the director have been allotted to this script?

SISSON: Quite early on, but he would tend not actually to come in on it until the script is in a really strong first draft. So the director doesn't take any part in the subplotting or in the "Shall I do this and shall I do that?" bit—he comes in when it's drafted.

With all the dialogue written?

SISSON: Absolutely complete. Then again we have the nice system by which the director, script editor, producer, and writer sit round together on the draft script and everybody contributes, because we know each other well enough for them to be absolutely honest.

How much change would there be at that stage, in "Joke Over" for instance?

SISSON: In "Joke Over" very little. My scripts tend to be too long, and it was chiefly, I think, a matter of cutting.

THE DIRECTOR

What are the stages by which you come to direct a given script?

BAIN: They'll say, "Can you do x number of *Upstairs, Downstairs*, on these dates?" and either this is agreeable to you or not, either you're doing something else or you're not. Sometimes you are committing yourself to dates a year or more ahead. It seems the luck of the draw finally which episodes you do. One's name goes down against certain items and there's very little chance of appeal. I don't think there's ever actually come an occasion when I've wanted to appeal.

The next thing is, you get one script, you never get a lot together. I get a script with just enough time in advance to prepare it, though they do produce a synopsis—which is quite rightly not always kept to—as to where the series is going to go. But very rarely have you got more than one script to be going on with. One of the nice things is that they let you in on the discussion. It's not a feeling that they've got to keep the director out of it till everybody else is happy; you throw in your two bobs' worth quite early, and that's awfully nice, because if you feel that a script ought to have a certain style you can help to embed the style in the writing. You can get them to change the location of a scene, for example, to achieve a different feeling or atmosphere.

You discuss that with the writer?

BAIN: It's generally a four-handed meeting, with the writer, producer, and script editor. I did a lot with Hazel in Series III. There came a stage when I seemed to know more about how Hazel had been getting on with people in the house than an individual writer might know. I'd pick up a script and say, "No, she can't be as cordial as this with Hudson, because I've just done one where she and Hudson were at daggers drawn, and anyway they always have been, and here it has all gone very cozy." From a character point of view you can affect a script because you've worked on a number of scenes with these people, and you know by now how they would react to each other because of their past history. I think, too, this is why John likes to have few writers and directors, because you're able to make a radical contribution; whereas if I were coming into it for the first time, well, I'd accept a script and shut up, because I'd think that with their experience of it, they'd know best.

How much control over costume do you get?

BAIN: I don't choose the clothes. I see them for the first time on the morning of the first day, unless there's something specific that I want asked for.

Could you, on the basis of the script, say something like, "I would like her to be very luridly dressed in this scene"?

BAIN: I could and I would.

Do you get in on minor casting—the widow at the inquest, for example?

BAIN: I do that. It's like sets—you can influence the one-off set, but not the permanent ones. The widow is mine, and also the young people, apart from Lady Dolly, who has been in the series before. I am responsible for the choice, always subject to John Hawkesworth's approval. He's terribly particular—and so he should be, in this series— about class. He could think someone was a marvelous actor but unsuitable because of belonging neither upstairs nor downstairs but rather on the landing.

At what stage do you sketch in your camera directions in the script?

BAIN: I like to spend the inside of a week on my own before I start rehearsal, working out for myself the mechanics of the piece and the sort of shots I'd like to see. I know some directors work differently and have a camera script absolutely accurately marked out before they go into rehearsal, but to do this seems to turn your back on the contribution which the cast can make to a scene, which it's very silly of a director to refuse. I never like to commit myself to a series of shots until I've worked with the actors for some time, to make sure that what we're doing is a truthful thing to do and not an arbitrary one. To me, the performances begin to dictate their own sort of shooting after a while, if you can explore with the actors, and luckily in this series we've got some splendid people—they all have a lot to offer. You feel sometimes you're of more use as a referee than as a director because they're so familiar with their characters now, and with the set, that it needs a radical piece of direction to make them go in an opposite way.

But do you have to stop them getting too comfortable?

BAIN: Absolutely—I think that's part of what I'm hired to do. What one tries to do all the way through, from the time you get a script to the time you finish rehearsing it, is try to fathom its depths and try to play those out without smashing the container that you've got, and also give it as much variety as you can within the series it belongs to. I think you can go too far *with* the script sometimes. You've got to play against parts of it for the benefit of the total experience, or ask an actor to play sometimes against what is written.

Is the initial read-through an occasion for spotting difficulties in the script that are apparent only when you begin to act it, or do you feel that your own reading of the script has already given you that?

BAIN: No, I keep finding things out about scripts. Some scripts—often they're by Freddie Shaughnessy—have a dimension to them that only becomes apparent when you start rehearsing. You take it at a certain value when you read it, and then as you play it, it casts longer shadows. That's always fun to do. Some scripts get thinner the more you work on them, and you realize you were walking on eggshells.

After the read-through, I usually spend an hour with the writer, the script editor, and the producer. They've discovered things in the script they weren't aware of, or that need changing: things that have been said wrong, or said twice; things that have to be cut because they will clash with something in a later episode. They never consider that the text is finally complete until it's recorded. It can be a bloody nuisance, but I think it's healthy, in that there is always some improvement possible right up to the time you tape it.

After the read-through, are you on your own?

BAIN: Yes, me and the actors, and no one comes near us until two days before we are due in the studio.

How much do you have the camera in mind as you plot moves in rehearsal?

BAIN: All the time. I must say it taxes the ingenuity sometimes, particularly when you're working in the morning room. The limitations in there are immense—you find you're trying to find a fresh way of shooting the same set of circumstances all the time, and it's just not possible to be inventive when the mechanics of the scene are very like the mechanics of all scenes in there.

You're not nearly as free as in films to use a fourth wall, or suddenly to reverse all the positions. One has got to be sympathetic to the needs of the people who are lighting the thing. I think the lighting man's job in television is a hell of a job. He's got to light for all the occupying positions within a set and yet make it seem as if it's been lit for each shot.

People talk about the differences between film and television in terms of definition and screen size, but this lack of flexibility in lighting is one of the major distinctions?

BAIN: Absolutely. To be able to light every setup is the greatest thing that filming has to offer. These boys in television do a marvelous job when you consider it—to light that morning room so that everything that happens from the beginning of the play to the end can be done within one afternoon, and yet they've got to light it so that it's got character and style and beauty.

How much flexibility have you within that? Could you say, "We're only going to have one table lamp lit"?

BAIN: One factor is that I have to be terribly aware of what the camera tubes will carry. When you're working with areas of darkness it's not really like film at all. On the very first shot of "Joke Over," I had to battle very hard with the lighting man—he's a very sympathetic man, but he could see the problem immediately, that they come in from a lit hall into a dark room and I take them across the dark room, panning with them, until one lamp is turned on. Now it doesn't seem difficult, but in terms of television it's *bloody* difficult, because if you hold a wide shot and pan with dark figures in a dark background, then the figures seem to carry a sort of halo with them, they streak out from behind in magenta and green.

He would have very much preferred me to set up a wide shot looking the other way, in which they would enter and walk without the camera moving at all, because it's much simpler to do, and he was pressed by the people who balance the cameras that there should be a great deal more light if we were going to pan with them. It takes a lot of negotiating to get really set-down dark, and I noticed that the light level was coming up on the first studio day, and indeed on the morning of the second day. In fact, on the recording, when I had a shot of them coming down the stairs into the kitchen, a few minutes into the story, suddenly they were being lit from a side window. I said, "Trevor, what are you doing to me? That was pitch-black this morning." "Oh, they've been on at me upstairs, they think the light level's too low and people will start complaining they can't see." And I said, "Well, let's do it again and try and get it like it was this morning." And he said, "Well, your head'll roll as well as mine when they come down on us." We did it and it looked lovely to me. But there is this basic problem with television, that you cannot do what you can do so sweetly and seemingly effortlessly on film. It's such a compromise, at so many levels.

In view of the compromises that come up out of four-camera shooting, is it unthinkable to shoot on one?

BAIN: It's unthinkable in terms of the time management give you, because you would then have to edit, and video-editing time would be like film-editing time. And it's the scarcity of videotape-editing machines . . .

What about the "ten-minute take"?

BAIN: Do you know, hardly anyone ever writes a ten-minute scene anymore. They're written so fragmented. Fifty-one minutes is the running time for a show like this, and I've done ones with over a hundred scenes, which means on average any scene is going to take less than thirty seconds. As for the chance of doing a lovely long take where you follow people around with cameras—I don't think you can apply that to just any scene that comes along; it needs to be written in a particular way.

We're all trying to compete with the film product with the resources that we've got. That's where it can be very difficult, because an audience at home doesn't know that it should put on one hat to watch *Kojak*, which is all done on film, and then put on a different one to watch *Upstairs, Downstairs*, which isn't.

What is your schedule now when you go out and film scenes for the series on location, as in "Joke Over"?

BAIN: Absolute murder. I have no first assistant, which is like trying to operate with my hands tied behind my back. There is no such thing as a first assistant in a television company. I rely on whoever is handy to run and get something, or call someone, or run up over the hill and wave the car forward or stop the traffic. It's murder.

During the day and a half in the studio, leading up to recording, to what extent are you testing and realizing in practical terms the scheme you have worked out, and to what extent are you still taking in suggestions?

BAIN: By this stage I know pretty well what I've had to settle for. I've had to produce a document for the lighting man; I *could* suddenly decide to do it round the other way, but it's a terribly time-wasting business, because he's then got to use that time to rig rather than to refine it. I think it's a matter of improving and refining within the way you've already seen the piece fall together in your mind. It's not a time for making up your mind how it should look.

But do you get any sparks off the actors, as you see them within the sets? Or from the writer, as he or she now sees them?

BAIN: No, it's pretty well too late unless it's something so superb that you simply must do it. In any case, the actors by that stage are pacing themselves: they're very sweet about it, and they almost perform, but it's not basically using up their psychic energy. Neither should it be, otherwise you'd never get a recording of any quality, they'd be exhausted. Their real work has been done in rehearsal.

You seemed to be recording the play in a fairly fragmentary way—are there more tape stops than a few years ago?

BAIN: Yes, but very often the script dictates this, particularly when you have stairs. The way plays are written now, characters often go from scene to scene to scene in different sets and you've got to stop to get them there, or you've got to stop to change their clothes; that's mostly within the germ of the piece itself. If I can, I like to do less fragmentary recordings than we do, but it's often not possible.

What do you do after the recording day? You seem to have quite a lot of loose ends, and bits to be cut in—is that unusual?

BAIN: Well, a lot of that is particular to the courtroom scene because of the fourth-walling on the jury—the fourth wall was "floated in" behind the jury and certain sections of the script reshot using that angle.

But planned edits are one thing; you get a lot of unplanned edits, too. If an actor is ill, for instance—we have a large running cast, and this can happen—we may reshoot some of their lines individually. Or when actors fluff, or when they go to pick up a whisky decanter and knock over glasses . . . and one is forever picking up shots to obviate a boom shadow over someone's head, or a bit of soft focus, or something. They're not planned but they have to happen.

So you become more like a film director, picking up shots and storing them away?

BAIN: Yes.

Do you have a lot of time for the editing?

BAIN: No, we get a copy on cassette of everything we've recorded and spend an afternoon, or a day, or two days, spooling through the cassette, selecting the exact take, or the exact shot that's going to be cut in: that way we cut down the time we actually need with the editing operator, who's tying up two of the company's machines for a set period. We go there with sheets and sheets of stuff, with every take nominated.

Several times you ended a scene with two silent close-ups: was this to leave your options open, when you come to handle the transition between two scenes in the editing?

BAIN: Yes, one can then choose to keep both, or one, or to chop both off. Of course one of the hardest things in television is that not only has it got to be a good show and look lovely, it's got to run fifty-one minutes. I don't know why we do it! After everything, we've got to come out with a show that runs fifty-one minutes. It's extraordinary.

Will you normally trim within scenes, or at the end of scenes, rather than take out a substantial block?

BAIN: It depends. Sometimes you get a feeling during rehearsal that it's a scene that you could very well drop if the whole thing is going to be over length. Mostly, the way scripts turn out, it's not so much the whole scene that can go, as that you can come into the middle of a scene, or leave it in the middle, when you're editing. Or you take a couple of shots at the end which will allow you to make a different ending to a scene and jump the other half of it, if the show is too long. The problem comes if it's too short—because you find you haven't got the material unless you make every scene ending and beginning so slow, and make the pace die. I think the whole business of coming out at fifty-one minutes is a Procrustean bed, absolutely.

During the studio rehearsal day we were struck by the extraordinarily long business of Hudson laying out tea in the morning room, and all the action stopping while he did so. Did that worry you, or is that what you wanted?

BAIN: That's what I wanted. Did it seem interminable?

Yes, we thought: "Obviously it's got to take a certain amount of time, but how is he going to cover the time?" and you seemed to be doing nothing at that stage to cover it.

BAIN: I think this is partly what the series is about. There they all are, having this intense discussion about the girl having to appear in court, and in the middle of the bloody thing, they've all got to sit there while the butler and maid come in and put the tea down. There was a certain pressure in rehearsal, in that the table the tea gets served on was already beside Virginia, and Hudson didn't have to fetch it for her, but that seemed to me far too pat. I mean, you don't just have it there, the butler comes in, and he puts the tea on it. On the first day, possibly it did run too long; maybe you'll still hate it when you see it. But I thought that was part of what the scene was about, that you have to stop and bottle it all up till the servants have finished. And they're not going to hurry: they haven't been told, "Get in and get out fast, kids, because they're talking important business." I hope you don't drop off when you see it.

You seemed to be under a bit of pressure at the end of the actual recording: Is that always so?

BAIN: It seems to be happening more and more. Every one of them seems to be a cliff-hanger.

Do you have to negotiate if you want to go beyond seven o'clock on the day of recording?

BAIN: It's very expensive to go beyond seven, because by that stage you've broken everybody's meal—the extent to which the union says they can go without meal breaks. The production manager will go round and ask very sweetly if they will give the director another quarter of an hour. If it's more than that, you're in for the most enormous overtime payment up and down the line. If you say, "Oh, but . . ." the answer people will give you is, "But you know the recording period finishes at seven: you have got to pace yourself up to that." And the way the business is going, we'd rather do it and keep the management in business than all dig our heels in and put the management out of business, in which case where the hell are we? I think that now people are readier to accept the limitations placed on them, and that the time of the maverick director in television is over.

Was there a time when they flourished?

BAIN: I think we've all done it. I don't mean that you set out to do it, but we've all said, "I'm not going to budge off this scene until I get it absolutely perfect in all regards even if I have to stay here all night." Those days are over. It just isn't on anymore.

Because you wouldn't get the jobs again?

BAIN: That's part of it. It's also true that people working in television don't want to see what's happening to the film industry happening to television. One wants the management to be able to continue, and with rising costs in every department, you know that if you outprice drama by being self-indulgent, then it's a very sad thing, because they will say, "We can't afford to do it anymore." I think we're all aware of the fact that we need commercial television more than commercial television needs us.

Are you under very great pressure to work all the time? Do you get on a sort of treadmill, doing a show a month?

BAIN: I suppose it is a treadmill. It doesn't feel like one because I enjoy it, but it is a terrific lot of pressure.

Is it a problem not having time to get the thing as fully worked out as you would like?

BAIN: Oh, well, how long is a piece of string? One would love to be Roman Polanski sometimes and be given *carte blanche* to finish *Macbeth* in one's own time, but I think there's a certain virtue sometimes in the discipline that's applied: maybe you work more vividly because you've only got a certain amount of time to do it in, I don't know. Everybody knows you've only got that amount of time, so they knock themselves out to do it.

CONVENTIONS

How far are you aware of conventions in the series?

SHAUGHNESSY: I think we are aware of appealing to a very wide family audience; and I don't think, really, that the occasion arises to go outside what might be considered rather old-fashioned conventions.

I think the series has got its own style, let's put it that way, and we don't have terrific and high-pitched hysterical scenes very often, nor do we have gruesome bloodshed and nasty things to look at, if we can avoid it. John Hawkesworth and I are of a generation that believes in a certain restraint and taste in things; therefore it would be going against our own feelings. You could easily in an Edwardian series have gone very erotic and depraved and shown all sorts of things if you wanted to.

When Upstairs, Downstairs *was first planned, one important aim was to deal with social and political questions: How far do you feel you have moved away from that into something slightly different? How far have the family and servants tended to outweigh the things happening around them?*

SHAUGHNESSY: Yes, perhaps one started off with a rather general platform, to examine the kind of life that was led by these kinds of people in this period, and the relationship between servants and masters, and the way they lived. But if you're going to generalize, you can only make a documentary; if you decide to deal with the same thing by taking a sample family in a sample house, and a sample staff working for them, what inevitably happens if you work with playwrights is that we all, as writers, become fascinated by the characters themselves, and they become so alive and real and have lives which seem to be real. You end up with a set of fifteen people whom the public get to know so well that they really do care what happens to them—it's the secret of the family saga on television.

You find that in a given situation you know more or less what Hudson's attitude would be because you know him as a man—that he will object to or disapprove of something, whereas Edward, who's younger and a bit cheeky, will say, "I don't see why not . . ." and Hudson says, "Nonsense, my boy," and all that . . . Their attitudes emerge out of their characters, and in fact they do behave predictably, most of the time. We have on a few occasions tried to make people behave unpredictably, but it must be a genuinely valid piece of behavior, arising out of character. But you're quite right to say that the family and their staff have taken the thing over and become central. What one is really interested in is what *they* feel, what will happen to *them*, how they will react, whether Mrs. Bridges will approve of this or not—rather than a kind of general, documentary approach to a social problem.

BAIN: One of the things I had to learn when I first came onto the series is that in essence it's a comedy. You can't play that music before and after and it not be somehow comedy: whatever its content—in the war particularly—it's still in a sort of comedy framework, not funny ha-ha, but it's not geared to be a deeply searching piece. And therefore you've got to hang back a bit, I think, with the way you shoot it. The second one I ever did had Sarah, the housemaid, upstairs in the attic, going through labor, while the King had come to dinner. Well, I'd not long before been with my wife when she had a baby; I knew what a horrifying business it really is to be with someone who is in labor, and I tried to introduce into that scene what I felt about the pain and everything. I realized it was a wrong thing to do when I saw it all together. I wasn't making a document about how in 1908 a housemaid screamed and had her knees up near her earholes, because the structure of the piece, the way it fits into a series, is wrong for that sort of attitude.

That's interesting. It is a kind of comedy, but it's almost a genre of its own, dictating a certain kind of mood, because you never get too far with comedy either—it's never wildly funny.

BAIN: No, I suppose it's a kind of high comedy that requires chuckles rather than belly laughs, that depends on style and niceties. And it's got its sad moments and its happy moments, but not its harrowing moments. I had to learn to tuck my elbows in a bit when I started working on it, it wouldn't stand just any sort of treatment.

As an Australian, do you find the specific Britishness of the series, the cult of restraint, almost, in British drama as much as in British life, a stimulus or a problem? A lot of the potentially anguished movements in "Joke Over" are rigorously excluded from the script. For example, you don't see Robert Stockbridge going through his crisis of confidence about whether he should go to court or not, you don't see Sir Geoffrey being put on the spot—precisely the moments that could be really "peaky" are out. Is that something you have to negotiate in this series?

BAIN: I had to negotiate similar points when I first joined the series. It's a bit like Sarah and the baby and wanting to be anguished and finally realizing, "No, save that up for another time in another series, it doesn't belong here." I think one has got into the way of it: also, getting to know the producer and story editor so well over a time, one knows the sorts of conventions they will use, and I respect them. It's a most particular kind of storytelling, and it's mostly about manners. It's extraordinary to me that there are enough people who recognize the rigorous class distinctions nowadays. I don't think England's really come very far.

THE LAST SCENE

The way the last scene of "Joke Over" was worked out illustrated the multiple pressures referred to in the interviews. Georgina is visited by Robert Stockbridge, the "new young man" of the story, after her appearance at the inquest. The scene between them lasts over a minute and was shot without a break, cutting between three cameras. This was the consummation of work done the week before in the rehearsal room, then with sets and cameras in the studio the previous day, and finally in the dress rehearsal the same morning.

As seven o'clock, the time when recording should be finished, drew closer, there was some delay on the penultimate scene (between Edward and Daisy): the pressure on the actors, and everyone else, to get the final scene right at the first attempt was considerable. They managed it successfully, with a minute to spare.

What does "getting it right" involve in this context? At an obvious technical level, not fluffing, and realizing the scheme of framing and cutting worked out in rehearsals. Beyond this, the actors had to achieve a difficult transition in feeling, to round off the play. The script required from Georgina a delicate shift between pleasure, remorse, hope. One question is whether, under these conditions of pressure, the first area of challenge—the technical one—doesn't tend to push the other into the background, to the extent that the necessary preoccupation with getting the mechanics right, on recording, allows the quality of the scene itself to stick at a rather mechanical level. Clearly this does happen with a lot of series television. Equally clearly, much depends on what is brought *to* the recording, that is, on the quality of the writing and the rehearsal work.

A complicating factor in "Joke Over" was that the relationship developed in it was to be taken up in a later story, written by John Hawkesworth. "Joke Over" was Rosemary Anne Sisson's final script for the series. The ending she wrote was for Georgina and Robert to kiss: this was in the script. In terms of "Joke Over" itself, Bill Bain had doubts about this: "To begin with, I thought that their background and upbringing would not allow it at this point, and I also thought that dramatically it was the wrong way to end." Bain also had to be aware of the wider implications: "At the time we shot 'Joke Over,' John was still in the process of writing the next one between Georgina and her young man. And he knew that so many doors would be closed to him if we came to too complete an understanding between them." So, on studio rehearsal day, a series of conversations took place around the control gallery between writer, director, producer and script editor—usually two at a time. It was agreed that the story should end without the kiss. Bain decided to "put in an extra shot" in its place. In the camera script, the last few lines of dialogue were down to be played in two-shot, profiles close to the camera; when it came to the scene, Bain inserted a frontal close-up of Robert. "I caught the look in his eyes, which I thought was very charming and said as much as ought to have been said." And the scene did at once acquire a quite different rhythm and tone. By the time of recording, reverse close-ups of Georgina had been added.

This small episode illustrates two kinds of interaction which seem to be basic to this form of television. Firstly, between the particular event and the series as a whole. Shaughnessy: "We get these things all the time. It's not like one author developing a relationship, it's really several authors developing a relationship under the guidelines of a script editor. It's more difficult to get it exactly right."

The second interaction is between writer and director. In an operation like this, the script, for a complex of reasons, has considerable authority. Once written, it is subject to relatively little change. The director, compared with what is common in the cinema, has little scope for choosing scripts or for helping to shape them. Nor—again for a complex of reasons—does he have as much scope in working on the visual texture of the image. But, as well as guiding the actors, the director does organize the layout of shots, an area of work which the end of "Joke Over" brought into sudden focus. One of the questions for television criticism to explore must be how this contribution of the director operates over television narrative in general—how it is made, and how it can be "read."

We had considered printing a section of "Joke Over" as initially scripted, then in camera script, then as finally shot and edited, so as to allow discussion of the process by which it assumed the visual/dramatic shape it has on the screen. No very striking example presented itself (though this ought to remain a project for the future). Bain, modestly, said that this particular script had "directed itself." Nonetheless, it was continuously interesting to watch him, on the first studio day, making adjustments to the rhythm of a sequence as he ran it through with the cameras, perhaps altering the framing of a shot, or inserting or taking out a close-up. As is normal, the writer was present; while she was consulted over anything to do with the lines, and more than once had changes made in costume, the layout of shots was left entirely to the director.

We asked Rosemary Anne Sisson if she put any camera directions in the script. "I do often indicate close-ups. Because when I started writing for television instead of the stage, the first lesson I learnt was the director saying to me, 'Let's cut this line, because we can do it with the camera.' So now I don't write the line, as I used to, but I do write the camera. So that when we say 'Hudson thinks,' I would originally have written, 'Hudson says, "Goodness me, we can't have that,"' or something. I don't do that now, I just say, 'Hudson's face.'"

There was an early scene in "Joke Over" in which she had written, "Hudson looks embarrassed" (at finding Georgina and friends fooling about below stairs in the middle of the night), and Bain hadn't used a close-up, playing against expectation by leaving Hudson's reactions to be read within a general shot. Many other such instances of directorial nuance could be cited, illustrating the way the director/writer relation seemed to be operating in this play. Sisson admitted a preference for a lot of close-ups, Bain wanted to be relatively sparing with them. She felt that in this play, as was usual, her own visualization of the action was being very exactly realized by the director, yet she agreed that another director might have realized it quite differently and left her feeling just the same.

AN ACTOR'S VIEW: GORDON JACKSON

Gordon Jackson has been a film actor since the early 1940s, initially as a contract player with Ealing Studios. In *Upstairs, Downstairs* he has played the role of Hudson, the butler, since the first episode in 1971.

Is your discussion of the character done more with the director or the writer?

JACKSON: No one. No one's ever talked to me about Hudson and I've never talked to them. You just bring your thing. I think it's basically the original casting, same as in anything. Some of the best film directors just say nothing to you on the floor: if you work in a part it's simply that they have cast correctly.

So except at a technical level you don't discuss with the director?

JACKSON: No, we have no time for that. Too busy just getting the moves sorted and learning the lines. Now and again you get the odd person who comes in and all rehearsal stops while they discuss the commas and the buts and the ifs, and you want to tell them, "Come on, come on! We're all waiting!" You haven't got time for that, quite honestly, in a series, going at this sort of speed.

Do you know in fact at each moment whether you're in close-up or long shot or whatever?

JACKSON: Not usually. Now and again I'll glance at a camera script to think how to get a certain point over; they don't encourage actors to see camera scripts, which I think is awfully wrong, as if you're like Little Noddies, just you leave it to us . . .

Do you ever find any conflict between your experience of the character over sixty or so episodes, and a director who has done only a small proportion of them and thus might not know it all so well?

JACKSON: Perhaps a mild one. One thing I remember is a director who once suggested I should play a scene slightly drunk. I said, "But I can't, because Hudson doesn't drink." He said, "Well, imagine you've secretly been at the port." I said it would be completely dishonest and wrong. But I'm sure he thought I was being unambitious as an actor, unexciting, that this was a great challenge to give another side of Hudson; but you don't know where to stop in that sort of thing. If you establish an integrity, a man who wouldn't steal the master's port, you can't possibly start doing that. I know it seems a trivial thing, but these are the sorts of things you can't possibly do.

I think it's important that I never change my frock. I've never seen any of *Upstairs, Downstairs*—well, I've seen the odd little bit of it now and again before I disappear to my room—but people tell me that this is the strength of Hudson. All the others get into different suits and dresses, things like that. The idea is to have your suit of armor on, your uniform, so they always identify you, know what they're getting —it's a really strengthening thing for a character.

I'm going to miss the *Upstairs, Downstairs* script coming through the door, very much. I wanted to keep it on like *Coronation Street*. I would have been happy to stay in it for another ten years.

14. THE RISE AND FALL OF FM ROCK

by Steve Chapple and Robert Garofalo

If there was a medium that characterized the 1960s, it wasn't film, it wasn't television, it wasn't even records; it was FM radio, especially as it flourished in union with "progressive rock." A 1966 FCC ruling forced broadcasters to program their FM stations separately from their AM bands. Previously, most FM programming had been an exact duplicate of AM. The sound quality was immeasurably better, of course, but Edwin Armstrong's dream was moribund. So long as station owners simply duplicated already available AM shows, there was little impetus for consumers to spend the extra money on FM. Thus the FCC decision proved a classic example of how government regulation of broadcasting can have powerful, positive effects.

FM became the tie that bound the counterculture. TV and film were still stuck in the fifties; AM radio consisted of simplistic two-minute popular singles and news (the call-in show, which has dominated the seventies, did not become popular until years later). In conjunction with the growing trend toward more complicated, "progressive" albums, FM helped to define the counterculture. It still exists, and is still profitable; but like the counterculture, FM rock is more a memory than a reality. The most popular of the low-key, personal FM disc jockeys, Jonathan Schwartz, eventually gave up in the mid-seventies and now broadcasts on AM only in New York, playing his excellent collection of Frank Sinatra, show tunes, and popular music of the thirties, forties, and fifties.

Chapple and Garofalo's piece, which appeared in one of the earlier issues of the post-counterculture magazine *Mother Jones* (advertised as "a magazine for the rest of us"), is the best overview I've seen of the FM phenomenon. Having a New York bias, however, I would quarrel with them over a few historical details. Contrary to popular opinion, culture does not start on the West Coast and flow east, and "summer of love" not withstanding, Progressive Rock FM first appeared in the Big Apple. On July 31, 1966, WOR-FM switched to rock. Owing to a strike, the station had no disc jockeys until the middle of October that year, when Scott Muni, Rosko, Murray the K (a major figure in AM radio and "the fifth Beatle" in the early sixties), and Johnny Michaels established the laid-back style that was to dominate the medium. Wolfman Jack may have been apotheosized by George Lucas's *American Graffiti,* but it was Murray the K who set the AM style on the East Coast. His drastic switch from high-pitched patter to low-key talk marked the end of one era and the beginning of another.

On October 31, 1967, Muni and Rosko resigned on the air after a dispute about playlists and prearranged programming. Almost immediately, they moved to WNEW-FM in New York and were soon joined by Jonathan Schwartz, the premier FM storyteller.

It was November 1967 when San Francisco DJ Big Daddy Tom Donahue, the founder of FM rock, delivered the epitaph to AM Top 40 radio, the jangley-jingle medium that until then had monopolized the airways, bringing you All the Hits, All the Time. "Top 40 radio, as we know it today and have known it for the last ten years," intoned Donahue, "is dead, and its rotting corpse is stinking up the airways." Now, less than a decade later, Donahue's own creation, "free-form revolutionary radio," has been laid to rest, as well.

Since World War II several waves of creative radio have emerged and been co-opted in the United States. In the mid-fifties, thumping, ranting and independent rock 'n' roll DJs like Alan Freed replaced the polished announcers working at established network stations. Freed's rock 'n' roll radio brought popular singers like Chuck Berry and Elvis Presley to a youth audience that had been stifled by the old-fashioned crooning of singers like Perry Como and Patti Page. In the early sixties, as rip-roaring rock softened to Philadelphia schlock, rock 'n' roll radio tightened its format considerably to include only "the hits" in a rigidly structured rotation known as Top 40. When folk rock, psychedelic music, and complicated British rock emerged in the mid-sixties, Top 40 AM stations refused to play it. This new music found its medium on FM radio. But in a replay of the fifties, FM rock, too, is being co-opted. Competition from FM stations that play Top 40 singles, or a highly commercial mixture of singles and album cuts, is squeezing the creativity from progressive FM rockers. Other factors besides competition are at play: corporate ownership, censorship, and the out-of-hand financial success of the medium.

THE FLOWERING OF FM

FM rock radio of the sixties was a child of fortunate coincidence: a meeting of new music with the revitalization of an old medium—frequency modulation. In 1966 the Federal Communications Commis-

Jonathan Schwartz, probably the leading FM disc jockey of the late sixties and early seventies, seated at his typewriter. Schwartz, who has since given up FM for AM, prefers the image of the writer (he's the author of a book of short stories).

sion ruled that broadcasters owning FM as well as AM stations in cities with populations of more than 100,000 could not duplicate their AM programming on FM more than 50 percent of the time. Since programming an FM station half of the broadcasting day costs nearly as much as changing the broadcasts for the entire day, most owners moved to split off their FMs entirely. Dozens of FM stations were subsequently opened to innovative programming directed at new audiences.

At almost the same time, especially on the West Coast, the new folk rock of Bob Dylan and the Byrds, and the psychedelic music of the Grateful Dead, the Jefferson Airplane, and others was knifing through the bubblegum sounds of the time. Trying to appeal to the lowest common denominator in its audience, AM radio continued to play schlock.

Although thirty-eight, Tom Donahue was no stranger to the 1967 rock scene. He had produced the first Beatles concerts in San Francisco and formed Autumn Records, an artistically strong San Francisco label that had first recorded the Beau Brummels and Grace Slick and the Great Society. After Autumn Records folded, Donahue lay low for a year in San Francisco's North Beach and formulated an idea for a new type of radio. He was able to develop his new radio concept for only eight years, until his death in April 1975, at the age of forty-six.

The radio format Donahue conceived would play stereo rock with a minimum of commercials and be introduced by low-key disc jockeys, speaking in a normal tone of voice. The DJs were to act as if they were at home entertaining friends. It was to be the opposite of strident Top 40 formula radio. Donahue took the concept to KMPX-FM in San Francisco and began to broadcast the 8 P.M. to midnight show. The program was an immediate success, and Donahue soon extended the format to the rest of the station's broadcasts; within a short time he flew to Los Angeles to establish the second FM rocker at KPPC.

In New York, executives at Metromedia (a sophisticated radio and television conglomerate originally based in the food brokerage firm of Kluge & Co.) were biding their time in the wake of the FCC edict on split programming, and searching for potentially successful formats for their FM stations. They realized that Donahue was onto something, and in October 1967, Metromedia changed the format of WNEW, their New York FM, to progressive rock. When Donahue and his staff struck at KMPX over starvation wages and "the whole long hair riff," Metromedia invited them to KSAN, their FM station in San Francisco, which until then had run a tepid "lively arts" mixture of jazz and classical music.

From the original stations in San Francisco, Los Angeles, and New York, FM rock spread to the Northeast and the Midwest, and into the colleges. By 1969, independent FM rockers had sprung up in Boston, St. Louis, and Sacramento, and Metromedia had reprogrammed its affiliates in Cleveland, Philadelphia, and Los Angeles, in addition to those already in San Francisco and New York.

During the initial flowering of FM rock, the stations were highly responsive to new music and to the burgeoning youth communities that formed the bulk of their audiences. The stations experimented musically, embracing, as Donahue put it, "the best of today's rock 'n' roll, folk, traditional and city blues, raga, electronic music, and some jazz and classical selections." Black rhythm-and-blues music, or soul, was integrated with the exploding white music in a mixture unheard since the early days of rock 'n' roll radio in the fifties.

FM disc jockeys were hardly the "happy-sounding cretins poured from a bottle every three hours" that Donahue had railed against on Top 40 AM stations. DJs on FM laughed, gave long introductions about musical origins of the songs, and talked to their audience as friends. Unlike AM disc jockeys, who were told what to play by the music director (in part because music directors were worried about charges of payola and thus careful to ensure a uniform station sound), DJs on the new progressive FM stations had near total freedom to play whatever they wanted.

Some progressive FM station owners were slower than others to fathom the popularity of "free form." At the Boston FM, WBCN, for instance, co-owner Ray Riepen was angered when fledgling DJ John Brodey played Blind Faith's "Do What You Like." In the middle of the song Riepen called Brodey on the studio hot line. "Hey, hotdog!" he boomed. "Nobody wants to listen to a drum solo on a Sunday afternoon!" Brodey was cowed, but the disc jockey who followed him,

AM predecessor of the FM personality "Wolfman Jack" as he was immortalized in American Graffiti.

Charles Laquidara, was incensed. Laquidara, who was tripping on mescaline at the time, retold the incident over the air in dramatic detail, then put on one of his favorite records, the long version of Ginger Baker's drum solo "Toad." He followed the cut with other drum songs: Aynsley Dunbar's "Mutiny" and some selections from Buddy Rich. WBCN listeners were ecstatic and jammed the switchboard for hours afterward with congratulatory messages. Free-form programming stayed.

To handle audience response, FM stations established switchboards that provided listeners with rides, addresses of places to spend the night, and news of concerts and demonstrations. San Francisco's KSAN was "information central," Donahue remembered in 1973. "The station was just where people would call when they were in trouble. The classic was at KMPX, where a kid called one day who'd been busted in Sacramento for grass. They allotted him one phone call, so he called us, 'cause we were the only friend he had. You had a lot of that." Many FMs built radical news departments that did not simply "rip and read" the wire service releases as AM did, but gathered their own news from a variety of sources.

Internally, FM stations ran more democratically than AM outlets. Disc jockeys met in music meetings to decide on new records; newscasters did not need approval by station managers and network officials to air controversial material. A few FMs, like KZAP in Sacramento and KMPX in San Francisco, abolished the program director position, distanced the staff from the general manager, and acted as a collective of DJs and newspeople.

Even commercially, the original stations, especially the non-chain independents, were often responsive to the anti-materialism of the youth communities. Many progressive FMs, like WBCN, refused to advertise cigarettes, or the products of particularly conspicuous war-making corporations. In the aftermath of the burning of the Santa Barbara Bank of America branch, KZAP, among others, turned down Bank of America ads.

Limitations were inherent in "revolutionary rock radio" from the beginning, however. The audience may have consisted of high school and college dropouts with nontraditional life-styles, but it was largely white. And the music itself, full of "Midnight Ramblers" and "backdoor men," was hardly sensitive to the burgeoning women's movement. FMs, as a whole, took years to hire women DJs. Allegedly antimaterialistic ad policies were still commercial. They simply favored record companies and small, hip businesses, such as vegetarian restaurants, over national corporations, oil companies, and banks. Such policies were also untested in these early years, because with small and isolated audiences, most FMs had few national advertisers knocking on their doors.

SLEEPING WITH THE DEVIL

The first large advertisers to recognize the commercial value of FM rock radio were the record companies. For the most part the record companies, denied access to AM with their newer rock acts, were searching for ways to promote their Dylans, Zappas, Butterfields, and Garcias. The commitment of the DJs to their music combined with the audio superiority of FM made FM the ideal vehicle for sophisticated rock music. The record industry was becoming a very big business during the late sixties and early seventies. In 1956, when Elvis Presley began to record for RCA, record sales had reached only $377 million annually. With the Beatles, who represented the dawning of the golden era, 1965 sales climbed to $862 million. But by 1970—between the car stereo market and the explosion of new rock—sales of recorded music approached $2 billion a year. The record business had millions of advertising dollars to pump into FM radio.

FM rock became the showcase, introducing Jimi Hendrix and Frank Zappa to every American backwater town with two bands on its radios. Today, even with the addition of huge new national advertisers, the record companies, along with stereo component manufacturers and concert promoters, are still the largest advertisers in many FM cities. In San Francisco, for example, record and hi-fi equipment companies take up 40 percent of the advertising on KSAN, still the most popular FM station in town.

As FM rockers demonstrated their hold on the high-spending eighteen- to thirty-four-year-old market, other consumer industries joined the music advertisers. Airlines, soft-drink companies, breweries, cosmetics manufacturers, auto makers, and even Army recruiting centers began to replace small community businesses. Local businesses were, for the most part, shut out by rising prices. The price for a sixty-second, prime-time slot on a Los Angeles or San Francisco progressive FM station shot from ten dollars in 1967 to seventy-six in 1976.

Staffers at some stations protested the change to high-powered national ads, but were often overruled by salespeople and station management. When a newscaster complained that KSAN should refuse an ad for the Standard Oil additive F-310 because the independent tests showed it did nothing to improve auto performance, Tom Donahue, then the station manager, laid out the basic truth: "Radical community stations are supported by advertisers with money. If you get in bed with the devil, you better be prepared to fuck."

During the shift to national advertisers, stations helped to co-opt themselves. National advertisers at first sent over offensive-sounding commercials that had been taped for Top 40 or even Easy Listening stations. FM stations, like KSAN and WNEW, rewrote the ads to jive them with rock music and laid-back DJ patter. "Why do you advertise McDonald's hamburgers?" asked a New York interviewer. "Well, doesn't everybody eat hamburgers?" replied Scott Muni, WNEW-FM's program director. "It's the sound, the *sound* that creates the problems." The upbeat ads were liked by DJs because they sounded good and by national advertisers because they sold products better. Thus FM rock was integrated more securely into the corporate economy.

By 1974 a major FM station on the West Coast was grossing close to $2 million annually. In the huge New York market, revenues were topping $4 million. Five years before, most FMs were barely breaking even. Overall, FM ad revenues climbed from $40 million in 1967 to about $260 million in 1975. There are more than 2900 commercial FM stations in the United States, but the bulk of revenues is concentrated in the forty largest FMs, centered in eleven city markets: the ABC and Metromedia chains dominate, along with a few important independents, such as Boston's WBCN.

FM followed a familiar media dynamic. Its music brought it a mass audience. A mass audience increased its ratings. Higher ratings brought bigger ad accounts and more expensive ads. High-priced ads meant vastly increased revenues—FM rock had suddenly become big business, underground no longer. As a large business, each FM rock station began to hire more salespeople, invest in better equipment, fund expanded news staffs and raise DJs' salaries. In some cases, increased revenues led to plusher quarters; WBCN, for instance, moved to the penthouse suite of the fifty-two-story Prudential Tower, Boston's most prestigious office building.

THE DEATH OF FREE FORM

Mass audiences and higher ratings did not mean greater freedom for DJs to play more of the music they wanted. Ironically, success put limitations on both DJs and music. With new high overheads, the program directors, station managers, and chain executives were running scared; to support the stations at the level they had reached, the ratings had to be maintained at all costs.

"Now we have to eliminate sludge," explains Norm Winer, the program director at Boston's WBCN, "the self-indulgence and excess that is one of the hallmarks of this type of radio. We're not saying 'Compromise,' but we are saying, 'Don't waste any time; don't take any chances; play a record you *know* is good.' " Of course playing a record that has proven to be "good" means, as in AM, playing a record that sells.

WBCN does not play All Hits All the Time, but three years ago the station introduced what is called an "emphasis section." The emphasis section consists of high-selling records, determined by trade magazine national charts and surveys of twenty Boston record stores; records being given heavy air-play at other progressive FMs across the country; records by artists appearing in Boston; and new records by superstars. In all, the section comprises seventy-five to eighty albums. According to Winer, a DJ does not have to play emphasis records if he or she doesn't want to. But DJs are *encouraged* to, and logs of their shows are checked at intervals by station managers.

The music has been tightened even at San Francisco's KSAN, long regarded by programmers as the most free form of the big commercial stations. At KSAN the emphasis section is large and the pressure to play from it subtle. But management constantly reminds DJs to cater to young, white rock fans, who make up the bulk of the station's audience. The emphasis section, known as the "red-dot file," consists of several hundred "meat-and-potatoes records," as station manager Jerry Graham describes it. DJs are not actively encouraged to play from the red-dot file, but the word gets to those who consistently stray too far from playing rock selections.

"They didn't *make* you do anything," recalled Dusty Street, a KSAN DJ who played mostly rhythm and blues, and soul. "But Donahue wanted more rock. He was right because he wanted a radio station that was successful." Street switched her daily show to weekends to avoid demands from young rock fans that she play less soul and, according to her, "more Iron Butterfly." Then she left the station altogether, refusing to compromise with management by cutting back on black music.

TOP 40 FMs MUSCLE IN

A new fear now is causing programmers at FM rock stations to regulate the music they play: Top 40 FMs. Top 40 FMs play single hits with a liberal smattering of album cuts. They tend to suck away younger listeners, those eighteen and nineteen, from the progressive stations just down the dial.

After abandoning its syrupy love-song format in 1970, ABC experimented with a free-form approach but jettisoned it when the network found that "too many people were getting carried away with freedom." ABC was beset with DJs "ignoring regulations, uttering obscenities over the air, and talking about marijuana, cocaine, and heroin. I was spending all day with the legal department trying to bail out one station or another," remembers Shaw. In search of marketable "taste" and control over music and news programming that would not embarrass parent ABC, Inc. in Washington, ABC radio imposed a strict, blander format in 1971.

The new format mixes fifteen to twenty hit singles each week with some twenty to thirty albums from which two to four cuts have been chosen. Each single is repeated every five hours. To a large degree the records are selected centrally in the New York office, with input from the local stations to cover regional differences. ABC follows this format on its stations in New York, Los Angeles, Chicago, and Detroit. Significantly, the ABC formula is succeeding against progressive FM stations in some cities, particularly New York and Los Angeles, where Shaw claims ABC is beating Metromedia's WNEW and KMET.

SOFTENING THE NEWS

Metromedia has been more patient than ABC. It sank several million dollars into FM rock back in 1968, waiting, in some cities like San Francisco, until 1972 to turn a profit. By granting relative autonomy to individual stations, Metromedia gained a reputation for hip capitalist enlightenment. Tom Donahue said last year that Metromedia "wants us to keep our nose clean and make money. Not necessarily in that order." The company has stuck with an approximation of the original free-form music programming. But like ABC it has fired outspoken newscasters who overstepped the bounds of what might be called its "free-form corporate format."

At KSAN, Metromedia fired newscasters regularly during the turbulent early seventies. First to go was Roland Young, a black DJ and newscaster who read over the air a telegram defending Black Panther Chief of Staff David Hilliard. Hilliard had angrily told a "peace and love" crowd at the San Francisco Moratorium that "We will kill President Nixon. We will kill any motherfucker that stands in the way of our freedom." The telegram urged listeners to duplicate Hilliard's message in their own letters to the White House, so that Hilliard could not be singled out. Young was quickly fired by the station manager. "Roland Young was *released* from KSAN for a number of reasons, and that was one," recalled George Duncan, president of Metromedia Radio. "You don't incite to riot on a radio station. It's against the law."

Next to be "released" was Scoop Nisker. Nisker had become famous in the Bay Area for his news collages that wove music into the news. The technique, hardly sensational now, was seen as highly provocative in the early seventies. In the aftermath of a demonstration in Berkeley, which heavily trashed downtown stores, Nisker's collages were blamed by the Berkeley police chief for inciting rioters. KSAN, explained the chief, had become a bulletin board for demonstrators. Nisker was told that his collages had to go, although he was given the option of staying if he agreed to read the news straight. He left. Nisker was replaced as news director by Larry Bensky, now station manager of the non-commercial Pacifica station KPFA-FM. Bensky was fired from KSAN five minutes after he offended Jeans West, a $5,000-a-month advertiser. On his newscast Bensky interviewed two employees of Jeans West, who alleged that the company forced its workers to take regular lie-detector tests in which they were asked whether they had ever smoked marijuana or whether they stole.

Metromedia is willing to employ radicals like Bensky or Right Wingers like George Putnam, who worked a Los Angeles talk show, so long as ratings stay high and advertisers are happy. Corporate owners can tolerate radical newscasts as long as they, in Duncan's words, "strive to be objective," do not become too rigorously analytical, and above all do not call on listeners to *do* anything.

If somehow local newscasters go much too far and draw fire from the FCC, high-priced corporate lawyers are put into action. Metromedia has played it doubly safe in recent years by hiring Herb Klein, the former director of communications in the Nixon White House, as its vice president for corporate relations. Since Metromedia is a diversified conglomerate with sales of more than $250 million a year through radio, television, and entertainment advertising, it must, like ABC, do little to jeopardize the parent corporation's relations with regulatory agencies such as the FCC.

In recent years corporate owners have been just as quick to silence anti-commercial DJs as they have been to shut up newscasters. A year ago, for example, the Concert Network Corporation, which owns WBCN in Boston, suspended DJ Charles Laquidara, who got into trouble again for commenting, after an ad for Honeywell Pentax cameras, that the parent firm was a major war-making corporation that had helped "kill all those Cambodian babies."

Now very few DJs would risk their jobs by attacking advertisers. Laquidara is an exception. At this point few DJs would even think to criticize sponsors and corporate owners. But outright censorship and periodic firings over controversies involving advertisers have played only a minor part in softening the voices of progressive FM DJs. Their integration into the hipboisie of the music and broadcasting industries has quelled their dissent considerably. Being a disc jockey at an FM rock station is a very pleasant occupation. Whereas seven years ago disc jockeys and newscasters at KSAN made $100 a week, now they earn at least $400. At WNEW in New York, or at its ABC counterpart, WPLJ, the average salary is about $600 a week.

High salaries do not automatically weaken DJs' commitments to their audience, but the money they make puts them in a different milieu from the students or factory workers who listen to the station.

With the immense growth of the music industry, DJs often identify more with silver-spoon-carrying producers, concert promoters, promo people, and rock critics than they do with any former countercultural community. "There's too much money and status and dope for them to change and fight now," says Dinah Vaprin, a former announcer at WBCN. "The only time an FM staff would hold a struggle meeting now," echoes Larry Bensky, "is if there was a pound of cocaine that needed dividing."

HOW TO START YOUR OWN FM STATION

If establishment radio seems hopelessly apolitical and meaningless, a possible solution exists: build your own non-commercial FM station.

Commercial FM stations are virtually unobtainable today in any major city. All commercial frequencies (between 92 and 108 on the FM dial) were long ago snapped up, and to buy an operating commercial FM station would cost from $500,000 to $2 million.

Out of 3,601 operating FMs in the U.S., only 816 are designated non-commercial (occupying the 88 to 92 spectrum). Of these, only twenty or twenty-five are not controlled by state and federal governments, or by universities or religious groups. Although the bands in major cities are full, plenty of room exists in surrounding towns, many high enough in elevation to allow good broadcasting to nearby cities. "All you have to do," claims FM pioneer Jeremy Lansman, who has taken part

in setting up some five FM stations, is find a hole in the broadcasting spectrum and pop a transmitter in there."

Sound easy? Here's what you need to do to set up a bare-bones, non-commercial, 30- to 40-watt station which can broadcast over a 2- to 20-mile radius for well under $5,000:

1. Get hold of a copy of *Sex and Broadcasting*, a handbook on starting community radio stations written by Lorenzo Milan, $5 from Dildo Press, 2516 Maple Avenue, Dallas, TX 75201. (The book is entirely about broadcasting; the title is just a come-on.) Then find a dedicated First Class chief engineer who is fed up with commercial radio and willing to donate her or his time.

2. Apply for a construction permit by filing form 340 with the FCC in Washington. But first, check out the public file of any local educational FM station to find out how to fill out a *successful* application.

It must demonstrate financing adequate to construct the station and operate it for one year.

3. Incorporate. On form 340 you will see that you are required to have a non-profit corporation as the licensee of the radio station and that it must comply with FCC and IRS requirements. You'll probably need a lawyer to incorporate, especially to reach the tax-exempt status you'd like to have once you're on the air. But there are a few lawyers who'll do it for no more than the cost of filing the forms with the state—anywhere from no charge to $100.

4. Scrounge up a used 10-watt transmitter for under $300. What you want is a nice old tube-type monaural exciter. A more powerful station recently converted to stereo may want to unload one cheap.

5. As soon as the FCC grants you a construction permit, rig a four-bay (multiple-section) antenna on a cheap plot of high ground. Be sure your tower is at least 50 feet tall. Height is crucial because of FM's tendency to broadcast in "line of sight." You will also need a power divider, because you're using more than one bay, and this will set you back another couple of hundred.

6. Rent cool and quiet studio space, as close to the transmitter as possible, so that you cut the costs of the phone lines you'll be using to transmit program material and control the

transmitter. Rent shouldn't cost more than $50 a month, and phone equipment another $20 to $50 a month.

7. Buy good used audio equipment, not hi-fi stuff. You'll need a low-rumble turntable, at least one rugged tape machine, a couple of microphones and stands, cables, headphones, and, most important, a control board. Shure has a series of mixers, two of which can be assembled into a passable control board for $300. For your record library, figure $1.25 a record. All this might cost anywhere from $800 to $1,000, depending entirely on how much in-house work your chief engineer and techie crew can do.

8. You've now spent two grand and are laying out, say, $100 a month before your first broadcast. For additional operating costs, like tape and razor blades, add another $100, plus salaries for two people at $300 a month each. This puts it up to $800 a month to operate, or $2,400 for your first three months. Count on having ten to fifteen volunteers working as programmers, DJs, assistant engineers, receptionists, janitors, and corporation board members.

Grand total: $4,400 with a three-month head start on scaring up the funding to keep you on the air. A slightly bigger station, San Francisco's KPOO community radio, which was cleverly slipped into the broadcast band by engineer Ben

Dawson, cost $20,000 to set up and it now needs only $1,500 each month to operate with an all-volunteer staff. But Jeremy Lansman says that, "for a 10-watt station, if you scale it really small, scrounging giveaway equipment from big stations and building it in your attic, you can go on the air for practically nothing—under $1,000." Give it a try.

—*Steve Chapple and
Joan Medlin*

Not all DJs have been seduced, and not all newscasters silenced. Like their counterparts at the alternative news weeklies, many principled DJs were disillusioned by the Left cultural drift in the mid-seventies. Radical journalists in print or broadcasting keep their politics more easily when they are linked to ongoing movements. There have been signs at KSAN, for example, that a few newscasters are fighting again for stronger-toned news analysis.

Could "free-form revolutionary radio" ever have been viable? Probably not. Despite the motives of radical, community-oriented disc jockeys and newscasters, FM radio was from the beginning a corporate venture. Within months after Tom Donahue started KMPX, the Metromedia conglomerate recognized the potential commerciality of FM rock. Within a year and a half, giant ABC had stepped in. The media corporations were willing to allow radical community responsiveness so long as it built a mass audience; they balked when DJs and newscasters chose to define responsiveness on the basis of politics rather than commerciality.

"Our concept at ABC," said Allen Shaw, "was to take the positive side of the cultural revolution rather than the revolutionary side, to create a radio format that would express those values rather than revolutionary values." Free-form FM could have survived, perhaps, but only if station owners, DJs, and newscasters had been willing to limit their own success.

15. THE GREAT TOILET PAPER WAR
by Ron Rosenbaum

A media anthropologist working, say, a thousand years from now would have an interesting picture of this civilization. Mr. Whipple, after all, has had more airplay than Nixon, Ford, and Carter combined. Moreover, commercials are by far the most intensely designed—and expensive—pieces of entertainment product on television. If an hour-long dramatic series (c. fifty minutes of screen time) costs an average of $350,000 to produce, commercials are often budgeted at one third of that amount for sixty seconds of screen time! Mr. Whipple was a perfect subject for Ron Rosenbaum, who did this piece for *MORE* in late 1975.

No story shows better how advertising *creates* a product out of, as it were, whole cloth.

One of the more curious of the recent Charmin toilet tissue TV spots gives us a rare glimpse of supermarket manager George Whipple in a reflective, even tender, mood. Quite uncharacteristically, this particular Charmin commercial takes us far from the familiar setting of the series—the paper products aisle of Jerry's supermarket—where we are accustomed to see Whipple engaged in one after another frustrating struggle against Charmin-squeezing housewives. No, in this spot we find ourselves in the untroubled interior of Whipple's own home as George, surrounded by wife and children, reflects on how it all began.

"There I was, a young man just starting out," Whipple says. "Had my own store."

"Did you stop the ladies from squeezing the Charmin, Dad?" young Whipple Junior asks.

"You betcha!" Whipple recalls proudly.

Then one day, Whipple continues, a bit dreamily now, he saw a special woman in the toilet paper aisle. She was squeezing, like the others, but somehow she was different from all the others.

"I was about to tell her, please don't squeeze the Charmin, when I took one look at her and fell in love."

Romantic music swells in the background. The family Whipple grows misty-eyed. "And you let me squeeze the Charmin, didn't you, George?" says Mrs. W.

"Yep," Whipple tells the kids. "And until this day your mother's the only one I've let squeeze the Charmin."

More is going on here than the obvious allegory linking Charmin and sexual fidelity. There's turmoil in toilet paper marketing these days, turnover in toilet tissue ad campaigns. There are signs—the unusual Whipple-family-at-home spot, just one of many—that the uncertainties of the marketplace are beginning to affect one of the single most successful, most notorious, longest-running ad campaigns ever to appear in any medium. There are even intimations that, after a full decade on the air, George Whipple's days in the toilet paper aisle are numbered. Perhaps there's a foreshadowing of this in Whipple's sentimental journey into the past. Maybe it's time to take a look at the media phenomenon the Charmin campaign has become, focusing first, like Whipple, on how it all began.

The time had come to kill off Gentle the Dog. The year was 1964. For two years, Gentle the Dog had been the number one spokescreature for Charmin toilet paper. Commercials for Charmin featured the fluffy animated animal romping around with other gentle animated souls—a gentle juggler who juggled only soft things, a gentle movie star named Belinda Beautiful who played only gentle roles, even a gentle dog-catcher. But the Procter & Gamble people who produced Charmin and the Benton & Bowles people who produced the commercials decided that Gentle the Dog just didn't fit in with the big marketing plans P&G had for Charmin. P&G production people had devised a new toilet-paper-making process, one they felt P&G could use to push its then-tiny Charmin brand into full-scale competition with the giant of the toilet paper industry, Scott. A February 1973 P&G report explains the secret of this history-making toilet paper breakthrough:

> The fibers from which tissue is made enter the paper machines in a very dilute water solution. Nearly all of this water has to be removed. Previously, the only way to remove the excess water from the tissue was to "squeeze" it out [which] compressed the tissue fibers, taking away from their fluffiness and softness . . . [T]he solution was relatively simple—eliminate as much of the physical pressing as possible and substitute a flow of hot air [which] would actually "fluff it up" . . . This allows for a deeper, more cushiony texture. An added benefit . . . is that less wood fiber per roll is required to make the same amount of this improved tissue.

In other words, in this new process, each square of one-ply Charmin toilet paper had less paper in it, but *looked* softer. (Whether it *felt* more "cushiony" is a hot dispute we will get into later.) The master marketing strategists at P&G thought this process could give them the opening they wanted in their plot against Scott: they could "position" this fluffed-up cheaper tissue between the rougher low-cost one-ply papers (dominated by Scott tissue) and the softer, more expensive "facial quality" two-ply tissues dominated by Scott's "Soft-Weve"). Thus they would be offering greater fluffiness to the one-ply buyers and lower price to the two-ply people, thereby taking the trade of both away from Scott and making big money because they use less pulp per sheet. It would take just the right ad campaign to introduce this fluffed-up Charmin into big-league competition and it looked as if Gentle the Dog couldn't hack the new responsibility. P&G needed a barker of a different sort. Oh, they gave the fluffy mutt a chance. They experimented with an ad in which Gentle trots into a courtroom, asks a judge to have his name changed from "Gentle" to "Gentler," and explains to the puzzled magistrate that new Charmin toilet tissue is "Gentler than ever." This commercial had the effect of putting many people to sleep. Also one dog.

So, in the summer of 1964, Benton & Bowles assigned a three-person creative team to come up with a brand-new concept for selling Charmin. The job that faced creative director Jim Haines, group supervisor Flora Fifield, and junior copy writer John Chervokas is generally considered one of the toughest in the ad business because of certain built-in limitations on toilet paper advertising. Obviously you can't do on-camera comparisons. No before-and-after demonstrations. In fact, at one time toilet paper people had a rough time convincing broadcasters toilet paper commercials should even be permitted on home screens because of their inherent indelicacy. So from the beginning toilet paper was soft-peddled on TV, and most toilet papers found 1001 indistinguishable ways to peddle themselves as soft.

Charmin started at a bit of a disadvantage in the soft parade, because for a long time it was one of the few tissues that hadn't cultivated a soft image. And with good reason: it wasn't that soft. When P&G acquired the Charmin tissue-making factory in Green Bay, Wisconsin, back in 1957, Charmin tissue was sort of a rough-hewn, backwoods toilet tissue, sold mainly in rural North Country counties. (Skeptics at the time of the purchase, unaware of Charmin's place in P&G's grand design, wisecracked that the main reason for the acquisition must have been to get season tickets to Packers games for executives from P&G's Cincinnati headquarters.)

In keeping with the rough-and-ready quality of early Charmin, the pre-P&G ads for the brand featured a crude, euphemistic absorption test. "They dropped two tissues into a pot of water to see which one sunk first," is the way Jim Haines recalls an early Charmin turkey. (Since similar tests usually advertise the toughness of heavy-duty paper towels these days, one can speculate on what Charmin felt like back then.) The first series of P&G-produced commercials de-emphasized the stiffness but still gave the impression that it was a heavy-duty institutional, even *outdoorsy*-type toilet tissue: there were endorsements from the housekeeper of an Alpine Chalet-Inn and the housekeeper of a riverboat.

It didn't take P&G's market research people long to establish that there was a great hunger in the growing American middle class for more softness in their toilet tissue, that there was a correlation between moving up in economic class and moving "up" from one-ply to two-ply tissue because two-ply was soft, and for one reason or another—advertising being one big reason—soft white tissue was an emblem of the soft white-collar life. But it wasn't until 1960 that P&G production people had softened up Charmin enough to bring Gentle the Dog and his gentle friends to announce that Charmin was "fluffed, buffed, and brushed," presumably like Gentle the Dog's fluffy coat. But comparing a toilet tissue to dogs' hair is risky business considering the popularity of wirehaired terriers.

And in any case *gentle* is still not *soft*. *Gentle* still has a residue of averted pain in it (as in "Don't hurt, please be gentle"). *Gentler* is not soft, either. Even *soft itself* wasn't enough for the brand-new ad P&G and B&B wanted from the creative team they assigned to the Charmin account. Everyone was soft already. And Scott's "Soft-Weve" had already beaten everybody to "Softer than soft." Had the whole soft thing reached a dead end, or was there some way to say *softer than softer-than-soft*, and to say it in a way that made a shopper, sated by so many similar softs, select it from the shelf?

There are two versions of the moment of discovery. There may be a third. Flora Fifield, the only one of the Benton & Bowles creative trio no longer in advertising, is reportedly living somewhere in Vermont, teaching school, and I was unable to locate her. (Both Procter & Gamble and Benton & Bowles, interestingly, claimed no memory and no records of the three people who created the momentous Mr. Whipple campaign and offered no help in finding them, or in supplying storyboards.)

Jim Haines, the creative head of the trio at the time, is now a partner in an ad agency in Johannesburg.* I spoke to him during one of his visits to New York. The way he remembers the big movement, it began with the three of them crammed into copywriter Chervokas's cubicle at Benton & Bowles's Fifth Avenue office, tossing a roll of toilet paper to and fro. They were at their wit's end, none of the ideas they'd tried had worked. They had run out of new ideas and they were running out of time. "It was one of those Grade B movie situations," Haines recalls. "We were having a think session, you know, a frustration session and we were not only kicking ideas around we were tossing

---

* Among other things, he's in charge of advertising a South African toilet tissue brand called "Cushy." The campaign for "Cushy" features, as I recall Haines's description, an Afrikaaner grandmother who is so obsessed with squeezing soft "Cushy" that she takes it to her bedroom with her; her family is constantly finding itself without tissue in time of need and pleading the brand's slogan, "Please keep the Cushy in the Loo."

Mr. Whipple, circa *1977.*

the roll around, and we started to get the giggles." The Muse must
have kissed the airborne Charmin in midflight because suddenly, "John
[Chervokas] caught the roll and started to squeeze it and somebody
said, 'Don't squeeze it,' and John said, 'Please don't squeeze it,' or
'Please don't squeeze the Charmin,' and it just happened. The thing
just rolled off his tongue. . . ."

The way John Chervokas tells it, there was no roll of toilet paper in
the air. "I don't remember tossing any roll around, no," Chervokas told
me when I spoke to him in his big new office at the Warwick, Welsh &
Miller agency. Chervokas has just received another of the many promotions that have marked his career since the Charmin creation, the
latest being a move from creative director at William Esty to senior
vice-president–creative director at Warwick. Back in 1972, Chervokas
wrote for *Advertising Age* a tongue-in-cheek "confession" about his
key role in writing Mr. Whipple into advertising history, but he concedes the Charmin conception has "definitely been a plus" in his career.

Like Haines, Chervokas sets the scene of the historic discovery in his
junior writers' cubicle at Benton & Bowles, but Chervokas recalls a
more elaborate operation of the creative process. Chervokas says the
discovery grew out of their feeling that instead of just *saying* soft, or
showing soft people and things, they should figure out a way to *demonstrate* soft. What follows is Chervokas's reconstruction in *Ad Age* of
the free-association process that led to the birth of Whipple:

How to demonstrate softness? A feather is soft, but suggests tickling.
A baby's behind suggests softness, but that's "too restrictive." Silk is
soft, but comparing Charmin to silk risks "overpromising." What
about a fall? A soft fall. A fall on a pillow? Hugging a pillow? Squeezing a pillow? Squeeze a banana!?

Wait a minute. Here was something. What does a woman do in a supermarket? She squeezes melons, tomatoes, bread . . . Squeeze *Charmin!*

There it was. Just one hitch remained, according to Chervokas, and in the ingenuity of its solution was the birth of George Whipple. Someone pointed out that if the ad told women to squeeze Charmin in the store, "supermarket managers will go crazy. The answer was to tell them *not* to squeeze it." But how to tell them not to squeeze it? You have a crazy supermarket manager tell them not to squeeze it, that's how. "In an hour and a half," Chervokas wrote, "America's most universally despised advertising campaign became a reality."

Unlike the physicists working on the Manhattan Project, who knew the magnitude of the terror they were about to unleash upon the world, the three people in that cubicle were unaware of the advertising explosion they had on their hands. According to Haines, "We were having a lot of laughs and we thought this was just another laugh until the substance of it was allowed to sink in." They liked the don't-squeeze idea, but the idea of the supermarket manager obsessed with protecting his Charmin from squeezers seemed a bit madcap at the time, particularly for a relatively cautious and conservative client like Procter & Gamble. The higher-ups at Benton & Bowles were a little nervous about it, too. "We encountered some abrasion," Haines recalls. "It may have been inside the agency. They considered it terribly harebrained; it took a lot of convincing inside to get them to convince Cincinnati to test the thing. Somebody had to go out there to fight tooth-and-nail for the campaign."

Even when P&G executives in Cincinnati grudgingly agreed to shell out for production of three sixty-second sample scripts of the "Don't squeeze" concept, there was no guarantee any one of them would ever make it on the air. Everything depended on the execution, as they say in the ad business, and the success of the execution, most everyone agreed, depended on how successfully the slightly mad character of the supermarket character could be brought off. According to Haines, Chervokas "had a very definite brief in mind. He wanted a Milquetoast character; a bit, I suppose, effeminate in his way, nervous, intimidated, but a champion of Charmin." Chervokas remembers, "I was originally thinking of an Edmund Gwennish kind of character—you know, *Miracle on 34th Street*—you know, a lovable little fraud, maybe a little dumpy. . . ." Whoever it turned out to be, they needed just the right actor to do it just the right way. The agency put out a casting call to both coasts and started compiling a reel of filmed auditions for the part.

Most comedy drunk acts these days are gassy drunk acts—the loud-mouth, the weeper, the burper. But the classic drunk acts of the golden age of vaudeville were the dancer acrobatic drunk acts. That's what Dick Wilson, the man who plays Mr. Whipple, told me. He was a dancer acrobatic drunk act. This meant he'd go up on a tightrope and make all sorts of funny heart-stopping drunken near-falls. "I worked with tails. I was classy, a lot of class, but a drunk," he said. He toured the best Canadian and English vaudeville circuits, played drunks for Olsen and Johnson, and ended up in America after the war. TV was good to him. "I must have done over 350 TV shows as a drunk. I'm the drunk in *Bewitched*, I was the drunk on *The Paul Lynde Show*, I did a lot of Disney's drunks." He almost got his first big break in a non-drunk part when some TV people were all set to cast him as the sidekick of *Sergeant Preston of the Yukon*. At the last minute, however, the part got written out and Sergeant Preston was given a dog named "King" as a substitute sidekick. "I was supposed to be the dog," Wilson said.

Despite these and other disappointments in non-drunk parts, Wilson knew he was capable of more in show business. Maybe he wouldn't play Hamlet, but he wouldn't be satisfied with just playing drunks. He'd begun doing some free-lance stage show producing in 1964. That summer he was in Las Vegas producing a Shirley MacLaine Revue at a place called "The Kings Road Tally Ho" when he got a call from his agent. "He asked me: 'What do you think of toilet paper?' " Wilson recalls. "And I told him I think everybody should use it." " 'No, no, no,' " the agent said, according to Wilson, who I suspect has polished this Big Break scene into a little routine over the years. " 'I'm asking you how would you like to do a commercial for toilet paper, there's an audition tomorrow.' " "How do you audition toilet paper?" Wilson asked. And his agent said, " 'Please go and take a screen test,' and I said a screen test would be a permanent record. But I went and they liked me because five days later we were making the first Charmin commercial in a supermarket in Flushing."

"Dick Wilson was kidding me when he says you made the first ones in Flushing, wasn't he?" I asked Howard Magwood, the man who directed them.

"No, no, no. It was Flushing," Magwood insisted.

"It wasn't Flushing," says John Chervokas, who was there to watch the filming of his scripts. "I think it was Astoria."

By the time director Magwood and his ten-person production crew set up for shooting in the Flushing/Astoria market, the original scripts drawn up at Benton & Bowles had undergone two interesting modifications. The name George Whipple, for instance, was a late change. I had always harbored a suspicion that it was no accident that "Whipple" sounded like a sinister fusion of "Whip" and "nipple," and that perhaps some devious motivational research person had created the name as an emblem of a submerged sadomasochistic element in the relations between Whipple and the housewives who risk his punishment for the pleasure of a squeeze.

Alas, the true story seems more innocent. I was able to acquire a copy of a hand-sketched storyboard draft of one of those original Charmin scripts, this one dated September 24, 1964, and titled "Digby to the Rescue." In this draft, the store manager is named not Whipple, but "Edgar Bartholomew," a far less provocative choice. The switch to Whipple was made, according to Chervokas, not to make the name more kinky, but because a real Edgar Bartholomew could not be found to sell the rights to his name. (When an ad agency gives commercial characters names, it makes a point of finding real persons with that name and persuades them to sell the use of their name for a token fee, so that *other* real persons with that name won't have legal standing to argue that *their* name is the one being used.) Back in 1964, the public relations director of Benton & Bowles was a well-liked man named George Whipple. Whether or not the hints of whip and nipple had anything to do with it, the creative people liked his name as a replacement for Bartholomew and the real George Whipple sold his agency the use of his name for one dollar.

There *is* one kinky aspect of the first-draft sketch of "Digby to the Rescue" that never made it into the final shooting script. It's the bit in which Digby the cop sticks his nose into the core of the toilet paper roll. The way it happens in the draft I have, store manager "Edgar Bartholomew" finds himself so overwhelmed with Charmin-squeezing women that he summons the local cop, Officer Digby, to restore order. The women insist that Digby give the Charmin a squeeze himself to see why they find it so irresistible. Over Bartholomew's protest ("You're on duty!") Digby takes a squeeze. He's visibly impressed, but the women insist that he sniff it, too. (P&G had been perfuming the cardboard core of Charmin rolls for some time.) The sketch calls for the fully uniformed cop to unwrap the paper and plunge his nose into the scented core, take a deep sniff, say "Ummmm . . ." and come up for air totally won over to the Charmin ladies' cause. The big sniff was eliminated from the final shooting—at least on camera. In the storyboard made from the final filmed version of "Digby to the Rescue" the camera tactfully shifts away from Digby as he checks out the fragrance.

Despite this evidence of concern for taste, the original Flushing/ Astoria Charmin commercials are not without some less than chaste moments. One script, entitled "Mrs. Logan," has a hidden Whipple staring at a certain Mrs. Logan squeezing tomatoes, melons, and, finally, Charmin, at which point Whipple exposes himself to view and bursts out with the familiar admonition "Please don't squeeze the Charmin." Then Whipple sneaks off by himself and chortles, "If you only knew, Mrs. Logan. I can't resist it myself. I like to sneak a squeeze on the sly."

"Wasn't that a bit of an innuendo," I asked John Chervokas.

"No, those were pre-innuendo days," Chervokas maintains, innocently. However, it seems clear that one advantage of pre-innuendo innocence was that ad men could get away with saying some very blatant things without the advertising acceptability departments imagining anyone would be dirty-minded enough to think of its innuendo implications (viz., the cigarette ad "It's not how long you make it, it's how you make it long.")

Maybe you don't immediately think of Shakespeare when you watch a Charmin commercial, but according to director Howard Magwood it was the Bard himself who suggested the solution to the single most perplexing problem in producing the original Charmin dramas. "It was a theatrical problem," says Magwood, who left a theatrical career to become a successful commercial director. "The problem was how to play the Charmin-squeezing women. These three broads had to be believable. We'd turn people off if they looked too stupid. The audience has to believe it's fun, crazy, but you can't have actors gagging it up; you have to believe it's real when you do it."

Out in Flushing/Astoria that day, the actresses Magwood had cast for the Charmin-squeezers were having trouble *believing* in their part. There were repeated run-throughs where Wilson/Whipple was fine, but the ladies just weren't right. Suddenly the Shakespearean solution suggested itself to Magwood. "I told them, 'Try to think of this as the three witches in *Macbeth*, because they're kind of wild and crazy,' and they said, 'Oooh, that's *it*.' "* They fell to their frenzy with immediately successful and believable results—all too believable, perhaps, in the long run, because the demented witchlike quality of their behavior has earned the Charmin campaign considerable hostility from the women's movement.

Even when the three original Charmin spots were finally "in the can," as they say in the film business, not many people believed they'd get out for long until the astonishing statistics from the first recall test came back. Procter & Gamble believes in careful testing before committing itself to a campaign. The company gave the Charmin spots a tryout then known as the Burke Recall Test. Benton & Bowles quietly slipped a sample sixty-second Charmin spot, reportedly "Digby to the Rescue," into the regular TV programming in a selected midwestern market. The following day, a consumer research firm called a sample of home viewers and asked them what they watched the day before and if they remembered any particular commercials.

Previous tests of other concepts for a new Charmin campaign had produced recall scores ranging from a mediocre 27 to a humiliating 2, according to Chervokas. Then, one day that winter, in another Grade B movie development, junior writer Chervokas (the Charmin campaign was his first assignment at Benton & Bowles) got a call from a B&B

---

* They're not talking about tissue wound on a roll, of course, but at one point in *Macbeth* the three witches cry out in unison, "The charm's wound up!" Perhaps the real Shakespearean parallel, if one is to be made at all, lies in the structural similarity of the Charmin commercial to the plots of the "problem comedies" *Measure for Measure* and *All's Well that Ends Well*, in which hypocritical tyrants and buffoons who make and enforce decrees against sexuality end up getting caught sneaking a squeeze on the sly themselves.

biggie. " 'Sit down, John,' he said," Chervokas recalls. " 'Your Charmin commercial scored 55.' " That was a record smasher, the highest recall score of any commercial tested up until then.

The *Wall Street Journal* (October 20, 1971) described the marketing mayhem that followed the full-scale debut of the new Charmin campaign as "the great toilet paper war" of the sixties. The *Journal* recognized the importance of Mr. Whipple, calling him "no mere foot soldier" in the war, but gave chief credit for P&G's stunning victories over Scott to P&G's big battalions—the billion-dollar company's "awesome marketing muscle" and its "sales force like an invading army." The P&G battle plan was to conquer the country with Charmin one region at a time. First the Midwest, then south to Texas, finally around 1970 attacking the East Coast and the Southwest, and not until just this year moving its troops across the Rockies into California. The strategy in each region was to soften the territory up with massive airstrikes—in 1970 P&G spent $2 million on air time for Whipple spots—then bring the "invading army" into the supermarkets with marketing muscle to command big displays and premium shelf space placement.*

It worked. By 1970, Charmin had gone from nowhere to equality with the market share of Scott Tissue, the largest selling one-ply in the country. Not only that, Charmin began to steal customers away from Scott's "Soft-Weve" and other two-ply tissues. In the five years between 1969 and 1974, production of two-ply tissue increased by only 7 percent, or 36,000 tons, while one-ply production went up 160,000 tons, nearly 20 percent. The growth of Charmin was responsible for much of that increase. Charmin was changing the nation's toilet habits.

Meanwhile, a whole other war broke out in the advertising industry over the *meaning* of it all. At first Whipple had the worst of it: the new, hip wildman-genius types, and the cerebral, sophisticated creative types all attacked the Charmin campaign and made it a symbol, a catchword, for all that was stupid, degrading, and meretricious about the old-fashioned hard sell, particularly the hard-sell school that believed simple irritation and reiteration were the key to consumer recall. "If I ever get a chance to meet the man who did those god-awful, terribly bad 'Don't Squeeze the Charmin' commercials—and he turns out to be small—I just may slug him," said outspoken ad whiz Jerry Della Femina. (According to John Chervokas, who is not small, they've never met.)

But lately the tables have been turned on the critics. Charmin and Whipple have been around so long, have been successful so long, that ad men of the old school are beginning to use the campaign against the clever young wiseguys, rubbing their noses in Charmin, chortling that

---

* In 1974, Procter & Gamble spent $3.8 million to advertise Charmin. The best recent account of how this $5 billion company pays $325 million a year to market its forty-two brands of household products can be found in a special issue of *Television/Radio Age*—June 9, 1975.

the Whipple pitch proves that the so-called creative softer-than-softsell stuff may win praise and awards but the old-fashioned abrasive hard sell makes the big bucks for the client. Just this year, Benton & Bowles took a big ad in *Advertising Age* to push this theme. It featured a sketch of Whipple looking far more censorious and mean-spirited than he ever does in the actual commercials, almost as if he were sneering triumphantly at the hippie malcontents who criticize his ad. IT'S NOT CREATIVE UNLESS IT SELLS, the big type boasts.

It sells, but why? Arcane alternatives to the Simple Irritant Theory abound. The Sex in the Supermarket Theory advanced by Faith Popcorn, for instance. Popcorn, currently president of Brain-Reserve, an agency that makes use of some advanced new creative techniques, attributes the success of Charmin to the sensuality of the squeeze: "It established tactile contact between the consumer and the product, which is very rare in television. It lets you experience the product right there in the store. It's the old, 'Lemme feel the material' thing, like people used to feel cloth before they bought it. Just that they let you squeeze it and touch it is a very sexy thing," she says. "Very, very sexy."

Then there's Professor Wilson Bryan Key, who thinks the whole secret is "soft stool." Professor Key is the author of a strange book called *Subliminal Seduction* (NAL) in which he allows that almost all print advertising is "embedded" with obscene words and pictures. "Mr. Whipple, with his bow tie and his effeminate mannerisms, is almost a perfect anal stereotype," Professor Key told me on the phone from Ontario where, he said, the University of Western Ontario had just fired him because of pressure from advertising agencies enraged at his book. "Go back and look at Freud's description of the anal personality. The idea of squeezing the tissue is the soft stool syndrome."

Dick Wilson has some less portentous theories about Whipple's phenomenal success. First of all, he rejects the idea that the Whipple series is old-fashioned and abrasive. He cites one TV breakthrough Whipple made in 1965: "Back then I was the first one to wear a mustache in a commercial." And he insists: "The stuff we do is not nauseating, it's cute." But the secret of Whipple's success, according to Wilson, is in the careful delineation of his character: "The director and I worked out his character between us, and we guard him very well. We'll try something and then say, 'No, no, Whipple wouldn't do that.' For instance, we never let him be nasty. He's not nasty, he's prissy but he's not nasty."

Wilson himself is a likable character, with the dignity of a vaudevillian who has aged well. I reached him by phone at a hotel in Kansas City where he was rehearsing a production of *The Unsinkable Molly Brown*. "I just finished making eleven new Charmin spots in L.A.," he said, "four of them in Spanish, where I'm Señor Whipple. That makes 204 in all, although we've remade some of them every once in a while." Charmin has been good to Dick Wilson. He's a certified celebrity now. "I get instant recognition everywhere I go. I have these cards I hand out that have a picture of me and say, 'Don't Squeeze the Charmin. Squeeze Me.' And they do. I get a lot of squeezes that way." Procter & Gamble certainly squeezes the most out of Whipple. They pay him to travel around to supermarket openings, sales conventions, warehouses and factories to boost sales and morale. They even sell Whipple Tee-shirts.

However, a new round of escalation in the toilet paper war is just beginning, and the possibility must be considered that P&G will come to consider Whipple a liability in the heat of the coming battle. He has his enemies out there. Feminists attack the Charmin commercial for degrading women; NOW pickets at a recent P&G shareholders meeting called on the company to "Squeeze out Mr. Whipple." A nun in Wisconsin who relentlessly monitored 150 hours of soap-opera programming to prepare an analysis of P&G's treatment of women for a shareholders' group doesn't find Whipple nearly as degrading as some other P&G ads, "merely asinine," but Whipple has become an emblem of all that critics find wrong with P&G, with advertising in general, with American culture. Mr. Clean doesn't get that kind of bad press.

Meanwhile other brands have been taking aim at Charmin, homing in on certain vulnerabilities Whipple can't camouflage. First, there was Scott's "roller derby" commercial, which pictures a "race" between two frantically unwinding rolls of tissue: Scott and a roll identified as "the other leading brand," clearly Charmin. Scott always loses the "roller derby" because, the spot points out, Scott Tissue has a full 1000 sheets to unwind from its roll while the other leading brand has only 650.

While Scott was skillfully exploiting Charmin's short-sheeted disadvantages among one-ply tissues (Charmin claims it can't fit as many sheets on a roll without the roll swelling to monstrous size because each of its sheets is fluffier than ordinary one-plys), an aggressive East Coast two-ply tissue named Marcal was attacking the apparent flimsiness of one-ply Charmin in comparison with a good two-ply. The Marcal spot mentions Charmin by name and consists of a demonstration in which a sheet of Charmin held up in front of a candle flame is found to be so diaphanous as to be almost transparent, while a sheet of Marcal virtually blocks the light with its staunch two-ply thickness.

Nor were the Whipple commercials responding effectively to these challenges. In fact, they seemed to have lost direction in the past couple of years. There were excursions into Whipple's home life which seem designed to lay to rest suspicions that there was something deviant about his devotion to Charmin. Not all these efforts to promote Whipple's wholesomeness were totally successful. One short-lived spot introduced us to Whipple's own mother, who was played by Wilson himself in Whipple drag: "I shaved my mustache off, dressed in girl's clothes and a white wig and high-heeled shoes and everything else that went with it," Wilson recalled. "They pulled that off the air fast. It was cute but a little grotesque." Then, in early 1974, the copy line for the spots underwent an odd change. A Charmin storyboard filed with the

FTC and dated December 1, 1973, describes Charmin as "Deep Down Squeezably Soft." Now I'd never been able to figure out deep down *where* it was squeezably soft, but the new copy line is even more puzzling. It describes Charmin's softness as "rich and fluffy"— language whose evocation of taste would be more appropriate to an Oreo cream filling than to a roll of toilet tissue. And in some of the more recent commercials, strange things are seen to be going on within Whipple's own psyche.

"Whipple's Dream" opens with Whipple and three ladies flagrantly squeezing Charmin together, with Whipple brazenly declaring, "Charmin's so rich and fluffy it's irresistible," as he squeezes away. Well, it turns out Whipple's actually at home in bed with his wife, who shakes him into realizing this debauch is only a dream. "Ooh, that explains it," Whipple says. "I'd never squeeze Charmin while I was awake." "Certainly not, George," says the wife, who then reveals that Whipple has taken a roll of Charmin to bed with him to squeeze. "Whipple's Temptation," dated January 1 in the FTC files, presents Whipple vigorously urged by a devilish figure to go ahead and squeeze the Charmin, while a haloed Whipple conscience feebly opposes the squeeze. Whipple succumbs, right before our eyes.

Does this new predilection of Whipple for fevered religious visions and erotic dreams reflect a psyche under severe strain after all those years of repression and guilt over forbidden pleasures? Why was Whipple doing things like taking rolls of tissue to bed with him? Why was he permitted full frontal squeezes rather than the sneaky ones on the sly? The answer, I'm afraid, is that Whipple may be going through the same last-chance testing period they gave Gentle the Dog. Because a decade has passed and all signs indicate that Procter & Gamble is getting ready to introduce another toilet paper development that may equal or exceed the hot-air fluffing that Whipple made famous. At this very moment in certain sections of America, P&G is slipping onto supermarket shelves a new-new Charmin that represents a whole *new* concept in softer-than-softer-than-soft.

It's a tricky new marketing ploy, so try to follow closely. New-new Charmin takes the same weight of paper pulp as old-new Charmin to make a roll. However, a roll of new-new Charmin has only 500 sheets instead of the 650 in old-new Charmin. That means there is more paper pulp per sheet on each of the 500 sheets than before this improvement. So each sheet is somewhat thicker and the hot air blower dryers have even more pulp fuzz to puff up. So what results is 500 extra-fluffy, plush feather-pillow-type sheets of tissue, but 150 fewer sheets for the money. In some markets—Northern California, Oregon, and St. Louis, among others—P&G is reportedly testing an extra-extra-plush sheet of toilet tissue with only 400 sheets of plumped up, pulpy tissue per roll.

The object here is to convince the consumer that fewer plush sheets will last just as long as more, flimsier sheets. P&G refuses to discuss marketing strategy, but a spokesman for Scott, which is also coming out with an extra-plush one-ply to be called "Cottenelle" (soft as cotton), puts it this way: "The assumption in all these new tissues is that people grab off what feels right in their hand, so if you have thicker sheets you have a thicker feeling in your hand from fewer sheets and you won't use as many."

A consumer affairs commissioner in New York's Suffolk County, where some of the new, plush Charmin is being tested in the supermarkets, claims that Charmin's explanation of the reduction in sheet-count was just a lot of hot air and pulp. "If they did do market research, I would like to know the parameters they used—used sheets?" says Commissioner James Lack, who threatened to take civil action against Charmin for misleading the public. "I maintain people use the same number of sheets that they started to use when their toilet habits were born," Lack said. "My staff researched this on an informal basis and the number of sheets doesn't change. I don't like corporations hiding misleading facts." Whatever the facts, if P&G does decide to go full force into the plush and extra-plush toilet market it's going to be a tough advertising job.

Does P&G think that Whipple, with all his notoriety, his enemies, and his ten-year-old pitch can handle the new responsibility? There's one spot being tested on the air right now which already seems to be easing him off center stage. The people at the Television Monitoring Institute of Huntington Station, Long Island, brought it to my attention. (They make their living taping TV commercials and programming 'round the dial 'round the clock, often for ad agencies who want to know what their competitors are putting on.) This new spot plugs the new plush Charmin being introduced into Long Island supermarkets with a promise never before made in toilet paper advertising: "You can *hear* the difference in New Charmin." (Since you can already smell it, feel it, see it, and it's so "rich" you can almost taste it, what was left but to hear it?)

But even more interesting than the sound of the roll is the size of the role they've given Whipple. The ladies in the market take up the opening moments of the spot chatting about New Charmin and listening to it. Whipple comes on to deliver a rather perfunctory version of his litany: "Ladies, I don't care if you can see, hear, feel, or smell the difference, but please don't squeeze it." His only line in the spot, barely a walk on. He's not given the opportunity to deliver his customary soliloquy on the squeeze; instead, a peremptory voice breaks in, says "Excuse me, Mr. Whipple," cuts him off, and takes over the difficult job of explaining the improvement in the new plush product. Whipple merely seems to be in everyone's way. And if this indignity is not enough, I've heard reliable reports that in one spot being tested the script actually calls for Whipple to *urge* the ladies to squeeze the Charmin.

When I heard that sad bit of news, I began to wonder seriously if Whipple was on the way out. If he's not there to tell people *not* to squeeze, any jerk can tell them to *listen* to the toilet paper or whatever the client wants. I wondered if P&G was testing to see if anyone noticed, if anyone cared any more that Whipple *didn't* care if they squeezed.. I called up Whipple, I mean Wilson, in California, and asked if it were true that in a new spot he actually does urge the women to go ahead and squeeze.

"Yes, it's true," he said. "But it's only a test, it's only one spot."

I hope so. After all these years, I'd hate to see Whipple go the way of Gentle the Dog.

16. THE BOBBY BISON BUY
by George W. S. Trow

Advertising sells products. But what sells advertising? Numbers sell advertising. Statistics of all sorts. And jargon. Would you expect anything less from a $33 billion industry? George W. S. Trow caught the tone and style of ad ads in full flight in this piece from *The New Yorker*, which appeared in November 1976. Take the subject seriously, and there's room for a book on it.

Bobby Bison wants to give you Upscale Families. Bobby Bison wants to give you Affluent Purchasers. Bobby Bison wants to give you the best. You want to reach the Young Affordables—that group of thin-skinned influentials who make *63 percent* of all cordial liquor purchases. What are your options? You *could* try for a television buy. You could buy three hundred ten-second spots. You could buy five thousand five-second spots. You could position a pre-prime saturation glut in the "shoulder" periods. *Or* you can make the Bobby Bison Buy.

BUY THE BOBBY BISON AFFORDABLES

Buy the Bobby Bison Affordables. Buy them outright. Tell Bobby how many you want. Tell Bobby what you want them to do. Bobby Bison wants to help.

LOOK AT THE BOBBY BISON AFFORDABLES

The Bobby Bison Affordables are on the beach. The Bobby Bison Affordables are in their loft bed. The Bobby Bison Affordables are covering themselves with special unguents and lotions. The Affordables are using their pretty colored telephones; the Affordables are employing an unusual appliance to uncork a bottle; the Affordables are taking their trust officer to lunch. The Bobby Bison Affordables are *three times as likely to have a personal trust officer as the viewers of the two most popular "shoulder" period family-access television programs.*

Bobby Bison controls the kind of up-target pliable you just can't reach with television. Look at the numbers. Ninety-two per cent of the Bobby Bison Affordables experience some form of anxiety during the day; over 60 percent refuse to talk to their Moms, nearly 40 percent break into unexplained weeping as a matter of habit. And the Bobby Bison Affordables are *twice as likely* to experience a crippling sexual disorder as the viewers of the most popular daytime TV shows. It seems incredible. But look at the numbers:

	%	%
CRIPPLING SEXUAL DISORDER		
DAYTIME TV VIEWERS:	NO	YES
"Day After Tedious Day"	84.5	15.5
"Ryan's Lunch"	73	27
"Don't Count on It"	71.2	28.8
BOBBY BISON AFFORDABLES:	42	58

BOBBY BISON DELIVERS HIS AFFORDABLES

With television you're supposed to be getting boxcar numbers. But just where are they? A lot of those television Affordables are leaving their sets on and going out. Make a television buy and you are paying for these unresponsive "viewers." Bobby Bison delivers his Affordables. Bobby Bison *owns* his Affordables. Outright. If a Bobby Bison Affordable refuses to buy your product you just tell Bobby Bison, and that Affordable better watch his or her step. *Bobby Bison Affordables do what they're told.* Whenever you actually want Affordables delivered to your door, Bobby Bison Can Do. Bobby will deliver boxcar after boxcar of Affordables to your point of purchase. Try getting that kind of response even from a prime-time television buy!

ONE MORE WORD ABOUT QUALITY

As a media man you are concerned with the intrusion of Low Reach undesirables into your prime-zone boxcar numbers, are you not? And you should be worried about tandem-ad gluts. You know that after two or three tandem-ad gluts the television Affordables "tune out," leaving you with an audience of Oldsters and welfare mamas. In this atmosphere, doesn't it make sense to make the Bobby Bison Buy?

MAKE THE BOBBY BISON BUY

A Young Affordable will contact you. Call Bobby Bison and he will send a Young Affordable to your office. The Young Affordable will explain the Bobby Bison Buy. If you like, the Young Affordable will bring you a little lunch. And a little bottle of Vichy water to wash it down. This is the Affordable life-style—fabulous little sandwiches with the crusts cut off and a pleasing bottle of Vichy water to wash them down. Your Young Affordable will explain the Affordable life-style. He'll tell you about the super little trips, the cunning plans for apartment living, the expensive therapies, the outrageous outlays for liquor and other stimulants. He'll tell you about the futile impulse purchases that keep each Young Affordable deep in debt. You will agree that you need to reach this fabulous Young Affordable. And if you want to reach this fabulous Young Affordable, you'll find him in Bobby Bison's hip pocket—lonely and ready to buy.

17. MASTERMIND OF THE INSTANT LOTTERY
by Tom Stevenson

Media psychology invades every area of life. Not only are products sold, ideas and people are marketed, even money—as this piece by Tom Stevenson (*The New York Times*, January 1977) interestingly demonstrates. The game theory John Koza uses to construct profitable state lotteries is not unlike the game theory that makes audience involvement shows, video games, and talk-back television so financially rewarding. In the late seventies, even state budgets are creatures of the media.

New York officials swear there is no way to unlock the secret to the state's upcoming instant lottery and walk away with the $1,000-a-week grand prize or the rest of the $60 million in booty. But when New York's second and, with projected sales of $150 million, the nation's biggest instant lottery gets under way Tuesday, one sure winner will be John R. Koza.

For the new lottery is one of thirty-six existing or prospective state lotteries that Mr. Koza, a thirty-three-year-old entrepreneur from Atlanta who has a Ph.D. in computer sciences, has helped design since he set up the nation's first instant lottery for Massachusetts in 1974. In return for his consulting and printing services, Mr. Koza gets nearly two cents a ticket. In 1976 his three-year-old privately held Scientific Games Development Corporation grossed around $10 million.

Mainly because of Mr. Koza's innovation, lottery officials who in 1973–74 were anxiously watching per capita sales drift down from twenty-three cents to eighteen cents are now happily pointing to 1976 sales of $1.5 billion—more than twice 1974 sales of $668 million. Sixty percent of the 1976 revenues came from the so-called "instant" lotteries—those that pay off immediately.

Mr. Koza's computer expertise got him into the lottery business. While he was a twenty-five-year-old graduate student at the University of Michigan, he landed a consulting job with Chicago-based J. & H.

International, a now defunct firm that merchandised the then-rampant supermarket and gas station games. Mr. Koza's responsibility was to develop the computer algorithms that determined the winning tickets for such games as National Supermarkets' Lucky Spots and Shell Oil Company's Bingo for Cash.

Most computer specialists would probably have been happy to stick to technical chores. Mr. Koza, however, became intrigued with the contrast between the spectacular popularity of the flashy, fast-paced commercial games and the tepid interest in the state lotteries.

"I realized that the state lotteries didn't really have a clear concept of mass merchandising," says Mr. Koza. "They never would have succeeded in the commercial field." Mr. Koza went to work trying to sell lottery directors on his idea of how a lottery should be run. Mainly, he urged the states to pay off winners immediately. Until then, the states had used a system developed in 1971 by Mathematica, a Princeton, New Jersey, consulting firm, where winners were determined by weekly drawings.

In contrast, the supermarket and gas station game promoters awarded instant prizes, an approach that Mr. Koza was certain could be adapted to the state lotteries. "We were confident because when you run a lot of commercial games you learn what works and what doesn't," he says. "What the industry needed above all was faster action."

Massachusetts was the first state to agree. In 1974 its Instant Game, as the first version was called, grossed $17 million in 10 weeks, nearly twice the sales of the weekly lottery. Other states quickly imitated Massachusetts. Today, all thirteen states with legal lotteries have run at least one instant game.

All use the same concept. On each $1 ticket there are a half-dozen or so panels covered with a tamper-proof latex coating. When the coating is rubbed off with a coin or other implement, numbers (or, in some lotteries, letters) appear. In some games, getting numbers that total seven, eleven, or twenty-one is the objective. In the first New York game, uncovering three identical numbers resulted in a prize. Still others are based on bingo.

The basic idea, however, is always the same: once the coating has been removed, the purchaser knows immediately whether the ticket is a winner or a loser. Such a simple concept calls for imaginative marketing, particularly considering the odds against winning.

While the percentage returned to bettors averages 94.7 percent in roulette, 94.1 percent in blackjack, 83.4 percent to 98.6 percent in dice, 75 to 97 percent in slot machines, 82 percent in horse racing and 77 percent in off-track betting, the prize money in state lotteries ranges from about 50 percent (in Delaware and New Hampshire) to 40 percent (in New York). Only illegal number games, bingo, and the Irish Sweepstakes (which pays back 37.5 percent) have comparably low rates of return.

Fortunately for the future of Scientific Games, although Mr. Koza's training is in computers, he has the soul of a Procter & Gamble brand manager. Since sales tend to drop rather sharply after the first two or three weeks of a game, most instant lotteries run no more than twelve to sixteen weeks. Then a four- to six-week breather is usually introduced. "We have found that total annual sales will be higher if you leave the stage while everyone is still interested than if you wait until the audience gets restless," says Mr. Koza.

To whet the public's appetite further, Mr. Koza has come up with a blizzard of game variations, such as Maine's Daily Double, Michigan's Landmark, Pennsylvania's Instant Dollars, and New Hampshire's High Card Instant Sweeps, to merchandise what is essentially the same game. Massachusetts, for example, is now on its sixth game in two and a half years. New York plans at least three games this year. "It doesn't matter which game you switch to," says Mr. Koza. "What is important is that it has a new face."

One of the biggest problems in marketing lotteries is that while most adults have purchased at least one ticket, only about 30 percent buy tickets regularly (one or two a week) while roughly 15 percent purchase tickets once or twice a month.

Mr. Koza focuses a good deal of his effort on trying to convert the monthly player into a regular weekly player. To do this he leans heavily on what he calls a "continuity feature" that tempts the one-ticket buyer to purchase additional tickets. For example, in the recently completed Massachusetts Instant Bingo lottery, a purchaser had to buy at least five tickets to complete a bingo card. The trick was to get N-39, which appeared on only one in 250,000 cards. In New York's just-completed game, each ticket contained either an E, K, N, O, R, W or Y. To win $2,500 in groceries it was necessary to spell N-E-W-Y-O-R-K, which meant purchasing at least seven tickets.

One of the most critical marketing decisions facing a lottery is the prize structure. Initially, many of the lotteries offered a large number of prizes in the $100 to $1,000 range. Mr. Koza, however, favors what he calls a "concave prize structure," with the bulk of the prize money going to the $2 and $5 winners and most of the rest to the $10,000 or higher prizes.

The main reason for beefing up the size of the big prizes is publicity. While, for example, two thousand $500 winners would generate no media coverage, the same amount awarded in a single $1 million jackpot can draw worldwide attention. "The middle prizes don't do anything for you," says Mr. Koza. "But when the New Jersey lottery gave away $1,776 a week for life, people were reading about it as far away as England."

Shifting a large proportion of the prize money to the small winners produces, of course, another kind of publicity: word of mouth. In New York, for example, 66 percent of the prize money went to $2 and $5 winners, or one out of 10 tickets. "The small prizes are what makes winning credible and reinforces the desire to play," says Koza. "It is like the two cherries in the slot machine. It feeds the action."

Another way to multiply the number of small winners without increasing the size of the pot is to give free tickets as prizes. That can mean that instead of one in ten or twelve tickets being prizewinners, as many as one in six are "winners." Usually a free ticket also entitles the winner to a shot at the grand prize drawing. "So it is not a valueless prize," says Mr. Koza. Indeed, in Michigan the free ticket strategy was so successful that it boosted sales of the state's fourth instant lottery up to the levels of its first.

Perhaps the most important characteristic of a successful instant lottery, however, is what Mr. Koza calls its "play value." It would be far simpler, he concedes, to set up a lottery with only a single panel indicating whether or not the card was a prizewinner. But that would eliminate the excitement of matching a series of panels or tallying a group of numbers. "Games that have play value sell much better than those that don't," says Mr. Koza.

The recently completed New York game, he says, had a high play value. The card contained six panels, each of which hid a number ranging from $2 to $5,000. If the ticket contained three identical dollar amounts, the purchaser won that amount.

Three matches were just the proper number for maximum play value, says Mr. Koza. If the ticket had required four matches, many people would have regarded the game as too difficult. If, on the other hand, matching only two panels had been required, each losing ticket would have contained a jumble of six different numbers.

Three matches was just right, asserts Mr. Koza, because even losing tickets then had pairs of $100 panels or $5,000 panels which, though valueless, created the illusion of a near win. Mr. Koza calls such cards "heartstoppers," and he uses them frequently. In the 7-11-21 game, for example, many of the cards add up to 20 or 22. "You have to make sure that the game is not boring," says Mr. Koza. "Heartstoppers are one of the best ways of doing this."

Whatever the psychology of the "heartstopper," the fact is that the instant lottery player, unlike a roulette player or a racetrack gambler, cannot influence the outcome of the game. What Mr. Koza would like to have done, and what many state lottery officials are still interested in, is to develop lotteries where a purchaser can indeed influence his chances of winning.

But Mr. Koza's first attempt to create what is called a "probability game" has caused his only embarrassing setback so far. Last summer Maine introduced the Incredible Instant Game, where, in order to win, the numbers on the ticket had to total 21.

However, instead of requiring the purchaser to rub each of the panels, as in all of the other instant lotteries, the Maine ticket holder was required to select only three of twelve panels. Each card was a winner—provided the player selected the correct three panels. "A player had his destiny in his own hands," says Mr. Koza.

Unfortunately for Scientific Games, a Maine shopkeeper, who later explained that mathematics had been his favorite subject in high school, detected a pattern in the sequence of tickets which enabled him, by buying books of two hundred tickets, to substantially increase his chances over the anticipated 220 to one. Shamefaced state officials ended up with 29,000 winners instead of the 5400 Mr. Koza had predicted. "It was a fiasco," says Mr. Koza, who adds that he presently has no plans to introduce other probability games.

Despite the success of the instant lottery, some believe that once their novelty wears off sales may tend to slip as they did with the weekly lottery. "I think that the excitement of the instant lottery is dropping very dramatically right now," says Max Goldman, who heads the lottery operations of Mathematica, the leading firm in weekly lotteries and, with an estimated 20 percent of the market, Scientific Games' only significant competitor in the instant field.

Mr. Goldman thinks that the industry must develop further player selection games, such as Maine attempted, to broaden the gambling market. Mathematica introduced a weekly football betting game in Delaware this fall, which, like the illegal game, permits buyers to select from four to twelve weekly pro games and win anywhere from $10 to $1,200 for a $1 wager.

That, too, ran into trouble in early December when reports began to circulate that the point spreads which the state published in newspapers each Wednesday were as much as nine points off the Las Vegas odds. On the weekend of December 11 and 12 the lottery commission cancelled the game—only to be overruled by the Delaware Attorney General several days later.

Mathematica has had far more success in Rhode Island with a lottery based on the illegal numbers game. For fifty cents, a bettor purchases an I.B.M. card and selects a number ranging from 000 to 999. Payoffs are made daily and about 50 percent of revenues are returned in prizes.

Many lottery officials are eager to add the numbers game to their product line because they believe it attracts a completely different group of players and will not cannibalize existing weekly or instant lotteries. Massachusetts, for example, runs all three games. "They appeal to completely different segments of the market and hardly compete with each other at all," says a Massachusetts lottery official.

The most sophisticated version of the numbers game is marketed by American Totalisator, which is best known for its parimutuel track boards. It has installed computerized systems in Maryland and New Jersey which are aimed squarely at the same market as the illegal numbers games. Similar systems are planned by Pennsylvania, Connecticut, and Michigan.

In Maryland the American Totalisator system has been particularly successful with a weekly gross of $2.2 million, roughly twice the per capita numbers revenues in Massachusetts and New Jersey. The reason, one source speculates, is that Maryland officials have been particularly effective at marketing the program to Maryland's black community.

Jack DeVries, chairman of American Totalisator, predicts these figures will hold up. "There tends to be a gradual decay in the weekly and instant lotteries," says Mr. DeVries. "In our game there is a sustained level of interest."

At the moment, however, Mr. Koza isn't worried about competition from new kinds of games. With Colorado and Vermont getting ready to launch lottery operations in 1977 and a dozen or so other states actively considering the idea, Scientific Games has plenty of action ahead.

Indeed, Mr. Koza claims that his one regret is that since he now sells lottery tickets to most states, it is hard for him legally to purchase a ticket himself. "Of all the forms of gambling I know," he says, "it is my best chance of doing what I would like to do—make $1 million."

As things are going now for Mr. Koza, who in November printed his billionth ticket (for Massachusetts), it appears he has found a surer way of making $1 million than playing a lottery game.

18. THE NEXT MEDIUM: INTERSEX
by Robert Russel

Robert Russel's parody of the media revolution hype of the late sixties and seventies is obvious (I hope), but it cuts close to the bone. Our own sense of sex is, even now, mainly dominated by images and fantasies the media convey. It's no accident that the "skin books" are, aside from *Reader's Digest* and *TV Guide*, the only general mass-circulation magazines remaining. "Intersex" is only one small step away.

Russel wrote a column on "The Next Medium" for *Take One* magazine for a couple of years in the late sixties. In case you doubt his prognosticative abilities, let me quote you a paragraph from a later column. Titled "Superdoc," its forecast took off from the film studios' already-demonstrated interest in real-life materials and "properties" from other mediums. Russel tried to figure out how the documentary form could be hyped to higher popularity, and the conclusion that he drew was to mix judiciously documentary materials with dramatic form. He called this new genre the "superdoc." When it finally arrived on television in the mid-seventies it was better known as "docudrama." He had the title wrong (he thought the blockbuster would be called "Negro") and he had the medium slightly wrong (he was still thinking in cinema terms), but eight years later . . .

Russel describes "Negro":

> During the next two and a half hours, the audience is taken back to the roots of Black Africa, through the slave raids, into the timbered holds of the slaveships, through the Caribbean plantations, into the magnificent manors of the South—with their fields of cotton—and up the freedom train to Windsor and Halifax, then back to Liberia, across again to Harlem and Watts, recreating the spectacular events of a race's history, re-exploring the currents of sex and song and fire and despair that have troubled this race's past—all with a dignity and sweep new to the cinema.

This was in 1969. Alex Haley was already at work.

Bio-Cybernetic Institute,
Tokaida University, Japan,
July 16, 1967

Dear Mr. Robert Russel,

If you will remember, we had several conversations at the Film Festival in Vancouver, 1963, while I was preparing a television program on Canadian culture for NHK. Our mutual friends in the CBC film unit in Vancouver have sent me your three most interesting articles about "The Next Medium." At the Bio-Cybernetics Institute where I am now working with an interdisciplinary team on feedback communications technology, it had not occurred to us that the personal communicator will be a complete and separate new medium in the same sense as Radio and Television. The idea is original; accordingly, I would like your permission to translate your articles to Japanese for our Bio-Cybernetics Communications Review.

In exchange, perhaps you might be interested in learning of our experiments in "The Next Medium" at the Institute, since they represent an unusual extension of the work you are describing in North America. For I, like you, have left film and television to work in communications. But whereas you are concerned exclusively with visual and auditory areas—print, images, sounds—we are exploring the transmission of other forms of sensory information. For an example, the communication of electrocardiograms from various regional hospitals over telephone lines to our FOCAM computer for interpretation and diagnosis. You are of course familiar with this procedure. Our projects are a development of this, are somewhat unusual, and grow out of the medical-sexual work of the Americans William Masters and Virginia Johnson: *The Human Sexual Response* (Little, Brown and Co., 1966), at the Reproductive Biology Research Foundation in St. Louis. We are working on the development of a group of systems for the two-way transmission of sensory-sexual information. The project is difficult to name in English. "Intersex" is too vague, while the more accurate "Interfuck" has a vulgarity in English it lacks in Japanese. I shall use the more decorous term in hope that it will provoke you to suggest a more felicitous phrase.

"Intersex" uses a modified and somewhat more sophisticated version of the equipment developed by Masters and Johnson in their sex-measurement studies. The sensory input devices are attached to the subjects to enregister heartbeat, respiratory rhythm, perspiration through skin conductivity, and emotional activity in the brain through scalp electrodes. These devices permit the registering and communication of the sensations and excitement of the subject during the sexual cycle. We use closed circuit television (color) to record and transmit facial expression, and other visual releasers such as tumescence. We are also using the autoeroticism machine, the motorized penile camera which in the Masters and Johnson experiments was inserted and controlled and manipulated by the subject (female). In our experiment, the manipulator is connected by cable to a male subject in another laboratory, as are the various sensory receivers and transmitters, and the two-way voice and video channels.

The object of the experiments is to gather data on a possible system for the remote communication of the complete sexual experience, through feedback communications technology. Each partner is able to see the other on the various closed circuit cameras, feel the sensations the other is undergoing through the system of remote sensors, exchange verbal data via the telephone circuits, and control the other partner's manipulator through telechiric transmission of pelvic and other body movement. Through a system of PCM (pulse-coded modulation) the four visual channels, the telechiric instructions and the sensory information can be transmitted in both directions simultaneously on two 6-megaherz channels.

At first, our research on this project was supported by an Air Force grant (AF63-8759) from the American Government, and later by the Hikari group of companies, who maintain a Pan-Asian unit similar to your American Express Company. Hikari are already extensively in computers and computer networks interconnecting their travel bureaus for the transfer of data and money, and they eventually foresee establishing "Intersex" studios at a number of principal travel bureaus throughout Asia, on a trial basis, to service traveling businessmen.

If I may leave "Intersex" for a moment, I would like to describe a second group of experiments commissioned by Hikari, under the project name of "Cybersex," wherein we plan to program our FOCAM 230-20 computer with a complete set of sensory and manipulative responses from a single subject, recorded during a number of varied sexual encounters. As you know, remote broadband lines and microwave links are very expensive, costing almost two thousand yen or a dollar per kilometer. In this way, the partner need not be connected to his mate via the "Intersex" hookup, but need merely enter a "Cybersex" studio, put his partner's program tape on the computer, attach the sensors and manipulators, and proceed as if in direct contact with her from a remote studio. Any action, feeling, or response he might make will be instantly interpreted by the computer, which will then examine the woman's memory tape for the appropriate images, vocalizations, sensory responses and movements prerecorded by the absent partner, and transmit them directly to the subject in the studio.

Thus, through "Intersex" for direct sensory contact with a distant partner, and "Cybersex" for relating personally to the tapes of distant partners, communications science may banish loneliness, separation, and even death, and according to our collaborators in the Philosophy Department, may even bring a meaningful variety to the sexual life of the couple, as they will be able to record on tape and repeat experiences from their earliest courtship, most happy holidays, right through their maturity and older age.

Various faculties and departments at Tokaida are taking part in discussions of the new possibilities, some of them quite amusing. For an example, the possible use of the equipment in sex education has quite discountenanced the pedagogical faculty. But it is too soon for the real meaning, the implications, of our work to appear. In fact it is for this reason that we do not conduct our experiments in privacy. For when (and if) our system is placed on the commercial market in several years' time, it will have the most profound effect on our social mores, and penetrate every aspect of communications from advertising to cinema, from furniture and fashion to the law. The legal faculty are examining the laws concerning divorce and adultery, for these will have to be most carefully reformulated in the light of the possibility that a husband or wife may lend or borrow a tape from someone outside the partnership. Great precautions must be taken to prevent bootlegging of tapes. Prominent individuals who might avail themselves of Cybersex recordings of themselves and their partners would have to be assured that technicians would not abuse their confidence by dubbing or otherwise using a tape destined for the exclusive use of another. Also, bugging of Intersex cables would become an intolerable invasion of privacy.

By the end of the century, Hikari expects to see commercial Cybersex tapes, recorded by prominent male and female celebrities, generally available, much as one buys a phonograph recording today. This would undoubtedly enhance the market for home units which would attach to the home communicator or even, if the market has evolved that far, to a home computer.

In a more traditional artistic vein, our manipulators and sensors attached to standard color television receivers, and operated through pulse-coded-modulation signals carried along with the normal television signal would permit a most affective form of drama to emerge—a new art form right in one's own home. The viewers, if we can still call them that, would participate directly in the physical action and reaction of the drama, feeling the sensations, partaking of the adventure, in a much more involving manner than 3-D or Smellovision ever dreamed of offering. Such a system was described thirty years ago by the Anglo-American writer Aldous Huxley in *Brave New World*. However, his "feelies" preceded the television era, and he imagined this new type of entertainment taking place in a darkened public auditorium rather than in the privacy of one's home.

The evolution of the next medium, with ALL that it implies (information retrieval, computer instruction, demand broadcasting, and Intersex) thus depends on the development of a feedback cable system, connecting each individual house and remote station with a central computer. I wonder if North Americans still share our national prejudice against the cable companies who bring remote television programs to our homes? It is they, not the television stations, who hold the key to the future. They should be encouraged to experiment with computers and feedback technology. The intellectuals should support them in this direction through research, programming, and through writing in the press about the nature, meaning, and importance of feedback technology and all that it could bring to our lives.

If there is any morality to our actions in this work, it seems to me to lie in the use of cybernetic technology to support and fulfill the individual by the specialized and personalized services only the computer and cable can bring, rather than (as we to date have applied our technology) for the "mass communication" of standardized information and the control of people. With each new development we should ask ourselves the question, "Does this system increase the freedom, understanding, and enjoyment of the individual, or does it merely serve the administrator's desire to maintain order?" From this point of view our two budding developments, Intersex and Cybersex, are truly moral, as they involve the creative participation of the individual in the artistic and human-sexual experience.

I am most anxious to read your comments on our work.

Yours most respectfully,
Donald Kenzotaki, Bio-Cybernetic Institute,
Tokaida University, Tokyo.

19. WHERE WILL THEY GO FROM HERE?
by Roy Blount Jr.

We don't have intersex yet, but we sure do know how to "show pink" these days. Incest is the hottest media topic of 1978. And the escalation in the skin books has hit a momentary plateau. After you show pink, what's left? Show bone? By the time you read this . . . Or maybe Blount's boyhood friend has the ticket. This piece served as a conclusion to *Esquire*'s detailed survey of the sex magazines which appeared in the November 1976 issue. The context is important. *Esquire* had begun as a men's magazine and had served as a model for *Playboy* et al. The men's books of the sixties preserved *Esquire*'s interest in big-name writers and hot interviews, but greatly emphasized the sex. Even as Blount wrote, W. R. Simmons was doing his work. There's a not inconsiderable tone of annoyed envy in the special *Esquire* report on magazines that had taken its formula and done so much better with it. The few nudes *Esquire* prints were always too artful to be salable commodities. In mid-1977, when Clay Felker bought *Esquire*, he announced immediately that the subtitle "The Men's Magazine" would be restored, and that *Esquire* would henceforth begin to retake some of the territory it had lost to the skin books.

Even when we were kids and *navels* were really something, Eddie Utterbund foresaw that the magazines we perused in his garage would go further than the rest of us dreamed. The day would come, he kept telling us, when we could walk right into a nice drugstore where everyone knew us, put down half a dollar and see *everything*.

"Aw, naw," we'd say.

"Yeah, yeah, they will. They'll show the hair and everything."

"Of old hoars and things." That was the way we thought you spelled it. Because we'd never seen it spelled.

"Naw. Of majorettes." We didn't believe him. I don't think we even

wholeheartedly wanted to believe him. It was too much. But Utterbund, except that he didn't figure inflation, was right.

And he grew up to be a media consultant, so I still run into him
occasionally. He has maintained a strong interest in skin magazines. I
remember he predicted a couple of years ago, "Next they'll show
pink."

I was ashamed to admit I even understood what "show pink" meant.
"Aw, no," I said. "Who really wants to *look at* pink? Anyway, pictures
of it."

"Hm," he said, as if to imply that I protested too much. "They'll
show pink. They'll show purple."

"Why?"

"Because it's there."

Utterbund's concern with that kind of thing has always struck me as
too explicit or something. But after all, one does wonder these days—
just as one once wondered about logical positivism or dissent—where
dirty magazines can go next. So when Utterbund called me the other
day and said he was himself planning to start a new "breakthrough"
dirty magazine and needed a contributing editor, I agreed to meet him
for lunch.

"What is *left* for dirty magazines?" I asked him.

"Well, obviously," he said, "there are lines that still haven't been
crossed." He was having the huevos foo yung. He likes Cuban-Chinese
restaurants because they remind him of an act an uncle of his once
saw in pre-Castro Havana, featuring a donkey and bound feet. "We
haven't had glossy intromission yet. Or even a full erection in the
slicks.

"I'm talking over-the-counter right-there-next-to-*Commentary*-and-
McCall's now, of course. At that level, frankly, I don't know that
magazines will ever go to screwing. No. I'll tell you what the next *big*
thing is. I'll tell you what the next *breakthrough* skin magazine is going
to be." Utterbund pushed aside his beans. His eyes were unusually
bright. He said, he hissed almost: *"Inspired."*

He looked off into the distance, such as it was in the restaurant
there. *"Felt. Complex.*

"Achieved."

There was a pause. In keeping with the cuisine, he looked both
inflamed and inscrutable.

I got the feeling Utterbund had been working on his prospectus.

"Let me just give you an idea of what could be done. A class act.
Name of the magazine: *Myrrh*. We get that, as we make clear every
month beneath the masthead, from the *Song of Songs*:

> *I rose up to open to my beloved;*
> *And my hands dripped with myrrh,*
> *And my fingers with sweet-smelling myrrh,*
> *Upon the handles of the lock."*

"You'd use the Bible?"

"Who's going to sue? And incidentally, you could sell a lot of actual myrrh itself, mail order. But that's incidental.

"Features. A little *imagination.* Recreate a 1936 *Life Goes to a Party* spread, same hairdos, same decors, same skin tones, only it gets out of hand. Everybody loses their heads and gets naked, right?

"Here's another. Modeling session, right? Starts out okay, first page she's going along, gradually slipping out of things and rubbing herself with a velvet pillow and a bunch of grapes and musing; but then, turn the page, *she's outraged.* 'You want me to *what?* What kind of girl . . .' *Furious.* Eyes flashing, hair rumpled. Shot of her throwing her blouse and skirt back on; shot of her stomping out half buttoned with bra in hand. *She's gone. She never gets naked.* For months, letters. 'Can't you talk Candy Veronese of your August issue into coming back?' 'Who does this Candy Veronese think she is, holding out on us? Signed The Sixth Fleet.' Does she come back? Maybe. Maybe not. Negotiations ensue. Some months, we report, she seems mollified. Sometimes she's pouting.

"I know what you're going to say. We'd never find a model who'd actually get outraged. But the readers don't know that. We could find one who could fake it.

"Letters. No more 'I never believed any of those letters you print about prolonged bouts of passionate oral lovemaking right on top of the teacher's desk while everyone in the room looked on; that is, until my History of Western Civ class yesterday.' That stuff is played out. You need to attract a different tone of letters. You might get a few that sounded like letters to *The Times* of London on sighting the first cuckoo of the spring, only they would be about vulvas. We could get lively controversies going between top authorities, in which they could call each other filthy names.

"Service articles. Edible panties—how are they nutritionally? Simple methods for keeping count of your climaxes in a swimming pool. What to do for snakebite of the cervix. How to regain your footing on Wesson Oil. Again: imagination.

"Advice column. It's 'Ask Our Amy.' All kinds of gamy questions come in—and *Amy doesn't understand any of them.* She has grown up sheltered, refers to beaver as 'down there,' gives incredibly naïve advice. Gets so embarrassed finally she says she thinks she's going to cry. So now everybody is writing in, explaining things to *her.* Nicely. Gently. Affectionately.

"Gradually, gradually, over a course of months, she begins to get hip. Opens up to things. Wears more and more revealing clothes in her picture. Even gets a little rowdy in an unaffected way. Everybody is *hot.* Everybody's heart *opens. She drives everybody in the country CRAZY!*

"Then . . . she begins to go over the edge. Bit by bit her advice, her features, coarsen. She gets into and advocates hard liquor, drugs, every kind of group and individual debasement. People write in: 'Amy, don't cheapen yourself!' She advises them to shove it. Finally, above her last column, she sits there brazenly spread and smeared all over with margarine and making a pun about it. Well. It's what America for so long has been dying to see. But now, somehow, it isn't so great. Her face is not the same. Her advice has become jaded, glazed over. Next month we announce we had to let her go. She is reported doing French Dominant in a Newark massage parlor, for free. Then she drops out of sight entirely. So many people haven't been moved to tears since the death of Little Nell."

I didn't know what to say.

"It's tough," Utterbund conceded. "It's life. Her kid sister takes over the column."

I told him I thought a job on a magazine like that would be too much for me emotionally. "But, Eddie," I said, "you're a visionary."

"That's not what you said," he replied, "when I told you they were going to show pink."

20. FIRST CLASS MAIL EXHIBITION #14 by The New York Graphic Workshop

The New York Graphic Workshop

announced its

FIRST CLASS MAIL EXHIBITION #14

from

The Museum of Modern Art

———

Summer 1970

LUIS CAMNITZER, JOSÉ GUILLERMO CASTILLO, LILIANA PORTER

Media are commodities in the seventies; they're also art. Conceptual art depends heavily on media concepts. Here's an example, which we print as an homage to the postal service as well as an artifact of media culture. The New York Graphic Workshop announced this artwork at a major show of conceptual art at the Museum of Modern Art in the summer of 1970. Spectators were presented with blue legal-size envelopes upon which they could write their names and addresses. Three months later, this came in the mail. I'm not sure which was the work of art—the announcement, the filling out of addresses on the envelopes, or the actual mailing of this post-announcement announcement of the announcement. At any rate, it has something to do with announcements. And with mail.

THE EFFECT

21. THIS TYPEFACE IS CHANGING YOUR LIFE

by Leslie Savan

Of all the media—concrete media, that is—type is perhaps the most attractive. There isn't much to enjoy about a broadcast signal, per se. Film has a good feel to it, but no variety. Vinyl records smelled much better in the fifties than they do today. But print— print you can sink your teeth into, as it were.

Paradoxically, most of the print a reader confronts is designed essentially conservatively. Readability depends on easily and quickly recognizing the shapes of letters. The typeface in which most of this book has been printed is, for example, a very popular "serif" face called Times Roman. (The headnotes are set in a "sans serif"—Permanent. Chapter and part titles are Helvetica.)

Display type—signs, headlines, ads—offers more room for creation. There are fashions each year or two that run their course on Madison Avenue, and a student sensitive to type design can probably come within two years of placing the date of an advertisement by analyzing the display type. Helvetica, which Leslie Savan analyzes in this *Village Voice* piece from 1976, started out as a popular ad type in the sixties (tough, clean, direct, honest—like Doyle, Dane, Bernbach's Volkswagen ads of the time). While Helvetica has continued to dominate sign type, advertising display typefaces in the seventies have become more elegant—they fit the camp chic style of the decade. Souvenir has been dominant. But Tiffany is coming up strong. The names tell you what to think about the faces.

The quest for a clean public restroom is usually in vain. We assume a restroom to be dirty and disease-ridden, and settle for what we have to. Occasionally, though, I've found a restroom that, before I'd even entered, I've assumed with relief was not dirty but clean. I realize that it was a restroom sign, with its modern, Teflon-smooth letters spelling "women," that led me to expect a clean toilet. Although it was surely no different from any other toilet, I thought it had to be more sanitary. It was similar to the way an attractively packaged cleansing cream, like Helena Rubinstein's "Deep Cleanser," could convince me that what was inside was the best of all possible creams. It was those same clean, modern letters on the package.

These letters seem to be everywhere. They tell us, "This is a dial-tone-first phone," this box is for "U.S. Mail," and to "Enjoy" Coke. "It's the real thing."

Along with NBC's well-publicized logo change, the typefaces used on all NBC-produced programs and printed material are being converted to this style.

This lettering style, or typeface, is graphically renovating or co-ordinating everything from newspapers (including *The Village Voice* logo) to "new towns" to multinational corporations.

The typeface is called Helvetica. From more than 9000 widely varying typefaces, a few "modern" ones have become designers' favorites. But Helvetica is by far the most popular and biggest selling typeface in the last ten years.

It comes in a variety of widths, weights, and spacing arrangements. The basic form is Helvetica Medium, and it seems "most itself" in lowercase letters.

The "signs of the times" can be found on the literal signs of the times. The use of Helvetica on so many of them expresses our need for security, for visual proof—if nothing else—that the world's machinery still runs. Subliminally, the perfect balance of push and pull in Helvetica characters reassures us that the problems threatening to spill over are being contained.

Helvetica was designed by a Swiss, Max Meidinger, and first produced by the Haas Typefoundry in 1957. Haas says it was designed specifically for the Swiss market (*Helvetica* means Swiss), and was intended to be a "perfectly neutral typeface without any overly individual forms and without personal idiosyncrasies."

Helvetica is a "sans serif," as it lacks the little extra strokes, called serifs, at the end of its letters' main strokes. Since serifs lead the eye from one letter to the next, they are supposedly more legible, particularly for small print. But the difference is minimal for most sign-size letters, and many designers say they use Helvetica precisely because it's so easy to read. As Ed Benguiat, a leading typeface designer and the art director of Photo Lettering, Inc., says, "You don't read the word, you read power. . . . For that one- or two-word display message, for buckeye and force, you use sans serif."

But why is Helvetica the most popular of the sans serifs? "It's beautiful," said Benguiat. "It's a pure letter."

Other designers describe Helvetica as "contemporary," "easy to read," "no-nonsense," "neutral," and even "cold." The first word that comes to their lips, though, is "clean."

It is not surprising, then, that when Walter Kacik redesigned New

The clean authority of Helvetica.

York City's garbage trucks in 1968, he used Helvetica. The trucks are all white except for one word, which is in black, lowercase Helvetica: "sanitation." Photographs of them were exhibited at the Louvre and at the Museum of Modern Art. Kacik chose Helvetica, he said, "because it was the best of the sans serifs and it didn't detract from the kind of purity we wanted." The result was that "people trusted these trucks."

Indeed, cleanliness implies trust. We've been brought up to associate the two ("I'm clean, officer.") and their opposites ("You dirty, rotten, two-timing dame!").

Cleaning up images is the main business of some marketing and design firms. Probably the most influential of them is Lippincott and Margulies (L&M). It is not an advertising agency; it bills itself as a "pioneer in the science of corporate identity."

Finding a corporation's identity almost always means redesigning its graphics. (Occasionally a name change itself is in order—L&M gave us such newspeak sounds as Amtrak, Pathmark, Cominco, and Uniroyal.)

In their own brochures (in Helvetica), L&M denies that it offers "face-lifts" or "standardized solutions." They claim to work from the inside out. Considering the expense to their clients ("Coca-Cola spent over a million dollars for the little squiggle," a former L&M executive said), their soundproof-room confidentiality, and their scientific bent, they might be regarded as a corporate shrink.

L&M's list of more than 500 identity-seeking clients includes American Motors, General Motors, Chrysler, Exxon, Amtrak, Chase Manhattan, First National City Corporation, Bowery Savings Bank, Chemical Bank, American Express, U.S. Steel, ITT, the Internal Revenue Service, the New York Stock Exchange, RCA, NBC, MGM, J. C. Penney, Coca-Cola, and Con Ed.

Only a few of these companies, such as Amtrak or Con Ed, use Helvetica for the logo itself—a logo is almost obliged to be unique and most are specially designed. But as a supporting typeface (and, in most cases, *the* supporting typeface) on everything from annual reports to cardboard boxes, nearly every one of the companies listed above uses some form of Helvetica.

For instance, "Coca-Cola" is distinctive, but Helvetica says "It's the real thing." The new American Express logo is specially drawn, but everything else is in Helvetica. (And when non-Roman alphabets like Chinese cannot take direct Helvetica letters, they will be drawn as closely as possible to it.)

L&M vice-president in charge of design, Ray Poelvoorde, said Helvetica "already has sort of become an unofficial standard." Asked if using such a pervasive typeface wouldn't undermine the costly corporate identity, he said, "You're offering a very nice courtesy to the general public, who is bombarded with many messages and symbols every day. And for a company not well-known, to ask the public to memorize more symbols . . . is fantasy."

But if he is right, then the companies that are remembered, that are finding their identities, are doing so by looking more and more alike—almost like one big corporation. A unilook for Unicorp.

Some designers do think Helvetica is overused. Some are even bored with it. But few believe that it is a mere fad. Most companies choose Helvetica in the first place because they expect it to remain contemporary for quite a while. And most companies cannot afford more than one identity change. This is especially true for New York's Metropolitan Transportation Authority.

Since 1967, the MTA has been gradually standardizing its graphics from about a dozen typefaces to a combination of Helvetica and Standard Medium. (The two are almost identical, but the latter was more available to the MTA.)

In contrast to the subway's filth and potential for violence, the cleanly and crisply lettered signs lend a sense of authority. They assure us that the train will come, and diminish the chaos created by the graffiti-scrawled walls. (It's no accident that the designer of Norman Mailer's *The Faith of Graffiti* branded the book's covers with Helvetica.) The subway-sign renovation alone, less than a quarter complete, is conservatively estimated to cost from $500,000 to a million dollars.

This MTA graphic system was originated by Massimo Vignelli, who founded, and has left, an appropriately named design firm, Unimark International, with Walter Kacik, the man who revamped the garbage trucks. Vignelli created Bloomingdale's logo and, more recently, the graphics, in Helvetica, for the Washington D.C. Metro, still under construction. He thinks Helvetica is not merely a fad but that it can be used faddishly. "As good as it is when used properly, it becomes very bad-looking when used badly," as, he suggested, in a wedding invitation.

What is its proper usage? "All kinds of signage are fine." In fact, a system of "symbol signs," with supporting Helvetica letters, intended to replace the numerous sign systems around the world, has been devised by Vignelli and other leading designers. (The design committee is headed by Thomas Geismar, whose firm Chermayeff & Geismar is L&M's chief competitor for the corporate identity market.)

Symbol signs are simple silhouetted pictures that act as signs, a knife and fork will mean restaurant, a question mark an information booth. The symbols are scheduled to be tested at various terminals in New York, Boston, Philadelphia, Williamsburg, Virginia, and the state of Florida. Helvetica is already used at airports such as Seattle, Dallas-Fort Worth, and Kennedy, but the symbol system might usher it into other transportation facilities.

The symbols will often need lettered support, but, in deference to varying cultural styles, its guideline manual does not recommend any one typeface. When other cultures shop around for a typeface, however, they will probably be influenced by the example used throughout the manual itself, one deemed "legible, aesthetic, and compatible" with the symbols: Helvetica.

Helvetica Light

ABCDEFGHIJK
LMNOPQRSTUVWXYZ
abcdefghijklmnopqrstuvwxyz
1234567890
&?!ß£$(;)≈»«

Helvetica Outline
(Helvetica Med. Outline) HAAS

ABCDEFGHIJKL
MNOPQRSTUVWXYZ
abcdefghijklm
nopqrstuvwxyz
1234567890
&?ß£$(;)«»

Helvetica has become such a dominant influence in type design during the last fifteen years that in some respects it is a state of mind as much as it is a particular typeface. The Univers family, designed by Adrian Frutiger, and first produced by Deberny and Peignot in 1957, is a similarly clean sans serif face which has perhaps been nearly as popular as Helvetica, although it has received less publicity.

In terms of advertising and "display" typography, Helvetica and similar authoritative faces, although they are still quite common, have given way to less conservative designs. Souvenir, a weighted serif face that combines a freehand flourish with the clean design of the sans serif, has been extraordinarily popular in the seventies and has given rise to a host of imitators (such as Tiffany). Meanwhile, new methods of phototypesetting have vastly increased the number and style of typefaces available. Many of them are idiosyncratic designs, such as Milton Glaser's Glaser Stencil, which, despite its strong personality, also happens to reveal the influence of Helvetica. Computers have had their influence as well. Microgramma (designed by A. Butti and A. Novarese) and its lower-case equivalent eurostile (A. Novarese) were first produced by Nebiolo in 1952 and 1962 respectively. Their square shape suggests computer printout style. They also have some hand-drawn characteristics.

Univers 55

ABCDEFGHIJKLM
NOPQRSTUVWXYZ
abcdefghijkl
mnopqrstuvwxyz
1234567890
&?!ß£$(·)

GLASER STENCIL

ABCDEFGHIJKLMN
OPQRSTUVWXYZ
1234567890
&!?£$

MICROGRAMMA

ABCDEFGHIJ
KLMNOPQRS
TUVWXYZ
1234567890
&?!£$

eurostile medium

abcdefghi
jklmnopqrstu
vwxyz

An automotive writer once described driving a rather well-known domestic luxury sedan as "...the ultimate act of motoring passivity."

One steers, selects forward or reverse, tunes the radio, stops—little else is required.

This point is quite central to the difference between a BMW and the majority of the world's automobiles.

A BMW is built to be driven. It is a car designed by German engineers who believe that driving is a thing that should be taken seriously and done well.

A

Indeed it does. As the 5-Car Showdown will testify. First of all, in tests of cornering flatness and steering quickness, none of the competitors out-ran Opel. And in tests of acceleration and gradability, only the VW Rabbit (a car much-ballyhooed for its fuel-injected engine) was able to nose out our Opel for top honors.

Opel's strong showing in these areas isn't surprising when you consider its own accoutrements. Like the dynamic overhead-cam, 4-cylinder hemi engine. Four-coil-spring-suspension. Front stabilizer bar. Rear track bar. Floor-mounted, full-synchronized, short-throw, 4-speed manual transmission (with 5-speed and automatic available). Rack-and-pinion steering. And lots more.

Nevertheless, it still may surprise you. But then, up to this point, maybe you haven't considered Opel.

Maybe you should.

B

All for $4399! (Manufacturer's Suggested Retail Price not including destination charges, taxes, license or title fees and optional tape stripe and mag type wheel cover package.)

Tough sport.

Solid, all-steel unibody is but one example of how the Datsun 200-SX is put together to stay together. Fact is, when we made this fun little car, we made sure of one thing.

The fun would last.

Suddenly it's going to dawn on you. C

Type in action: Ads that want to convey a feeling of efficiency and "no nonsense" performance still depend heavily on Helvetica and other sans serifs, as these three recent examples show. But Souvenir and other "humanized" 1970s faces are moving up quickly. BMW (A) and Opel (B) want a clean, technical image, but Datsun (C) is pushing "this fun little car"—Souvenir works better in that context. Helvetica, of course, makes no sense at all for products like frozen french fries (D), so Souvenir rules triumphant.

Maybe you've never thought about it, but frozen french fries don't really fry. They go on a cookie sheet, into your oven, and just warm up. That's why they taste less than terrific. To get good and crispy on the outside, stay nice and meaty inside, turn golden brown and all those good things—french fries oughta fry.   D

Souvenir Light

INTERNATIONAL TYPEFACE CORPORATION

ABCDEFGHIJKLMN
OPQRSTUVWXYZ
abcdefghijklmn
opqrstuvwxyz
1234567890 &!?£$

Souvenir Bold

INTERNATIONAL TYPEFACE CORPORATION

ABCDEFGHIJKLMNO
PQRSTUVWXYZ
abcdefghijklmnop
qrstuvwxyz
1234567890&!?£$

According to Arthur Congdon, head of design for Lippincott & Margulies, the trend in corporate logos is away from the austere authority of Helvetica and toward more humanized faces. Handwritten faces, "slab serifs," and even Typewriter have all come into their own recently. The A&P logo above, for example, manages to convey some of the flavor of the traditional nineteenth-century image at the same time as the design of the type's background presents a forward-looking image.

The U.S. Department of Transportation, which commissioned the system, will ask other federal agencies and state governments to adopt it. Then, in order to become an official standard, the symbols will be submitted to two standardization organizations (the American National Standards Institute and the International Organization for Standardization), which certify and promote standards in everything from abbreviations to industrial parts. Helvetica, riding the back of a symbol, might pass through a well-guarded standards stronghold.

Meanwhile, it already headlines all publications of the Departments of Labor and Agriculture. It's also the only standard style for the U.S. Post Office. With an eagle it appears on the new mailbox stickers saying "U.S. Mail" and "Air Mail."

Governments and corporations rely on Helvetica partly because it makes them appear neutral and efficient, partly because its smoothness makes them seem human.

This chic, friendly aspect of the typeface bothers one designer. James Wines, co-director of SITE (Sculpture in the Environment) and a Pulitzer Prize winner for graphics (the category has since then been discontinued), said about Helvetica, "It represents an update authority. Not old government, but new government." He goes further: "Helvetica is part of a psychological enslavement. It's a subconscious plot: getting people to do, think, say, what you want them to. . . . It *assumes* you accept some system. It means it's predetermined that you're on their route, that it's not casually happening to you."

Helvetica signs ease us not only through building corridors, but through mental corridors as well. Ready for any mistaken move in a modern maze, a sign greets us at the point of decision, a mental bell rings in recognition, and down we go through the right chute! A slick-looking sign lubricates our grooves of thought and taste, making the product whose name it bears easier to accept. After transforming ugly garbage trucks into slick sanitation vehicles, Walter Kacik should

Typography

Typography

Typography

Typography

Typography

Typography

Typography

Typography

Typography

Typography

Typography

Typography

In addition to opening up the floodgates of type design, phototype-setting has resulted in an almost infinitely flexible spectrum of possi-bilities within any particular design. These examples from Typo-Graphics Communications, Inc. (in Helvetica Medium) show how spacing can be varied between letters to any desired extent and how even the shapes of the letters can be adjusted through photographic techniques. One basic font produces all twelve of these examples (and many more). In the days of "cold" lead type, twelve separately de-signed and separately executed fonts would have been necessary— and prohibitively expensive.

know when he says, "Helvetica enhances things that normally wouldn't work."

It serves to tone down potentially offensive messages: "Littering is filthy and selfish, so don't do it!" And Lenny Bruce's autobiography is packaged in Helvetica.

Helvetica skims across all categories of products and places to stamp them "sanitized," "neutralized," and "authorized." Cleanly trimmed of all excess until only an instant modern classic remains, its labels seem to say, "To look further is in vain." As Vignelli said, "What you see is different from what you perceive. You see Helvetica and you perceive order." With more unusual lettering, "you perceive fantasy."

Fantasy and a well-ordered society have always been at odds. And, as James Wines says, by designing fantasy out of our society, we are headed in a dangerous direction. "Our world is a designed extension of service," he said. "Other worlds are an aesthetic extension of spirit."

The writing's on the wall.

22. MISSING HAZEL
by Nora Ephron

During the mid-seventies, most general-interest magazines started covering media regularly. No one has written about the diffuse subject with more wit and style than Nora Ephron in *Esquire*. See Chapter 13 if you want to learn a little about how *Upstairs, Downstairs* is put together, but Ephron's piece describes perfectly, I think, the effect a developing serial has on viewers.

As I write, we have not yet been informed of Ephron's reaction to the suicide of James, Hazel's husband, which (along with a couple of marriages—not to be too downbeat) put a blunt period to the series. Alfred Hitchcock used to say, "It's only a movie." But a television serial, that's something else.

My friend Kenny does not feel as bad about the death of Hazel as I do. My friend Ann has been upset about it for days. My friend Martha is actually glad Hazel is dead. I cried when Hazel died, but only for a few seconds, partly because I wasn't at all surprised. About three months ago, someone told me she was going to die, and since then I have watched every show expecting it to be her last. Once she stuck her head into a dumbwaiter to get some food for James, who had finally recovered enough from his war injuries to have an appetite, and I was certain the dumbwaiter was going to crash onto her head and kill her instantly. Another time, when she and Lord Bellamy went to fetch James from a hospital in France (and Hazel and Georgina had a fight over whether he should be moved), I was sure the ambulance would crash on the way back. Hazel lived on, though, show after show, until there came the thirteenth episode. As soon as they mentioned the plague, I knew that would be it. It was. The particular plague Hazel died of was the Spanish influenza, which, according to Alistair Cooke, was the last true pandemic. I was sorry that Alistair Cooke had so much more to say about the plague than he did about the death of Hazel, but perhaps he has become wary of commenting on the show

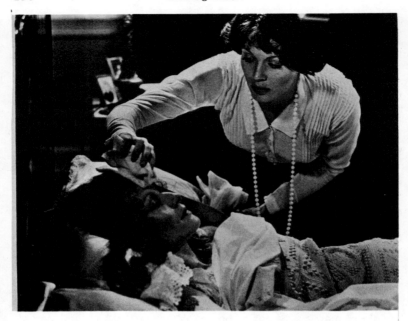

Georgina (Lesley-Anne Down) attends the dying Hazel (Meg Wynn Owen). The ostensible cause of death was influenza, but Hazel's real problem was a curious epidemic that struck many of the female stars of Upstairs, Downstairs *(lucky Georgina excluded) during its five-year run.*

itself after everyone (including me) took offense at some of the things he had to say about George Sand.

Of course, Hazel should never have married James Bellamy in the first place. James is a big baby. Hazel should have married Lord Bellamy, which was impossible since Lady Marjorie had just gone down on the *Titanic*. Or she should have run off with the upwardly mobile air ace, which was impossible since he was killed on the very next show after she met him, along with Rose's fiancé, Gregory. (I never laid eyes on Gregory, but Kenny tells me he was a very interesting man, a natural radical, who met Rose by sitting on her cake.) Hazel's finest moment was the show when she met the ace, and they went dancing, and she wore a dress with tiny, delicate beaded straps, and turned out to have the most beautiful back I have ever seen. But other than her back, and her fling with the ace, and her occasional success in telling Hudson off, and her premature death, Hazel left something to be desired. Not as far as Ann is concerned, but certainly as far as Martha is concerned. "Let's face it," said Martha. "Hazel was a pill." In fairness, we might all be pills if we had had to spend our lives sitting on a chesterfield couch pouring tea, but that's no excuse, I suppose. Hazel *was* a pill (though not nearly as terrible a pill as Abigail Adams and her entire family), and she really ought to have married an older man who wanted nothing more than to go to bed early. Still, James had no cause to treat her so badly. Kenny is the only person I know who has a kind word to say for James, and here it is: "Somewhere there must be something good about him that we'll find out about eventually." Actually, James did have a couple of good weeks there, when he returned from the front to report the army was dropping like flies, but I am told by a reliable source that his behavior was derivative of Siegfried Sassoon, and in any case, he shortly thereafter reverted to type. The worst James ever treated Hazel—aside from when she was sick and dying of the plague and he was playing rummy with his father's new fiancée, the Scottish widow—was when she had her miscarriage, and he totally ignored her, and went off dancing with Cousin Georgina.

Which brings us to Cousin Georgina. Martha doesn't much like Georgina either. This puzzles me. I can understand not liking Hazel and liking Georgina, or not liking Georgina and liking Hazel, but not liking both of them? Georgina was a true ninny when she arrived in

The young parlormaid Sarah (Pauline Collins) was written out of the series after the first season, although she had been one of its major attractions. She was soon joined by the first Mrs. Bellamy, Lady Marjorie (Rachel Gurney), who went down ignominiously off-camera on the Titanic.

Perhaps the greatest loss to the show was daughter Elizabeth (Nicola Pagett), seen here with her father (David Langton). A budding feminist and the strongest-willed of all the female characters, Elizabeth was unceremoniously packed off to New York after the first season and never seen again, although she did perform useful duty for four years more as a destination for characters who were to be written out for awhile (or for good, in the case of her mother). Only Mrs. Bridges (Angela Baddeley) survived for the full five-year run against creator Jean Marsh's Rose. (In an ironic twist, Baddeley herself died only months after the completion of the last episode.)

In retrospect, it's very clear who the star of Upstairs, Downstairs was.

the Bellamy household, and she hung around with Daisy, who is the most unrelenting ninny in television history. (For example, when Rose found out that Gregory had left her twelve hundred pounds, Daisy said: "Some people have all the luck." I rest my case.) But Georgina has become a wonderful nurse, and I'm proud of her. Also, her face is even more beautiful than Hazel's back. As for the burning question proccupying us all—will Georgina marry James now that Hazel is dead?—I say no. (Martha says yes.) Georgina sees through James. I know it. I see her marrying the one-armed officer she went off to Paris with, if only because she is the only person on the show saintly enough to marry a man with one arm. Ann, on the other hand, does not trust Georgina as far as she can spit. "I know she was a great nurse," says Ann, "but she reminds me of those bitchy women you went to college with who were great biology students. She has no heart." There is indeed some recent evidence pointing to Georgina's heartlessness: when Hazel died, she went off to a party. But the war was over, and who could blame her? I was far more shocked at the la-di-da way Lord Bellamy behaved; he got off an Alistair Cooke-like remark about the plague itself, and that was that. Only Rose was magnificent about it. Ann thinks the reason everyone (except Rose) behaved so unemotionally about Hazel's death was that she was a petit bourgeois and they had never accepted her. I disagree. I think it's possible that the same person who tipped me off about Hazel's death tipped off the Bellamy household, and they just weren't all that surprised when it finally happened.

Even Martha loves Rose. Rose reminds me, in some metaphysical way, of Loretta Haggers. She is so good, so honest, so pure, so straight, and so plucky. Kenny worries that Rose is going to leave the show now that she has come into all this money, but I say she'll never leave: the actress who plays Rose created the show itself, so she'll never be got rid of. I sometimes wonder how they do get rid of people at that show. They sank Lady Marjorie, I read somewhere, because the actress playing her wanted to take a vacation in Europe. But what about Hazel? Did they know all along? Did they hire her in the beginning and say, "Look here, Hazel, we'll carry you through World War One, but then you're through"? Or did they hire her, planning to use her straight through the Depression? Did she do something to antagonize them? Did she know she was going to die, and if so, when?

We all know that Mrs. Bridges and Hudson are going to get married at the end of the next batch of episodes, which have already been shown in England. The reason we all know this is that the information was mentioned in the obituary of the actress who played Mrs. Bridges, who died of the flu in real life in Essex a couple of weeks before Hazel died of the flu on television in America. Was this planned, too? Did they say to her, "Well, Mrs. Bridges, we'll give you a nice fat part for the entire series and marry you off to the butler in the end, but shortly thereafter you'll have to die"? I wonder. I also wonder how I'm going to feel about Mrs. Bridges and Hudson getting married. There's something a little too neat about it. Besides, Mrs. Bridges is a much better person than Hudson, who has become a mealymouthed hypocrite as well as a staunch defender of the British class system. All of this would probably be all right and deliciously in character except that it is beginning to look as if Hudson is going to personify, in microcosm, the entire rise of Fascism in Europe. Ann is more concerned on this point than I am.

As for Edward and Daisy, they talk a lot about leaving the Bellamy household, but it is Kenny's theory that they are beginning to sound more and more like the three sisters and Moscow. Which is a shame, because I wish they would leave.

Here are some things we all agree on:

We are all terribly worried that Rose will never find a man.

We all miss Lady Marjorie a lot more than the Bellamys do, and are extremely apprehensive about meeting the Scottish widow's children.

We all think the best show of the year was the one with the scene in the train station with the dying and wounded soldiers. The second-best show was the one in which Gregory and the ace died. We would all like to know some of the technical details of the show—how the writers are picked, how much of the plot is planned ahead of time— but it is too dangerous to find out. Someone, in the course of giving out the information, might let slip a crucial turn of the plot. We would all rather die than know what is going to happen.

Mostly, we all wish *Upstairs, Downstairs* would last forever.

23. WHAT TV DOES TO KIDS
by Harry F. Waters

For twenty years, television critics railed periodically on the effect of television violence on children. The furor usually reached a peak shortly after an assassination or a mass murder. Congressional hearings were held, reports were issued, and gradually the controversy subsided for another couple of years. In fact, the relationship between television violence and real-life violence is not all that clear. Like other forms of pornography (those more directly connected with sex), the dramatized violence may just as likely work cathartically to defuse real passions as to inspire them.

Recently, attention has shifted away from the message and to the medium. Marie Winn's 1977 book *The Plug-In Drug* was perhaps the most explicit statement of this new approach. Harry F. Waters' February 1977 *Newsweek* cover story is a good summary of the argument. It *feels* true. The problem is that it's almost impossible to prove that, in effect, the medium is the message.

This one's for Froggy.

His first polysyllabic utterance as "Bradybunch." He learned to spell Sugar Smacks before his own name. He has seen Monte Carlo, witnessed a cocaine bust in Harlem, and already has full-color fantasies involving Farrah Fawcett-Majors. Recently, he tried to karate-chop his younger sister after she broke his Six Million Dollar Man bionic transport station. (She retaliated by bashing him with her Cher doll.) His nursery-school teacher reports that he is passive, noncreative, unresponsive to instruction, bored during play periods and possessed of an almost nonexistent attention span—in short, very much like his classmates. Next fall, he will officially reach the age of reason and begin his formal education: His parents are beginning to discuss their apprehensions—when they are not too busy watching television.

The wonder of it all is that the worry about television has so belatedly moved anyone to action. After all, the suspicion that TV is turning children's minds to mush and their psyches toward mayhem is almost as old as the medium itself. But it is only in recent years—with the first TV generation already well into its twenties—that social scientists, child psychologists, pediatricians, and educators have begun serious study of the impact of television on the young. "The American public has been preoccupied with governing our children's schooling," says Stanford University psychologist Alberta Siegel. "We have been astonishingly unconcerned about the medium that reaches into our homes. Yet we may expect television to alter our social arrangements just as profoundly as printing has done over the past five centuries."

The statistics are at least alarming. Educators like Dr. Benjamin Bloom, of the University of Chicago, maintain that by the time a child reaches the age of five, he has undergone as much intellectual growth as will occur over the next thirteen years. According to A. C. Nielsen, children under five watch an average of 23.5 hours of TV a week. That may be less than the weekly video diet of adults (about forty-four hours), but its effects are potentially enormous. Multiplied out over seventeen years, that rate of viewing means that by his high-school graduation today's typical teenager will have logged at least 15,000 hours before the small screen—more time than he will have spent on any other activity except sleep. And at present levels of advertising and mayhem, he will have been exposed to 350,000 commercials and vicariously participated in 18,000 murders.

The conclusion is inescapable: after parents, television has become perhaps the most potent influence on the beliefs, attitudes, values, and behavior of those who are being raised in its all-pervasive glow. George Gerbner, dean of the University of Pennsylvania's Annenberg School of Communications, is almost understating it when he says: "Television has profoundly affected the way in which members of the human race learn to become human beings."

A QUESTION OF AIR POLLUTION

Unquestionably, the plug-in picture window has transmitted some beneficial images. The January 1977 showing of *Roots*, for example, may have done more to increase the understanding of American race relations than any event since the civil-rights activities of the sixties. And the fact that 130 million Americans could share that experience through the small screen points up the powerful—and potentially positive—influence the industry can have on its audience. In general, the children of TV enjoy a more sophisticated knowledge of a far larger world at a much younger age. They are likely to possess richer vocabularies, albeit with only a superficial comprehension of what the words mean. Research on the impact of *Sesame Street* has established measurable gains in the cognitive skills of preschoolers. And many benefits cannot be statistically calibrated. A New York preschooler tries to match deductive wits with Columbo; a Los Angeles black girl, who has never seen a ballet, decides she wants to be a ballerina after watching Margot Fonteyn perform on TV.

Nonetheless, the overwhelming body of evidence—drawn from more than 2300 studies and reports—is decidedly negative. Most of the studies have dealt with the antisocial legacy of video violence. Michael Rothenberg, a child psychiatrist at the University of Washington, has reviewed twenty-five years of hard data on the subject—the fifty most comprehensive studies involving 10,000 children from every possible background. Most showed that viewing violence tends to produce aggressive behavior among the young. "The time is long past due for a major, organized cry of protest from the medical profession in relation to what, in political terms, is a national scandal," concludes Rothenberg.

An unexpected salvo was sounded in 1977 when the normally cautious American Medical Association announced that it had asked ten major corporations to review their policies about sponsoring excessively gory shows. "TV violence is both a mental-health problem and an environmental issue," explained Dr. Richard E. Palmer, president of the AMA. "TV has been quick to raise questions of social responsibility with industries which pollute the air. In my opinion, television . . . may be creating a more serious problem of air pollution." Reaction was immediate: General Motors, Sears Roebuck, and the Joseph Schlitz Brewing Co. quickly announced they would look more closely into the content of the shows they sponsor.

The AMA action comes in the wake of a grass-roots campaign mobilized by the national Parent-Teacher Association. The 6.6 million-member PTA recently began a series of regional forums to arouse public indignation over TV carnage. If that crusade fails, the PTA is considering organizing station-license challenges and national boycotts of products advertised on offending programs.

"THE FLICKERING BLUE PARENT"

In their defense, broadcasting officials maintain that the jury is still out on whether video violence is guilty of producing aggressive behavior. And they marshal their own studies to support that position. At the same time, the network schedulers say they are actively reducing the violence dosage. "People have said they want another direction and that's what we're going to give them," promises NBC-TV president Robert T. Howard. Finally, the broadcast industry insists that the responsibility for the impact of TV on children lies with parents rather than programmers. "Parents should pick and choose the shows their kids watch," says CBS vice president Gene Mater. "Should TV be programmed for the young through midnight? It's a real problem. TV is a mass medium and it must serve more than just children."

*Commercial children's television in the U.S. has developed a complex—
and possibly dangerous—attitude toward the relationship between fantasy and reality. Far more so than in adult entertainment, a number of
distinct levels of fact and fiction are inextricably interwoven. Children
enjoy the muddle as much as adults might—but does this steady diet of
video environment affect their collective ability later in life to distin-
guish between essentially different levels of truth?*

*By far the great majority of commercial children's television is
animated. Some of the characters, such as Wile E. Coyote (A), the*

Roadrunner's perennial victim, come from movie cartoons. The Pink Panther (B), star of his own Pink Panther's Laugh-and-a-half Hour-and-a-half *Saturday mornings, was born as a logo for the film of the same name, not as a character per se. Live-action characters such as the indestructible Tarzan (C) are metamorphosed into cartoons, as well. Mr. Jaws (D) is, of course, a shark, and harks back to the movie of the same name, but he acts more like Charlie the Tuna, the television commercial character, than he does like "Bruce," the star of* Jaws.

Kids know the line between commercials and entertainment is erasable. The Flintstones segue neatly from performance to sales with

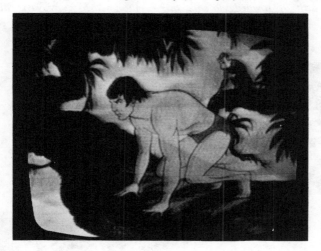

a bowl of "Cocoa Pebbles" (the milk turns "chocolately" brown before your very eyes! (E) and Ronald McDonald (F), the live clown, exists solely for the sake of children's commercials. On the other hand, dolls must be as lifelike as technology can make them, possibly to compensate for the lack of reality and the overdose of fantasy in the entertainment portion of the media package. Dolls that cry and wet their disposable diapers (G) have been commonplace for years. In the early seventies, Macy's offered a doll that menstruated. Celebrity dolls, miniature wax museum images, have risen greatly in popularity in the last few years.

    The attitude toward violence this cartoon world conveys is still an

important issue, despite the reams that have been written about it during the last twenty-five years. Nitroglycerine comes in cute little bottles, neatly labeled (H), and all it does, really, is make the victim sooty for a quick shot. The Roadrunner's magnificent perspective chasm (I), into which Wile E. Coyote is perpetually falling, whistling with a Doppler effect as he goes, might serve as an emblem of the vertiginous descent into fantasy that commercial U.S. television perpetuates for children from the time they are old enough to sit up straight and focus on the tube until the time some years hence when—possibly, but not necessarily—they begin to figure out for themselves that some things in this world are more real than others.

But the blight of televised mayhem is only part of TV's impact. Beyond lies a vast subliminal terrain that is only now being charted. The investigators are discovering that TV has affected its youthful addicts in a host of subtle ways, varying according to age and class. For deprived children, TV may, in some cases, provide more sustenance than their home—or street—life; for the more privileged, who enjoy other alternatives, it may not play such a dominating role.

Nonetheless, for the average kid TV has at the very least preempted the traditional development of childhood itself. The time kids spend sitting catatonic before the set has been exacted from such salutary pursuits as reading, outdoor play, even simple, contemplative solitude. TV prematurely jades, rendering passé the normal experiences of grow-

Meanwhile, for the last nine years public television for children has worked to clarify some of the issues involved. Sesame Street *has used many of the manipulative techniques of commercial television, but ostensibly to a better end: education. No doubt it has been just as effective in selling the alphabet as Ronald McDonald has been in selling gray meat patties. Children's Television Workshop, creators of* Sesame Street, *defends the approach on the basis of simple utilitarianism. Diametrically opposed has been the more ethically conscious approach of Fred Rogers'* Mister Rogers' Neighborhood. *Some adult critics find him too meek, but that is, I think, a carefully calculated personality. For Rogers, ever since the late sixties, the object has been not to overwhelm his viewers but to involve them; and his educational aim, contrary to* Sesame Street's *has been to expose and examine ethical, moral—even quasi-political—issues: to teach children how to think rather than simply to drill them in the use of linguistic and mathematical tools.*

Here Judy Collins, guest star, cringes in mock pain at Oscar the Grouch's "music" in a Sesame Street *episode from the 1976–77 season (A). Fred Rogers listens to some of his fans during a visit to New York in 1974 (B).*

ing up. And few parents can cope with its tyrannical allure. Recently, Dr. Benjamin Spock brought his stepdaughter and granddaughter to New York for a tour of the Bronx Zoo and the Museum of Modern Art. But the man who has the prescription for everything from diaper rash to bed-wetting could not dislodge the kids from their hotel room. "I couldn't get them away from the goddamned TV set," recalls Spock. "It made me sick."

Small wonder that television has been called "the flickering blue parent." The after-school and early-evening hours used to be a time for "What did you do today?" dialogue. Now, the electronic box does most of the talking. Dr. David Pearl of the National Institute of Mental Health suspects that the tube "has displaced many of the normal interactional processes between parents and children. . . . Those kinds of interactions are essential for maximum development." One veteran elementary-school teacher in suburban Washington, D.C., has noticed that her students have grown inordinately talkative when they arrive for class. "At home, they can't talk when the TV is on," she says. "It's as if they are starved for conversation."

THE PASSIVE GENERATION

Even more worrisome is what television has done to, rather than denied, the tube-weaned population. A series of studies has shown that addiction to TV stifles creative imagination. For example, a University of Southern California research team exposed 250 elementary students —who had been judged mentally gifted—to three weeks of intensive viewing. Tests conducted before and after the experiment found a marked drop in all forms of creative abilities except verbal skill. Some teachers are encountering children who cannot understand a simple story without visual illustrations. "TV has taken away the child's ability to form pictures in his mind," says child-development expert Dorothy Cohen at New York City's Bank Street College of Education.

Parenthetically, nursery-school teachers who have observed the pre-TV generation contend that juvenile play is far less imaginative and spontaneous than in the past. The vidkids' toys come with built-in fantasies while their playground games have been programmed by last night's shows. "You don't see kids making their own toys out of crummy things like we used to," says University of Virginia psychology professor Stephen Worchel, who is the father of a six-year-old. "You don't see them playing hopscotch, or making up their own games. Everything is suggested to them by television."

Too much TV too early also instills an attitude of spectatorship, a withdrawal from direct involvement in real-life experiences. "What television basically teaches children is passivity," says Stanford University researcher Paul Kaufman. "It creates the illusion of having been somewhere and done something and seen something, when in fact you've been sitting at home." *New York Times* writer Joyce Maynard, twenty-three, a perceptive member of the first TV generation, con-cludes: "We grew up to be observers, not participants, to respond to action, not initiate it."

Conditioned to see all problems resolved in thirty or sixty minutes, the offspring of TV exhibit a low tolerance for the frustration of learning. Elementary-school educators complain that their charges are quickly turned off by any activity that promises less than instant gratifi-cation. "You introduce a new skill, and right away, if it looks hard, they dissolve into tears," laments Maryland first-grade teacher Eleanor Berman. "They want everything to be easy—like watching the tube." Even such acclaimed educational series as *Sesame Street, The Electric Company*, and *Zoom* have had some dubious effects. Because such shows sugarcoat their lessons with flashy showbiz techniques, they are forcing real-life instructors into the role of entertainers in order to hold their pupils' attention. "I can't turn my body into shapes or flashlights," sighs a Connecticut teacher. "Kids today are accustomed to learning through gimmicks."

For the majority of American children, television has become the principal socializing agent. It shapes their view of what the world is like and what roles they should play in it. As the University of Penn-sylvania's Gerbner puts it: "The socialization of children has largely been transferred from the home and school to TV programmers who are unelected, unnamed, and unknown, and who are not subject to collective—not to mention democratic—review."

What does TV's most impressionable constituency learn from prime-time entertainment? No one can really be sure, but psychologists like Robert Liebert of the State University of New York, one of the most respected observers of child behavior, don't hesitate to express sweep-ing indictments. "It teaches them that might makes right," Liebert says flatly. "The lesson of most TV series is that the rich, the powerful, and the conniving are the most successful."

THE VIEW FROM THE VICTIMS

Whatever the truth of that, the tube clearly tends to reinforce sex-role stereotypes. In a Princeton, N.J., survey of sixteen programs and 216 commercials, it was found that men outnumbered women by three to one and that females were twice as likely to display incompetence. By and large, men were portrayed as dominant, authoritative, and the sole source of their family's economic support. "These roles are biased and distorted, and don't reflect the way a woman thinks or feels," complains Liebert. "And it's just as bad for blacks."

It may, in fact, be even worse for blacks. Not only do black children watch more TV than white, but they confront a far greater disparity between the illusions of videoland and the reality of their own lives. Two yet-to-be-published studies conducted by University of South Carolina psychology professor Robert Heckel found that young black viewers regard whites as more competent than blacks, and model their conduct accordingly. In one study, black children were shown a TV film of an interracial group of peers choosing toys to play with—and then given the same toys to pick for themselves. All the blacks selected the toys chosen by whites in the film, even though many of those toys were smaller or inferior in quality. "On TV, the competent roles tend to go to whites, particularly young white males," explains Heckel. "Thus black children regard whites as someone to copy."

A classic example of such racial imprinting is Rowena Smith, a fourteen-year-old Los Angeles black who remains glued to the tube from school recess to eleven each night. Rowena's favorite TV characters are CBS's Phyllis and her teenage daughter. "They get along so good," she sighs. "I wish me and Mom could talk that way." When Rowena was scolded for getting her clothes dirty, she indignantly told her mother that "the kid in the Tonka truck ad gets dirty all the time." Rowena's first awareness of the facts of non-TV life came after she ran away for two days—and her mother gave her a licking. "When TV shows runaways," she complains, "they don't show the part about being beaten." Nowadays, Rowena is more skeptical about television, but she has become increasingly concerned about her eight-year-old brother. He wistfully talks about getting seriously injured and then being reassembled like the Six Million Dollar Man. "This kid really *believes* TV," sighs his sister. "I gotta keep an eye on him twenty-four hours a day."

Indeed, call on the children themselves to testify and the message comes through clear—and sometimes poignantly. A vidkid sampler:

- FOURTEEN-YEAR-OLD, LOS ANGELES: "Television is perfect to tune out the rest of the world. But I don't relate with my family much because we're all too busy watching TV."
- ELEVEN-YEAR-OLD, DENVER: "You see so much violence that it's meaningless. If I saw someone really get killed, it wouldn't be a big deal. I guess I'm turning into a hard rock."
- NINE-YEAR-OLD, SAN FRANCISCO: "I'd rather watch TV than play outside because it's boring outside. They always have the same rides, like swings and things."
- FIFTEEN-YEAR-OLD, LAKE FOREST, ILL.: "Sometimes when I watch an exciting show, I don't blink my eyes once. When I close them after the show, they hurt hard."
- THIRTEEN-YEAR-OLD, GLASTONBURY, CONN.: "When I see a beautiful girl using a shampoo or a cosmetic on TV, I buy them because I'll look like her. I have a ton of cosmetics. I play around with them and save them for when I'm older."
- TEN-YEAR-OLD, NEW YORK: "It bugs me when someone is watching with me. If your friend is bored, you have to go out or make conversation. That's hard."

*   *   *

On the whole, Rogers' more thoughtful and less utilitarian approach seems to be gaining adherents in the late seventies. Most PBS shows that have been added to the schedule since Sesame Street premiered in 1969 have eschewed excessively fantastic formats in favor of a more conversational realism. ZOOM (A) was one of the first and most successful of this new breed. The cast of relatively real children changes regularly and the format is simple and direct: kids entertain kids, and the audience at least has a theoretical chance to join in.

Studio See (B) takes participation one logical step further, demystifying the television process by showing kids how the technology works and even allowing them to use it themselves. Producer Jayne Adair is shown here with young "videotographer" James Howard.

It would be preposterous, of course, to suggest that television alone is responsible for everything that is wrong with America's young. Permissiveness at home and in school, the dispersion of the extended family, confusion over moral standards, and the erosion of traditional institutions—all help explain why Dick and Jane behave as they do. Moreover, any aspect of child psychology is enormously complex, especially when it comes to measuring cause and effect. There is always the temptation among social scientists to set up their experiments in a way guaranteed to reinforce their preconceptions. Nevertheless, there is one thrust of reliable study—into video violence—that has produced an unmistakable pattern of clear and present danger.

PARANOIA AND PROPAGANDA

The debate over the link between TV violence and aggressive behavior in society has had a longer run than *Gunsmoke*. Today, however, even the most chauvinist network apologists concede that some children, under certain conditions, will imitate antisocial acts that they witness on the tube. Indeed, a study of a hundred juvenile offenders commissioned by ABC found that no fewer than twenty-two confessed to having copied criminal techniques from TV. Last year, a Los Angeles judge sentenced two teen-age boys to long jail terms after they held up a bank and kept twenty-five persons hostage for seven hours. In pronouncing the sentence, the judge noted disgustedly that the entire scheme had been patterned on an *Adam 12* episode the boys had seen two weeks earlier.

Convinced that they have proved their basic case, the behavioral sleuths on the violence beat have switched their focus to less obvious signs of psychic dysfunction. They are now uncovering evidence that the tide of TV carnage increases children's tolerance of violent behavior in others. In one experiment, several hundred fifth-graders were asked to act as baby-sitters for a group of younger kids—shown on a TV screen—who were supposedly playing in the next room. The baby-sitters were instructed to go to a nearby adult for assistance if their charges began fighting. Those who had been shown a violent TV film just before taking up their duties were far slower to call for help than those who had watched a pro baseball telecast. "Television desensitizes children to violence in real life," observes University of Mississippi psychology professor Ronald Drabman, who helped conduct the study. "They tolerate violence in others because they have been conditioned to think of it as an everyday thing."

Beyond that, some researchers are finding that TV may be instilling paranoia in the young. Three years of tests directed by Gerbner, who is perhaps the nation's foremost authority on the subject, established that heavy TV watchers tend to exaggerate the danger of violence in their own lives—creating what Gerbner calls a "mean-world syndrome." As for children, he reports that "the pattern is exactly the same, only more so. The prevailing message of TV is to generate fear."

And now a word about the sponsors. The late Jack Benny once quipped that television is called a medium because nothing it serves up is ever well-done. But as the child watchers see it, the not-so-funny problem with TV commercials is precisely that they are so well put together. "Everybody has had the experience of seeing a two-year-old playing on the floor, and when the commercial comes on, he stops and watches it," notes F. Earle Barcus, professor of communications at Boston University. "TV ads probably have more effect on children than any other form of programming."

JUNK FOOD FOR THOUGHT

The hottest battle involves the impact of child-directed commercials on their audience's eating habits. More than 70 percent of the ads on Saturday and Sunday-morning "kidvid" peddle sugar-coated cereals, candy, and chewing gum. Laced with action-packed attention grabbers and pitched by an ingratiating adult authority figure, such messages hook children on poor eating habits long before they develop the mental defenses to resist. "This is the most massive educational program to eat junk food in history," charges Sid Wolinsky, an attorney for a San Francisco public-interest group. "We are creating a nation of sugar junkies."

Research has also established that as the kids grow older their attitudes toward commercials move from innocent acceptance to outrage about those ads that mislead and finally to a cynical recognition of what they perceive as adult hypocrisy. According to a study by Columbia University psychology professor Thomas Bever, TV ads may be "permanently distorting children's views of morality, society, and business." From in-depth interviews with forty-eight youngsters between the ages of five and twelve, Bever concluded that by the time they reach twelve, many find it easier to decide that all commercials lie than to try to determine which are telling the truth. Concludes Bever: "They become ready to believe that, like advertising, business and other institutions are riddled with hypocrisy."

Who is to blame and what, if anything, can be done? The networks argue that the number of violent incidents portrayed on TV has declined by 24 percent since 1975. That figure has been challenged, but there is little question that the networks have instituted some reforms. The number of "action-adventure" series has decreased of late, and the weekend-morning kidvid scene is gradually being pacified. Such super-hero cartoon characters as CBS's *Superman* and NBC's *Granite Man* have been replaced with gentler fare; ABC even canceled *Bugs Bunny* and *Road Runner* because of their zap-and-whap antics.

There is also considerable merit to the broadcasters' argument that parents are to blame if they don't regulate their children's viewing habits. By the time the Family Hour experiment was struck down by the courts last year, it had already proved unworkable because so many parents refused to cooperate. Neilsen found that 10.5 million youngsters under the age of twelve were still hooked to the tube after 9 P.M., when the Family Hour ended. And a recent Roper study reported that only two fifths of the parents polled enforced rules about what programs their children could watch. "Parents who take active charge of most of the elements of their children's upbringing allow a kind of anarchy to prevail where television viewing is concerned," says Elton Rule, president of ABC, Inc.

THE PUBLIC STRIKES BACK

In rebuttal, public-interest groups point out that TV stations have been granted federal licenses to ride the public airwaves—a highly lucrative privilege that carries a unique responsibility. In addition to the nationwide pressure being exerted by the AMA and the PTA, local organizations like the Lansing (Michigan) Committee for Children's Television have persuaded local stations to drop gory shows from their late-afternoon schedules. But no one has achieved more reform than the activist mothers of Action for Children's Television, based in Newtonville, Massachusetts. ACT is largely credited with persuading the networks to reduce time for commercials on children's weekend shows from sixteen to nine and a half minutes an hour, to halt the huckstering of vitamins on kidvid and to end the practice of having the hosts deliver the pitches. ACT's ultimate—perhaps chimeric—goal is to rid kidvid of all advertising. "We feel it is wise to separate children from the marketplace until they are ready to deal with it," explains Peggy Charren, ACT's indefatigable president.

The shrewdest reform movement is aimed at persuading network programmers and advertisers that violence really doesn't sell. J. Walter Thompson, the nation's largest advertising agency, has begun advising its clients to stop purchasing spots on violent series—pointing out that a sampling of adult viewers revealed that 8 percent of the consumers surveyed had already boycotted products advertised on such shows, while 10 percent more were considering doing so. To help viewers identify the worst offenders among the shows, the National Citizens Committee for Broadcasting now disseminates rankings of the most violent series. At last body count, the bloodiest were ABC's *Starsky & Hutch* and *Baretta*, NBC's *Baa Baa Black Sheep*, and CBS's *Hawaii Five-O*.

On the brighter side, some educators have begun harnessing commercial TV's power in positive ways. The movement first took hold a few years ago in Philadelphia's school system, which started tying reading assignments to TV offerings. For example, scripts for such docudramas as *The Missiles of October* and *Eleanor and Franklin* were distributed to more than 100,000 Philadelphia students in advance of the TV dates.

FROM VIOLENCE TO SOCIAL VALUES

The children watched the shows while following along in the scripts, and discussed them in class the next day. The program has worked so well—some pupils' reading skills advanced by three years—that 3500 other U.S. school systems are imitating it.

Prime Time School TV, a nonprofit Chicago organization, has come up with the most innovative approach: PTST uses some of TV's most violent fare to implant positive social values. In one seven-week course, pupils were given questionnaires and told to fill them out while watching *Kojak, Baretta*, and the like. The questions, which were subsequently kicked around in class, dealt with everything from illegal search and seizure to forced confessions. "One boy told us that we had ruined television for him," reports PTST official Linda Kahn. "He couldn't watch a police show any more without counting the number of killings." Says PTST president William Singer: "We are saying that there are alternatives to merely railing against television, and this is just one of them."

LIFE WITHOUT THE TUBE

Unfortunately, the options available to the individual parent are considerably more limited. A few daring souls have simply pulled the plug. Charles Frye, a San Francisco nursery-school teacher and the father of five boys, decided he would not replace his set after it conked out in 1972. Frye's brood rebelled at first, but today none of them voices regret that theirs is a TV-less household. Fourteen-year-old Mark fills his afternoon hours with tap-dancing lessons, Sea Scout meetings, and work in a gas station. Kirk, his thirteen-year-old brother, plays a lot of basketball and football, and recently finished *Watership Down* and all four of the Tolkien hobbit books. "I know of no other children that age who have that range of interests," says their father.

Short of such a draconian measure, some parents are exercising a greater degree of home rule. Two years ago, the administrators of New York's Horace Mann nursery school because distressed over an upsurge of violence in their students' play. Deciding that television was to blame, they dispatched a letter to all parents urging them to curb their children's viewing. "After we sent the letter, we could see a change," recalls Horace Mann principal Eleanor Brussel. "The kids showed better concentration, better comprehension, an ability to think things through." Sheila Altschuler, one of the mothers who heeded the school's request, noticed that her four-year-old son began making up his own playtime characters instead of imitating those on the tube. "If I didn't feel it was kind of freaky, I wouldn't own a set," allows Altschuler. "But these days it's a matter of conformity. Kids would be outcasts without TV."

Clearly, there is no single antidote for the vidkid virus. For the children of the global village, and their progeny to come, TV watching will continue to be their most shared—and shaping—experience. Virtually all the experts, however, agree on one palliative for parents of all socioeconomic levels. Instead of using TV as an electronic baby-sitter, parents must try to involve themselves directly in their youngsters' viewing. By watching along with the kids at least occasionally, they can help them evaluate what they see—pointing out the inflated claims of a commercial, perhaps, or criticizing a gratuitously violent scene. "Parents don't have to regard TV as a person who can't be interrupted," says behavioral scientist Charles Corder-Bolz. "If they view one show a night with their kids, and make just one or two comments about it, they can have more impact than the whole program."

Reduced to the essentials, the question for parents no longer is, Do you know where your children are tonight? The question has become, What are they watching—and with whom?

ALL ABOUT KIDVID

In their less circumspect moments, the people who create, manufacture, and market weekend-morning children's shows refer to their audience as "mice." Last year, advertisers laid out more than $400 million for commercials ingeniously designed to lure those mice to the corporate cheese. And in return for delivering its most captive audience, the television industry reaped no less than 25 percent of its annual profit from children's video. Nowhere else on TV is the medium more the message, and the programming so much wrapping around the huckster's package. To watch kidvid is to be engulfed in a tide of sugary glop—Kit Kat chocolate bars, Starburst Fruit Chews, Charm's Blow Pops, Fruit Stripe gum, Moonstones, and Honeycombs. The look of kidvid is that of a mouth doomed to dental catastrophe.

What about the shows that interrupt the sales spiels? Reform is fleetingly visible. Those mindless cartoons now make up less than half of the kidvid schedule. And some of the newer shows, such as CBS's *Ark II* and *Fat Albert*, gently weave in benign messages: international brotherhood, the perils of smoking and drugs, and the joys of facing up to bullies. Of late, the networks' news departments have classed up the act. ABC's *Animals Animals Animals* is a sort of peewee *60 Minutes* with a zoological theme. CBS's periodic *In the News* introduces its audience to such adult concerns as environmental pollution and bankrupt school systems.

Spunky:

And then there is *Muggsy*. This NBC series about an orphaned teenage white girl adrift in an inner-city slum realistically deals with growth pains that afflict all races. In one episode, Muggsy straightened out a black youngster who was being mercilessly harassed by his supercool friends for joining the Boy Scouts. "Why you jivin' around with those honkies?" demanded one tormentor. Sensitively played by 13-year-old Sarah MacDonnell, who has more freckles than Sissy Spacek, Muggsy is spunky, vulnerable, and—unlike the polyethylene Disney clones who populate most of kidvid—altogether real.

Unfortunately, the rest of children's video has matured woefully little since the days when Howdy Doody flashed his bicuspids. NBC's *Big John, Little John* stereotypes parents as incorrigible klutzes, while the network's *Speed Buggy* is nothing but a weekly lesson in reckless driving. There are even kiddie game shows to install avarice early. On Metromedia's *Guess Your Best*, the audience of moppets screams in a *Let's*

Make a Deal frenzy as its panelist peers compete for AMF sports equipment and Panasonic tape recorders. "Kids are people, too . . . wackadoo, wackadoo," warbles the show's unctuous emcee.

The schlock depths, however, are reached by *The Krofft Supershow*. With a stupefyingly silly music group called Kaptain Kool and the Kongs acting as host, this one-hour ABC adventure series focuses on Dr. Shrinker, a mad scientist who reduces his victims to six-inch miniatures. The quality of the special effects would draw boos at a student film festival. The series also features two female magazine reporters who, when evildoers appear, transform themselves into Electra Woman and Dynagirl, outfitted in costumes apparently picked up at a Woolworth's post-Halloween sale. When last observed, the superheroines had been ensnared by Glitter Rock, an epicene Elton John type who sported a green Afro coiffure set off by a spangled body stocking. Perhaps this show's most heinous crime is that each episode costs nearly $200,000 to produce.

Lessons:

Relief, of course, can still be found on the public-TV channels. Non-commercial television's best new offerings are *Rebop*, which imparts lessons in interracial harmony, and *Infinity Factory*, aimed at inner-city adolescents who have trouble fathoming math. *Infinity Factory* is after an older audience than *Sesame Street* and it understands the turf. A jive-spouting disk jockey announces: "Let me tell you all about this weird dude—the number 36." A man-in-the-street survey to introduce the concept of six-digit figures asks adults and children how much money the President of the U.S. makes. "I dunno," shrugs a Harlem housewife, "but we sure ain't making none of it here."

No one is proposing that kid-vid should be nothing but a sixth day of school. The four-teen million youngsters who use it to unwind on weekends are just as entitled to their video Martinis as their elders. But they are also entitled to nourishment for their imaginations, even a brief message of their thought glands, and on those counts commercial children's programming flunks the test. If there is such a thing as the evil of banality, then it is seeping through the looking-glass with every Saturday's dawn. Even mice, after all, deserve an occasional change in diet. How about something truly wackadoo—or at least a spin-off of *Muggsy*?

24. THE COMMUNITY OF *ROOTS*
by Charlayne Hunter-Gault
and Thomas A. Johnson

That's the bad news, now for the good. At its best, television is an unbelievably powerful medium of instruction that provides a sense of community unmatched since the rise of cities. This happens rarely. Sports contests sometimes unify a city, but the nation as a whole only seems to come together in mourning. ABC's telecast of Alex Haley's *Roots* in January of 1977 was a unique experience. It doesn't matter how good a telefilm it was, it doesn't matter that it was scheduled in the dead of winter when most people are likely to be watching TV anyway, it doesn't matter that the competing networks didn't feel it necessary to counterprogram during the eight-day week of *Roots*, nor does it matter finally that Haley was later criticized for doing what everyone understood that he did; that is, fictionalize experiences. . . . None of this matters: the ratings records *Roots* set are a valid index of the degree to which the U.S.— black and white—was moved by a television show.

" 'ROOTS' GETTING A GRIP ON PEOPLE EVERYWHERE"

by Charlayne Hunter-Gault

The New York Times, January 28, 1977

"My children and I just sat there, crying," said a black public relations director in Nashville. "We couldn't talk. We just cried."

"It has made the brutality of slavery more vivid for me than anything I've seen or read," said a black economist in Philadelphia.

"It's so powerful," said a white secretary in New York. "It's so distressful, I just feel awful, but I'm glad my children are watching."

All across the country this week, millions of people have been drawn to the unfolding drama of *Roots*, the eight-part television adaptation of the book by Alex Haley, tracing his origins back to an African village. It has produced the largest audiences in television history.

Nearly eighty million people have sat before their television sets in penthouses and tenements, bars and brownstones, fraternity houses and dormitories, as the saga of Kunta Kinte had flashed before them night after night since last Sunday.

Doubters and enthusiasts, whites as well as blacks, young and old, wealthy and poor, had reactions they wanted to share.

Some laughed when a hungry Kunta Kinte, who was thought to have learned no English, suddenly thrust his plate toward the older slave, Fiddler, and said, "Grits, dummy."

Some cried as Kunta Kinte finally gave in to the whip's lash and accepted the slave name Toby.

And some got angry at the long, deep scars on his back in a later episode.

But however different their reactions might have been, people everywhere, even those who had not seen it, were talking about *Roots*.

Doubleday reports that sales of *Roots*, now in its 13th printing since publication in October, have soared even higher since the television serial went on the air. The best-selling book is Mr. Haley's narrative account of his twelve-year search for his origins—a search that started with stories of family members and a handful of African words, including the name Kinte.

The search ended in Gambia, a tiny state in West Africa, where, with the help of the *griot*—the oral historian—Mr. Haley went back in time to 1750, when Kunta Kinte, his ancestor, was born.

The story dovetailed with the one Mr. Haley had heard from his family.

The people of Gambia embraced "Meester Kinte" immediately, telling him, "Through our flesh, we are you, and you are us."

After a young black writer from the West Coast watched the first two-hour episode on Sunday, he shook his head and, referring respectively to the author of the book and the director of the television adaptation, said:

"Haley, yes. [David] Wolper no."

The production, he said, was "too Hollywood," lacking in both depth and truth to the original narrative.

After Monday night's showing, which included the scene where Kunta Kinte is whipped by the white overseer to force him to give up his African ancestral name and accept the slave name Toby, the writer, smiling, said to his host:

"Haley, yes. Wolper, maybe."

A black man carrying an attaché case stepped into the elevator of the predominantly white company where he worked.

"Good morning, Kunta Kinte," said a white colleague, cheerfully.

The black man lowered his head, smiled, and said, "Toby."

In one middle-class white Queens household there was a lively debate over coffee and bagels after the second installment.

"It doesn't show any good white people," said the wife. "There must have been some decent white people, and it should have been more balanced."

"No, the good whites had their day with *Gone With the Wind*, said the husband. "Anyhow, how good could any whites look to a slave? And that's whose eyes we're seeing it through. All the white bosses must have looked pretty bad, like Nazi Party members did to Jews."

"They were terrible," shouted the eighteen-year-old son. "Slavery was evil and this shows how bad it was, stealing those people from their homes and carrying them far away and buying and selling them."

A group of six young black men and women gathered at a counter as the short-order cook, her jaw set firmly, commented tersely about *Roots*.

"I had to cut the thing off about halfway through and go to bed," she said. "It was getting to me."

"I cried like a baby," said another of the women. "I just never thought it was so bad. I never thought they could treat you so bad."

"I tell you one thing," injected a somber young man in the group, "Those white folks better not mess with me today. I just might have to stomp one."

"Don't do that," another of the group snapped. "Things ain't changed that much. And jobs don't grow on trees."

It took a little while for the four- and five-year-olds in the kindergarten class at the Patterson School for Heritage and Education in Harlem to come alive, since most of them had stayed up way past their normal bed time to watch *Roots*.

"I was having a hard time getting my four-year-old up," said one young mother, "but, at one point I said, 'Okay, Mandinka warrior. Time to go hunting in the forest.' He smiled, opened his eyes and rolled out."

"It's just incredible," Mr. Haley, the author of *Roots*, said from O'Hare Airport in Chicago yesterday during a stopover between lectures. "ABC has preserved the integrity of the thing as best they could. And I think they've done a fantastic job.

"A young white boy told me yesterday in Texas that his father had always hated my people, but after seeing *Roots*, he said, 'I watched my father cry for the first time in his life.'

"A black man saw me in the airport, and for a long time didn't say anything. Finally, he turned to me and said, 'Look, man, I just can't be cool. I've just got to say thank you.'"

Jock's, a popular Harlem bar and restaurant with a TV has been jammed all week with patrons like Ronald Guy, a lawyer, who "wanted to watch it with other people around."

Joe Kirkpatrick, the owner, said that one night viewers got so angry over the treatment of Kunta Kinte that they would not allow the juke box to be turned on even after the show had ended.

Roots: *O. J. Simpson and Ren Woods are shown here as an African tribesman and his daughter, a powerful and very effective image of a race in history.*

"They just wanted to talk it out," he said, "and it wasn't until they had talked and talked for a very long time that they finally remembered they were in a bar.

"That's when they started drinking up."

John Henrik Clarke, the black historian, said there were some "cultural inaccuracies" in the television series, "but those are minor."

"Overall," he said, "I think it has opened up a delicate situation that will probably cause some embarrassment on both the black and white sides. But it has paved the way for a much needed, long overdue discussion."

" 'ROOTS' HAS WIDESPREAD AND INSPIRING INFLUENCE"

by Thomas A. Johnson

The New York Times, March 19, 1977

Kunta Kinte Reid, a 7-pound, 11-ounce baby boy, was born to John and Nefhertiti Reid in Harlem Hospital on February 18.

The child was named after the main character in *Roots*, the best-selling book in the eight-segment record-breaking television series, because "we want him to be somebody," his mother said.

"Like Kunta Kinte, he should be free, and he should be somebody and know that he is somebody," she said.

With the production of *Roots*, the show has attracted the largest audience in the history of the medium; now six weeks into history, the naming of children for its main characters has emerged as one of the most interesting aspects of this phenomenon.

Other offshoots of the interest spurred by *Roots* include significant increases in interest in travel to Africa, in the studies of Africa and slavery in the Western Hemisphere, and in genealogy.

The Reids, who have a railroad apartment at 117 West 138th Street in Central Harlem, have long shared an interest in Africa and have also had a "strong desire" to travel there. There is little possibility that they will be able to make the trip, however.

Mr. Reid, twenty-five years old, was last employed in 1974 as a laborer with the New York City Parks Department. He was laid off during a fiscal cutback and has "reported every other week to the employment office—there are never any jobs, so they stamp my book and send me home."

The baby was one of twenty newborn black boys and girls in New York City last month who were given the names Kunta Kinte or Kizzy. Kizzy was the name of Kunta Kinte's daughter.

Officials in the health departments of several cities reported that fifteen babies last month had been named Kunta Kinte or Kizzy in Los

Angeles, ten in Detroit, and eight in Atlanta. In Cleveland, male and female twins were named after the two characters.

Their welfare check covers the rent of about $150 a month and gives them a little more than $100 to feed themselves and their other two children, John Jr., three, and their daughter, Lashawn, two.

"Of course, we dream of Africa," said Mrs. Reid, who is eighteen, "but if I had any money at all, I would buy a carriage so I could get the children out more when John is looking for work—we could go to the park."

Mr. and Mrs. Reid, who both were born in Harlem and are high-school dropouts, agreed on the choice of the name, Kunta Kinte, during the television series.

"It is a name with some pride to it," Mr. Reid said, "because we're going to do all we can to make him be somebody."

"He's going to have an education," Mrs. Reid said, "and get out and do things. He's not going to hang out there on those streets—there's nothing out there on those streets."

Roots represented twelve years of research and writing by Alex Haley, who started with his grandmother's memories of Kunta Kinte, "the African." Working his way through old records in the United States and in England, Mr. Haley was able to trace the roots of this, his earliest ancestor in America, to a remote tribal village in Gambia, West Africa. It was near there that "the African" was taken captive at the age of sixteen and sent off to America on a slave ship.

The appearance of the book and the showing of the television series has had varied effects on people, interests, and industries.

"It has produced a virtual explosion of American interest in travel to Africa," said Charles Librader, who is based in New York as the marketing manager for Air Afrique, which is owned by ten French-speaking African nations, and is black Africa's most heavily traveled airline.

"I have been promoting travel to Africa for about eight years," he said, "and it has been a long, drawn-out effort. Now, suddenly, *Roots* hits the industry like a bomb, a very positive bomb."

Mr. Librader and officials of several travel agencies seeking to capitalize on the phenomenon said it was not yet possible to evaluate the interest "in dollars and cents" but that they were hoping for a literal boom in travel.

Jake Henderson, Jr., president of Henderson Travel Service in Atlanta, a pioneer black-owned agency that has specialized in trips to Africa for two decades, reported "a substantial increase in interest in trips to Africa."

The Henderson agency has inaugurated a special tour called "Roots" that begins in Senegal and touches on the small farming village of Juffure, in Gambia, the birthplace of Mr. Haley's ancestor, Kunta Kinte.

And officials of the Cleveland-based American Forum for International Study, a ten-year-old teacher-training organization that takes hundreds of educators to Africa on travel-study tours in the summer, reported that they have noted "an unprecedented increase of interest" on the part of teachers and the foundations that help sponsor the trips.

"Africa has become a real place in the minds of many Americans," one official said.

Roots was published by Doubleday, but another publishing company, Random House, has moved to take advantage of some of the economic fallout.

It has reissued *Generations*, its own popular 1973 book on the importance of family histories.

Random House has also published the book *Freedom to Freedom, African Roots in American Soil*, a book of "selected readings based on *Roots: The Saga of an American Family*." Mr. Haley wrote the forward to the Random House publication and served as a consultant on the project.

And another, thinner book, with the same title, but called "a student's guide," has also been published by Random House.

The new books, explained Barry Feteroff, the college department editor, are part of a joint venture between Random House Films and Miami Dade Junior College created to market a variety of books, tapes, films, and courses based on *Roots*.

Joe Morse, Random House's marketing manager for colleges, said *Roots* courses had been sold to 150 institutions and "the interest is burgeoning."

A survey of college and high school teachers has also shown an increase in the interest of the study of history and genealogy.

The much-studied Sea Islands off the coast of South Carolina and Georgia, which contain numerous elements of African languages, customs, and extended family patterns, are again being studied by groups and visited by curiosity-seekers, residents of the region have reported.

The islands were once famous for the production of fine-quality "sea island cotton," and they retained many African elements because they were cut off from the mainland and the black, former slaves spent several generations there.

The Sea Islands, in addition, were the landing sites for some of the last-known slave ships operating in the middle 1800s.

Scholars from Oakes College of the University of California at Santa Cruz, led by Dr. J. Herman Blake, the provost, are now in the Sea Islands conducting interviews with descendants of slaves taken to the region by the New York-based slaveship *The Wanderer*.

Shipping records show that this ship picked up about 750 Africans, who ranged in age from about thirteen to eighteen, from the region that is now Zaire in central Africa and sold the human cargo near Brunswick, Georgia, on December 1, 1858.

Although abetted financially by the popularity of the book and the television program, Dr. Blake's studies grew out of "the need for new information about the structure and organization of the black family at different historical periods and in different regions of the United States. We need new and better information," he said, "about values, attitudes, and social and economic conditions which have affected family development."

James Dyer, a program officer for the Carnegie Foundation, secured the financing for a variety of foundation-sponsored historical and genealogical studies after he heard Mr. Haley lecture on preparation of the book *Roots*.

Mr. Dyer secured a $12,000 grant for a "Family Heritage Program" at James Madison High School in Brooklyn, "a defusing mechanism" to combat the growing ethnic tensions that developed in the fall of 1975.

The program, in one of New York City's most ethnically mixed high schools, provided for twenty-five juniors and seniors to take tape recorders home to interview parents and grandparents about their ancestors and their places of origin. Reports on the students' findings were later made to parents and student groups.

"The enthusiasm on the part of the parents, grandparents, and students was incredible," said Ira Ewen, the principal of Madison. "The students not only developed close bonds with one another but they also became important participants in our student human-relations team.

"We want to repeat the program, it is one of my highest priorities, but we have run out of money and have not been able to get more money for it."

A number of educators are seeking such funds, including Allyn Field, a teacher who recently mounted a project to have his mostly low-income, ethnically mixed students in a Waltham, Massachusetts, high school trace their family histories and then publish the results.

The phenomenon has inspired new attempts to search out family backgrounds and has brought to light a number of older efforts, especially among blacks.

Among the newer searchers is twenty-four-year-old Harry B. Matthews, assistant dean of students at MacDuff Hall, the New York State University Campus at Oneonta. Discussions with family members and a review of documents has taken him back to the point where his forebears had been slaves in the late 1700s.

He wants to continue the search and said, "I have the energy, desire, and need to trace my ancestry before I become a father."

Barbara C. Clark, district manager for the American Express Company's travel division in Chicago, has been searching for her ancestral roots for years, and has traced her father's lineage into the early 1800s in the Louisville, Kentucky, area. Her mother's side was traced to their black and American Indian ancestors in the Tuscaloosa, Alabama, area in the late 1700s.

"One very interesting aspect of searching old archives," Mrs. Clark said, "is that blacks do not appear in many of them before the 1870s.

After that time, blacks are listed as if they materialized out of thin air."

Not everyone has been influenced so positively by *Roots*.

David Duke, national director of the Knights of the Ku Klux Klan, charged in a letter to the ABC-TV network that the program had been a "vicious malignment of the white majority in America and a serious distortion of the truth."

Mr. Duke asked for equal time on the network to respond.

The request was denied.

25. AUTHENTIC SOURCES AND THE MEDIA
by Virginia B. Platt

Roots may have succeeded as a television program in creating a sense of community and history as it never could have in print. Ironically, however, most of us don't have *griots* to hand down history orally. Despite the immeasurable value of the electronic media and film as anthropological tools, history still depends on writing. Historian Virginia B. Platt is a specialist in authentic sources. She discusses the problems the shift from writing to the electronic media has created for historians in this piece written especially for inclusion here.

I speak for the preservation of the written word.
"Hear me for my cause!"

The recent presentation of a televised version of Alex Haley's *Roots* and the profound impact it seems to have exerted on the way its millions of viewers perceive a portion of the American past raise a number of questions about source materials for programs for the present and especially for the future. Rarely will the person doing research on which to base a documentary or an entertainment be able to devote twelve years of persistent labor to the verification of the subject under study. Even more rare is the probability of finding in this country a series of family papers—journals, diaries, letters—such as that upon which *The Adams Family* was based. John and Abigail Adams established a tradition of respect for the written word that served the family well; John's long absences from home encouraged the practice of journal keeping and letter writing at the same time that he was in immediate contact with events of great significance to the future of America, as his descendants continued to be for generations; and the family has remained based in Quincy, Massachusetts, in a position to retain its great heritage. Such great collections are likely to become fewer as electronic methods of communication become more universal. I would like to make a plea not only for the continuation of the practice of journal and diary keeping but also for personal communication by letter.

When Alex Haley began his personal search, his initial information consisted of tales told to him in childhood by his maternal grandmother, a woman who possessed what Jervis Anderson refers to in *The New Yorker* as "an improbably long memory."* Following up the clues contained in her tales, he reached the tradition-bearing *griot* of the village of Juffure in Gambia, who made it clear that there once was such a man as Kunta Kinte and that he must have been Haley's ancestor. Official shipping and court records and early newspapers of Annapolis, Maryland, completed the authentication of the grandmother's tales. It seems that the adjective "improbably" should not precede "long" in describing her memory. Oral tradition has served an essential function for thousands of years in preserving the continuity and the values of folk history, as witness the millennium during which Vedic philosophy was transmitted orally by the priestly Brahmans of India. The Brahman, the *griot*, and the grandmother were serving essentially preliterate groups not only as transmitters of the folk memory but also as entertainers for people who had few other forms of entertainment and hence fewer distractions. In such circumstances, repetition, often in poetic form, and intense concentration on the part of the hearers, make retention of information almost inevitable.

It is when Haley leaves authentic tradition and official documents and has to depend on research in the general history of American slavery to flesh out his picture of the lives of the Kinte descendants that his book becomes what he calls "faction." This is, he says, a mixture of fact and fiction, a "novelized amalgam" rather resembling, to my mind, E. L. Doctorow's *Ragtime.* Had his ancestors been literate and had there been any opportunity for them to keep records, he would have been in a position to make his account of this later period much closer to actuality. Family dispersal could have been specifically documented, and the gradual decline in the relationship of master with slave during the antebellum period would have become apparent, as it does in the diaries and journals kept by the master class.

When *Roots* reached television, it did so, to paraphrase the words of the Man of La Mancha, in the form of an "entertainment": the dramatic and the violent were emphasized, and stereotypes frequently replaced individualized characters, notably in the case of the Southern white women. Yet what Nicholas Pronay calls "the illusion of actuality" was maintained, and a semi-fictionalized world that never actually existed became "reality" to millions of viewers, much as other millions of Americans accept another "world that never was," which is perpetuated as a set piece at Colonial Williamsburg.

Haley was fortunate in his search for his African origins. He garnered significant "clues" from his grandmother's oral recitations and he

* *The New Yorker*, Feb. 14, 1977, pp. 112–122.

searched in Africa at a time when men were still acting as *griots*. There are many indications, however, that the bearers of oral tradition are becoming less numerous; literacy long ago reduced the audience of the storyteller in the Western world; the transistor radio is spreading rapidly in countries still largely illiterate and is assuming the function of entertainer and informer for millions of people; and grandmothers themselves, in our fluid and less family-oriented society, lose their circles of receptive children as they take up residence in rest homes and in other ghettos for the aged.

In developed Western civilizations the function of the preliterate tradition-bearer was long ago superseded by written records as oral tradition declined. Conceivably, however, usable written records are today on the brink of a slide into similar obscurity. Increasingly we are told that "Johnny can't write," and more and more Johnny doesn't seem to need to do so. For years now, even the literate communicate with their families and their business associates more by telephone than by mail, and information is increasingly transmitted electronically. Literacy itself may be in an obsolescent stage. Truly private papers, so essential to a sensing of the quality of life at any given time, seem likely to dwindle almost to the vanishing point.

What, then, will be the sources available for the development of future programming along the line of *Roots*? More importantly, how will the conscientious researcher for such programs as *60 Minutes* and the Canadian *Soixante* go about preparing his analyses?

Conceivably, the tape recorder will provide man's memory bank. It may be possible to overcome the suspicion that what goes on tape will fall easy prey to the manipulator who erases easily and splices skillfully. There may be means of obtaining information through interviewing prominent persons that is not too structured by the nature of questions asked or too colored by the natural desire of the individual to appear intelligent, omniscient, and simon-pure. Assuming these givens, how then does the media researcher cope with the sheer mass—not to mention the basic dullness—of a corpus of the dimension of the Nixon tapes?

The uses of film are of course myriad in preserving a record of major—and minor—events. Its serious limitations are subjected to sophisticated analysis by William Hughes in an essay entitled "The Evaluation of Film as Evidence."* He mentions the plasticity of films, which makes possible their shaping and reshaping "to produce a variety of meanings," and he quotes a great Soviet director, V. I. Pudovkin, in the same vein: "This celluloid is entirely subject to the will of the director who edits it." (pp. 53–54). Questions of sponsorship, of censorship, of motive, immediately arise.

One can appreciate the contribution of live broadcasting of public

* Paul Smith, ed., *The Historian and Film*, Cambridge: The Cambridge University Press, 1976, pp. 49–79.

events to our knowledge of history while at the same time questioning the fundamental integrity of the finished product. Congressional hearings should be observed with the reservation in mind that the participants are men with political—hence oral—experience, themselves always aware of the camera as an "affecting presence" and of the audience as never to be forgotten. Occasionally, it is true, great emotional stress has resulted in unguarded remarks by hearings participants, notably in the course of the Army-McCarthy hearings. Attorney Joseph L. Welch, infuriated by a gratuitous attack on a young friend, mounted a counterattack: "Until this moment, Senator, I think I had never gauged your cruelty or your recklessness . . ." and, "Let us not assassinate this lad further, Senator. You've done enough. Have you no sense of decency, sir, at long last? Have you left no sense of decency?" Senator Stuart Symington in turn helped to dispel the miasma of fear created by McCarthy when, after being accused of cowardice, he burst out: "You said something about being afraid. I want you to know from the bottom of my heart that I am not afraid of anything about you or anything you've got to say any time, any place, anywhere." Of such is history made.

No claim can be made that the use of traditional written materials for the reconstruction of the past and the understanding of the present is without its limitations and, in fact, its pitfalls. Verification of government documents, of wills and inventories, of diplomatic correspondence, of journals, diaries, and letters has been a perennial occupation of scholars from the time of Herodotus. Centuries of effort have produced an expertise that affords considerable protection against the fraudulent, the sins of omission and commission, the excessive claims of possession of "inside information," and the personal foibles of prominent and not so prominent writers.

One great advantage of dealing with journals, diaries, and letters is that one is analyzing the activities and objectives of an identifiable individual, not those of nameless members of a film-editing team or of a group of careless or indifferent "word processors" at a computer center. Journals and diaries have the additional advantage of being of manageable size, although Nigel Nicolson reports that the diaries of Harold Nicolson and the letters between him and his wife ran to about twenty times the length of the three thick volumes of selections that have been published. Nicolson composed his diaries on the typewriter, a word-extender not available less than a century earlier, when journal writers were more limited by time factors in writing by hand.

The problem of authenticity is the first to be faced in using such personal papers. Defoe's *Journal of the Plague Year* is the classic example of the verisimilitude that can be achieved by a clever fabricator. A series of letters known as the Minor papers appeared in the *Atlantic Monthly* in 1928 and purported to have been written by Lincoln and some of his friends, including Ann Rutledge; Paul Angle, a distinguished Lincoln scholar, analyzed these letters with great care and concluded that they were forgeries.

Once authorship is confirmed, there must be analysis as to whether the materials have been altered, either by the original writer or by some well-intentioned or not-so-well-meaning person: Gideon Welles, Lincoln's Secretary of the Navy, revised his diary at least twice and became more perceptive in the process. The elisions from the Nicolson diary could, for example, alter the sense of some of the commentary, although Nicolson himself read and approved the version printed, and his son believes that almost nothing has been lost "by discretion."

A most important question that must be asked when proposing to use a diary or a group of letters is, of course, why they were written. The log or journal kept by a perceptive traveler or by a person domiciled in an area foreign to him has a certain authenticity insofar as it is intended as a kind of modern equivalent to the medieval "King's Remembrancer," to help the writer retain his impressions. Without the original journal, there could be no thoughtful and analytical study covering a long sojourn away from home such as Hedrick Smith's recent book *The Russians.*

Should the writer at any time speculate on the possibility of ultimate publication, the value of his diary or letters as evidence must inevitably decline. One cannot even assume that Leonardo da Vinci or William Byrd II wrote their diaries in personal shorthand to keep them forever private; one might suspect that Byrd hoped that the record of his peccadilloes would lighten the hours of some future reader. Harold Nicolson may not have anticipated the publication of his diary, but he stated that such a document should be written · "for one's greatgrandson. . . . One should have a remote, but not too remote, audience." Among men of the generation of our founding fathers, the wish for fame, current and posthumous, was very strong, and John Adams allowed his personal vanity to color his otherwise extremely valuable commentary on his times, as he assumed, quite correctly, that the papers of a president—himself—would be published.

The immediacy of daily recording of events and impressions makes diaries much more valuable than memoirs or autobiographies. The diarist, for example, can throw quick light on an unfamiliar way of life, as the Scottish "Lady of Quality," Janet Schaw, did when she reported her impressions of slave life in North Carolina as she saw it in 1775:*

> The Negroes are the only people that seem to pay any attention to the various uses that the wild vegetables may be put to. . . . The allowance for a Negro is a quart of Indian corn pr day, and a little piece of land which they cultivate much better than their Master. There they rear hogs and poultry, sow calabases, etc., and are better provided for in every thing than the poorer white

---

* Evangeline Walker Andrews, ed., in collaboration with Charles McLean Andrews, *Journal of a Lady of Quality* . . . New Haven: Yale University Press, 1927, pp. 176–177.

people with us. They steal whatever they can come at, and even intercept the cows and milk them. They are indeed the constant plague of their tyrants, whose severity or mildness is equally regarded by them in these Matters.

Albigence Waldo, Miss Schaw's contemporary, was all too familiar with the realities of existence at Valley Forge while he served as a surgeon in the Connecticut forces, and he transmitted them with remarkable effectiveness to the pages of his diary:

Dec. 21st 1777—Preparations made for hutts. Provision Scarce. Mr. Ellis went homeward—sent a Letter to my wife. Heartily wish myself at home—my Skin & eyes are almost spoil'd with continual smoke.

A general cry thro' the Camp this Evening among the Soldiers— "No Meat!—No Meat!"—the Distant vales Echo'd back the melancholly sound—"No Meat! No Meat!" Immitating the noise of Crows & Owls, also, made a part of the confused Musick.

What have you for our Dinners, Boys? "Nothing but Fire Cake & Water, Sir." At night—"Gentlemen the Supper is ready." What is your Supper, Lads? "Fire Cake & Water, Sir." Dec. 22d.—Lay excessive Cold & uncomfortable last Night—my eyes are started out from their Orbits like a Rabbit's eyes, occation'd by a great Cold—and Smoke.

What have you got for Breakfast, Lads? "Fire Cake & Water, Sir." The Lord send that our Commissary of Purchases may live on, Fire Cake & Water, 'till their glutted Guts are turned to Pasteboard.

A diarist does not necessarily always strive scrupulously for the truth. A classic diary of the Civil War period was kept by a South Carolinian, Mary Boykin Chesnut, and it has been edited by Ben Ames Williams under the title *A Diary from Dixie*. Williams calls Mrs. Chesnut a "chronicler of the contemporary," and she herself confessed, "I write current rumour. I do not vouch for anything." At the same time, she was able to reflect a society that was more sophisticated than has generally been assumed, and the recording of rumor has its uses, since people react to what they believe to be true rather than to an unknown truth. As much a part of the master class as anyone in the South, this intelligent, informed woman was as opposed to slavery as any black, though for different reasons. An entry of August 27, 1861, reads as follows:

I hate slavery. You say there are no more fallen women on a plantation than in London, in proportion to numbers; but what do you say to this: A magnate who runs a hideous black harem with its consequences under the same roof with his lovely white wife, and his beautiful and accomplished daughters? He holds his head as high and poses as the model of all human virtues to these poor women whom God and the laws have given him. From the height of his awful majesty, he scolds and thunders at them, as if he never did wrong in his life. Fancy such a man finding his daughter reading "Don Juan". "You with that immoral book!" And he orders her out of his sight. You see, Mrs. Stowe did not hit the sorest spot. She makes Legree a bachelor.*

Persons of political prominence have contributed hundreds of thumbnail sketches of the great. It is interesting to compare such a sketch of Franklin D. Roosevelt with another of Winston Churchill. Raymond Moley, one of the original "Brains Trust," described FDR in a letter written to his sister early in 1932, a year before Roosevelt became president:

When he wants something a lot he can be formidable—when crossed he is hard, stubborn, resourceful, relentless. . . . He seems quite naturally warm and friendly . . . because he just enjoys the pleasant and engaging role, as a charming woman does. . . . Broad, never really witty . . . and seldom even funny, but bold and cheerful. . . . The man's energy and vitality are astonishing. . . .

As I look back at what I have scribbled here I see I haven't conveyed any sense of his gallantry, his political sophistication, his lack of the offensive traits of men who have a bloated sense of personal destiny. But then I know you get that from the speech.†

Raymond Moley became alienated from the Roosevelt administration, whereas Harold Nicolson remained devoted to Churchill. Nicolson's diary entry of October 17, 1940, records the following:

I go to the smoking-room with Harry Crookshank and Charles Waterhouse. Winston is at the next table. He sits there sipping a glass of port and welcoming anyone who comes in. "How are you?" he calls gaily to the most obscure Member. It is not a pose. It is just that for a few moments he likes to get away from being Prime Minister and feel himself back in the smoking-room. His very presence gives us all gaiety and courage. People gather round his table completely unawed. They ask him questions. Robert Cary makes a long dissertation about how the public demand the unrestricted bombardment of Germany as reprisals for the raids on London. Winston takes a long sip at his port, gazing over the glass at Cary. "My dear sir," he says, "this is a military and not a civilian war. You and others may desire to kill women and children.

---

* Ben Ames Williams, ed., *A Diary from Dixie*, by Mary Boykin Chesnut, Boston: Houghton Mifflin, 1949; Sentry ed., pp. x, 122.

† Raymond Moley, *After Seven Years*, New York: Harper and Brothers, 1939, pp. 10–11.

We desire (and have succeeded in our desire) to destroy German military objectives. I quite appreciate your point. But my motto is 'Business before Pleasure' . . ." We all drift out of the room thinking, "That was a man!"*

Interestingly, Nigel Nicolson notes that Churchill wrote in *Their Finest Hour*, describing this period of the Blitz: "The abandonment by the Germans of all pretence of confining the air war to military objectives had raised this question of retaliation. I was for it, but I encountered many conscientious scruples." As Daniel Aaron has remarked, "every recollection is suspect."

One final example of the fascinating and diverse resources contained in diaries and letters appears in a holograph letter of August 4, 1863, written by Lieutenant John Bedingfield of Gordon's Georgia Brigade to his "Dear Ma," wife of a tenant farmer in southern Georgia. He describes the depression that has touched the Confederate Army of Northern Virginia in the wake of Gettysburg, and asks:

> Why continue longer against such fearful odds? What prospect is there for us, and what encouragement? Gen. Lee has a grand and gallant army, and I am proud to belong to it, and am willing to go wherever old Bob says go, but this army can not accomplish everything. I must confess that I find the spirits of the soldiers greatly depressed. Most of them were opposed to going over into Maryland, fearing that they would meet with another bloody reverse. They went over into the rich Cumberland valley of Pennsylvania, and Gordon's Brigade reached as far North as the Susquehannah River. There they saw the richest and most delightful country their eyes ever beheld. There they could procure every luxury their appetites could crave, generally for nothing and always for small price. . . . The men saw in fact that the war was in no way injuring the people of that country. They sow and reap and enjoy life the same as before the war, and in fact they live so much better than our people do in the best of times, that the men became discouraged, and could not but exclaim, "How is it possible for us to war against such a people?" . . . And then when the Army was repulsed and compelled to recross the Potomac, the spirits of the men were well nigh broken."†

Hundreds of letters such as this one have been printed in dozens of periodicals during the course of our national history. The Library of Congress and other great repositories, state and local historical societies, and private collections hold public and family papers that are now measured by the "linear foot." Amongst these, the most valuable

* Nigel Nicolson, ed., *Harold Nicolson: The War Years, 1939–1945*, New York: Atheneum, 1967, pp. 121–122.

† One of a group of manuscript letters in possession of V. B. Platt.

for purposes of obtaining a sense of a vibrant and often colorful past and an empathy for those who lived in earlier periods are journals, diaries, and personal letters. Hopefully the present generation and generations in the future will produce similar testaments and will see that they are preserved. Persons who are active in the media, engaged as they are in daily contact with events and persons of significance to all, seem to me to be in an unusually favored position to provide such records. Logs, methodically maintained, should be accompanied by daily summaries of events and of impressions of those events and persons with which the individual has had contact. These would be invaluable for the preparation of later media programs, both documentary and entertaining. Effective use of their journals and those of hundreds of other Americans should make possible a closer proximation to Ranke's ideal history; namely, that the past should be presented "as it actually was."

THE LAST WORD

26. POST-MODERNISM IS DEAD
by Donald Barthelme

Like most *New Yorker* writers, Donald Barthelme often contributes (anonymously) to the "Talk of the Town" section of that magazine, where this piece appeared originally. In the end, systems of analysis cease to be of prime interest, and our attention turns to an analysis of those systems (of analysis). This we might call "analography," which either means "writing about analysis" or "anal writing," one isn't quite sure.

In any event, it is a problem peculiar to media culture, and "Post-Modernism Is Dead" is the last word.

Letter to a literary critic:

Yes, you are absolutely right—Post-Modernism is dead. A stunning blow, but not entirely unanticipated. I am spreading the news as rapidly as possible, so that all of our friends who are in the Post-Modernist "bag" can get out of it before their cars are repossessed and the insurance companies tear up their policies. Sad to see Post-Modernism go (and so quickly!). I was fond of it. As fond, almost, as I was of its grave and noble predecessor, Modernism. But we cannot dwell in the done-for. The death of a movement is a natural part of life, as was understood so well by the partisans of Naturalism, which is dead. That was a great category, Naturalism (was it not you, my friend, who did the first Swedish translation of Zola's *Le Roman Expérimental*?).

I remember exactly where I was when I realized that Post-Modernism had bought it. I was in my study with a cup of tequila and William Y's new book, *One-Half*. Y's work is, we agree, good—*very* good. But who can make the leap to greatness while dragging behind him the burnt-out boxcars of a dead aesthetic? Perhaps we can find new employment for him. On the roads, for example. When the insight overtook me, I started to my feet, knocking over the tequila, and said aloud (although there was no one to hear), "What? Post-Modernism, too?"

So many, so many. I put Y's book away on a high shelf and turned to the contemplation of the death of Plainsong, 958 A.D.

By the way: Structuralism's tottering. I heard it from Gerald, who is at Johns Hopkins and thus in the thick of things. You don't have to tell everybody. Frequently, idle talk is enough to give a movement that last little "push" that topples it into its grave. I'm convinced that's what happened to the New Criticism. I'm persuaded that it was Gerald, whispering in the corridors. Don't tell him I said so.

On the bright side, one thing that is dead that I don't feel too bad about is Existentialism. Which I never thought was anything more than Phenomenology's bathwater anyway. It had a good run, but how peeving it was to hear all those artists going around talking about "the existential moment" and similar claptrap. Luckily, they have stopped doing that now. Similarly, the Nouveau Roman's passing did not disturb me overmuch. "Made dreariness into a religion," you said, quite correctly. I know this was one of your pared-to-the-bone movements and all that, but I didn't even like what they left out. A neat omission usually raises the hairs on the back of my neck. Not here. Robbe-Grillet's only true success, for my money, was with *Jealousy*, which I'm told he wrote in a fit of.

Well, where are we? Surrealism gone: got a little sweet toward the end, you could watch the wine of life turning into Gatorade. Sticky. *Hélas!* Altar Poems—those constructed in the shape of an altar for the greater honor and glory of God—have not been seen much lately: missing and presumed dead. The Anti-Novel is dead; I read it in the *Times*. The Anti-Hero and the Anti-Heroine had a thing going that resulted in three Anti-Children, all of them now at Dalton. The Novel of the Soil is dead, as are Expressionism, Impressionism, Futurism, Vorticism, Regionalism, Realism, the Kitchen Sink School of Drama, the Theatre of the Absurd, the Theatre of Cruelty, Black Humor, and Gongorism. You know all this; I'm just totting up. To be a Pre-Raphaelite in the present era is to be somewhat out of touch. And, of course, Concrete Poetry.

So we have a difficulty. What shall we call the New Thing, which I haven't encountered yet but which is bound to be out there somewhere? Post-Post-Modernism sounds, to me, a little lumpy. I've been toying with the Revolution of the Word II, or the New Revolution of the Word, but I'm afraid the Jolas estate may hold a copyright. It should have the word "new" in it somewhere. The New Newness? Or maybe the Post-New? It's a problem. I await your comments and suggestions. If we're going to slap a saddle on this rough beast, we've got to get moving.

THE DATA:
Who Owns the Media?

APPENDIX 1: THE SHAPE OF THE MEDIA INDUSTRY

TABLES

TABLE 1: MEDIA REVENUES

	1976 (\$billions)	Notes
Newspapers	11.2[1]	Subscriptions and single-copy sales: 22%, Advertising: 78%.
Books	4.6[2]	Publishers' revenues: \$3.8 billion, retail markup: \$0.8 billion.
Periodicals	4.6[1]	More than 60,000 periodicals of all kinds are listed in the Standard Periodical Directory. Of these, only 500 or so are considered commercial enterprises.
Total Print	20.4	The entire graphic arts market (including commercial printing, business forms, etc.) had revenues of more than twice this amount in 1976—\$42 billion.
Audio	2.74[3]	These figures represents potential "list"-price retail sales. Taking into account the widespread but unmeasurable practice of price cutting, most observers consider \$1.8 billion a more realistic gross. The wholesale gross for 1976 was approximately \$1.5 billion. Additionally, \$125 million was returned to authors and artists in the form of ASCAP and BMI performance royalties.
Recordings	1.908	
Discs	.829	
Tapes		
Radio	2.27[4] est.	Subscription radio revenues are minimal. This figure represents advertising sales entirely.
Television	7.58[3]	Broadcast total ad revenue: 6.533. Local figure includes only top 75 markets, but revenues from other markets are minimal.
Network	5.22[5]	
Local	1.313[5]	
Cable	0.9[6]	
Export	0.15[7]	

	1976 ($billions)	Notes
Video Recordings	—	Minimal in 1976. The videotape industry had just entered the hardware stage (35,000 Betamax recorders were sold). The videodisc industry was still in development stage.
Film Domestic Export	2.96 est. 2.36[8] 0.6[7] est.	The domestic box office gross includes entertainment taxes. Distributors receive, in general, less than half of this money. Approximately 47% of distributors' gross sales are export.
Legitimate Theater	0.071[7]	This figure does not include more general performance-entertainment, which is a far larger industry. Campus entertainment grosses (including music performances) for 1976 were $500 million[9] while state and county fairs grosses were $50 million, for example. A safe estimate would be more than $2 billion for the entire performance industry, including music performance, ballet, concerts, Las Vegas, night clubs, campus entertainment, fairs, etc.
Total Audiovisual	15.624	This figure, of course, does not include hardware revenues. The production and sale of audiovisual equipment is a major industry itself. Whereas no equipment is necessary to use print media, the investment by consumers in audiovisual equipment is significant, and should be recognized in judging the total financial commitment of the society to nonprint media.
TOTAL MEDIA	36.024[10]	
Advertising and Promotion	33.420[10]	Approximately 65% of this money—$21 billion—is fed into communications media. The remainder goes to pure advertising media, such as direct mail, and production and talent.

Sources: [1] U.S. Census Bureau. [2] *Publishers Weekly.* [3] Recording Industry Association of America. [4] Radio Advertising Bureau. [5] BAR Reports. [6] National Cable Television Association. [7] *Variety.* [8] Motion Picture Producers' Association of America. [9] National Entertainment Conference. [10] McCann-Erickson advertising survey.

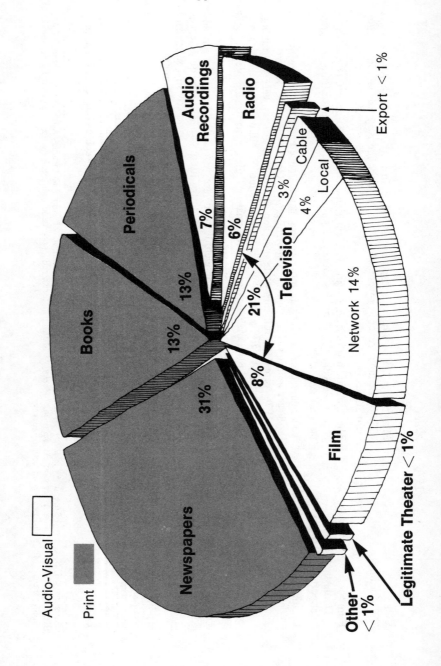

TABLE III: ADVERTISING BREAKDOWN

1976	%	$billion
Newspapers	30.0	10.022
Periodicals	5.3	1.775
Television	19.7	6.575
Radio	6.7	2.228
Direct Mail	14.1	4.725
Business Publications	3.0	1.020
Outdoor	1.2	.388
Farm journals	0.3	.085
Other	19.8	6.602
Total National Advertising Budget		33.420

NOTE: These figures include production and talent, as well as ad time and space.
SOURCE: McCann-Erickson survey.

TABLE IV: FILM INDUSTRY BREAKDOWN

Company	1976 Rank	1976 Share	1975 Rank	1975 Share
Warner Bros.	1	18.0%	6	9.1%
United Artists	2	16.2%	5	10.7%
20th Century-Fox	3	13.4%	2	14.0%
Universal	4	13.0%	1	25.1%
Paramount	5	9.6%	4	11.3%
Columbia	6	8.3%	3	13.1%
Buena Vista	7	6.7%	7	6.0%
AIP	8	3.8%	8	3.4%
Independents		11.0%		7.3%

These figures reflect domestic rentals only. They do not include export sales, nor do they take into account actual box-office grosses. The ranks of the six majors vary from year to year (Universal's precedent-setting showing in 1975 was due mainly to *Jaws*), but they consistently control 80% of the domestic market. Of the six, Warner's has had the most consistent showing, ranking either first or second in four of the last six years.

Film exhibition is considerably less centralized, although chains such as ABC-Paramount own a significant number of the nation's 15,000 theaters.

Film production is more complicated to analyze. Although production facilities are now widely available to anyone who cares to use them, and although a significant number of films are now produced more or less independently of the studios (and then acquired for distribution by them), the six major distributing organizations still exert powerful control over the product that reaches the screens. In order to finance a theatrical feature, it is usually necessary to have either the commitment in advance of one of the studios or personnel (star, director, producer, writer) who are trusted by studio executives.

SOURCE: *Variety.*

TABLE V: BOOK INDUSTRY BREAKDOWN

1976

Type	Revenue (in millions)	Units	Unit Cost	% of Total Revenue	Market Units	Revenue Rate of Growth %/yr.
Trade	$867	201	$4.30	18.7	15.9	5.1
Religious	277	75	3.68	6.0	5.9	11.3
Professional	568	85	6.59	12.2	6.7	12.5
Book Clubs*	329	104	3.15	7.0	8.2	11.2
Mail Order	358	31	11.61	7.7	2.5	24.6
Mass Market Paperback	661	442	1.50	14.3	35.0	16.6
University Presses	60	8	7.40	1.3	0.6	9.7
Elementary/Secondary Text	616	234	2.64	13.3	18.5	—0.6
College Text	623	83	7.47	13.4	6.6	7.6
Subscription Reference	279	1	253.73	6.0	0.1	11.4
Total	$4638	1264	$3.67	100.0	100.0	9.6

Paperback books continue to gain on hardcover books. Their share of market revenue increased 3.4% in 1976. Paperbacks now account for 73% of all books sold in the U.S., although hardcover books still bring in 60% of all revenues due to their higher price. The average hardcover trade book price in 1976 was $7.46, the average paperback trade book approximately $2.90.

* Ten companies accounted for 89% of all book club sales in 1976.

Appendix 1

Channels of Domestic Book Distribution

	1976 Revenue (in millions)	Units	% of Market Revenue	Units	% Increase over 1975 (Revenue)
General Retailers	$1351	484	29.1	38.3	14.0
College Stores	855	184	18.4	14.6	7.4
Libraries, Institutions	410	77	8.8	6.1	6.9
Schools	801	299	17.3	23.7	1.9
Direct to Consumer	1157	185	25.0	14.6	15.7
Other	64	35	1.4	2.8	−23.3
Total	$4638	1264	100.0	100.0	9.6

There are approximately 10,000 retail bookstores in the U.S. "Direct to Consumer" includes publisher and book club sales to individuals as well as to industry and government. "Other" includes mainly special and "remainder" sales. An average of 30,000 new titles are published each year in the U.S., together with 10,000 new editions of older titles.

SOURCE: *Publishers Weekly.*

TABLE VI: BROADCASTING INDUSTRY BREAKDOWN

25 Largest U.S. Corporations with Station Ownership
(ranked by 1975 sales)

Rank	Company	Total Sales ($billions)	Stations: Radio	TV	Principal Industry
1	Westinghouse Electric	5.86	7	5	electrical equipment
2	RCA Corp.	4.79	8	5*	electronics
3	CBS, Inc.	1.94	14	5	broadcasting
4	General Tire & Rubber	1.75	17	4	rubber, plastics, chemicals
5	American Broadcasting Co.	1.06	12	5	broadcasting
6	Kaiser Industries Corp.	1.02	—	5	engineering, steel
7	Times-Mirror Co.	.80	—	1	publishing
8	Schering-Plough Corp.	.79	12	—	pharmaceuticals
9	Avco Corp.	.65	7	5	mixed
10	Knight-Ridder Newspapers, Inc.	.59	8	1	newspapers
11	Fuqua Industries, Inc.	.54	2	3	broadcasting
12	McGraw-Hill, Inc.	.54	—	3	publishing
13	New York Times Co.	.41	2	1	publishing
14	Gannett Co.	.36	2	1	newspapers
15	20th Century-Fox Film Corp.	.34	—	2	film
16	Columbia Pictures Industries	.33	5	4	film
17	Washington Post Co.	.31	2	4	publishing
18	Fairchild Industries, Inc.	.22	1	—	aircraft
19	Metromedia, Inc.	.21	12	6	broadcasting
20	Wometco Enterprises, Inc.	.18	1	3	broadcasting
21	Capital Cities Communications	.17	13	6	broadcasting
22	Media General, Inc.	.17	2	1	broadcasting
23	Meredith Corp.	.16	6	5	various
24	Cox Broadcasting Corp.	.11	7	4	broadcasting
25	Storer Broadcasting Co.	.11	6	7	broadcasting

* Individual companies are limited by law to ownership of five local television stations. Ownership is now in flux and these figures may change as a result, owing to recent court decisions regarding "cross-ownership" of broadcasting stations by newspapers. The companies listed are publicly owned, only. Total Sales includes all enterprises, of which broadcasting is only a minor part (even for RCA, CBS, and ABC).

Sources: *Fortune* and *Madison Avenue* magazines.

TABLE VI:
BROADCASTING INDUSTRY BREAKDOWN (cont'd)

Network Station Affiliation

Networks	Radio	Television
ABC	1504	182
CBS	260	200
NBC	225	215
Mutual	—	—
PBS	—	265
NPR	181	—

NOTE: These figures subject to change as ABC acquires additional television affiliates.

U.S. Broadcasting as of July 1, 1974

	On Air	Authorized by FCC
AM	4409	4467
FM	2547	2713
Educational FM	684	764
UHF TV (commercial)	192	239
VHF TV (commercial)	514	520
UHF TV (educational)	143	150
VHF TV (educational)	91	96

Television Station Group Ownership in the U.S.

Rank		Stations	Homes
1	CBS o&o*	5†	15,077,600
2	NBC o&o	5	14,493,800
3	ABC o&o	5	14,452,900
4	Metromedia	6 (inc. 1 UHF)	11,655,000
5	RKO-General	4	8,723,200
6	Westinghouse	5	8,550,600
7	WGN-Continental	4	7,349,200
8	Kaiser	7 (inc. 2 UHF)	6,217,600
9	Capital Cities	6 (inc. 1 UHF)	5,098,700
10	Storer	7 (inc. 2 UHF)	5,016,600

* "o&o"—owned and operated.
† Limited by law to 5 VHF and 2 UHF.
SOURCE: Herbert H. Howard, "The Contemporary Status of Television Group Ownership," *Journalism Quarterly*, Autumn 1976.

TABLE VII: RECORDING INDUSTRY BREAKDOWN

Total Industry Gross Dollar Volume: 1976

	($ billions)	*($ billions)*
LPs	1.663	
Singles	.245	
Total Disc Sales		1.908
8-track	.678	
Cassettes	.146	
Quad (8-track and reel-to-reel)	.005	
Total Prerecorded Tape Sales		.829
Total Gross Dollar Volume		2.737

Increase over 1975 Sales: 17%

SOURCE: RIAA.
NOTE: These figures are based on retailer list prices. The widespread but unmeasurable practice of price cutting must be taken into account in arriving at a real figure. Most observers consider $1.8 billion to be a more realistic total gross dollar volume. The wholesale gross for 1976 was approximately $1.5 billion. The remainder represents retail markup, real or imagined.

Estimated International Sales	.350

SOURCE: CBS Records International.

Most figures for revenue and income from sales of recordings are masked in the annual reports of the major media conglomerates, and industry groups have no hard figures on the division of the marketplace among the leading companies.

Even though the statistics are "soft," however, it is clear that the recording industry is effectively dominated by two conglomerates. Measuring stated revenues against RIAA net dollar volume, for example, CBS, Inc. appears to control 37.6% of the 1976 market, while Warner Communications, Inc. controls 27.0%. These are undoubtedly the two leading recording conglomerates with a total share of the market approaching, perhaps, 65%. But other media giants have significant slices of the market as well. Again, measuring stated revenues against adjusted wholesale dollar volume: American Broadcasting Companies, Inc. has a 12.5% share; MCA, Inc. a 7.5% share; and RCA Corp., although its figures are buried in the category of "Consumer Products and Services," probably at least a 10% share. A little arithmetic shows that, even taking inflated revenue figures into account, there is little room for competition against these five giants.

Channels of Recording Distribution

Outlet	Percentage of Total Sales
Department and Discount Stores	67.7
Retail	15.6
Drugstores	7.4
Variety Stores	5.2
Service PXs	2.2
Supermarkets	0.8
Miscellaneous (book, electronic, automotive stores, etc.)	1.1

SOURCE: NARM (National Association of Recording Merchandisers).

TABLE VII:
RECORDING INDUSTRY BREAKDOWN (cont'd)

Market Taste Analysis

Type	Percentage of Total Sales
Contemporary (rock, soul, etc.)	62.0
Country	12.1
Middle-of-the-Road	10.5
Jazz	5.3
Classical	3.4
Children's	3.2
Comedy	1.5
Miscellaneous (spoken word, ethnic, language, etc.)	2.0

SOURCE: NARM.

TABLE VIII: RANKING FILMS

Rank	Film	Director	Distributor	Distributor's Gross*
1	Star Wars	Lucas	20th C.-Fox	127,000,000
2	Jaws	Spielberg	Universal	121,356,000
3	The Godfather	Coppola	Paramount	86,112,947
4	The Exorcist	Friedkin	Warner Bros.	82,200,000
5	The Sound of Music	Wise	20th C.-Fox	78,662,000
6	The Sting	Hill	Universal	78,090,000
7	Gone With the Wind	Fleming	MGM-UA	76,700,000
8	One Flew Over the Cuckoo's Nest	Forman	UA	58,300,000
9	Rocky	Avildsen	UA	54,000,000
10	Love Story	Hiller	Paramount	50,000,000
11	Towering Inferno	Guillermin	20th C.-Fox	50,000,000
12	The Graduate	Nichols	Avco-Embassy	49,078,000
13	American Graffiti	Lucas	Universal	47,308,000
14	Doctor Zhivago	Lean	MGM-UA	46,550,000
15	Butch Cassidy and the Sundance Kid	Hill	20th C.-Fox	46,039,000
16	Airport	Seaton	Universal	45,300,000
17	The Ten Commandments	DeMille	Paramout	43,000,000
18	Mary Poppins	Stevenson	Buena Vista	42,250,000
19	The Poseidon Adventure	Neame	20th C.-Fox	42,000,000
20	Smokey and the Bandit	Needham	Universal	39,744,000
21	A Star Is Born	Pierson	Warner Bros.	37,100,000
22	MASH	Altman	20th C.-Fox	36,720,000
23	Ben-Hur	Wyler	MGM-UA	36,650,000
24	Earthquake	Robson	Universal	36,094,000
25	King Kong	Guillermin	Paramount	35,851,283

SOURCE: *Variety.*
* As of December 31, 1977. Distributor's Gross includes total rental received from U.S. and Canada markets only. Foreign sales often match or exceed this figure. Box-office receipts are often twice the distributor's gross (the remainder goes to the exhibitor).

TABLE IX: RANKING TELEVISION SHOWS

Rank	Program Date	Network	Household Audience
1	Roots (January 30, 1977)	ABC	36,380,000
2	Gone With the Wind Pt. 1	NBC	33,960,000
3	Gone With the Wind Pt. 2	NBC	33,750,000
4	Roots (January 28, 1977)	ABC	32,680,000
5	Roots (January 27, 1977)	ABC	32,540,000
6	Roots (January 25, 1977)	ABC	31,900,000
7	Super Bowl XI (1977)	ABC	31,610,000
8	Roots (January 24, 1977)	ABC	31,400,000
9	Roots (January 26, 1977)	ABC	31,190,000
10	Roots (January 29, 1977)	ABC	30,120,000
11	Super Bowl X (1976)	ABC	29,440,000
12	Super Bowl IX (1975)	ABC	29,040,000
13	Roots (January 23, 1977)	ABC	28,840,000
14	Airport (November 11, 1973)	ABC	28,000,000
15	Super Bowl VII (1973)	ABC	27,670,000
16	World Series Game 7 (1975)	ABC	27,560,000
17	Super Bowl VIII (1974)	ABC	27,540,000
18	Super Bowl VI (1972)	ABC	27,450,000
19	Love Story (October 1, 1972)	ABC	27,410,000
20	All in the Family (January 5, 1976)	CBS	27,350,000

SOURCE: National Nielsen Audience Estimates through February 1, 1977.

NOTE: Household Audience estimates do not measure number of viewers, only number of sets tuned in. *Roots*'s domination of the rankings is all the more remarkable when one realizes that, beside the one *All in the Family* episode listed, it is the only television show in the top twenty that is not either a sports broadcast or a previously popular film.

TABLE X: "ALL THE NEWS THAT'S FIT TO PRINT"

The New York Times *News and Advertisements, Daily Paper*
Wednesday, April 20, 1977

	Pages	Percentage of Total Space	Percentage of Total Non-ad Material
COPY			
News	*11.23*	*12.2*	*31.6*
National	3.38	3.7	9.5
Local	2.02	2.2	5.7
International	1.62	1.8	4.6
Science/ Environment	0.30	0.3	0.8
Crime/ Disaster	0.54	0.6	1.5
Financial/ Business	3.37	3.7	9.5
Feature	*11.72*	*12.7*	*32.9*
Arts	2.76	3.0	7.6
Sports	2.80	3.0	7.9
Gossip	1.13	1.2	3.2
"Living"	3.20	3.5	9.0
Op/Ed	1.83	2.0	5.1
Financial Listings	*5.00*	*5.4*	*14.0*
Pictures	*4.56*	*5.0*	*12.8*
Advertising	*56.40*	*61.3*	
Display	43.98	47.8	
Classified	12.72	13.8	
Design Space	*3.09*	*3.4*	*8.7*
Totals	92.0	100.0	100.0

The New York Times *News and Advertisements, Sunday Paper*
Sunday, April 24, 1977

	Pages	Percentage of Total Space	Percentage of Total Non-ad Material
COPY			
News		*17.60*	*4.2*	*16.7*
National	4.18	1.0	4.0
Local	3.21	0.8	3.0
International	3.49	0.8	3.3
Science/Environmental	0.79	0.2	0.8
Crime/ Disaster	0.33	0.1	0.3
Financial/ Business	5.6	1.3	5.3
Feature		*28.87*	*6.9*	*27.4*
Arts	10.85	2.6	10.3
Sports	6.98	1.7	6.6
Gossip	2.23	0.5	2.1
"Living"	7.17	1.7	6.8
Op/Ed	1.64	0.4	1.6
Financial Listings		*5.67*	*1.4*	*5.4*
Pictures		*13.10*	*3.1*	*12.4*
Supplementary Features		*24.53*	*5.8*	*23.3*
Magazine	15.30*	3.6	14.5
Book Review	9.23*	2.2	8.8
Advertising		*314.59*	*74.9*	
Display	171.05	40.7	
Classified	70.15	16.7	
Free-standing Inserts	13.71*	3.3	
Magazine	45.46*	10.8	
Book Review	14.22*	3.4	
Design Space		*15.64*	*3.7*	*14.8*
Total	420.0*	100.0	100.0

* Magazine, Book Review, and Free-standing advertising inserts are odd sizes. Columns and pages have been adjusted to be equivalent to standard page size (126

TABLE XI: THE TEN LARGEST NEWSPAPER CHAINS

Rank	Chain	Total Daily Circ.	No. of Dailies	Total Sunday Circ.	No. of Sundays	1976 Revenues ($millions)
1	Newhouse (Booth)	3,695,699	30	3,823,312	22	1,080.4
2	Knight-Ridder	3,642,213	32	4,209,954	22	682.3
3	Chicago Tribune	3,047,450	7	4,269,174	5	839.4
4	Gannett (Speidel)	2,227,327	54	1,655,890	29	412.2*
5	Scripps-Howard	1,837,839	17	1,517,594	7	350.0
6	Dow-Jones	1,782,257	14	259,430	6	273.6
7	Times-Mirror	1,749,870	4	2,068,320	4	964.3
8	Hearst	1,435,527	8	2,241,432	7	472.8
9	Cox Enterprises	1,111,742	14	1,094,693	9	190.5
10	New York Times	972,452	10	1,551,253	6	462.1
	Totals	21,502,376	190	22,691,052	117	5,727.6

SOURCE: H. L. Masters, *MORE* magazine. As of early 1977.
* This revenue figure does not include the recently acquired Speidel chain.

column-inches). The *Times* is particularly low on Crime/Disaster coverage, compared with the average American newspaper, and concurrently stronger than most on national and international coverage.

In the newspaper business, the number of column-inches of news and feature material that can be printed in any single issue is called the "news hole" and is directly determined by the amount of advertising linage sold. The *Times* news hole for the Wednesday issue analyzed (28.7%) seems unusually large. A normal ratio would be 25% news to 75% advertising. Many papers run even higher.

Arts coverage is unusually extensive, but it should be noted that much of the arts reporting runs to personality interviews, which might just as easily be included in the Gossip category. The "Living" category also spreads over into Gossip, and includes such staples of feature copy as recipes, restaurant reviews, and how-to articles. Although the daily issue analyzed happened to include the weekly special "Living" section (others are Sports, Home, and Weekend), the ratio of the feature materials is not much changed from day to day.

TABLE XII: THE CABLE TELEVISION INDUSTRY

The Ten Largest Cable Operators

Rank		Subscribers
1	Teleprompter Corp.	1,070,000
2	Tele-Communications, Inc.	551,661
3	Warner Cable Corp.	550,000
4	American TV & Communications Corp.	550,000
5	Cox Cable Communications, Inc.	413,000
6	Viacom International, Inc.	303,814
7	Sammons Communications, Inc.	286,956
8	Communications Properties, Inc.	255,165
9	UA-Columbia Cablevision, Inc.	203,395
10	United Cable TV Corp.	188,699
	Total	4,372,690

Total Cable Homes Served: 11,900,000
Top Ten Percentage of Market: 37%
Number of Cable Systems in U.S.: approx. 3,700
Number of Communities Served: 8,000
Penetration (ratio of homes served to homes passed): 65%
Saturation (ratio of cable subscribers to total TV homes): 16.8%
Total Capital Investment: approx. $1 billion.

Five Largest Cable Systems

Rank		Subscribers
1	San Diego, CA (Mission Cable TV, Inc.)	116,012
2	New York, NY (Manhattan Cable TV, Inc.)	83,000*
3	Los Angeles, CA (Theta Cable of California)	78,899
4	Oyster Bay, NY	65,000
5	Suffolk County, NY	64,749

SOURCES: *TV Factbook, TV Digest*, National Cable Television Association. As of Autumn 1976.
* Manhattan is served by two cable franchises; the second, Teleprompter, has 50,566 subscribers for a total of 133,566.

TABLE XIII: BOOK INDUSTRY CONGLOMERATES

The Major Book Publishing Groups*
(in alphabetical order)

There have been more than 300 major mergers and acquisitions in recent years. Here are some major ones:

CBS, Inc. owns Holt, Rinehart and Winston (a major textbook house); Popular Library (paperbacks) and Fawcett Publications, Inc. (major paperback and magazine publisher, privately owned until its sale); BFA Educational Media; W. B. Saunders Co.; Winston Press; NEISA. Holt, Rinehart and Winston acquired Praeger Publishers (trade) in 1977.

Doubleday & Co. owns Dell (major mass-market paperback house), which owns Delta (trade paperbacks), Delacorte (hardcover), and The Dial Press.

Elsevier, N.V., is basically a Dutch company which owns sixty-four different companies involved in book publication, distribution, and retail sales, and magazine publication and distribution. The company is divided into four major groups (General, Scientific, Journals, Miscellaneous) and operates in ten countries. Elsevier is also involved in printing. Elsevier, N.V., owns Sequoia-Elsevier, N.V., which owns the American publisher E. P. Dutton & Co., as well as reference book and distribution divisions.

Englehard-Hanovia, Inc. bought American Heritage from McGraw-Hill, Inc. in 1976.

"Fiat." Gianni Agnelli owns Institorio Finanziale Internazionale, which owns 49% of Bantam, a major mass-market house, which did $70 million in sales in 1976. In 1977, IFI sold 51% of Bantam to Bertelsmann Publishing Group, a German company.

Filmways owns Grosset & Dunlap, which owns Ace.

Gulf + Western Industries, Inc. owns Simon & Schuster, Pocket Books, Monarch Books, Washington Square Press, Globe Books, magazines, 25.5% of Esquire, Inc. (but not *Esquire* magazine), and paper mills.

Harcourt Brace Jovanovich, Inc. owns Pyramid (Jove), Academic Press, and Harvest, and publishes many magazines, including the Modern Medicine Group, recently acquired from NYT.

Harper & Row owns Thomas Y. Crowell (acquired in 1977 from Dun & Bradstreet), and Barnes & Noble (bookstore operators as well as publishers) and Lippincott. Crowell owns Abelard-Schuman and Funk & Wagnalls.

* As of January 1, 1978.

Hearst Corporation owns Avon (mass-market) and Hearst Books, as well as magazines and newspapers.

ITT owns Howard W. Sams Co., which owns Bobbs-Merrill Co., Theodore Audel and Co., and other minor publishers.

Litton Industries owns Litton Educational Publications Inc., which owns the American Book Co. and Van Nostrand-Reinhold, as well as smaller companies.

Macmillan, Inc. owns Collier Books, Free Press, Hagstrom Map Co., Berlitz, Brentano's (book and artifact stores), G. Schirmer (music publishers and retail sales), and others.

McGraw-Hill Inc. owns Standard & Poor's corp.

MCA, Inc. owns G. P. Putnam's Sons, Coward, McCann & Geoghegan, and Berkley (mass-market paperbacks).

New York Times Co. owns Arno Press, Information Bank, Cambridge Book Co., Quadrangle, as well as Education and Information Services.

Penguin Books (an English corporation) owns Viking Press, which owns Grossman Publishers.

Prentice-Hall, Inc. (major textbook house) owns Appleton-Century-Crofts (a not-quite-so-major textbook firm), Parker Publishers, Goodyear Publishers, Responsive Environments Corp., and other minor interests.

RCA Corp. owns Random House (major trade firm) and Ballantine Books (medium-size mass-market paperback house). Random House owns Pantheon and Alfred A. Knopf (two highly respected trade houses), Vintage, and Modern Library.

Time Inc. owns Time-Life Books, Inc., Little, Brown & Co., New York Graphic Society Ltd., Book-of-the-Month Club, and Talent Associates, Ltd.

Times-Mirror Corporation owns New American Library (major mass market house), New English Library, Matthew Bender, Harry N. Abrams, magazines, newspapers, and distribution companies.

Warner Communications, Inc. owns Warner Books (formerly Paperback Library) and is involved in magazine production and distribution.

Xerox Education Group owns R. R. Bowker, Xerox Learning Systems, Ginn and Co. (textbooks), Xerox Educational Publishers, Xerox Family Educational Services, Unipub, and University Microfilms.

Minor connections: Cox Broadcasting Corp. owns Amphoto Publishers. Farrar, Straus & Giroux owns Hill & Wang. Capital Cities Communications owns Fairchild Publications (*Women's Wear Daily*).

Seven paperback publishers now control the bulk of mass market publishing. All are part of larger corporations.

APPENDIX 2: WHO OWNS WHAT?

THE MAJOR MEDIA CONGLOMERATES

	1976 Net Sales ($ billion)	Increase Over 1975
American Broadcasting Companies, Inc.	1.342	26%
CBS, Inc.	2.231	15%
Columbia Pictures Industries, Inc.	.332*	2%
Gulf + Western Industries, Inc.	3.396	30%
MCA, Inc.	.803	−1% †
New York Times Company	.446	14%
RCA Corp.	5.364	11%
Time, Incorporated	1.038	14%
Times-Mirror Company	.976	21%
Transamerica, Inc.	2.730	14%
Twentieth Century-Fox Film Corporation	.355	4%
Warner Communications, Inc.	.827	23%
Total	19.840	Mean 14%

NOTE: These are not necessarily the most profitable media companies, nor the ones with the highest revenues. They were chosen because they seem the dozen organizations that exert most control over American media. Several—Gulf + Western, Transamerica, for example—derive much of their income from non-media activities. Among them, these twelve companies control all television networks, all major film distributors, most major recording labels, and a good percentage—although possibly not the major part—of the book-publishing industry. They also control two of the three most powerful newspapers in the country and a smattering of magazines. Although Gulf + Western and RCA have larger revenues, CBS and WCI are better diversified over the whole spectrum of media and should therefore be considered the most powerful of the twelve.

Net sales include income from all operations, not just media.

* CPI's fiscal year ended June 26, 1976.

† MCA's revenues for the preceding year were artificially inflated by the enormous success of *Jaws*. Therefore, this apparent loss is misleading. 1976 revenues were 30% greater than 1974 revenues.

American Broadcasting Companies, Inc.

Revenues	1976	Percentage
Broadcasting	1,019,162,000	75.9
Theaters	63,258,000	4.7
Records	187,584,000	14.0
Motion Pictures	5,084,000	0.4
Publishing	31,178,000	2.3
Scenic Attractions and Other	35,915,000	2.7
Total	1,342,181,000	

OWNERSHIP AND SUBSIDIARIES

Broadcasting: ABC Television (ABC Television Network, ABC Owned Television Stations, ABC Entertainment, ABC Sports, ABC News, ABC Broadcast Operations and Engineering); ABC Radio (ABC Radio Network, 1500-plus stations; ABC Owned AM Radio Stations, ABC Owned FM Radio Stations; ABC Spot Radio Sales; American Contemporary Radio Network, 377 stations; American Information Radio Network, 496 stations; American Entertainment Radio Network, 431 stations; American FM Radio Network, 192 stations; 7 o&o ["owned and operated"] AM and 7 FM stations).
Records: ABC Records; ABC Record and Tape Sales; Word, Inc. (religious books and records). Mid-State Distributing Company (CB and audio equipment). Labels: ABC Dunhill, Impulse, Command, etc. Music publishing operations.
Publishing: ABC Leisure Magazines (*High Fidelity*, *Modern Photography*, numerous others). W. Schwann, Inc. ABC Farm Publications (4 magazines). Wallace-Homestead Book Company, *Los Angeles* and *American West* magazines, Nils Codes and Regulations, Inc. (insurance laws).
Theaters: ABC Theaters (formerly ABC-Paramount Theaters): 121 single-screen, 68 twin-screen, 1 triple-screen.
Scenic Attractions and Other Operations: Three outdoor family recreational facilities. ABC Entertainment Center (office, theater, commercial facility in Century City, California). ABC Films (involved in television distribution), ABC International.

CBS, Inc.

Revenues	1976	Percentage
Broadcast Group	1,042,800,000	46.7
Records Group	563,800,000	25.3
Columbia Group	393,300,000	17.6
Publishing Group	220,800,000	9.9
Other	9,900,000	0.4
Total	2,230,600,000	

OWNERSHIP AND SUBSIDIARIES

Broadcasting: CBS Television Network, CBS Television Stations, CBS Radio Network, 260 stations; CBS News, 7 o&o AM stations, 7 o&o FM stations.

Records: Largest producer, manufacturer, and marketer of records in the world. CBS Records, CBS Records International.

Columbia Group: Consumer products and marketing. Columbia House, Steinway pianos, Fender guitars, Gulbransen organs, Rhodes Electric pianos, Rogers drums, Leslie speakers, V. C. Squier strings, CBS Retail Stores division, Creative Playthings, Wonder Products Company (toys), Columbia Record and Tape Clubs, National Handcraft Institute, X-Acto tools, Pacific Stereo stores, Lyon and Healy, Inc. (world's largest maker of harps).

Book Publishing: Holt, Rinehart and Winston; Fawcett Publications, Inc.; BFA Educational Media; Popular Library; W. B. Saunders Co.; Winston Press; NEISA (scientific and medical books in Spanish and Portuguese), Frederick Praeger, Inc.

Magazine Publishing: Seven major special-interest magazines: *Field & Stream, Road & Track, Cycle World, World Tennis, Sea, PV4, Popular Gardening Indoors.* Twenty-one other magazines. Reader's Service Department (direct mail sales). Fawcett magazines: *Woman's Day, Mechanix Illustrated, Rudder,* and thirty other special-interest publications.

Other: Frank Music Publishers, Music Theater International, and affiliated companies. CBS Comtec (laboratories). Savin business machines. CBS no longer owns Cinema Center Films or The New York Yankees, and has spun off the Viacom group of companies, active in Cable television and TV program distribution.

Columbia Pictures Industries, Inc.

Revenues	1976	Percentage
Theatrical Films	152,200,000 ⎫	
Television Films	19,300,000 ⎬	52
Television Programs	67,800,000	20
Records	30,400,000	9
Other	37,800,000	11
Broadcasting	24,600,000	7
Total	332,100,000	

OWNERSHIP AND SUBSIDIARIES

Columbia Pictures, Columbia Pictures Television, Columbia Pictures publications (music, print), Columbia Pictures Pay Television, Columbia Pictures Merchandising, 8mm films division, D. Gottlieb Co. (pinball machines), Arista Records (Clive Davis), EUE Screen Gems (commercials), WNJU-TV, WWVA radio, WYDE radio, The Burbank Studios (with Warner Bros.), Independent Artists, Fred Levinson and Associates, Bill Alton Films, George Gage Productions, Marshall Stone Productions, Inc. (commercial production companies), Bob Abel & Associates (television graphics).

Gulf + Western Industries, Inc.

Revenues	1976	Percentage
Manufacturing	1,019,800,000	25
Consumer & Agricultural Products	444,400,000	11
Leisure Time	451,400,000	11
Natural Resources	177,500,000	4
Apparel Products	601,100,000	15
Paper and Building Products	430,200,000	11
Automotive Replacement Parts (the original G + W business)	277,700,000	7
Financial Services	641,200,000	16
Total	4,043,300,000	

OWNERSHIP AND SUBSIDIARIES

G + W owns more than 300 subsidiaries. These are the major ones:
Manufacturing: E. W. Bliss (Universal American), Collyer Insulated Wire, Eagle Signal, Bohn Metals, Taylor Forge, Michigan Plating and Stamping, Young Seating, Macintosh-Hemphill, Bonney Forge, Lenape Forge, Elco, Northern Stamping, Morse Cutting Tools, Sorensen, Guaranteed Parts.
Consumer and Agricultural Products: La Romana Sugar mill; Florigold Grapefruit; Romana, Casa de Campo, Hispaniola, and Santo Domingo hotels in Dominican Republic; Consolidated Cigar Corporation; South Puerto Rico Sugar Co. (275,000 acres in Dominican Republic); Schrafft's Candies; 117,000 acres devoted to livestock in D.R.; Industrial Free Zone at La Romana (industrial park), D.R.; Willem Cigars; interests in H. Upmann, Montecristo cigars. (In 1977 G + W agreed to sell its citrus and cattle operations in Florida.)
Leisure Time: Paramount Pictures, Cinema International Corp. (major international distributor), Simon & Schuster, Pocket Books, Monarch Books, Washington Square Press, Cinema Dominica, Esquire, Inc., Madison Square Garden Corp. (Madison Square Garden; Washington Park Race Track and Arlington Park Race Track, both Chicago; Roosevelt Raceway, Arena and Hotel; N.Y. Knicks; N.Y. Rangers; Madison Square Boxing, Inc.; hotels and real estate; International Holiday on Ice), part of Hughes Television Network, Famous Players (51% owned), Canadian theaters and real estate, Famous Music Corp., Sega Enterprises (95% owned, electronic and coin games), Paramount Pictures Television, Desilu, Oxford Films.
Natural Resources: The New Jersey Zinc Co., Marquette Co. (cement),

36% interest in Flying Diamond Oil Corporation, ⅓ of Quebec Iron and Titanium Corp.

Apparel Products: Excello, Kayser, Bostonian shoes, Paris belts and underwear, Cole of California, Catalina, Supp-hose, No Nonsense, Mojud, Interwoven hosiery (Kayser-Roth Corp.).

Paper and Building Products: 80% of Brown Company, which owns Peavey Paper Mills, Inc.; Symons Corporation; Livingston-Graham (building products).

Automotive Replacement Parts: Big A, American Parts System, Henrie & Bolthoff, Doyen, Vensu, Uranio, Newport Supply Co., Florida Cycle Supply Co., International Cycle Supply Co., Plavica, Overseas, S.A., Auto Body Parts, International Parts Service.

Financial Services: Associated First Capital Corp., Associates Corporation of North America, Capitol Life Insurance Co., Providence Washington Insurance Co., Emmco Insurance Co., Associates Financial Services Co., Associates Commercial Corp., G + W Realty Co., G + W Foundation, Columbus Circle Investors Corp.

MCA, Inc.

Revenues	1976		Percentage
Filmed Entertainment	507,000,000	{ Theatrical	27
		{ Television	31
Records and Music Publishing	112,000,000		. 14
Retail and Mail Order	117,000,000		15
Recreation Services	57,496,000	⎫	
Financial Services	56,000,000	⎬	13
Book Publishing	10,000,000 (?)	⎭	
Videodisc Operations	—		
Other Operations	—		
Total	859,496,000		

OWNERSHIP AND SUBSIDIARIES

Filmed Entertainment: Universal Films, Universal Television, Universal Studio Tour and Amphitheatre, MCA Merchandising, Universal City (420 acres), Cinema International Corp.

Records and Music Publishing: MCA Records, MCA Music, other labels: Coral, Europa.

Retail and Mail Order: Spencer Gifts (265 stores), Spencer catalogues.

Recreation Services: Studio Tour and Amphitheatre, Yosemite Park and Curry Co., Landmark Services and Mount Vernon Inn, Minibus (manufactures custom tram trains).

Financial Services: Columbia Savings and Loan Association (Colorado), Mid-Continent Computer Services (Denver).

Book Publishing: G. P. Putnam's Sons; Coward, McCann & Geoghegan; Berkley (paperbacks).
Videodiscs: In conjunction with the Dutch hardware manufacturer, N.V. Philips, MCA is developing one of two major competing Videodisc systems.
Other Operations: MCA New Ventures, Inc. (a minority enterprise small business investment company), Coca-Cola Bottling Co. of Los Angeles.

New York Times Company

Revenues	1976	Percentage
New York Times	290,058,000	65
Affiliated Newspapers	28,506,000	7
Publishing, other activities	32,560,000	7
Broadcasting	8,782,000	2
Magazines	85,779,000	19
Total	445,685,000	

OWNERSHIP AND SUBSIDIARIES

Newspapers: The New York Times, 13 affiliated newspapers in Florida and North Carolina, NYT News Services, ⅓ interest in *International Herald-Tribune* (Paris).
Magazine Publishing: Family Circle, Golf Digest, Tennis, Australian Family Circle, US (The Family Circle, Inc.).
Broadcasting: WREG-TV (Memphis), WQXR-AM, WQXR-FM (New York).
Book Publishing and Other Activities: Quadrangle, Arno Press, Cambridge Book Co., NYT Educational Services, NYT Information Services, NYT Information Bank, Microfilming Corporation of America, equity interests in three Canadian newsprint mills.

RCA Corp.

Revenues	1976	Percentage
Electronics—Consumer Products and Services	1,371,000,000	26
Electronics—Commercial Products and Services	689,000,000	13
Broadcasting	955,000,000	18
Vehicle Renting and Related Services	780,000,000	15
Communications	259,000,000	5
Government Business	368,000,000	7
Other Products and Services	942,000,000	18
Total	5,364,000,000	

OWNERSHIP AND SUBSIDIARIES

Electronics Divisions: Consumer Electronics; Global Communications; Government and Commercial Systems, Outdoor Electronics (Canada), and other foreign subsidiaries; Automated Systems; RCA Labs; RCA Ltd.; RCA Service Co. (repairs); Solid State Division; Electro Optics and Devices; RCA Sales.

Recordings: RCA, Red Seal, Sunbar; distributor of Buddha and others. RCA Record Club.

Publishing: Random House (and through Random House, Alfred A. Knopf, Pantheon, Vintage, and Modern Library), Ballantine Books.

Broadcasting: National Broadcasting Company, including television and radio networks and full complement of o&o stations; major interest in COMSAT. RCA Global Communications is an international common carrier. RCA American Communications operates SATCOM I and services NASA. RCA built the South Vietnamese television system (and many others), and bought ALASCOM (Alaska long lines telephone, formerly maintained by the Army and Air Force) from the U.S. government.

Other Operations: Hertz Corporation; Coronet Industries, Inc. (floor coverings); Banquet Foods Corp. (Frozen foods); RCA Institutes; Oriel Foods Group (U.K.).

Time, Incorporated

Revenues	1976	Percentage
Magazines	402,000,000	39
Books	192,000,000	19
Forest Products	306,900,000	30
Video and Film	54,700,000	5
Other Operations	82,600,000	8
Total	1,038,200,000	

OWNERSHIP AND SUBSIDIARIES

Forest Products: Temple-Eastex, Inc.; Eastex Pulp and Board: Temple Building Materials; Eastex Packaging; T-E Forests (timberland management); AFCO Industries, Inc. (wall products); Woodward, Inc. (bedroom furniture); Lumbermen's Investment Corp. (mortgage banking).

Magazines: Time, Fortune, Sports Illustrated, Money, People, Life Special Reports, magazine development.

Books: Time-Life Books, Inc.; Little, Brown and Co.; New York Graphic Society, Ltd.; Alva Museum Replicas, Inc. (sculpture and jewelry), Book-of-the-Month Club.

Video and Film: Time-Life Films, Inc. (major distributor of film and television programs); Time-Life Television; T-L Video; T-L Multimedia; T-L TV Books; Home Box Office (pay cable channel); Manhattan Cable TV, Inc.; WO-TV (Grand Rapids), Talent Associates, Ltd.

Other Operations: Sabine Investment Corp. (land development); minority interests in: Rowohlt Taschenbuch Verlag (German), Éditions Robert Laffont (French, 36%), Salvat Ediclub (Spanish, 40%), Organización Editorial Novano (Mexican), Shingakusha-Time International (Japanese). SAMI (Selling Areas-Marketing, Inc.), Pioneer Press Inc. (17 suburban Chicago newspapers), PDI (Printing Development—color scanners and typesetting).

Times-Mirror Company

Revenues	1976	Percentage
Newspapers	426,136,000	40
Newsprint, Forest Products	262,738,000	25
Book Publishing	173,057,000	16
Other Operations	188,640,000	18
Corporate	3,198,000	
Total	1,053,769,000	
Less Intercompany Sales	78,129,000	
Net Sales	975,640,000	

OWNERSHIP AND SUBSIDIARIES

Newspapers: Los Angeles Times, Newsday (Long Island), *Dallas Times-Herald, The Sporting News,* Orange Coast Publishing Co., L.A. Times-Washington Post News Service. *Stamford Advocate, Greenwich Time.*

Magazines: Outdoor Life, Ski, Golf, Popular Science.

Book Publishing: New American Library (New English Library), The Southwestern Company, Year Book Medical Publishers, Matthew Bender (law), Harry N. Abrams (art). (In 1977, T-M tried to buy the Random House companies from RCA, but rising sentiment against concentration blocked the deal.)

Other Activities: Publishers Paper Company, Jeppesen-Sanderson (charts), KDFW-TV (Dallas), KTBC-TV (Austin), Gousha/Chek-Chart, International Technical Graphics, Pickett (engineering supplies), Times-Mirror Press (directories), TM Communications (cable television in Mission Viejo, St. Louis, Long Island, and elsewhere).

Transamerica, Inc.

Revenues	1976	Percentage
Life Insurance	975,866,000	35.7
Property and Casualty Insurance	410,866,000	15.1
Title Insurance	69,127,000	2.5
Investment Income	168,230,000	6.2
Finance Service	134,066,000	4.9
Motion Pictures, Records, and Entertainment	374,486,000	13.7
Airlines	132,039,000	4.8
Manufacturing	281,311,000	10.3
Other	184,873,000	6.8
Total	2,730,884,000	

OWNERSHIP AND SUBSIDIARIES

Film: United Artists (which distributes M-G-M films as well); Cinegraphics, Inc.; United Artists Television; Hollywood Home Theater (a cable television service).

Records and Music: United Artists Records, United Artists Music.

Financial Services: Transamerica Computer Services; Pacific Finance Loans; Occidental Life Insurance Co.; Transamerica Life Insurance Co.; Transamerica Capital Fund; Transamerica Investors' Fund; Transamerica Title Insurance; Transamerica Real Estate Tax Service; American Life Insurance Co.; Occidental Life/Canada; Wolverine, Premier, and Automotive Insurance Cos.; Canadian Surety Co.; Transamerica Investment Management Co.; Transamerica Income Shares.

Other Activities: Lyon Moving and Storage, Transamerica Relocation Service, Transamerica Development Co., Bankers Mortgage Company of California, Transamerica Mortgage Advisors, Compagnie Européene de Banque, Trans-International Airlines (including Saturn Airways), Budget Rent-a-Car, Sears Rent a Car, Transamerica Film Service (processing), Delaval Turbine, Inc. (manufacturing), Delaval-Stork (Netherlands), IMO Pump Division, Wiggins Connectors Division, Transamerica Computer Co., Compass Computer Services (joint operation with Hilton Hotels Corp.), SynerGraphics (microfilm, micropublishing), Tafex Systems (computer systems).

Twentieth Century-Fox Film Corporation

Revenues	1976	Percentage
Feature Films	217,223,000	61
Television Programs	37,687,000	11
International Films	34,318,000	10
Film Processing	29,727,000	8
Television Stations	22,583,000	6
Records and Music Publishing	9,936,000	3
Nonoperating	3,564,000	1
Total	355,038,000	

OWNERSHIP AND SUBSIDIARIES

Filmed Entertainment: Feature Film Division, Television Program Division, Hollywood Home Theatre (jointly with UA, a pay cable operation), International Theatres Division (including Hoyts Theatre chain in Australia).
Broadcasting: United Television, Inc. (three VHF stations).
Film Processing: Deluxe General, Keith Cole Photography, Fox Movietone News.
Records and Publishing: 20th Century Records, 20th Century Music.

Warner Communications, Inc.

Revenues	1976	Percentage
Recordings and Music Publishing	406,100,000	49
Motion Pictures and Television	285,200,000	35
Publishing and Distribution	48,400,000	6
Cable Television	51,600,000	6
Electronic Games	35,500,000	4
Total	826,800,000	

OWNERSHIP AND SUBSIDIARIES

Recordings and Music Publishing: Warner Bros. Records; Elektra, Asylum, Nonesuch; Atlantic Records; WEA Corp. (marketing and distribution); WEA International (with eleven international affiliates); Warner Bros. Music (publishing).
Motion Pictures and Television: Warner Bros., Warner Bros. Television, The Wolper Organization, Panavision (equipment), Licensing Corporation of America, The Burbank Studios (with Columbia).
Publishing and Related Distribution: Warner Books (formerly Paper-

back Library), Independent News (magazine and paperback distribution), DC Comics, *Mad* magazine, E.C. Publications.
Cable Television: Warner Cable Corp. (2nd largest cable network), Star Channel (pay cable channel), new pay cable division.
Electronic Games: Atari, Inc.
Other Activities: Warner Fragrances Ltd. (with Ralph Lauren), 7% of Coca-Cola Bottling Co. of New York, 6¼% of Bausch & Lomb Optical Co., 63% of Garden State National Bank (with net income of $5.6 million), 95% of Cosmos North American Soccer League Team, Goldmark Communications Corp., Knickerbocker Toy Co.

WCI will, by law, be required to divest itself of its stock in Garden State National Bank by the end of 1980. WCI has closed Jungle Habitat, its theme park in New Jersey. WCI owns approximately 47% of the common stock and 100% of Convertible Preferred stock in National Kinney Corp., a company primarily engaged in providing building maintenance and construction services to the real estate industry. When Warner Bros./Seven Arts was acquired by (or merged with) Kinney in the late sixties, the company was known as "Kinney Services, Inc." Since 1972 it has used the name Warner Communications, Inc., and in 1975 announced its decision to dispose entirely of its interest in Kinney. Kinney's subsidiary, Uris Buildings Corp., formerly a major New York office building developer, has to this end sold nine of its ten New York City office buildings.

Sources for all data in Appendix 2: relevant annual reports.

THE BOTTOM LINE

- The twelve conglomerates listed in this appendix have total net sales equal to half the net sales for all media. Revenues from media operations for the twelve represent approximately 30% of net sales for all media.

- *Newspapers:* The ten largest newspaper chains listed in Table XI account for 51% of total newspaper revenues.

- *Records:* Warner Communications, Inc. and CBS, Inc. receive approximately 65% of all record and tape revenues (wholesale) in the U.S.

- *Television:* The three commercial networks account for 69% of total television revenues. Eighty-five percent of commercial television stations are affiliated with one or another of the three networks. Twenty-two cable operators cover 51% of the market.

- *Film:* In any year, three of the top five distributors receive more than half of film rental revenues. In 1976, Warner Bros., United Artists, and Twentieth Century-Fox accounted for 48% of total rental revenues; in 1975, Universal, Fox, and Columbia accounted for 52% of total rental revenues.

- In any year, six media companies—ABC, NBC, CBS, WCI, and any two other film companies—control more than half the total nonprint media market in the U.S.

APPENDIX 3: READING ABOUT MEDIA:
A Selective Guide to Books on the Subject

Here is a basic library of currently available books about print, film, video, and other media. Unless otherwise noted, all books are available in paperback editions. The list is arranged alphabetically; reference books are listed separately.

Erik Barnouw's classic history of broadcasting is by far the best introduction to nonprint media. Raymond Williams's books are most useful in terms of theory. John Tebbel's *The Media in America* covers the history of print media. Steinberg's *Five Hundred Years of Printing* provides a longer view. Herbert I. Schiller's *Mass Communications and the American Empire* is a landmark study of media domination. Gerald Mast's *A Short History of the Movies* is probably the best general survey of film history available. My own *How to Read a Film* covers a number of introductory topics in film and electronic media.

Altick, Richard D. *The English Common Reader: A Social History of the Mass Reading Public, 1800–1900.* Chicago: University of Chicago Press. 1963.

Andrew, J. Dudley. *The Major Film Theories: An Introduction.* New York: Oxford University Press. 1976.

Arlen, Michael. *Living-Room War.* New York: Viking. 1969. Arlen is one of the most respected television critics working today.

———. *The View From Highway One.* New York: Farrar, Straus & Giroux. 1976. More collected criticism.

Barnouw, Erik. *Documentary: A History of the Non-Fiction Film.* New York: Oxford University Press. 1974. Recommended.

———. *A History of Broadcasting in the United States.* New York: Oxford University Press. Vol. 1: *A Tower in Babel.* 1966. Vol. 2: *The Golden Web.* 1968. Vol. 3: *The Image Empire.* 1970. The standard work on the subject. Essential and highly recommended. (Hardcover.)

————. *Tube of Plenty: The Evolution of American Television.* New York: Oxford University Press. 1975. A one-volume revision of *A History of Broadcasting.* Recommended.

Barthes, Roland. *Elements of Semiology/Writing Degree Zero.* Trans. Annette Lavers, Colin Smith. Boston: Beacon Press. 1968. Semiotic media theory.

————. *Mythologies.* Trans. Annette Lavers. New York: Hill & Wang. 1972. More practical criticism.

Beckett, Samuel. *Cascando and Other Short Dramatic Pieces.* New York: Grove Press. 1975. Beckett analyzes various media within their own forms.

————. *Krapp's Last Tape and Other Dramatic Pieces.* New York: Grove Press. 1967.

Benjamin, Walter. *Illuminations.* Ed. Hannah Arendt. New York: Schocken Books. 1968. See especially "The Work of Art in the Age of Mechanical Reproduction," a seminal essay.

Bergman, Andrew. *We're in the Money.* New York: Harper & Row. 1973. America in the thirties.

Blake, Reed H., and Erwin O. Haroldsen. *A Taxonomy of Concepts in Communication.* New York: Hastings House Publishers. 1975.

Blum, Eleanor. *Basic Books in the Mass Media.* Urbana: University of Illinois Press. 1972. A basic bibliography.

Braudy, Leo. *The World in a Frame.* New York: Anchor. 1976. A theory of film.

Briggs, Asa. *The History of Broadcasting in the United Kingdom.* London: Oxford University Press. Vol. 1: *The Birth of Broadcasting.* 1961. Vol. 2: *The Golden Age of Wireless.* 1965. Vol. 3: *The War of Words.* 1970. Recommended.

Brown, Les. *Television: The Business Behind the Box.* New York: Harcourt Brace Jovanovich. 1972. Recommended.

Cater, Douglass, ed. *Television As a Cultural Force.* New York: Praeger Publishers. 1976. Aspen Institute anthology.

————. *Television As a Social Force.* New York: Praeger Publishers. 1975. Aspen Institute anthology.

Cirino, Robert. *Don't Blame the People: How the News Media Use Bias, Distortion, and Censorship to Manipulate Public Opinion.* New York: Vintage. 1971.

Enzenberger, Hans Magnus. *The Consciousness Industry.* New York: Seabury.

Fielding, Raymond. *The American Newsreel: 1911–1967.* Norman: University of Oklahoma Press. 1972.

————. *Focal Encyclopedia of Film and Television Techniques.* New York: Hastings House. 1969. Useful guide to technology.

————, ed. *A Technological History of Motion Pictures and Television.* Berkeley: University of California Press. 1967.

Friendly, Fred. *Due to Circumstances Beyond Our Control.* New York: Random House. 1967. Television from the inside.

Garnham, Nicholas, et al. British Film Institute *Television Monographs.*

1. *Structures of Television* (1973). 2. *Light Entertainment* (1973).
3. *Television and the February 1974 General Election* (1974). 4.
Football on Television (1975). 5. *Television News* (1976). 6.
Television Documentary Usage (1976). London: British Film Institute. New York: New York Zoetrope (31 East 12th Street, 10003).

Glessing, Robert J. *The Underground Press in America*. Bloomington: University of Indiana Press. 1970.

Gouldner, Alvin W. *The Dialectic of Ideology and Technology*. New York: Seabury Press. 1976.

Groombridge, Brian. *Television and the People: A Programme for Democratic Participation*. London: Penguin. 1972.

Guback, Thomas H. *The International Film Industry*. Bloomington: Indiana University Press. 1969. Recommended.

Handel, S. *A Dictionary of Electronics*, 3rd ed. London: Penguin. 1971.

Haskell, Molly. *From Reverence to Rape*. New York: Penguin. 1974. Women in the movies.

Innis, Harold A. *The Bias of Communication*. Toronto: University of Toronto Press. 1951. Precursor of McLuhan.

Johnson, Nicholas. *How to Talk Back to Your Television Set*. Boston: Little, Brown. 1970. By the former rebel FCC commissioner.

Key, Wilson Bryan. *Subliminal Seduction*. New York: Signet. 1973. Advertising.

Leonard, John. *This Pen for Hire*. New York: Doubleday. 1973. Collected criticism.

McLuhan, Marshall. *Understanding Media: The Extensions of Man*. New York: McGraw-Hill. 1964. Controversial but often seminal.

———. *The Gutenberg Galaxy*. Toronto: University of Toronto Press. 1962.

——— and Quentin Fiore. *The Medium Is the Massage: An Inventory of Effects*. New York: Bantam. 1967.

McQuade, Donald, and Robert Atwan, eds. *Popular Writing in America: Advertising, Newspapers, Magazines, Best Sellers, Classics*. New York: Oxford University Press. 1977. Interesting anthology.

McQuail, Denis, ed. *Sociology of Mass Communications*. London: Penguin. 1972.

Maddox, Brenda. *Beyond Babel: New Direction in Communications*. Boston: Beacon Press. 1972.

Marcus, Greil. *Mystery Train: Images of America in Rock 'n' Roll Music*. New York: E. P. Dutton. 1976. The best rock criticism yet to appear.

Mast, Gerald. *A Short History of the Movies*, 2nd ed. Indianapolis: Bobbs-Merrill. 1976.

——— and Marshall Cohen. *Film Theory and Criticism*. New York: Oxford University Press. 1974. Useful anthology.

Mayer, Martin. *About Television*. New York: Harper & Row. 1974.

Mayer, Michael. *The Film Industries*. New York: Hastings House. 1973.

Mellen, Joan. *Women and Their Sexuality in the New Film.* New York: Horizon Press. 1973.

Metz, Christian. *Film Language: A Semiotics of the Cinema.* Trans. Michael Taylor. New York: Oxford University Press. 1974. (Hardcover.)

Miller, Jonathan. *Marshall McLuhan.* New York: Viking Press. 1971.

Monaco, James. *How to Read a Film: The Art, Technology, Language, History, and Theory of Film and Media.* New York: Oxford University Press. 1977.

————, ed. *Celebrity.* New York: Delta. 1978.

Mueller, Claus. *The Politics of Communication.* New York: Oxford University Press. 1973.

Mumford, Lewis. *Technics and Civilization.* 1934. Reprint, New York: Harcourt Brace and World. 1966.

The Network Project *Notebooks.* 1. *Domestic Communications Satellites* (1972). 2. *Directory of the Networks* (1973). 3. *Control of Information* (1973). 4. *Office of Telecommunications Policy—The White House Role in Domestic Communications* (1973). 5. *Cable Television* (1973). 6. *Down Sesame Street* (1973). 7. *The Case Against Satellites* (1974). 8. *Cable Television—End of a Dream* (1974). 9. *Government Television* (1974). 10. *Global Salesman* (1975). (101 Earl Hall, Columbia University, New York 10027.)

Newcomb, Horace. *TV: The Most Popular Art.* New York: Doubleday. 1974.

————, ed. *The Critical View: Television.* New York: Oxford University Press. 1976.

Palmer, Tony. *All You Need Is Love: The Story of Popular Music.* New York: Grossman Publishers. 1976.

Petersen, Clarence. *The Bantam Story: 30 Years of Paperback Publishing,* 2nd ed. New York: Bantam. 1975.

Pollak, Richard, ed. *Stop the Presses, I Want to Get Off!* New York: Delta. 1975. Anthology of *MORE* magazine articles. Recommended.

Schiller, Herbert I. *Communication and Cultural Domination.* New York: International Arts & Sciences Press. 1976.

————. *Mass Communications and the American Empire.* Boston: Beacon. 1969.

Schneider, Ira, and Beryl Korot. *Video Art.* New York: Harcourt Brace Jovanovich. 1976.

Schwartz, Tony. *The Responsive Chord: How Radio and TV Manipulate You. . . .* New York: Anchor. 1973.

Shamberg, Michael, and the Raindance Corp. *Guerrilla Television.* New York: Holt, Rinehart and Winston. 1972.

Shanks, Bob. *The Cool Fire: How to Make It in Television.* New York: Norton. 1976.

Shapiro, Andrew. *Media Access.* Boston: Little, Brown. 1976.

Sklar, Robert. *Movie-Made America: A Cultural History of American Movies.* New York: Random House. 1975.

Sloan Commission on Cable Communications. *On The Cable: The Television of Abundance*. New York: McGraw-Hill. 1971.

Smith, Ralph Lee. *The Wired Nation: Cable TV: The Electronic Communications Highway*. New York: Harper & Row. 1972.

Steinberg, S. H. *Five Hundred Years of Printing*, 3rd ed. New York: Penguin. 1974.

Swanberg, W. A. *Citizen Hearst*. New York: Bantam. 1971.

———. *Pulitzer*. New York: Scribner's. 1972.

Tebbel, John. *A History of Book Publishing in the United States*. New York: R. R. Bowker. 3 vols. 1972, 1975, 1977.

———. *The Media in America*. New York: Mentor. 1974.

Tomkins, Calvin. *The Scene: Reports on Post-Modern Art*. New York: Viking Press. 1976. (Hardcover.)

Tunstall, Jeremy. *The Media Are American*. London: Constable. New York: Columbia University Press. 1977.

———, ed. *Media Sociology*. London: Constable. 1970.

Warshow, Robert. *The Immediate Experience*. 1962. Reprint: New York: Atheneum. 1970. One of our first and best critics of popular culture.

Watzlawick, Paul. *How Real Is Real? Confusion, Disinformation, Communication*. New York: Vintage. 1977.

Williams, Raymond. *Communications*, 3rd ed. London: Penguin. 1976. Probably the most useful theoretical work on print media.

———. *Keywords: A Vocabulary of Culture and Society*. New York: Oxford University Press. 1976.

———. *Television: Technology and Cultural Form*. New York: Schocken Books. 1975. Highly recommended. Most useful television theory of recent times.

Winn, Marie. *The Plug-In Drug: TV, Children, and the Family*. New York: Viking. 1977.

Wright, John, ed. *Admass*. New York: Delta. 1977.

Wood, Michael. *America in the Movies*. New York: Basic Books. 1975.

A BASIC MEDIA REFERENCE SELF

Film:

Bawden, Liz-Ann, ed. *The Oxford Companion to Film*. London and New York: Oxford University Press. 1976.

Cawkwell, Tim, and John M. Smith, eds. *The World Encyclopedia of Film*. London: Studio Vista. New York: A&W Visual Library. 1972.

Halliwell, Leslie. *The Filmgoer's Companion*, 4th ed. New York: Hill & Wang. 1974.

Manvell, Roger, and Lewis Jacobs, eds. *The International Encyclopedia of Film*. New York: Crown Publishers. 1972.

Roud, Richard, ed. *A Critical Dictionary of the Cinema*. London: Secker and Warburg. New York: Viking Press. 4 vols. 1978.

Thomson, David. *A Biographical Dictionary of Film.* London: Secker and Warburg. New York: Morrow. 1975, 1976. Worth reading for itself.

Television:
Brown, Les. *The New York Times Encyclopedia of Television.* New York: Quadrangle. 1977.
David, Nina. *TV Season 74–75.* . . . Annual. Phoenix: The Oryx Press. (3930 East Camelback Road, 85018.) Reliable.
Terrace, Vincent. *The Complete Encyclopedia of Television Programs.* 2 vols. Cranbury, N.J.: A. S. Barnes. 1976.

Radio:
Buxton, Frank and Bill Owen. *The Big Broadcast 1920–1950.* New York: Avon. 1966, 1972.
Dunning, John. *Tune in Yesterday: The Ultimate Encyclopedia of Old Time Radio: 1925–1976.* Englewood Cliffs, N.J.: Prentice-Hall. 1977.
World Radio T.V. Handbook. New York: Billboard Publications. Yearly.

Recordings:
Roxon, Lillian. *The Complete Encyclopedia of Rock.* Paper. New York: Grosset & Dunlap. 1971, 1974.

Periodicals:
Trade journals are still the best sources of information about the media. *Publishers Weekly* covers books; *Broadcasting,* radio and television; *Billboard,* the recording industry; and *Advertising Age* and *Madison Avenue,* advertising. *Variety* covers all the media, but pays most attention to film and television. *American Cinematographer* is the most useful technical journal.

General interest magazines have begun to pay more serious attention to the media. Here are several lesser-known journals that are recommendable: *MORE: The Media Magazine* pays more attention to journalism than to the "entertainment" media. *The Columbia Journalism Review* is slightly more academic. *The Journal of Popular Culture* and *The Journal of Popular Film* are scholarly journals. *American Film, Sight and Sound,* and *Take One: The Magazine of Movies and Media* are film magazines first, but regularly include important articles on television and other media. *Rolling Stone* is of course the premier rock magazine, but usually has precious little to say about the medium, per se. *Folio* is a new magazine for professionals in the magazine business.

NOTES ON CONTRIBUTORS

ROBERT ALAN AURTHUR was a prolific writer and producer during television's golden age. He is currently working in film. *All That Jazz*, which he co-wrote with Bob Fosse, in his most recent film.

CHARLES BARR, JIM HILLIER, and V. F. PERKINS are English film critics associated with *MOVIE* magazine.

DONALD BARTHELME writes regularly for *The New Yorker*, teaches at City College, and has written nine books of fiction and nonfiction, including *The Dead Father* and *Amateurs*.

ROY BLOUNT, JR., writes for *Esquire* and is the author of *About Three Bricks Shy of a Load*, a chronicle of a season with the Pittsburgh Steelers, and *Trash No More*, about the South, where he was born and raised.

BO BURLINGHAM, an observer of the current scene, is based in Cambridge, Massachusetts. His articles have appeared in numerous magazines, including *Esquire* and *Mother Jones*.

STEVE CHAPPLE is coauthor of *Rock and Roll Is Here to Pay: The History and Politics of the Music Industry*, from which this article was excerpted. He is a free-lance journalist and novelist living in San Francisco. He contributes regularly to several magazines.

NORA EPHRON's most recent collection of essays is *Scribble, Scribble*. She is also the author of *Crazy Salad*, and a contributing editor at *Esquire*.

ROBERT GAROFALO is coauthor of *Rock and Roll Is Here to Pay*. He is director of students at Franconia College and a professional musician. He appears on the album *Red Shadow: The Economics Rock and Roll Band Live at the Panacea Hilton*.

JEFF GREENFIELD is a prolific journalist with special interests in politics and contemporary culture. His most recent book is *Television: The First Fifty Years.*

RUST HILLS alternates between careers as editor and writer. He has just returned for his third stint as *Esquire*'s fiction editor. He is also the author of the "Fussy Man" series: *How To Do Things Right, How To Retire at 40*, and *How To Be Good.*

ANDREW HOROWITZ was part of the Network Project at Columbia University when this article was written. Since the fall of 1975 he has been co-director of the Public Interest Satellite Association, an organization working to obtain access to new satellite technology, to assist citizen and community organizations, and affect satellite-use policy. The address for PISA is: 55 West 44th Street, New York, New York 10017.

CHARLAYNE HUNTER-GAULT has been a reporter for *The New York Times* and is a correspondent for *The MacNeil-Lehrer Report* on PBS.

THOMAS JOHNSON writes for *The New York Times.*

DAVID LINDROTH is a book designer and illustrator working in New York.

JAMES MONACO is General Editor of the Media Culture series for Delta Books. His most recent publications are *Celebrity* and *Alain Resnais.*

VIRGINIA BEVER PLATT, Professor Emerita of History at Bowling Green State University, is a trustee of The Ohio Historical Society. She has published widely in academic journals.

RON ROSENBAUM is a prolific and widely read journalist. His work has appeared in numerous magazines, including *The Village Voice, Esquire*, and *New York.* He is currently completing a collection of his pieces to be published this year.

ROBERT RUSSEL wrote for *Take One* magazine in the late sixties, where he correctly forecast a number of developments in his column "The Next Medium."

LESLIE SAVAN writes regularly about television for *The Star.* She is a free-lance writer whose work has appeared in *The Village Voice* and *Viva.* She lives in New York.

TOM STEVENSON has been an associate editor at *Forbes* and a free-lance writer. He is now executive director of Seminar Resources, where he develops seminar programs for colleges and universities.

GEOFFREY STOKES is a staff writer for *The Village Voice.* His book,

Star-Making Machinery, is about the economics of the rock and roll industry; it won the Deems Taylor Award for 1976.

DAVID THOMSON is the author of *America in the Dark: Hollywood and the Gift of Unreality* as well as *A Biographical Dictionary of Film*. He is also a novelist and currently teaches at Dartmouth.

GEORGE W. S. TROW's fiction regularly appears in *The New Yorker*. He is currently working on a play, *The Tennis Game*.

LUCIAN K. TRUSCOTT IV has written for numerous magazines, including *The Village Voice* and *New Times*. He lives and works in New York City and Sag Harbor, New York.

HARRY WATERS is a senior writer at *Newsweek* specializing in the media.

E. B. WHITE lives in Maine, composes the "newsbreaks" for *The New Yorker*, recently published his collected letters and his collected essays, and, as coauthor of *The Elements of Style*, has helped teach a generation to write.

INDEX